Grade Aid with Practice Tests

for

Butcher, Mineka, and Hooley

Abnormal Psychology

Twelfth Edition

prepared by

Laurie Mackenzie
San Diego Mesa College

PEARSON

Boston   New York   San Francisco
Mexico City   Montreal   Toronto   London   Madrid   Munich   Paris
Hong Kong   Singapore   Tokyo   Cape Town   Sydney

ISBN 0-205-40328X

Printed in the United States of America

10 9 8 7 6 5 4 3 2   08 07 06 05 04

TABLE OF CONTENTS

GRADE AID

Abnormal Psychology
Twelfth Edition

GENERAL INFORMATION

So, you have decided to take and abnormal psychology class. Congratulations, and welcome to a fascinating and intriguing world. But, first, a word of caution. As I tell my students, this is not a course that will help you figure out what's wrong with you, your families, or your friends. In fact, trying to be an amateur psychologist could cause you to lose some friends. Do not fall victim to the "medical student syndrome" and believe that you or they suffer the disorders we study here. Abnormal psychology is not an easy subject—it can't be. Few things can be more difficult than trying to understand the human mind, and what can go wrong with it—and why. Treating people who suffer from mental illness—as well as their families and, if appropriate, their friends—can be an equally difficult challenge.

The twelfth edition of *Abnormal Psychology,* provides you with a very comprehensive look at this subject. It gives you historical perspectives on the development of various disorders and, indeed, on the evolution of psychology itself. In addition, you are introduced to the wide array of mental disorders, their etiology, diagnostic criteria, and treatment methods.

So much is covered that you, as a student, could feel overwhelmed, if you don't know how to study. This book has but one purpose, to assist you in learning the information contained in your textbook. It is hoped that you will use it as a companion guide to your textbook throughout the semester.

HOW TO STUDY

There is an art to studying. Learning how requires developing and utilizing tools that will help achieve the goals of comprehending and retaining the course information. This book is called a "Grade Aid," not "study guide." It is hoped that it will aid you in developing methods/tools for study, which will translate into a good grade, and, in turn, further interest in psychology. It will provide you with a variety of exercises which allow you to experience different methods of learning. But, before I talk about the Grade Aid itself, I'd like to outline a few general guidelines for studying in general.

OUTSIDE CLASS:

No matter how often students hear that putting off reading/studying until the last minute isn't a good idea, there are still many who do just that. There are many reasons why this is the case—active social life, working while trying to go to school, family responsibilities, or just a habit that, perhaps, worked well in elementary and high school, but isn't going to cut it in college. So, the first step in learning how to study is to take a realistic look at your time and create a schedule that takes into account all of your responsibilities. It is estimated that for every three hours of class a student needs to study six hours. So you can see why scheduling is important. Of course, emergencies can arise, but a good schedule can help you oveercome them with minimum disruption to the rest of your life. Also, don't get trapped by thinking that you need large amounts of time to study. Much can be accomplished in half an hour or forty-five minutes. A practice test from this Grade Aid, should take about 20 minutes, if you have read the chapter. Setting aside that time, and taking the test, can be of great benefit in pointing out concepts you haven't comprehended. This, then, would allow you time to ask your instructor for clarification.

USING THE TEXTBOOK AND GRADE AID:

Reading the chapter and completing the Grade Aid exercises **before** going to class is very important. You can begin by skimming major headings and familiarizing yourself with the concepts in the textbook. Then, go back and read the chapter highlighting important points.

Outline important sections or points using your own words or memory tricks. Often if you put information into your own words, you will retain it better. Studies show this to be so.

After reading the textbook chapter, highlighting, and outlining, go to the Grade Aid and answer as many questions as you can. Note those areas that you missed or were confused about, then return to the text for clarification. Do this, and you will be prepared for class.

IN CLASS:

Taking notes, especially if the instructor talks fast, is a difficult task. There is no way that you will be able to write down everything an instructor is saying. Get the key points, what is on the blackboard, in overhead transparencies, or PowerPoint presentations. If you feel you have missed something important, leave a blank spot and ask to look at a fellow student's notes or ask your instructor after class.

PUTTING IT ALL TOGETHER:

Ok, so you have read the chapter, highlighted the important points, put information into your own words and completed the Grade Aid corresponding chapter. Now what? Back to the schedule. The purpose of this preparation is to make studying for an exam a review of what you have learned, not the initial learning itself. In preparing for the exam, allow enough time to look at notes, Grade Aid, outlines and highlighted sections of text.

HOW TO TAKE AN EXAM

Most students have test anxiety, but, as you will read in the textbook, not all anxiety is bad. Some anxiety can help you do better on test, if you use it to motivate yourself. So, perhaps the best way to cope with the anxiety of test taking is to "be prepared."

If you have studied the material and feel confident in your knowledge, you are in great shape to take a test. The first thing to do when you get the test is to scan it, answering the questions you are sure about. This will make you feel better and help lessen any anxiety you might be feeling about the test. With this confidence, you can go back and tackle the remaining questions. This method applies to all forms for test, multiple/choice, true/false, essay, etc.

Read the question very carefully, but, try not to read a lot into a question. Students frequently do this. They tend to look for hidden meanings, getting themselves caught up in cyclical thinking, which gets them no where. If you are confused about the wording of a question, ask your instructor for clarification. If he or she doesn't answer questions during a test, then go on to another question and come back to the problem after you have taken a bit of break from it.

There are different strategies for taking different types of test. If you are taking a multiple choice question test, eliminate the obvious wrong answers first then concentrate on the remaining answers. With true and false, look for the use of words like "all," "always," and "never." Things are rarely "always" or "never," which means that the answer is probably false. When taking an essay test, take a few seconds to briefly outline your answer. This will give you guidelines to follow and keep you from rambling.

Remember, however, that knowing the information above will really help only you if you have studied and know the material. In a course as comprehensive as abnormal psychology, knowledge and practice are the keys.

HOW TO USE THIS GRADE AID

As mentioned earlier, this book is an aide, a tool that will help you understand the concepts presented in the textbook. It is meant to give you a comprehensive, but concise, overview of the important aspects of each chapter. **Write in this book**, it is designed to be open and spacious, with lots of room for you to write notes, thoughts, ideas. Take it apart, if necessary, and otherwise use it to increase your knowledge. The various sections of the Grade Aid are designed to give you a variety of learning experiences and test-taking practice. The answers to the questions are provided in the back of the book. However, page numbers also follow each question or exercise, giving you optimum availability to check your answers. The following is a more detailed description of the sections provided in the Grade Aid.

BEFORE YOU READ

This section provides a brief overview and table of content of the chapter. Its purpose is to introduce you to the chapter before you begin to answer the questions in the Grade Aid. The table of content comes directly from the corresponding chapter in the textbook.

OBJECTIVES

These are goals you are expected to achieve after reading the chapter. They can be used as a measuring stick to determine your mastery of the subject.

AS YOU READ

The exercises in this section is meant to provide you with a variety of ways to remember the material. Given that not all people learn the same way, the selection of exercises hopefully will provide something for everyone. These sections include:

- **Key words:** use this part to define the important words identified by the authors. The page number that the word appears on is provided so that you may check your work. These are not in the answer section of your book.

- **Who's Who and What's What—Matching:** A matching section gives you the opportunity to become familiar with some important people, places, things, and ideas which are presented in each chapter. Again, it allows you to test your memory for important aspects of the chapter.

- **Short answers:** Writing is an important part of any class. This exercise is designed to see how well you can put your thoughts onto paper in a concise manner.

- **Fill-in the Blanks:** These are questions that are designed to help you focus in on specific details. They provide important concrete information regarding chapter content.

- **Picture This:** Hopefully, this section can be used as a memory tool. It asks you to write the word represented by the pictures. Use your imagination and have fun.

- **The Doctor Is In:** If you are taking an abnormal psychology class, perhaps you have aspirations of becoming a therapist. This section gives you an opportunity to test you diagnostic skill. Scenarios of disorders represented in the chapter are given, and you are asked to act as a "therapist" by diagnosing and treating the patient.

AFTER YOU READ

This section contains three practice tests. They are designed to give you experience test taking, roughly dividing the chapter into thirds—each test asking questions from a third of the text. Again, the page numbers are provided at the end of each question. Take these tests and see how well you do. Then go back and correct your answers. These test are to prepare you for the comprehensive test coming up next.

COMPREHENSIVE PRACTICE TEST

There are three types of test in this section, multiple choice, true/false, and essay. They cover the entire chapter and give you an opportunity to see how well you understand the concepts. Because there are several testing methods provided, you will have lots of practice before the real thing.

Web Links: A few web sites are provided for more information concerning topics covered in each chapter.

CRISS CROSS

Another tool provided is a crossword puzzle that uses key words from the chapter. This comes at the end of each Grade Aid chapter and is a way to see how well you remember the definitions to the key words. Enjoy.

SPECIAL THANKS

To the authors of the previous editions of this Grade Aid, thank you for showing the way. To my husband, Joe Holly, thank you for your support, hard work, and, mostly, thank you for your sense of humor. Students, if, some dark and stormy night, as you are working through this material in preparation for tomorrow's test, you come upon something which makes you smile, most likely that is Joe's gentle touch. You learn more when you are happy. Good luck.

Hello, student! Before starting Chapter 1, check out the Preface. It contains much information about this Grade Aid, including a comprehensive Table of Contents of your textbook. Also, you can pick up a few pointers on how to use this book, how to study, and how to take a test. Reading it could only be a good thing.

CHAPTER ONE

Abnormal Psychology: An Overview

BEFORE YOU READ

Most likely you have known someone with a mental disorder. We have all seen people "acting strangely" in a park or on a street corner. Or we have read or seen a movie about someone who has committed suicide because of depression. All around us are the elements of abnormal psychology. In Chapter 1, the world of abnormal is put into a context. This will help you understand how to separate the fact from the fiction. Psychology, as fact, is based on scientific research. To be able to define or classify mental disorders and create effective treatments, we must have knowledge of research methods and an understanding of the definitions used to describe what is being studied. This is the goal of Chapter 1, Abnormal Psychology: An Overview. It lays the foundation from which to approach the rest of your textbook and the fascinating world of abnormal psychology.

OBJECTIVES

After reading this chapter, you should be able to:

1. Explain the authors' approach to the study of abnormal psychology.
2. Discuss common topics and issues relevant to abnormal psychology.
3. Explain why we need to classify mental disorders.
4. Explain the DSM-IV definition of mental disorders.
5. Identify how cultural issues can influence the definition of abnormal psychology.
6. Identify the professionals responsible for working on the mental health "team."
7. Explain the difference between the prevalence and the incidences of mental disorders.
8. Discuss the prevalent rates for mental disorders.
9. Explain inpatient and outpatient treatment.
10. Describe and explain the benefits and dimensions of the various research approaches.
11. Describe the process of doing research.

AS YOU READ

Answers can be found in the Answer Key at the end of the book.

KEY WORDS

Each of the words below is important in understanding the concepts presented in this chapter. Write the definition next to each of the words. The page numbers are provided in case you need to refer to the book.

family aggregation (p. 3)

placebo (p. 4)

double blind (p. 4)

nomenclature (p. 5)

symptoms (p. 8)

syndrome (p. 8)

abnormal behavior (p. 10)

epidemiology (p. 11)

epidemiological studies (p. 11)

prevalence (p. 11)

incidence (p. 12)

lifetime prevalence (p. 12)

comorbidity (p. 13)

acute (p. 13)

chronic (p. 13)

case study (p. 14)

hypothesis (p. 15)

sampling (p. 16)

criterion group (p. 17)

observational research (p. 17)

retrospective strategy (p. 18)

prospective strategy (p. 19)

independent variable (p. 20)

dependent variable (p. 20)

experimental research (p. 21)

ABAB design (p. 21)

analogue studies (p. 22)

MATCHING
Who's Who in the Mental Health Field—Match each of the following people with her/his accomplishment or theory.

C Jerome Wakefield

F Kazdin (1998)

D Emil Kraeplin (1856-1926)

A Eugen Bleuler (1857-1939)

B Alois Alzheimer (1864-1945)

E Sigmund Freud (1856-1939)

A. Swiss psychiatrist who worked with Kraepelin to write about schizophrenia and manic depression

B. described disorder that was to become associated with a disorder common to elderly people

C. proposed idea of mental disorders as being "harmful dysfunctions."

D. German psychiatrist who worked with Bleuler to write about schizophrenia and manic depression

E. founder of psychoanalysis

F. "Methodology is not merely a compilation of practices and procedures. Rather, it is an approach toward problem solving, thinking, and acquiring knowledge."

What's What—Match each of the following professions with its definition. (p. 11)

E Clinical Psychologist

A Counseling Psychologist

D School Psychologist

B Psychiatrist

C Psychoanalyst

F Psychiatric Social Worker

H Psychiatric Nursing

I Occupational Therapist

G Pastoral Counselor

A. Ph.D. in psychology and internship in mental or student counseling

B. M.D. with residency in psychiatric hospital

C. M.D. or Ph.D. with emphasis on psychoanalysis

D. may or may not have Ph.D., but has extensive training regarding academic or learning problems

E. Ph.D. in psychology with research and clinical skills

F. M.S.W. or Ph.D. with clinical training in mental health settings

G. ministerial background and training in psychology

H. R.N. certification but could also have M.A. or Ph.D. specializing in care and treatment of psychiatric clients

SHORT ANSWERS

Provide brief answers to the following questions.

1. Discuss how the Developments in Research 1.1 "Do Magnets Help with Repetitive-Stress Injury?" demonstrate the importance of controlled research trials. (p. 4)

2. Describe the difference between inpatient and outpatient care for people with mental disorders. What are some of the changes that have occurred in treatment? (p. 13)

3. Discuss the strengths and limitations associated with using the experimental method when conducting treatment research. (p. 20)

4. Explain the problem with expanding the DSM to include all kinds of behavior that are undesirable, such as "road rage." (p. 24)

FILL IN THE BLANKS

Read the following and fill in the blanks. These questions are designed to help you focus on specific details.

1. The four drawbacks to a classification system for mental disorders are: _loss of information_, _stigmatizing_, _stereotyping_, and _labeling_. (pp. 5-6)

2. Prevalence estimates can be determined by several different methods: _point_ prevalence, estimates active cases in a given population at any instant; _one-year_ prevalence, number who suffered from the studied disorder at any time during a year, and _life time_ prevalence, the number of people who suffered the studied disorder any time in their lives. (pp. 11-12)

3. Correlational research looks at variables to determine if there is a ___*positive*___ correlation, where things vary together in a direct, corresponding manner, a ___*negative*___ correlation, where there is an inverse relationship between variables or ___*uncorrelated*___, where the variables are independent of one another. (p. 19)

4. The authors of your textbook focus on three significant aspects of disorders. These are the ___*symptoms*___, ___*syndrome*___ and ___*disorders*___. (p. 22)
    clinical picture   *possible causes*   *treatment*

5. Experimental research involves manipulating the ___*independent*___ variable and seeing what effect this has on the ___*dependent*___ variable. (p. 25)

6. Unfortunately, receiving a psychiatric diagnosis can lead a person to being ___*stigmatized*___, ___*stereotyped*___, and/or ___*labeled*___ by others. (p. 6)

7. By referring not to the causes of mental disorders, but to their characteristics, the DSM attempts to be ___*objective*___. (p. 7)

PICTURE THIS

Below are pictures that represent key people or concepts from the book. Write the answers on the line to the right of the clues.

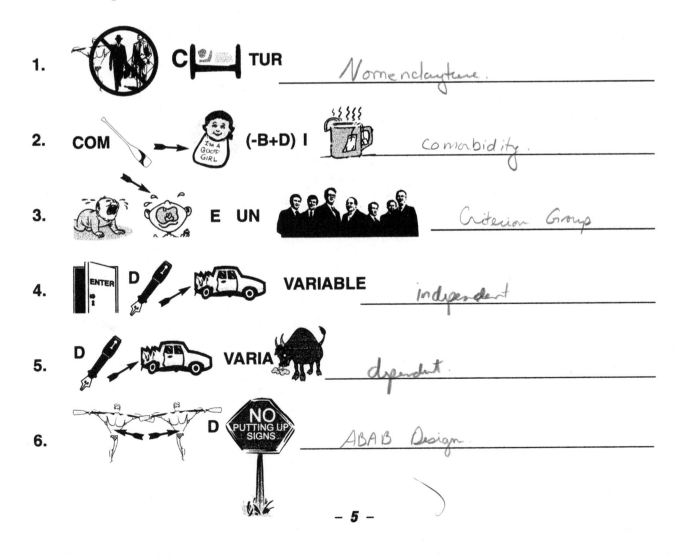

1. C[ ]TUR   *Nomenclature.*

2. COM → (-B+D) I   *Comorbidity.*

3. E UN   *Criterion Group*

4. ENTER D VARIABLE   *Independent*

5. D VARIA   *dependent.*

6. D NO PUTTING UP SIGNS   *ABAB Design.*

DOCTORAL CANDIDATE IS IN PROCESS—INTERN HELP 2.5 CENTS

You are a doctoral candidate in psychology and are starting your research. You are trying to decide what research design would be best for your work. The two you have decided to seriously consider are observational and experimental. Fill in the blanks for both methods below and write a brief description of both. (p. 20)

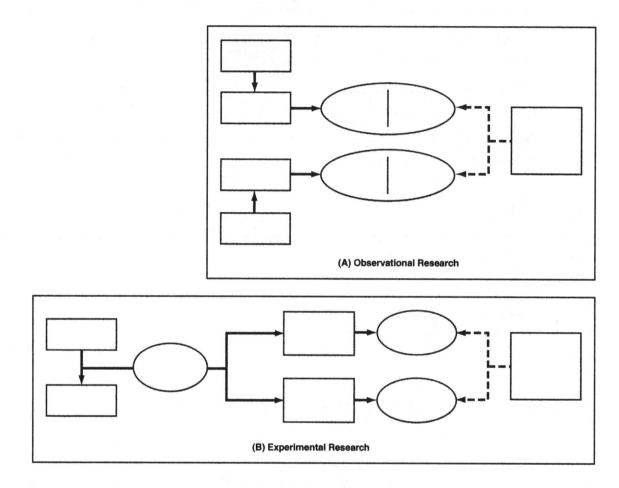

(A) Observational Research

(B) Experimental Research

OBSERVATIONAL:

EXPERIMENTAL:

AFTER YOU READ

PRACTICE TESTS

Take the following three multiple-choice tests to see how much you have comprehended from the chapter. Each represents roughly one-third of the chapter. As you study the chapter, use these to check your progress.

PRACTICE TEST NUMBER 1

1. To understand mental disorders, we need to (p. 3)
    a. ask questions that will help patients and their families.
    b. get to know people many people with mental disorders.
    c. watch several movies that deal with mental disorders, such as "A Beautiful Mind" or "As Good as it Gets."
    d. none of the above

2. An example of what is abnormal or deviant changes over time is the removal of _____ as a mental disorder from the DSM. (p. 5)
    a. depression
    b. pedophilia
    c. homosexuality
    d. voyeurism

3. A respectful way to classify the disorder, not the person, is by saying (p. 6)
    a. "The bipolar in room 325."
    b. "Suzie, who has schizophrenia, in Room 627."
    c. "Phobic John in Room 520."
    d. none of the above.

4. The most recent edition of the DSM is (p. 7)
    a. DSM-IV.
    b. DSM-IV-TR.
    c. DSM-V.
    d. DSM-III-R.

5. Mary is worrying excessively. This excessive worry is an example of a _____ which could indicate a larger problem. (p. 8)
    a. syndrome
    b. disorder
    c. symptom
    d. none of the above

6. John has been having trouble sleeping, feeling sad, having difficulty concentrating, and is losing weight. Together, all of these behaviors are referred to as a (p. 8)

    a. syndrome.
    b. disorder.
    c. symptom.
    d. none of the above

7. Koro, an anxiety disorder, is an example of a psychopathology that is specific to which culture? (pp. 9-10)

    a. Middle Eastern
    b. African
    c. Asian
    d. Hispanic

8. The World Around Us 1.3 "Personnel in Mental Health" describes professional and para-professional persons who work in the area of mental health. Two para-professionals described are (p. 11)

    a. pastoral counselor and community health worker.
    b. occupational therapist and alcohol- or drug-abuse counselor.
    c. community mental health worker and alcohol- or drug-abuse counselor.
    d. pastoral counselor and occupational therapist.

9. The ECH and NCS epidemiology studies cited in your book found that the most prevalent kind of psychological disorder in the United States is a(n) (p. 12)

    a. mood disorder.
    b. anxiety disorder.
    c. cognitive disorder.
    d. sexual disorder.

10. The NCS study found that _____ percent of people with one disorder also had one or more additional disorders. (p. 13)

    a. 28
    b. 12
    c. 56
    d. 68

PRACTICE TEST NUMBER 2

1. Early knowledge of psychopathological disorders come primarily from (p. 14)

    a. in-depth laboratory studies of many people.
    b. case studies of specific individuals.
    c. epidiomological studies of groups of people.
    d. surveys conducted by well-trained individuals.

2. Carol sits in a chair with several electrodes attached to her scalp. She is asked a series of questions. How her brain is processing information is being recorded. The method that is being used to collect information is (p. 15)

    a. direct observation.
    b. brain-imaging techniques.
    c. self-report.
    d. case study.

3. Research in abnormal psychology is concerned with (p. 16)

    a. gaining enhanced understanding.
    b. gaining control of abnormal behavior.
    c. a and b.
    d. none of the above

4. Although single case studies can be valuable, these do have drawbacks, one of which is (p. 16)

    a. generating a hypothesis.
    b. yielding enough information to make generalizations.
    c. causing us to think intelligently.
    d. a and c.

5. The most important thing to consider when conducting a research study is (p. 16)

    a. finding people who fit the criteria.
    b. passing out surveys.
    c. a and b.
    d. none of the above

6. A representative sampling is (p. 17)

    a. a small group of people drawn from a larger group, which meets criteria for the research.
    b. everyone who doesn't meet the criteria.
    c. every other person who meets criteria.
    d. random sampling of the entire population.

7. In doing research on childhood abuse experiences, David asked his subjects to recall certain incidents, but also relied on (pp. 18-19)

    a. siblings' memory.
    b. school reports.
    c. medical records.
    d. b and c.

8. A(n) _____ research approach collects information about a person's early life in an attempt to identify factors that lead to the development of a disorder. (p. 18)

   a. prospective
   b. retrospective
   c. introspective
   d. detective

9. The most basic experimental design in single-case research is the (p. 21)

   a. BABA design.
   b. DSM-IV-TR design.
   c. ABAB design.
   d. MINH design.

10. In a single-case research design, the same _____ is studied over time. (p. 21)

   a. population
   b. subject
   c. treatment
   d. all of the above

PRACTICE TEST NUMBER 3

1. A(n) _____ research approach focuses on individuals who have a higher-than-average likelihood of developing a psychological disorder and provide assistance before the disorder develops. (p. 18)

   a. prospective
   b. retrospective
   c. introspective
   d. detective

2. Drs. Abby and Normal are conducting experimental research on the effects of sound on student concentration. They will be manipulating the sound level in their experiment. The sound is known as the (p. 19)

   a. dependent variable.
   b. independent variable.
   c. correlational variable.
   d. co-existing variable.

3. The outcome of the above experiment is known as the (p. 20)

   a. dependent variable.
   b. independent variable.
   c. correlational variable.
   d. co-existing variable.

4. Pat was in a study in which she received a sugar pill instead of the experimental medication. Afterward she reported feeling better. Pat's reaction is a result of what? (p. 4)

    a. placebo treatment
    b. luck
    c. not having anything wrong in the first place
    d. being in the wrong group

5. A distinctive innovation since the DSM-III of 1980 has been the use of "operational" criteria for defining disorders. This means that the DSM now (p. 7)

    a. clearly specifies the causes or etiological factors.
    b. specifies the theoretical interpretation of the symptoms.
    c. identifies the adaptive function of the symptoms.
    d. specifies the exact behaviors that must be observed.

6. There is strong evidence for significant overlap between anxiety and depression. Still a patient receives two diagnoses: one for anxiety and one for depression. This is an example of (p. 13)

    a. synthesis.
    b. concurrence.
    c. convergence.
    d. comorbidity.

7. Which of the following terms refers to a mental condition of relatively short duration? (p. 13)

    a. episodic
    b. acute
    c. chronic
    d. factitious

8. In order to make sense of observed behavior, psychologists generate more or less plausible ideas called (p. 15)

    a. constructs.
    b. hypotheses.
    c. principles.
    d. theories.

9. The purpose of _____ is to ensure, in effect, that each member of the population has an equal chance of being included in the study's sample. (p. 17)

    a. increasing reliability
    b. hypothesis testing
    c. structured set sampling
    d. random selection

10. A psychologist identifies 50 children who have schizophrenic mothers. At adolescence, the researcher compares those who develop schizophrenia with those who don't. This is an example of a _____ study. (p. 18)

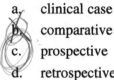

    a. clinical case
    b. comparative outcome
    c. prospective
    d. retrospective

COMPREHENSIVE PRACTICE TEST

The following tests are designed to give you an idea of how well you understood the entire chapter. There are three different types of tests: multiple-choice, true-false, and essay.

MULTIPLE-CHOICE

1. A classification system for mental disorders is advantageous because it gives us a way to (p. 5)

    a. structure information.
    b. advance research.
    c. create treatment plans.
    d. all of the above.

2. The DSM is published by the (p. 7)

    a. American Psychological Association.
    b. American Medical Association.
    c. American Psychiatric Association.
    d. American Social Work Association.

3. The number of active cases in a population during any given period of time is referred to as (p. 11)

    a. incidences.
    b. epidemiology.
    c. clinically significant.
    d. prevalence.

4. The number of new cases that occur over a period of time is referred to as (p. 12)

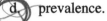

    a. incidences.
    b. epidemiology.
    c. clinically significant.
    d. prevalence.

5. Research in abnormal psychology helps to (p. 13)
   a. study the nature of the disorder.
   b. understand the causes.
   c. provide the best care.
   d. all of the above

6. Doing research on shopping behavior for her class, Sally sat on a bench in a busy mall making notes of what she saw. Sally was using what method to gather information? (p. 14)
   a. direct observation
   b. psychophysiological variables
   c. self-report
   d. case study

7. Dr. Casey has what she thinks is a unique client and has done extensive data collection when working with him, including taking photographs of the behavior. She plans to present this client's behavior at a national convention. Dr. Casey is using what method to gather this information? (p. 14)
   a. direct observation
   b. brain-imaging techniques
   c. self-report
   d. case study

8. Stan and Jim are eager to find out if college students at their school are typical with regard to the ever-increasing problem of binge drinking. To gather this information, they create a survey asking a number of questions about student's drinking habits. The method that Stan and Jim are using is (p. 15)
   a. direct observation.
   b. brain-imaging techniques.
   c. self-report.
   d. case study.

9. Jennifer is doing research on the effects of violent video games on children's behavior. Her observations have lead her to believe that possibly there is a connection. She wants to test this concept. Jennifer's idea is called a(n) (p. 15)
   a. projection.
   b. case study.
   c. hypothesis.
   d. finding.

10.   To test a hypothesis, researchers use _____ of people who don't exhibit the disorder being studied. (p. 17)

  a.   an interesting group
  b.   a control group
  c.   a loosely structured group
  d.   a variable group

11.   Unlike a controlled-research approach, observational or correlational research (p. 17)

  a.   manipulates variables.
  b.   uses a control group.
  c.   does not manipulate variables.
  d.   all of the above.

12.   The possible reason(s) two variables are highly correlated is/are (p. 18)

  a.   variable A causes B (or vice versa).
  b.   variable A and variable B are both caused by variable C.
  c.   variables A and B are both involved in a pattern of other variables that influence A and B.
  d.   all of the above.

13.   Chris is studying depression in animals. He hopes that his findings may be generalized to humans. Chris's work is referred to as a(n) (p. 22)

  a.   retrospective study.
  b.   prospective study.
  c.   case study.
  d.   analogue study.

14.   Observational research studies things as they (p. 25)

  a.   want to be.
  b.   seem to be.
  c.   are.
  d.   a and c.

15.   The New View Hospital is conducting a research study in which neither the experimenters nor the subjects know who is getting the experimental drug and who is getting the placebo. This is an example of what kind of study? (p. 4)

  a.   case study
  b.   experimental study
  c.   observational study
  d.   double-blind study

TRUE - FALSE

1. Two areas in which psychologists are specially trained are asking questions and doing research. (T)/ F   (p. 3)

2. There is consensus regarding the definition of "abnormality." (T)/ F   (p. 4)

3. Culture plays a role in how clients present mental disorders to clinicians. (T)/ F   (p. 9)

4. More than 18% of the U.S. population suffers from at least one mental disorder during the course of a year. (T)/ F   (p. 13)

5. People with psychological disabilities will always seek treatment from a trained psychologist. T /(F)   (p. 13)

6. Research is confined to the laboratory. T /(F) (p. 14)

7. The greater the number of people who are sampled or studied, the better the findings will be. (T)/ F   (p. 14)

8. The less representative the sample, the more the findings can be generalized to the larger group. T /(F) (p. 17)

9. Correlation proves causation. T /(F)   (p. 18)

10. Correlational studies can suggest causal hypotheses. (T)/ F   (p. 18)

11. The experimental research methods have proven valuable in treatment research. (T)/ F (p. 20)

12. Experimental research always involves testing hypotheses by manipulating variables across groups. (T)(F)(p. 21)

13. The authors of your textbook believe it is important to be respectful of scientific principles and patients who have psychopathological conditions. (T)/ F   (p. 23)

ESSAY QUESTIONS

1. Describe the elements of abnormality. (p. 6)

   Deviance
   Suffering
   Maladaptiveness
   Irrationality + Unpredictability.
   Social Discomfort
   Violations of Standards of Society.

2. Steve is doing research on how watching comedy will affect people who are depressed. Discuss how Steve will go about setting up his research. (pp. 15-19)

WEB LINKS TO ITEMS OR CONCEPTS DISCUSSED IN THIS CHAPTER

DSM-IV-TR

    www.geocities.com/morrison94/

    behavenet.com/capsules/disorders/dsm4TRclassification.htm

Sigmund Freud

    plaza.interport.net/nypsan/freudarc.html (Collection of links)

    plaza.interport.net/nypsan/ (Freud Net)

    freud.t0.or.at/ (Freud Society, Vienna)

CRISS-CROSS

Now that you know all there is to know about this chapter, here's your chance to put that knowledge to work.

CRISS CROSS CLUES

Across
5. Identifying two or more disorders in a psychologically disordered individual
7. Experiment wherein neither participants nor staff knows which group gets the placebo
10. Study of the distribution of mental disorders

Down
1. Sudden onset of a disorder, usually with intense symptoms
2. The process of selecting a representative subgroup
3. The proportion of active cases that can be identified during a given time period
4. Positive effect experienced after an inactive treatment is administered
5. Long-standing or frequent disorder, often with progressing seriousness
6. Occurrence rate of a given disorder
8. Patient's subjective description of a physical or mental disorder
9. Symptoms that occur together and represent the typical picture of a disorder

Puzzle created with Puzzlemaker at DiscoverySchool.com

CHAPTER TWO

Historical and Contemporary Views of Abnormal Behavior

BEFORE YOU READ

To understand what's happening in the present and to be able to look to the future, we need to know about the past. Why people behave the way they do is something that has been written about, researched, speculated over, and discussed for thousands of years. Abnormal behavior has fascinated humankind from its beginning, and various explanations of the causes of such behavior have developed over the course of history. Indeed, behavior also has been influenced by historical events and times.

This chapter presents a chronological overview of the many ways abnormal behavior has been viewed and treated, starting with ancient times and continuing through the modern era. This chapter enables you to learn how these different views of behavior have evolved. In so doing, it aims to help you understand the background for and basis of many of the fundamental issues in our field.

OBJECTIVES

After reading this chapter, you should be able to:

1. Explain why in ancient times abnormal behavior was attributed to possession by a demon or god and describe how exorcism was administered by shamans and priests as the primary type of treatment for demonic possession.

2. Describe the important contributions from 460 B.C. to 200 A.D. of Hippocrates, Plato, Aristotle, and Galen to the conceptualization of the nature and causes of abnormal behavior.

3. Discuss how mental disorders were viewed during the Middle Ages.

4. Give examples of mass madness or mass hysteria and summarize the explanations offered for this unusual phenomenon.

5. Outline the contributions in the late Middle Ages and early Renaissance of Paracelsus, Teresa of Avila, Johan Weyer, Reginald Scot, and St. Vincent de Paul, all of whom argued that those showing abnormal behavior should be seen as mentally ill and treated with humane care.

6. Describe the inhumane treatment that mental patients received in early "insane asylums" in Europe and the United States.

7. Describe the humanitarian reforms in the treatment of mental patients that were instigated by Philippe Pinel, William Tuke, Benjamin Rush, and Dorothea Dix.

8. Explain how the discovery of a biological basis for general paresis and a handful of other disorders (such as, the senile mental disorders, toxic mental disorders, and certain types of mental retardation), contributed in a major way to the development of a scientific approach to abnormal psychology, as well as to the emergence of modern experimental science, which was largely biological.

9. Distinguish between biological and non-biological versions of medical-model thinking about psychopathology.

10. Trace the important events in the development of psychoanalysis and the psychodynamic perspective.

11. Contrast the biological and psychodynamic views of abnormal disorders.

12. Describe how the techniques of free association and dream analysis helped analysts and their patients.

13. List the major features of the behavioral perspective.

14. Discriminate between classical and operant conditioning.

15. Explain the problems associated with interpreting historical events.

AS YOU READ

Answers can be found in the Answer Key at the end of the book.

KEY WORDS

Each of the words below is important in understanding the concepts presented in this chapter. Write the definition next to each of the words. The page numbers are provided in case you need to refer to the book.

insanity (p. 36)   mesmerism (pp. 45-46)

mass madness (p. 33)   Nancy School (p. 46)

tarantism (p. 33)   catharsis (p. 46)

Saint Vitus's Dance (p. 33)   unconscious (p. 46)

exorcism (p. 34)   free association (p. 47)

asylums (p. 36)   dream analysis (p. 47)

moral management (p. 38)   behavioral perspective (pp. 48-49)

mental hygiene movement (p. 38)   classical conditioning (p. 48)

deinstitutionalization (p. 41)   behaviorism (p. 49)

psychoanalytic perspective (p. 45)   operant conditioning (p. 49)

psychoanalysis (p. 45)

SHORT ANSWERS

Provide brief answers to the following questions.

1. Describe the contributions Hippocrates made to the understanding of mental illness. (pp. 28-29)

2. The occurrence of mass madness peaked in the 14th and 15th centuries. Why, according to the text, was mass madness so common during these years? (p. 34)

3. Describe the atmosphere and treatment methods at the early asylums. (pp. 36-37)

4. Discuss the reasons moral management of the mentally ill had been abandoned by the last part of the 19th century. (p. 38)

5. Explain the important events that lead to the biomedical breakthrough in discovering a cure for general paresis. (p. 44)

WHO'S WHO IN THE HISTORY OF ABNORMAL PSYCHOLOGY

From the list on the next page, write the number of the achievement or description on the line next to the corresponding name above, and list two or three relevant benefits or accomplishments of the era.

THE ANCIENT WORLD

Plato *(429-347 B.C.)* _____ 6

Galen *(130-200 A.D.)* _____ 19

13 _____ Hippocrates *(460-377 B.C.)*

27 _____ Aristotle *(384-322 B.C.)*

Accomplishments _____

THE MIDDLE AGES

Martin Luther *(1483-1546)* _____ 1

8 _____ Avicenna *(980-1037)*

12 _____ Paracelsus *(1490-1541)*

Accomplishments _____

THE 16th THROUGH THE 18th CENTURIES

Teresa of Avila *(1515-1582)* _____ 7

Riginald Scot *(1538-1599)* _____ 2

William Tuke *(1732-1822)* _____ 11

Benjamin Rush *(1745-1813)* _____ 22

26 _____ Johann Weyer *(1515-1588)*

17 _____ Robert Burton *(1576-1640)*

15 _____ Philippe Pinel *(1745-1826)*

Accomplishments _____

THE 19th AND EARLY 20th CENTURIES

Clifford Beers *(1876-1943)* _____ 10

Emil Kraepelin *(1856-1926)* _____ 26

Wilhelm Wundt *(1832-1920)* _____ 21

Lightner Witmer *(1867-1956)* _____ 14

William Healy *(1869-1963)* _____ 9

B. F. Skinner *(1904-1990)* _____ 25

4 _____ Dorothea Dix *(1802-1887)*

5 _____ Franz Anton Mesmer *(1734-1815)*

18 _____ Sigmund Freud *(1856-1938)*

3 _____ J. McKeen Cattell *(1860-1944)*

23 _____ Ivan Pavlov *(1849-1936)*

16 _____ John B. Watson *(1878-1958)*

24 _____ E. L. Thorndike *(1874-1949)*

Accomplishments _____

1. German theologian during the Reformation who held the belief, common to his time, that the mentally disturbed were possessed by the devil.

2. Englishman who refuted the notion of demons as the cause of mental disorders and was castigated by King James I.

3. American psychologist who adopted Wundt's methods and studied individual differences in mental processing.

4. American teacher who founded the mental hygiene movement in the United States.

5. Austrian physician who conducted early investigations into hypnosis as a medical treatment.

6. A Greek philosopher who believed that mental patients should be treated humanely.

7. Canonized Spanish nun who argued that mental disorder was an illness of the mind.

8. Islamic Arabian-born physician who adopted principles of humane treatment for the mentally disturbed at a time when Western approaches to mental illness were the opposite.

9. American psychologist who established the Chicago Juvenile Psychopathic Institute.

10. American who campaigned to change public attitudes toward mental patients after his own experiences in mental institutions.

11. English Quaker who established the York Retreat, where mental patients lived in humane surroundings.

12. Swiss physician who rejected demonology as a cause of abnormal behavior.

13. Greek physician who believed that mental disease was the result of natural causes and brain pathology, rather than demonology.

14. American psychologist who established the first psychological clinic in the United States, focusing on problems of mentally deficient children.

15. French physician who pioneered the use of moral management in La Bicétre and La Salpétriére hospitals in France.

16. Known as the father of behaviorism.

17. Oxford scholar who wrote *Anatomy of Melancholia,* in 1621.

18. The founder of the school of psychological therapy known as psychoanalysis.

19. Greek physician and advocate of the Hippocratic tradition who contributed much to our understanding of the nervous system.

20. German psychiatrist who developed the first diagnostic system.

21. German scientist who established the first experimental psychology laboratory in 1879.

22. American physician and founder of American psychiatry.

23. Russian physiologist who published classical studies in the psychology of learning.

24. Developed concept of instrumental conditioning.

25. Studied how consequences of behavior influences behavior operant conditioning.

26. German physician who argued against demonology and was ostracized by his peers and the Church for his progressive views.

27. Greek philosopher and a pupil of Plato who believed in the Hippocratic theory that various agents, or humors, within the body when imbalanced, were responsible for mental disorders.

FILL IN THE BLANKS

Read the following and fill in the blanks. These questions are designed to help you focus on specific details.

1. The four bodily fluids (humors) Hippocrates and Galen believed controlled health, and, when not in balance, caused mental illness were _____, _____, _____, and _____. (p. 29)

2. The Middle Ages in Europe lasted from about 500-1500 A.D. The Middle Ages can be characterized as _____ with respect to scientific thinking about the causes of abnormal behavior or enlightened treatment of mentally disordered persons. (p. 32)

3. Robert Burton, who wrote _____ in 1621, said there were two types of demonically possessed people—those who were _____ possessed and considered mad, and those who were _____ possessed and considered witches. (p. 34)

4. Henry VIII of England established a mental hospital in 1545 called St. Mary of Bethlehem, which soon became known as _____, adding a new word to our language. (p. 36)

5. The first hospital in the United States devoted exclusively to the mentally ill was _____, which was constructed in Williamsburg, Virginia, in 1773. (p. 36)

6. In the early 19th century _____, _____, or _____ were the acceptable medical treatment of "lunatics." These produced few objective results. (p. 39)

7. In the early 20th century, two people who were instrumental in helping Clifford Beers educate the public concerning the bad treatment still given the mentally ill were _____ and _____. (p. 40)

8. The development in 1956 of two psychotropic medications, _____ and _____, which was discussed in Developments in Research 2.3 "Historic Search for Medication to Cure Related Disorders," effected psychiatric hospitals by leveling admissions at 560,000, then dropping them to 300,000 by 1971. (p. 42)

9. In addition to an emphasis on the importance of brain pathology in mental disorders, the most important contribution of Kraepelin's 1883 textbook was his system of _____, which became the forerunner of today's DSM-IV. (p. 44)

10. In disagreement with the Nancy School, Charcot insisted that _____ _____ led to hysteria. (p. 46)

11. The Nancy School finally triumphed in its dispute with Charcot, representing the first recognition of a _____ caused mental disorder. (p. 46)

12. The debate between the Nancy School and Charcot was a step in recognizing that mental disorders could have a _____ basis or a _____ basis or _____.
    (p. 46)

13. The behavioral perspective is organized around a central theme: the role of _____ in human behavior. (p. 48)

14. John A. Watson's (1878-1955) behavioristic approach placed emphasis on the role of the _____ environment in _____ personality development and both _____ and _____ behavior. (p. 49)

THE DOCTOR IS IN...PSYCHIATRIC HELP—5¢

Read the following scenarios and diagnose the client. Remember to look carefully at the criteria for the disorder before you make a decision as to the diagnosis. Make a list of other information you might need to help you understand the causal factors.

1. You are an assistant to the great Greek physician, Hippocrates. A patient comes to you and is sad, not interested in anything, sleeping badly, and unable to take part in the active Greek social life. Hippocrates asks for your opinion on what is wrong with this patient, the cause, and the treatment. What would you say? (pp. 28-29)

2. You and Philippe Pinel have just taken charge of the asylum of La Bicétre in Paris. What experiment do you and Pinel conduct there? (p. 37)

3. As a psychiatrist in the early 19th century, you have just become affiliated with the local asylum. A young woman comes to the asylum and tells you she is feeling low, lacks energy, and has several physical symptoms: crying and pain in several areas of her body. How would you diagnose her and what would you consider the cause of her affliction? (p. 39)

4. It's 1912 and you have just been referred to Dr. Sigmund Freud. You have had symptoms of hysteria and he is the leading expert in the field. What would you expect Dr. Freud to tell you about the cause of your disorder and what treatments would he use? (p. 45)

AFTER YOU READ

PRACTICE TESTS

Take the following multiple-choice tests to see how much you have comprehended from the chapter. Once again, if you get stuck, the page numbers are listed at the end of the study aid chapter along with the answers.

PRACTICE TEST NUMBER 1

1. Stone-age cave dwellers treated mental illness by performing a crude operation known as (p. 28)
    a. tripoding.
    b. trephining.
    c. triazing.
    d. catharsis.

2. Abnormal behavior was attributed to what by the ancient Chinese, Egyptians, Hebrews, and Greeks? (p. 28)
    a. bad genes
    b. disobeying the state
    c. demon or god possessions
    d. bad humor

3. A person who "spoke with a god" in ancient China would have been considered to be (p. 28)
    a. possessed by evil spirits or demons.
    b. not him or her self.
    c. trying to get attention.
    d. possessed by good spirits.

4. If a person were considered possessed by a demon, treatment usually was (p. 28)
    a. confinement to an institution.
    b. dream analysis.
    c. exorcism.
    d. plenty of sleep.

5. Hippocrates and, later Galen, supported an early paradigm that stated _____ bodily humors were responsible for human behavior. (p. 29)
    a. five
    b. thirty-seven
    c. eight
    d. 4

6. The first person to consider dreams an important tool in understanding a patient's problem was (p. 29)
    a. Freud.
    b. Pinel.
    c. Hippocrates.
    d. Galen.

7. The first person to propose that people with mental disorders weren't responsible for their criminal behavior was (p. 29)
    a. Hipprocates.
    b. Galen.
    c. Freud.
    d. Plato.

8. The first to provide descriptions of consciousness and to write extensively on mental disorders was (pp. 29-30)
    a. Aristotle.
    b. Plato.
    c. Galen.
    d. Freud.

9. The ancient Roman physician, Galen, maintained a very scientific approach to psychological disorders by dividing their causes into _____ categories. (p. 31)

    a. spiritual and demonic
    b. practical and impractical
    c. known and unknown
    d. physical and mental

10. _____, known as the "prince of physicians," wrote *The Canon of Medicine* during the Middle Ages. (p. 31)

    a. Aleppo
    b. Avicenna
    c. Damascus
    d. Galen

PRACTICE TEST NUMBER 2

1. During the Middle Ages in Europe, people with mental disorders were (p. 32)

    a. treated with care and respect.
    b. given the most current treatment.
    c. studied in the light of scientific thinking.
    d. void of humane treatment.

2. Johann Weyer, one of the first physicians to specialize in mental disorders, is also know as the founder of (p. 35)

    a. modern psycholopathology.
    b. humanism.
    c. psychoanalysis.
    d. electrotherapy.

3. Who is considered the first person to begin humane treatment of the mentally ill in French asylums? (p. 37)

    a. Benjamin Franklin
    b. Philippe Pinel
    c. Henry VIII
    d. William Tuke

4. This man established the York Retreat, a country house where the mentally ill could live, work, and rest in a religious atmosphere. (p. 37)

    a. Philippe Pinel
    b. William Tuke
    c. Benjamin Rush
    d. Benjamin Franklin

5. He is the founder of American psychiatry. (p. 38)

    a. Benjamin Franklin
    b. James Watson
    c. Benjamin Rush
    d. Carl Rogers

6. *The Snake Pit* was written in 1946 by _____. It called attention to the need for more humane mental health care in the _____, not overcrowded mental hospitals. (p. 40)

    a. Mary Jane Ward, community
    b. Sigmund Freud, community
    c. Clifford Beers, private residence
    d. William James, private residence

7. The National Institutes of Mental Health was organized in (p. 40)

    a. 1925.
    b. 1946.
    c. 1950.
    d. 1492.

8. Beginning in the last part of the 19th century, technological discoveries helped start what is known today as the _____ view of abnormal behavior. (p. 43)

    a. scientific
    b. experimentally oriented
    c. sociological
    d. a or b

9. Emil Kraepelin, in his work to classify mental disorders, distinguished between mental disorders and thought the course of each was (p. 45)

    a. left to chance.
    b. predictable and predetermined.
    c. similar.
    d. at the whim of fate.

10. Freud's method of treatment, psychoanalysis, has its roots in the study of (p. 45)

    a. hypnosis.
    b. brain chemistry.
    c. individuals.
    d. groups.

PRACTICE TEST NUMBER 3

1. Franz Anton Mesmer (1734-1815), in his belief that people possessed magnetic fields that could be used to cure mental disorders, demonstrated most of the phenomena later associated with (pp. 45-46)

    a. dream analysis.

    b. psychoanalysis.

    c. hypnosis.

    d. a and b

2. Who was the first person to attempt to systematically answer the question as to how psychologically based mental disorders develop? (p. 46)

    a. Charcot

    b. Bernhein

    c. Liêbeault

    d. Freud

3. Toward the end of the 19th century, another school of thought about abnormal behavior, called _____, began to emerge that challenged the dominant theory. (p. 48)

    a. psychoanalysis

    b. humanism

    c. cognitive

    d. behaviorism

4. Ivan Pavlov (1849-1936) is noted for his work with dogs in which he demonstrated what was to become known as (pp. 48-49)

    a. operant conditioning.

    b. generalization.

    c. classical conditioning.

    d. a and c

5. Operant conditioning theory, developed by E. L. Thorndike (1874-1949) and B. F. Skinner (1904-1990), explores how behaviors are influenced by (p. 49)

    a. feelings.

    b. thoughts.

    c. family dynamics.

    d. consequences.

6. All of the following are reasons that have been offered as explanations for the abandonment of moral treatment in the latter part of the 19th century, **except** (p. 38)

    a. a rising tide of racial and ethnic prejudice.

    b. overextension of hospital facilities.

    c. general loss of faith among the general population.

    d. belief that mental disorders would yield to physical solutions.

7. Classical and operant conditioning differ primarily with respect to (p. 49)

    a. the types of reinforcers involved.

    b. an emphasis on animal versus human subjects.

    c. the number of trials to reach criterion performance.

    d. whether the outcome (reinforcer) is dependent on the animal's behavior.

8. To understand current events in psychology or any area, for that matter, it is important to have an understanding of the _____ developments. (p. 52)

    a. historical

    b. future

    c. concrete

    d. empirical

9. It is often difficult to study historical information and form accurate pictures. Why is this the case? (p. 53)

    a. events are open to reinterpretation

    b. bias on part of researchers

    c. cannot rely on direct observation

    d. all of the above

10. In 1917, Wagner-Jauregg introduced a treatment for general paresis involving (p. 44)

    a. prescribing laudanum.

    b. prescribing specific wild herbs.

    c. prescribing lithium.

    d. infecting the sufferer with malaria.

COMPREHENSIVE PRACTICE TEST

The following tests are designed to give you an idea of how well you understood the entire chapter. There are three different types of tests: multiple-choice, true-false, and essay.

MULTIPLE-CHOICE

1. Information dating back to the 16th century B.C. on the treatment of disease and mental disorders appears on (p. 28)

    a. the Edwin Smith and Ebers papyri.

    b. cave walls.

    c. the Rosetta Stone.

    d. tools used to perform treatment.

2. Early Chinese, Egyptians, Hebrews, and Greeks believed person who became excited or overactive and perhaps exhibited strange behavior to be (p. 28)

    a. possessed by evil spirits or demons.

    b. not him or herself.

    c. trying to get attention.

    d. possessed by good spirits.

3. Hippocrates said that mental illness could be classified into three general categories: (p. 29)

    a. spiritual, demonic, and exorcised.

    b. paranoid, depressed, and schizophrenic.

    c. blood, phlegm, and bile.

    d. mania, melancholic, and phrenitis.

4. According to ancient Greek and Egyptian medicine, hysteria was a result of a(n) (p. 30)

    a. imbalance of the four humors.

    b. wandering womb.

    c. demonic possession.

    d. godly possession.

5. _____ has been called the "Hippocates of China." (p. 33)

    a. Ben-Teans Ng

    b. Huang Ti

    c. Chung Ching

    d. Tai Chi

6. Who is considered a pioneer in the humane treatment of the mentally ill in England? (p. 37)

    a. Benjamin Franklin

    b. Philippe Pinel

    c. Henry VIII

    d. William Tuke

7. Dorothea Dix is noted for her highly successful campaign to do something about the (p. 39)

    a. inhumane treatment accorded the mentally ill.

    b. problem of heroin abuse during the Civil War.

    c. view that women were biologically inferior.

    d. overcrowded conditions in large mental hospitals in rural areas.

8. In the early part of the 19th century, psychiatrists were known as (p. 39)

    a. lay people.

    b. saints.

    c. alienists.

    d. scientists.

9. The last half of the 20th century saw a change in the mental hospital environment because of what scientific development? (p. 41)

   a. effective use of psychoanalysis

   b. understanding the need to rehabilitate people with mental illnesses

   c. effective medication

   d. effective use of group therapy

10. Believing that mentally disturbed people were better off in the community, which could provide integrated and humane treatment, the latter decades of the 20th century began a movement of (p. 41)

    a. communitization.

    b. deinstitutionalization.

    c. networking.

    d. modernization.

11. Advancing knowledge of anatomy, physiology, neurology, chemistry, and general medicine lead to the identification of _____ pathology underlying many physical ailments, as well as mental illnesses. (p. 44)

    a. psychological

    b. neurological

    c. biological

    d. sociological

12. He is acknowledged as the most frequently cited psychological theorist of the 20th century. (p. 45)

    a. Kraepelin

    b. Mesmer

    c. Freud

    d. Watson

13. Who is considered the founder of clinical psychology? (p. 48)

    a. Sigmund Freud

    b. William Healy

    c. Lightner Witmer

    d. Wilhelm Wundt

14. Who was the first person to expand the causes of abnormal behavior beyond inner psychological problems to include environmental or sociocultural factors? (p. 48)

    a. Sigmund Freud

    b. William Healy

    c. Lightner Witmer

    d. Wilhelm Wundt

15. Behaviorism emerged out of (p. 48)

    a.   experimental psychology.

    b.   the unconscious.

    c.   cathartic experiences.

    d.   Pavlov's experiments.

TRUE - FALSE

1. What once was known as hysteria, is referred to today as conversion disorder. T / F (p. 30)

2. Contrariis contrarius was a treatment plan used by ancient Roman doctors to treat patients. T / F (p. 31)

3. During the Middle Ages, Europe was more enlightened in its treatment of the mentally ill than the Middle East. T / F (p. 31)

4. Scientific questioning didn't emerge again until the first part of the 19th century. T / F (p. 35)

5. Johann Weyer (1515-1588) was a German physician and writer who used the pseudonym, Joannus Wierner, when he wrote *The Deception of Demons*. T / F (p. 35)

6. Asylums are often referred to as sane houses. T / F (p. 36)

7. Moral management was a success because antipsychotic drugs were used to help patients. T / F (p. 38)

8. The early period of the Middle Ages in Europe saw the mentally ill treated with kindness by the clergy. This later gave way to much more inhumane treatment. T / F (p. 34)

9. Early 19th century psychiatrists/alienists became the purveyors of morality by saying that Victorian morality was good for mental health. T / F (p. 39)

10. By the end of the 19th century, mental hospitals were accepted by society as well-run facilities. T / F (p. 40)

11. Wilhelm Wundt and Carl Jung are two names associated with the early rigorous efforts to objectively study psychological processes. T / F (p. 47)

ESSAY QUESTIONS

1. Discuss the motives behind and problems with deinstitutionalization. (pp. 41-42)

2. Explain the disagreement between the Charcot and the Nancy School. (p. 46)

WEB LINKS TO ITEMS OR CONCEPTS DISCUSSED IN THIS CHAPTER

Nancy School home page

       www.thenancyschool.com/

Tarantism

       www.webref.org/psychology/t/tarantism.htm

       www.wordreference.com/English/definition.asp?en=tarantism

Abnormal Behavior

       www.pbs.org/als/world_psych/wanpdescrip.htm

CRISS-CROSS

Now that you know all there is to know about this chapter, here's your chance to put that knowledge to work.

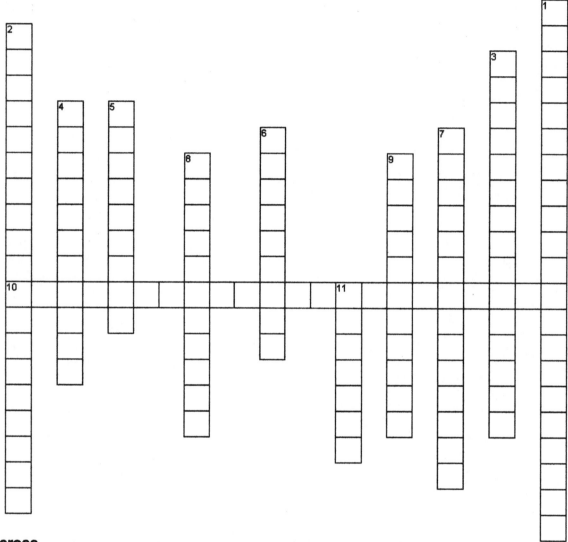

Across
   10.   Movement to close mental hospitals and treat patients in the community
Down
   1.   Basic form of learning using a neutral stimulus with an unconditioned stimulus repeatedly to eventually elicit a conditioned response
   2.   Form of learning in which a response is reinforced
   3.   Method for probing the unconscious by having patients talk freely about themselves
   4.   A major portion of the mind containing a hidden mass of instincts, impulses, and memories
   5.   13th-Century, Italian dancing mania
   6.   Theories of "animal magnetism" (hypnosis) developed by Anton Mesmer
   7.   Method Freud used to study and treat patients
   8.   Delusion of being a wolf
   9.   A school of psychology that formerly restricted itself primarily to study of overt behavior
   11.   Institutions meant solely for the care of the mentally ill

CHAPTER THREE

Causal Factors and Viewpoints In Abnormal Psychology

BEFORE YOU READ

This chapter discusses modern viewpoints and causal models of abnormal behavior. Within the biological viewpoint, several broad physiological causal factors are reviewed, ranging from brain and biochemical functioning to genetic/-constitutional vulnerabilities. The psychosocial viewpoint encompasses the psychodynamic, behavioral, and cognitive-behavioral models. The chapter then focuses on the importance of early psychosocial factors as powerful causes of abnormal behavior.

The sociocultural viewpoint reminds us that humans are part of larger social contexts, and our behavior cannot be fully understood without reference to the influences of the society in which we live. It is now widely recognized that no one model adequately explains every aspect of every form of abnormal behavior. Consequently, one needs to assess and deal with the interaction of biological, psychosocial, and sociocultural factors to develop the total clinical picture.

OBJECTIVES

After reading this chapter, you should be able to:

1. Discuss the different conceptual approaches to understanding the causes of abnormal behavior. These approaches will include: (a) necessary, sufficient, and contributory causes; (b) feedback and circularity models; and (c) the diathesis-stress model.

2. Summarize the biological theories of abnormal behavior, including neurotransmitter/hormonal imbalances, genetic and constitutional influences, and physical damage to brain structures.

3. Outline the major psychosocial theoretical approaches to abnormal behavior, including the psychodynamic, behavioral, and cognitive-behavioral perspectives.

4. Discuss the substantive contributions of the psychosocial factors of deviant cognitions (schema and self-schema), early deprivation or trauma (e.g., parental deprivation, institutionalization, abuse, etc.), inadequate parenting and pathogenic family structures, and problems with peer relationships.

5. Describe the sociocultural perspective and its contributions to understanding abnormal behavior.

6. Explain why the field needs a unified viewpoint and how the biopsychosocial viewpoint may fulfill that need.

AS YOU READ

KEY WORDS

Each of the words below is important in understanding the concepts presented in this Chapter. Write the definition next to each of the words. The page numbers are provided in case you need to refer to the book.

etiology (p. 56)   twin method (pp. 65-66)

necessary cause (p. 56)   adoption method (p. 66)

sufficient cause (p. 56)   concordance rate (p. 66)

contributory cause (p. 57)   linkage analysis (p. 66)

diathesis-stress models (p. 58)   association studies (p. 68)

protective factors (p. 58)   fetal alcohol syndrome (p. 69)

resilience (p. 58)   temperament (p. 69)

developmental psychopathology (p. 59)   developmental systems approach (p. 70) id (p. 72)

ego (p. 72)

libido (p. 72)

pleasure principle (p. 72)

primary process thinking (p. 72)

superego (p. 74)

reality principle (p. 74)

secondary process thinking (p. 74)

intrapsychic conflicts (p. 74)

ego defense mechanisms (p. 74)

psychosexual stages of development (p. 74)

Oedpius complex/Electra complex (p. 76)

castration anxiety (p. 76)

object relations theory (p. 76)

introjection (p. 76)

interpersonal perspective (p. 77)

attachment theory (p. 78)

classical conditioning (p. 80)

extinction (p. 80)

spontaneous recovery (p. 80)

reinforcement (p. 81)

generalization (p. 81)

discrimination (p. 81)

observational learning (p. 81)

cognitive-behavioral perspective (p. 83)

attributions (p. 83)

schema (p. 86)

self-schema (p. 86)

assimilation (p. 86)

accommodation (pp. 86-87)

WHO'S WHO AND WHAT'S WHAT—MATCHING

Who's Who–Match each of the following people with her/his accomplishment or theory.

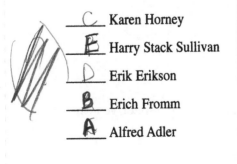

_C_	Karen Horney
_E_	Harry Stack Sullivan
_D_	Erik Erikson
_B_	Erich Fromm
_A_	Alfred Adler

A. believed that people are inherently social beings motivated primarily by the desire to belong to and participate in a group.

B. focused on dispositions that people adopt in their interactions.

C. vigorously rejected Freud's demeaning female psychology.

D. broadened Freud's psychosexual stages into more socially-oriented concepts.

E. maintained that the term "personality" was best defined in terms of an individual's characteristic way of relating to others.

What's What—Match each of the following terms with its definition.

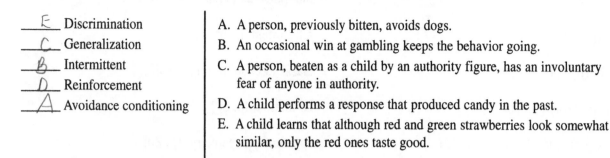

   E   Discrimination
   C   Generalization
   B   Intermittent
   D   Reinforcement
   A   Avoidance conditioning

A. A person, previously bitten, avoids dogs.

B. An occasional win at gambling keeps the behavior going.

C. A person, beaten as a child by an authority figure, has an involuntary fear of anyone in authority.

D. A child performs a response that produced candy in the past.

E. A child learns that although red and green strawberries look somewhat similar, only the red ones taste good.

What's What—Match each of the following terms with its definition.

C   Authoritative
D   Authoritarian
A   Permissive-indulgent
B   Neglecting-uninvolved

A. impulsive and aggressive; spoiled, selfish, inconsiderate, and demanding; exploit people for their own purposes

B. disruptions in attachment in childhood; moodiness, low self-esteem, and conduct problems later in childhood; problems with peer relations and academic performance

C. energetic and friendly, competent in dealing with others and the environment

D. conflicted, irritable, moody; poor social and cognitive skills

SHORT ANSWERS

Provide brief answers to the following questions.

1. List the five methods used in behavior genetics to study the heritability of mental disorders and give description of each. (pp. 65-68)

2. Briefly explain the cultural differences between Western and Japanese perspectives on attachment relationships. (pp. 98-99)

3. Define and give an example of each of the following defense mechanisms: (p. 75)

    a.   acting out

    b.   denial of reality

    c.   displacement

    d.   fixation

    e.   projection

    f.   rationalization

FILL IN THE BLANKS

Read the following and fill in the blanks. These questions are designed to help you focus on specific details.

1. A _neccessary_ cause is one that must exist for a disorder to occur, but it is not always a sufficient cause. (p. 56)

2. A _sufficient_ cause guarantees the occurrence of a disorder, but it may not be necessary for the disorder to occur. (p. 56)

3. A _contributory_ cause increases the probability of a disorder but is neither necessary nor sufficient. (p. 57)

4. Causal factors occurring relatively early in life that do not show their effects for many years are considered _distal_ causal factors that may contribute to a _proximal_ to develop a disorder. (p. 57)

5. Causal factors that operate shortly before the occurrence of symptom onset would be considered _proximal_ causal factors that, in some cases, may be no more than the "straw that breaks the camel's back." (p. 57)

6. A condition that tends to maintain maladaptive behavior that is already present is a _reinforcing_ cause (e.g., the extra attention, sympathy, and removal from unwanted responsibility that may be secondary to becoming ill). (p. 57)

7. Being raised by a parent who is warm and supportive is an example of a _protective_ factor. (p. 58)

8. Thomas Kuhn noted that theoretical orientations in science typically remain strong even in the face of evidence or alternate explanations. A theory typically lasts until a fundamental insight is achieved that appears to resolve problems left unsolved by existing theories. The new insights, also called _paradigm_ shifts, are complete reorganizations of the way people think about a particular issue or field of science. (p. 60)

9. The electrical nerve impulse travels from the cell body of a neuron to the terminal buttons via the ___axon___. (p. 62)

10. The ___terminal buttons___ or ___presynaptic terminals / axon endings___ are the sites where neurotransmitter substances are stored until needed. When the nerve impulse reaches the axon endings, the transmitter is released into the ___synapse___, a tiny fluid-filled gap between the axon endings of the ___presynaptic___ neuron and the ___dendrites___ of the postsynaptic neuron. (p. 62)

11. The neurotransmitter substances act on the dendrite of the postsynaptic neuron at specialized places called ___receptors___ sites. (p. 62)

12. The effect of the neurotransmitter on the postsynaptic neuron can be either ___positive___, which means it increases the probability that the neuron will fire, or ___negative___, which means that it decreases the probability that the neuron will fire. (p. 62)

13. The action of the neurotransmitter substance is time-limited either by deactivation by an ___enzyme___, such as monoamine oxidase, in the synaptic cleft or by a process called ___reuptake___, which takes it back into the presynaptic neuron and stores it in the synaptic storage vesicles. (p. 61)

14. Highly intelligent parents provide an intellectually stimulating environment. This is an example of what has been termed a(n) ___passive___ effect of the child's genotype on the environment, resulting from the genetic similarity of parents and children. (p. 65)

15. Happy babies evoke more positive responses from others than do passive, unresponsive infants. This is an example of a(n) ___evocative___ effect of the child's genotype from the social and physical environment. (p. 65)

16. Extroverted children may seek the company of others, thereby enhancing their own tendencies to be sociable. This is an example in which the child's genotype plays a more ___active role___ in shaping the environment. (p. 65)

17. If a given disorder were completely heritable, the ___concordance rate___ for identical twins with the disorder would be 100%. (pp. 65-66)

18. Those factors that would affect all children in a family similarly are known as ___shared environmental influences___ (p. 67)

19. The id operates according to the _pleasure_ principle. (p. 72)

20. The id generates mental images and fantasies referred to as _primary process_ thinking. (p. 72)

21. The ego operates according to the _reality_ principle. (p. 74)

22. The ego uses reason and intellectual resources to deal with the external world, which is referred to as _secondary process_ thinking. (p. 74)

23. The superego is the outgrowth of internalizing the _taboos_ and _moral values_ of society. (p. 74)

24. Freud's views replaced brain pathology with intrapsychic conflict and exaggerated ego defenses against anxiety as the cause of at least some mental disorders. One of his most noteworthy contributions was to emphasize the extent to which _unconcious_ motives and _defense_ mechanisms affect behavior, the importance of _early childhood_ experiences in later personality adjustment and maladjustment, and the importance of _sexual_ factors in human behavior and mental disorders. The second particularly noteworthy contribution was the realization that the same psychological principles apply to both _normal_ and _learned_ behavior. (pp. 78-79)

25. Two important criticisms of psychoanalytic theory have been offered. First, it fails to recognize the scientific limits of _personal reports_ as the primary mode of obtaining information. Second, there is a lack of _evidence_ to support many of its explanatory assumptions or the effectiveness of its therapy. (p. 79)

26. The roots of the behavioristic approach can be traced to the study of _Classical Conditioning_ by a Russian physiologist named Ivan Pavlov and to the study of _Instrumental Conditioning_ by Edward Thorndike. Promotion of the behavioral approach is credited to a young American psychologist named _Watson_. (pp. 79-80)

27. Identify the following statements as referring to classical conditioning (C) or instrumental (I) conditioning (i.e., place a "C" or "I" after each as appropriate). (pp. 80-81)
    a. As we mature, this type of learning becomes more important. _I_
    b. Many responses, particularly those related to fear or anxiety, are learned through this type of learning. _C_
    c. As we grow up, this type of learning becomes an important mechanism for discriminating the desirable from the undesirable. _I_
    d. Consists of simple strengthening of a stimulus-response connection. _I_
    e. The person learns a response-outcome expectancy. _I_

28. In operant or instrumental conditioning, initially a high rate of reinforcement may be necessary, but thereafter, it is especially persistent when reinforcement is _intermittent_. (p. 81)

29. Behaviorism has been praised for its precision and objectivity, its wealth of research, and its demonstrated effectiveness in _changing specific behavior_. (p. 82)

30. According to Beck, different forms of psychopathology are characterized by different _____ that have developed as a function of adverse early _____ and that lead to the _____ of _____, characteristic of certain disorders, such as anxiety, depression, and personality disorders. (pp. 83-84)

31. Cognitive-behavioral clinicians have shifted their focus from overt behavior to the _____ assumed to be producing that behavior. Then the clinician's goal becomes one of altering maladaptive _____. (p. 84)

32. Each psychosocial viewpoint of abnormal behavior depends on _____ from limited observations and research. (p. 84)

33. Bowlby found that, when children age 2 to 5 years are separated from their parents during prolonged periods of hospitalization, the acute effects include significant _____ during the separation and _____ upon reunion. (pp. 90)

34. _____ models of abnormal behavior state that many mental disorders or believed to develop as the result of some kind of stressor operating on a person who has a predisposition for that disorder. (p. 58)

35. The _____ viewpoint acknowledges the idea that biological, psychosocial, and sociocultural factors all interact and play a role in psychopathology and treatment. (p. 60)

36. The four neurotransmitters that have been studied most extensively in relationship to psychopathology are: _____, _____, _____ and _____. (p. 61)

37. When looking at shared and nonshared environmental influences, it was found that for many important psychological characteristics and forms of psychopathology, _____ environmental influences appear to be more important. (p. 67)

38. The effects of deprivation and rejection on a child was delineated by Bullard and his colleagues as a "_____" syndrome in which normal growth and development are seriously impaired and frequently required admission to a hospital. (p. 88)

39. Although there are some universal symptoms and patterns of symptoms for mental disorders appear, _____ do often influence which disorders _____, the _____ these take and their _____. (p. 96)

THE DOCTOR IS IN...PSYCHIATRIC HELP—5¢

Read the following scenarios and diagnose the client. Remember to look carefully at the criteria for the disorder before you make a decision as to the diagnosis. Make a list of other information you might need to help you understand the causal factors.

1. Roger comes to your office because he has recently been laid off from his job as a store manager. He is concerned because he has started to drink heavily as a result of this and finds himself feeling incredibly sad and depressed. His wife is supportive but he is afraid she will get tired of dealing with his moods and leave. Although she says she won't, he is becoming preoccupied with the idea of her leaving him. He tells you that his father abused alcohol and that his mother ended up leaving when she couldn't take it any more.

   His father always drank, according to Roger, would get really down, and, on at least one occasion, talked about suicide. Roger doesn't want to become like his father but finds himself acting in similar ways. He is thinking that maybe he should just tell his wife to leave him, then move to another state, and start all over.

   Look at Roger's situation from a psychodynamic, behavioral, and cognitive-behavioral perspective. What in Roger's story would you emphasize from each of these perspectives and how would you treat him? (p. 58)

AFTER YOU READ

PRACTICE TESTS

Take the following three multiple-choice tests to see how much you have comprehended from the chapter. Each represents roughly one-third of the chapter. As you study the chapter, use these to check your progress.

PRACTICE TEST NUMBER 1

1. Disorders could be classified and diagnosed better if their causes could be better understood instead of relying on (p. 56)
   a. clusters of symptoms.
   b. clusters of test results.
   c. interview techniques.
   d. unconscious motivations.

2. The etiology of abnormal behavior means the (p. 56)
   a. method of treatment.
   b. treatment outcome.
   c. causal pattern.
   d. all of the above.

3. The response of an individual to demands that he or she perceives as taxing or exceeding his or her personal resources is referred to as (p. 58)
   a. stress.
   b. fixated.
   c. socialized.
   d. diathesis.

4. The diathesis is a relatively _____ necessary or contributory cause. (p. 58)
   a. proximal
   b. distal
   c. unimportant
   d. a and c

5. Jimmy's parents use drugs and his father is often abusive toward his mother. In spite of this, Jimmy is doing well in school and has made the football team. Jimmy's success is a form of (p. 58)
   a. good genes
   b. good luck
   c. resilience
   d. diathesis

6. Jimmy had an uncle who took him under his wing and helped him get through some rough times. This uncle provided the warmth and support that Jimmy lacked at home. Jimmy's uncle provided a (p. 58)
   a. protective factor.
   b. relief to Jimmy's parents.
   c. proximal cause.
   d. distal cause.

7. When Sharon went to school, she was taught the theory and practice of the psychoanalytical viewpoint. The methods she used in her practice reflected this viewpoint and she believed totally in this perspective. At a conference, she was introduced to the cognitive-behavioral viewpoint and became intrigued by it. She went on to study this perspective and incorporate it into her practice. Sharon's new insights constituted a (p. 60)
   a. breakthrough.
   b. paradigm shift.
   c. break from tradition.
   d. cognitive shift.

8. Malfunction of the negative feedback system in the hypothalamic-pituitary-adrenal-cortical axis has been implicated in such psychopathologies as (p. 63)

    a. post-traumatic stress disorder.

    b. depression.

    c. OCD.

    d. a and b.

9. The fact that a number of disorders, such as depression, schizophrenia, and alcoholism, show heredity as an important predisposing causal factor is consistent with which perspective? (p. 63)

    a. biological

    b. behavioral

    c. cognitive

    d. psychoanalytical

10. The observed structural and functional characteristics that result from an interaction of the person's total genetic endowment and the environment are referred to as a person's (p. 64)

    a. phenotype.

    b. genotype.

    c. self.

    d. linotype.

PRACTICE TEST NUMBER 2

1. An example of a constitutional liability is (pp. 68-70)

    a. eye color.

    b. physical handicaps.

    c. temperament.

    d. b and c.

2. At what age can we identify approximately five dimensions of temperament development that may affect personality? (p. 69)

    a. one to two years

    b. two to three months

    c. six months to one year

    d. four to five years

3. The _____ acknowledges that genetic activity influences neural activity, which, in turn, influences behavior, which, in turn, influences the environment, and that these influences are bidirectional. (p. 70)

    a. brain activity approach

    b. neural regulatory approach

    c. developmental systems approach

    d. none of the above

4. Because biological treatments seem to have more immediate results than other available therapies, these have been seen as a possible (p. 71)

    a. cure-all.
    b. band-aid approach.
    c. short cut.
    d. answer to all of the problems with therapy.

5. When we adopt a perspective, it will influence (p. 85)

    a. our perceptions of maladaptive behavior.
    b. the types of evidence we look for.
    c. the way in which we interpret data.
    d. all of the above.

6. The process of working new experiences into existing cognitive frameworks, even if the new information has to be reinterpreted or distorted to make it fit, is known as (p. 86)

    a. integration.
    b. accommodation.
    c. assimilation.
    d. incorporation.

7. The process of changing existing frameworks to make it possible to incorporate discrepant information is known as (pp. 86-87)

    a. integration.
    b. accommodation.
    c. assimilation.
    d. incorporation.

8. Amato and Keith (1991a, 1991b) found that the negative effects of divorce seemed to be decreasing, particularly since 1970, because divorce was decreasing in (p. 93)

    a. stigmatization.
    b. number.
    c. amount parents blamed each other.
    d. availability.

9. Jill, who is 20 years old, is popular with many people and is comfortable in all settings. Jill has a good deal of (p. 94)

    a. luck.
    b. intuition.
    c. social competence.
    d. social ineptitude.

10. Jennifer, who is five years old and in kindergarten, is clueless when it comes to reading her peer's emotions, especially fear and sadness. This behavior can predict aggressive behavior toward peers in the (p. 95)

    a.   third grade.
    b.   first grade.
    c.   ninth grade.
    d.   the behavior really can't predict anything.

PRACTICE TEST NUMBER 3

1. Studies done by sociocultural researchers made it clear that there is a relationship between mental disorders and (p. 96)

    a.   individual schema.
    b.   cultural schema.
    c.   sociocultural conditions.
    d.   none of the above.

2. In our society, the lower the SES, the higher the incidence of (p. 99)

    a.   therapy.
    b.   intervention of some sort.
    c.   mental disorder.
    d.   a and b.

3. Many more women than men suffer from various emotional disorders. This may be in part due to sexual discrimination. The primary types of discrimination are (pp. 100-01)

    a.   work and wage.
    b.   access and treatment.
    c.   educational and career.
    d.   all of the above.

4. Estimates are that approximately _____ of the homeless are affected by mental illness. (p. 101)

    a.   one-half
    b.   one-quarter
    c.   75%
    d.   one-third

5. Since Kleinman and Good consider cultural factors so important to understanding depressive disorders, they have urged the psychiatric community to do what? (p. 101)

    a.   incorporate it into all therapeutic treatment
    b.   incorporate it into all educational programs
    c.   incorporate another axis in the DSM
    d.   create a new paradigm

6. Dr. Smith combines many different approaches/techniques when assessing and working with clients. What is Dr. Smith's approach? (p. 102)
    a. confusing
    b. eclectic
    c. puristis
    d. practical

7. A factor that increases the probability of developing a disorder without being either necessary or sufficient is a _____ cause. (p. 57)
    a. distal
    b. proximal
    c. reinforcing
    d. contributory

8. Which type of anxiety is a signal to the ego that the id's unacceptable impulse is threatening to break out? (p. 74)
    a. reality anxiety
    b. neurotic anxiety
    c. moral anxiety
    d. free-floating anxiety

9. The ability to discriminate may be brought about by (p. 81)
    a. classical conditioning.
    b. shaping.
    c. responding differently to similar stimuli, based on which ones are reinforced.
    d. avoidance conditioning.

10. Which of the following was not proposed as a strong factor in popularity among juveniles? (pp. 94-95)
    a. parents' income
    b. intelligence
    c. being seen as friendly and outgoing
    d. physical attractiveness

COMPREHENSIVE PRACTICE TEST

The following tests are designed to give you an idea of how well you understood the entire chapter. There are three different types of tests: multiple choice, true-false, and essay.

MULTIPLE-CHOICE

1. A predisposition toward developing a disorder is termed (p. 58)
    a. stress.
    b. fixated.
    c. socialized.
    d. diathesis.

2. The stressor is a more _____ cause. (p. 58)
   a. proximal
   b. distal
   c. unimportant
   d. b and c.

3. A rapidly growing field of psychology that focuses on determining what is abnormal at any point in development by comparing and contrasting it with normal and expected changes that occur in the course of development is called (p. 59)
   a. cognitive-behavioral psychology.
   b. psychodevelopment psychology.
   c. developmental psychopathology.
   d. cognitive-developmental psychology.

4. The belief that _____ in the brain can result in abnormal behavior is one of the basic tenets of the biological perspective today. (p. 61)
   a. diseases
   b. disorders of the central nervous system
   c. neurotransmitter imbalances
   d. none of the above

5. The _____ is referred to as the master gland of the body. (p. 63)
   a. adrenal gland
   b. hypothalamus
   c. endocrine gland
   d. pituitary gland

6. A person's total genetic endowment is referred to as her or his (p. 65)
   a. phenotype.
   b. genotype.
   c. self.
   d. linotype.

7. The _____ perspective views human nature as basically "good." (p. 73)
   a. existential
   b. behavioral
   c. psychoanalytical
   d. humanistic

8. The _____ perspective places more emphasis on the irrational tendencies and the difficulties inherent in self-fulfillment—particularly in a modern, bureaucratic and dehumanizing mass society. (p. 73)
   a. existential
   b. behavioral
   c. cognitive
   d. humanistic

9. Evidence suggests that disordered _____ make a significant contribution to child and adolescent psychopathology, especially to problems, such as depression, conduct disorder, delinquency, and attention deficit disorder. (p. 91)

    a. mothers
    b. brothers
    c. grandparents
    d. fathers

10. Your book mentions that, at present, the only unified perspective is called the (p. 103)

    a. unification viewpoint.
    b. cognitive viewpoint.
    c. cognitive-behavioral viewpoint.
    d. biopsychosocial viewpoint.

11. The specialized structure on the postsynaptic neuron at which the neurotransmitter exerts its effect is the (p. 62)

    a. synaptic cleft.
    b. synaptic vesicle.
    c. receptor site.
    d. enzyme.

12. After being released into the synaptic cleft, the neurotransmitter substance may be reabsorbed into the presynaptic axon button, a process called (p. 62)

    a. re-uptake.
    b. deactivation.
    c. recapture.
    d. active transport.

13. In genetic studies the subject, or carrier, of the trait or disorder in question who serves as the starting point is known as the (p. 65)

    a. proband.
    b. zygote.
    c. risk person.
    d. initiation point.

14. According to Freud's psychoanalytic perspective, the source of all instinctual drives is the (p. 72)

    a. ego.
    b. id.
    c. libido.
    d. superego.

15. Margaret Mahler focused on the process by which children come to understand that they are different from other objects. This process involves a developmental phase called (p. 76)
    a. assimilation-accommodation.
    b. introjection-identification.
    c. introversion-extroversion.
    d. separation-individuation.

16. Instead of Freud's concept of fixation, Erikson proposed that parental deprivation might interfere with the development of (p. 78)
    a. high self-esteem.
    b. tolerance for stimulation.
    c. self-control.
    d. basic trust.

17. The form of learning in which an individual learns to achieve a desired goal is (p. 80)
    a. classical conditioning.
    b. operant conditioning.
    c. modeling.
    d. avoidance conditioning.

18. The behavioristic tradition has been criticized for (p. 82)
    a. its precision and objectivity.
    b. its research orientation.
    c. its failure to demonstrate effectiveness.
    d. its over concern with symptoms.

19. The tendency to explain one's success as due to luck—as compared to hard work—is best categorized as an example of a specific (p. 83)
    a. attributional style.
    b. contributory effect.
    c. proximal schema.
    d. internal representation.

20. A basic goal of psychosocial therapies is (p. 87)
    a. accommodation.
    b. social skills training.
    c. reduction of anxiety.
    d. assimilation.

21. Bowlby found that when young children were separated from their parents during prolonged periods of hospitalization, their reaction upon reunion was (p. 90)
    a. strong dependence.
    b. detachment.
    c. joy.
    d. anger.

22. A _____ parental style is likely to produce a child who is impulsive and aggressive, spoiled, selfish, inconsiderate, and demanding, and who will exploit people for his/her own purposes. (p. 92)

    a. authoritative
    b. authoritarian
    c. permissive-indulgent
    d. neglecting-uninvolved

23. Epidemiological studies that have linked psychopathology with social class are (p. 99)

    a. based on controlled experimentation.
    b. correlational in nature.
    c. establishing a clear-cut cause-effect relationship.
    d. good examples of analogue studies.

24. According to the authors, the problematic proliferation of diverse viewpoints about psychopathology can best be solved by (pp. 84-85)

    a. adhering to a single point of view for consistency's sake.
    b. becoming an eclectic.
    c. developing a unified point of view.
    d. divorcing oneself from all major perspectives.

True - False

1. The behavioral sciences have no difficulty distinguishing between what is cause and effect. T / F (p. 57)

2. Protective factors are not necessarily positive experiences. T / F (p. 58)

3. Some forms of psychopathology have been linked to hormonal imbalances. T / F (p. 63)

4. Genes affect behavior directly. T / F (p. 63)

5. The most common birth difficulty associated with later mental disorders is low birth weight. T / F (p. 68)

6. Assimilation is the basic goal of psychosocial therapies. T / F (p. 86)

7. Children deprived of needed resources normally supplied by parents or parental surrogates may be left with irreversible psychological scars. T / F (p. 87)

8. Candy is a loner and Brian is a bully. Each of them will probably have healthy mental health outcomes. T / F (p. 94)

9. When social roles are conflicting, unclear, or difficult to achieve, unhealthy personality development may occur. T / F (p. 99)

10.   Prejudice against minority groups may play a role in explaining why these groups sometimes show increased prevalence of certain mental disorders. T / F   (p. 100)

11.   The sociocultural viewpoint has been readily embraced by the therapeutic community and incorporated into treatment. T / F   (p. 101)

ESSAY QUESTIONS

1.   List the misconceptions and stereotypes that exist about studies of genetic influences on behavior, traits and psychopathology, and give examples of each. (p. 67)

WEB LINKS TO ITEMS OR CONCEPTS DISCUSSED IN THIS CHAPTER

Psychopathology

    psychclassics.yorku.ca/Freud/Psycho/

    titles.cambridge.org/journals/ journal_catalogue.asp?historylinks=SUBJ&mnemonic=DPP

    pegasus.cc.ucf.edu/~gjacinto/6123.htm

Fetal Alcohol Syndrome

    www.nofas.org/

    www.acbr.com/fas/

    www.cdc.gov/ncbddd/fas/

    depts.washington.edu/fadu/

Sigmund Freud

    plaza.interport.net/nypsan/freudarc.html

    www.psychoanalysis.org

    www.freud.org.uk/

    freud.t0.or.at/

CRISS-CROSS

Now that you know all there is to know about this chapter, here's your chance to put that knowledge to work.

CRISS-CROSS CLUES

Across

3. mediates between the demands of the id and the realities of the external world
4. distinguishing between similar stimuli and responding differently to these
5. an internal process in which the infant or child incorporates symbolically
6. life instincts and death instincts
10. gradual lessening of a conditioned response, when the UCS is omitted
13. the outgrowth of internalizing the taboos and moral values of society
14. fitting new experiences into one's existing cognitive framework
15. causal pattern of abnormal behavior
16. the process of assigning causes to things that happen

Down

1. delivery of a reward or pleasant stimulus; aids in conditioning
2. changing existing cognitive framework to incorporate new discrepant information
7. one's reactiviy and characteristic ways of self-regulation
8. one's frame of reference through the complexities of modern living
9. when one stimulus (or set of stimuli) can be evoked by another, similar stimuli
11. the source of instinctual drives
12. the ability to adapt successfully

Puzzle created with Puzzlemaker at DiscoverySchool.com

CHAPTER **FOUR**

Clinical Assessment

BEFORE YOU READ

One of the most important activities of the mental health professional is to assess the nature and extent of the problem for which help is being sought. Chapter 4 is devoted to a discussion of the goals, methods, and issues involved in clinical assessment. For a clinician, the primary goals of clinical assessment include an identification, description, and diagnosis of an individual's presenting symptoms, as well as evaluation of variables that might influence treatment, including potential causal and protective factors. Clinical assessment depends on data from observation and interviews, as well as psychological, often neuropsychological, and, in some cases, neurological tests. This chapter describes what the different types of tests are, how these are constructed, and what types of information can be obtained from them.

After obtaining the information—what then? Chapter 4 also looks at how to integrate the data and the ethical issues associated with assessment.

Assessment of a mental disorder must be placed in a larger context. This is where the importance of classifying abnormal behavior comes in. The last part of Chapter 4 is devoted to understanding reasons for classifying behavior, how to determine its usefulness, and different models of classification ultimately focusing on the DSM, the standard used in the United States.

- **THE BASIC ELEMENTS IN ASSESSMENT**
  The Relationship Between Diagnosis and Assessment
  Taking a Social History
  The Influence of Professional Orientation
  Trust and Rapport Between the Clinician and the Client

- **ASSESSMENT OF THE PHYSICAL ORGANISM**
  The General Physical Examination
  The Neurological Examination
  The Neuropsychological Examination

- **PSYCHOSOCIAL ASSESSMENT**
  Assessment Interviews
  The Clinical Observation of Behavior
  Psychological Tests
  Advantages and Limitations of Objective Personality Tests
  A Psychological Case Study: Esteban

- **THE INTEGRATION OF ASSESSMENT DATA**
  Ethical Issues in Assessment

- **CLASSIFYING ABNORMAL BEHAVIOR**
  Reliability and Validity
  Differing Models of Classification
  Formal Diagnostic Classification of Mental Disorders

OBJECTIVES

After reading this chapter, you should be able to:

1. Describe the basic elements of clinical assessment, including: a) its nature and purpose, b) the relationship between diagnosis and assessment, c) the types of information sought, and d) the different types of data of interest.

2. Describe the influence of professional orientation on the assessment process.

3. Explain what is meant by rapport between the clinician and client, and outline the components of a relationship that leads to good rapport.

4. Summarize the various approaches to assessment of physical problems, including the general, physical, neurological, and neuropsychological examples.

5. List types of psychosocial assessments.

6. Discriminate between structured and unstructured interviews for the assessment of psychosocial functioning, and evaluate the relative merits of the two.

7. Discuss various approaches to the clinical observation of behavior and identify the advantages of each.

8. Explain the importance of rating scales in clinical observations.

9. Describe the major intelligence tests.

10. Discuss the advantages and disadvantages of projective personality tests.

11. Discuss the advantages and disadvantages of objective personality tests.

12. Summarize the process of integrating assessment data into a model for use in planning or changing treatment.

13. Explain the ethical issues involved in assessment.

14. Explain the purpose of classification systems for abnormal behavior.

15. Discuss reliability and validity as they relate to a classification system.

16. Describe the differing models of classification.

17. Explain the DSM classification of mental disorders.

AS YOU READ

Answers can be found in the Answer Key at the end of the book.

KEY WORDS

Each of the words below is important in understanding the concepts presented in this chapter. Write the definition next to each of the words.

electroencephalogram (EEG) (p. 109)   computerized axial tomography (CAT scan) (p. 109)

dysrhythmia (p. 109)   magnetic resonance imaging (MRI) (p. 109) positron emission tomography (PET scan) (p. 109)

functional magnetic resonance imaging (fMRI) (p. 109)

neuropsychological assessment (p. 110)

self-monitoring (p. 113)

rating scales (p. 113)

role playing (p. 113)

projective tests (pp. 114-15)

Rorshach Test (p. 115)

Thematic Apperception Test (TAT) (p. 117)

sentence completion tests (p. 118)

objective tests (p. 119)

Minnesota Multiphasic Personality Inventory (MMPI) (pp. 119-23)

actuarial procedures (p. 123)

reliability (p. 128)

validity (p. 128)

comorbidity (p. 129)

symptoms (p. 129)

signs (p. 129)

acute (p. 133)

chronic (p. 133)

mild (p. 133)

moderate (p. 133)

severe (p. 133)

episodic (p. 133)

recurrent (p. 133)

WHO'S WHO AND WHAT'S WHAT—MATCHING

Complete the chart below that compares the overall strengths and weaknesses of projective and objective tests.

Test	Strengths	Weaknesses
Projective	(p. 118)	Interpretations are subjective, unreliable, and difficult to validate, require trained staff to administer and score.
Objective	Cost effective, reliable, objective, administered and scored by computer	(p. 120)

Match the following psychological tests with the appropriate description of each test's purpose.

Psychological Test	Purpose
_____ Rorshach Test	A. Rating scale based on standardized interview
_____ Thematic Apperception Test	B. Intelligence scale for children
_____ Minnesota Multiphasic Personality Inventory (MMPI)	C. Intelligence scale for adults
	D. Projective test using inkblots
_____ WAIS-R	E. Projective test using pictures
_____ WISC-R	F. Structured personality test
_____ Brief Psychiatric Rating Scale (BPRS)	G. Test that pinpoints topics that should be explored
_____ Sentence Completion Test	

SHORT ANSWERS

Provide brief answers to the following questions.

1. Discuss the benefits of using computers in psychological testing and why some clinicians are reluctant to use these. (p. 115)

2. Compare the functions, advantages, and disadvantages of the CAT, MRI, fMRI, and the PET scans. (pp. 108-10)

3. Explain the purpose of classifying abnormal behavior. (p. 131)

4. Discuss the problem of labeling. (pp. 133-34)

FILL IN THE BLANKS

Read the following and fill in the blanks. These questions are designed to help you focus on specific details.

1. Data from clinical assessment is used for two purposes. First, it serves as a basis for treatment decisions. A less obvious, but equally important, function is that of establishing a ____baseline____ against which to evaluate progress made during and following treatment. (p. 106)

2. For clinical purposes, knowledge about an individual's ____history____, ____intellectual____ ____functioning____, personality characteristics, and environmental pressures and resources is more important than a formal diagnosis. (p. 106)

3. Medical examinations are necessary in some situations to rule out physical abnormalities or to determine the extent to which physical problems are involved. The two types of medical examinations that may be performed include the general _____ examination and the _____ examination, aimed at assessing the _____ (_____) and _____ (_____) integrity of the brain as a behaviorally significant physical system. (p. 108)

4. An EEG is a graphic record of the _____. Significant divergences from the normal pattern of brain impulses can reflect abnormalities of brain function, such as might be caused by a brain tumor or other lesion. (p. 109)

5. Neurological tests identify abnormalities in the brain's physical properties. In contrast, neuropsychological assessment identifies gross impairments in _____ and varied psychological _____. (p. 110)

6. The Halstead-Reitan battery consists of a standard set of tests that have been preselected to sample in a systematic and comprehensive manner a _____ known to be adversely affected by various types of brain injury. (p. 111)

7. Psychosocial assessment attempts to provide a realistic picture of the individual in interaction with the ___*social environment*___ (p. 112)

8. The main purpose of direct observation is to learn more about the person's psychological functioning through the objective description of behavior in various contexts. Ideally, such observations would occur in the individual's ___*natural environ*___, but are typically confined to ___*clinic*___ or ___*hospital*___ settings. In addition, many clinicians ask their patients to report their own behavior, thoughts, and feelings as these occur in various natural settings—a procedure called ___*self-monitoring*___ (pp. 112-13)

9. Psychological tests are standardized sets of procedures to obtain samples of a subject's behavior that can be compared to the behavior of other individuals, usually through the use of established test ___*norms*___ or test score ___*distribution*___. (p. 114)

10. Among the characteristics about which the clinician can draw inferences from psychological tests are coping patterns, motive patterns, personality characteristics, role behaviors, values, levels of depression or anxiety, and ___*intellectual functioning*___ (p. 114)

11. Projective tests are aimed at discovering the ways in which an individual's ___*past*___ ___*learning*___ and ___*personality structure*___ may lead him or her to organize and perceive ___*ambiguous*___ information from the environment. (p. 115)

THE DOCTOR IS IN...PSYCHIATRIC HELP—5¢

Read the following scenarios and diagnose the client. Remember to look carefully at the criteria for the disorder before you make a decision as to the diagnosis. Make a list of other information you might need to help you understand the causal factors.

1. You are a famous neuropsychologist, and a new patient has been referred to you. This patient's history leads you to believe that some sort of brain injury has occurred. You believe that a preselected battery of standard tests is the most beneficial. What test battery would you use? What are its component parts, and what are its limitations? (pp. 110-11)

2. Tim, a 21-year-old man, has just been admitted to the hospital. He had been found wandering the streets, talking to himself. It looks as if he has been homeless for some time. You are called in to do a clinical observation. What would you include in your observation of Tim? (p. 112)

3. You are seeing a new patient who has been referred to you by his primary-care doctor. Ben, a 29-year-old truck driver, went to his doctor thinking he was having a heart attack. When he drove across bridges, his heart would pound, his hands got sweaty, he would feel short of breath, and begin to hyperventilate. Several months ago, Ben was involved in an accident that left three people dead and several injured. Though it wasn't his fault (there had been heavy fog), he felt that as an experienced truck driver, he should have been able to prevent the accident. The symptoms began shortly after the accident and have lasted for six months. His primary doctor reports that Ben is not having any heart problems and is generally in good health.

    As Ben's psychologist, what type of interview would you conduct? What diagnosis would you give him on Axis I, II, and III? Why? (p. 130)

PICTURE THIS

Below are pictures that represent key people or concepts from the book. Write the answers on the line to the right of the clues.

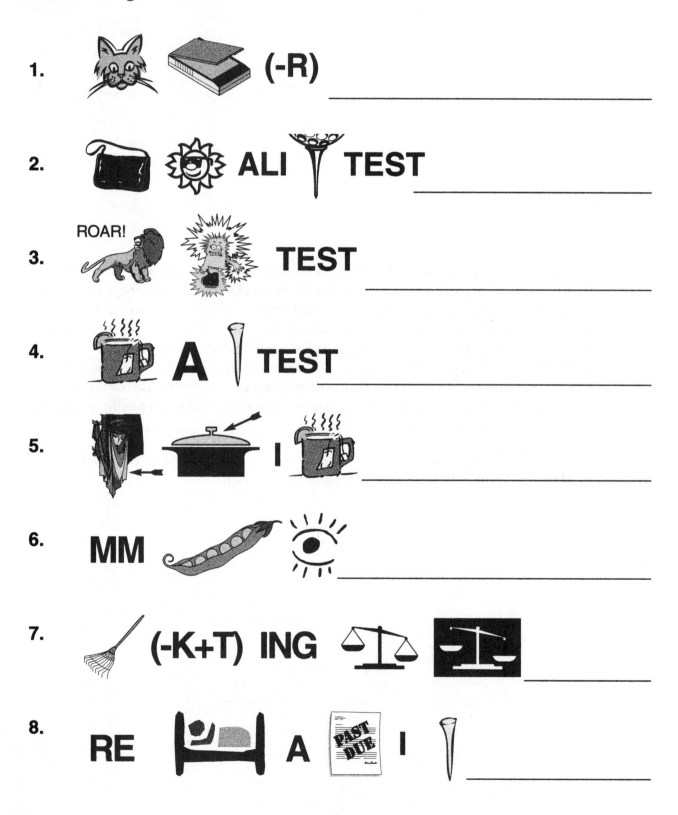

1.  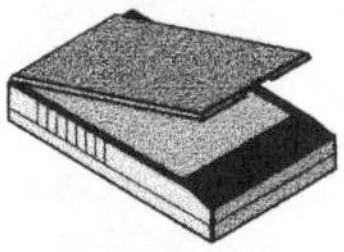 (-R)

2.   ALI  TEST

3. 

 TEST

4.  A  TEST

5.  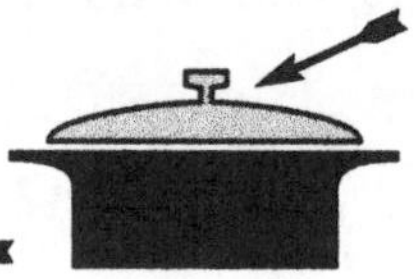 I 

6. MM 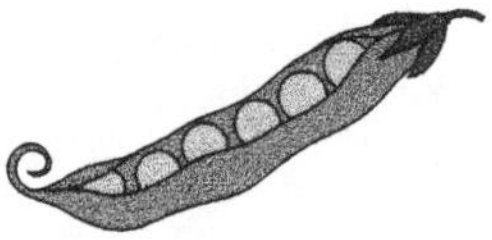 

7.  (-K+T) ING  

8. RE  A 

I 

AFTER YOU READ

PRACTICE TESTS

Take the following three multiple-choice tests to see how much you have comprehended from the chapter. Each represents roughly one-third of the chapter. As you study the chapter, use these to check your progress.

PRACTICE TEST NUMBER 1

1. Formal diagnosis is necessary after assessment for (p. 106)
   a. insurance claims.
   b. planning treatment.
   c. deciding on which treatment facilities would be best for the client.
   d. all of the above.

2. When taking a social history, the clinician notes key dimensions that help her/him to understand the individual's problem. The key dimensions are (p. 107)
   a. excesses, deficits, and appropriateness.
   b. excesses, desires, and dreams.
   c. behaviors, subconscious wishes, and fantasies.
   d. thought association and results of CAT scans.

3. After the assessment data is integrated into a consistent, meaningful picture, a _____ is developed about the client's behavior. (p. 107)
   a. Rorschach
   b. TAT
   c. dynamic formulation
   d. hypothesis

4. A significant divergence of normal brain patterns recorded on an EEG, which may be a result of some abnormality, is referred to as (p. 109)
   a. dysthmia.
   b. dysrhythmia.
   c. a brain tumor.
   d. none of the above.

5. Mrs. Smith, 73, is experiencing some significant difficulty with cognitive activities and has lost some coordination. She is referred to a specialist who will test her cognitive, perceptual, and motor performance. This specialist is a (p. 110)
   a. neuropsychologist.
   b. cognitive behaviorist.
   c. psychoanalyst.
   d. biologist.

6. Mrs. Smith is administered a battery of tests, consisting of a standard set of tests designed to systematically and comprehensively sample psychological competencies known to be affected by types of brain injuries. The test she probably was given was a (pp. 110-11)

    a. TAT.
    b. MRI.
    c. Brief Psychiatric Rating Scale.
    d. Halstead-Reitan.

7. You have scheduled an assessment interview for a new client. You have chosen a standardized interview format that you hope will yield a clear picture of your client's situation. This will be a(n) _____ interview. (p. 112)

    a. structured
    b. unstructured
    c. insightful
    d. constructed

8. You have scheduled an assessment interview for another new client. There are several questions you want the client to answer, but you want to be free to explore responses in more depth. This format is considered a(n) _____ interview. (p. 112)

    a. structured
    b. unstructured
    c. insightful
    d. constructed

9. Tim has been admitted to the hospital, and you, a renowned doctor, are about to administer several clinical observations using a rating scale. It is called the (p. 113)

    a. TAT.
    b. WISC-R.
    c. BPRS.
    d. MMPI-2.

10. You are going to conduct research on depression. You use what instrument to select your research subjects? (p. 113)

    a. TAT
    b. HRSD
    c. BPRS
    d. MMPI-2

PRACTICE TEST NUMBER 2

1. Which of the following is an example of an intelligence test? (p. 114)

   a. WISC-III

   b. WAIS-III

   c. Standard-Binel Intelligence Scale

   d. all of the above

2. Holding an inkblot picture in front of her client, Dr. Taylor asked the client to respond to what she saw in the picture. Dr. Taylor was administering the _____ test. (p. 115)

   a. Thematic Apperception

   b. Rorschach

   c. Sentence-Completion

   d. Stanford-Binet

3. Holding a series of pictures in front of his client, Dr. Zimmer asked the client to make up a story based on the picture. Dr. Zimmer was administering the _____ test. (p. 117)

   a. Thematic Apperception

   b. Rorschach

   c. Sentence completion

   d. Stanford-Binet

4. Dr. Jones gives her client the beginning of sentences and asks that she complete each one. This is known as the _____ test. (p. 118)

   a. Thematic Perception

   b. Rorschach

   c. Sentence completion

   d. Stanford-Binet

5. Unlike projective testing devices, these tests are more controlled and objective. This type of test is a(n) _____ personality test. (p. 119)

   a. subjective

   b. deductive

   c. objective

   d. carefully constructive

6. The MMPI consists of _____ clinical scales, each designed to measure tendencies to respond in psychologically deviant ways. (p. 119)

   a. 10

   b. 15

   c. 8

   d. Doesn't have clinical scales, because it is a projective test.

7. As a psychiatrist in a large mental hospital, you and several of your colleagues often work together to evaluate assessment data. You are part of a (p. 126)

   a.   collective-bargaining unit.

   b.   ward-management team.

   c.   administrative team.

   d.   interdisciplinary team.

8. The degree to which a measuring device produces the same results each time it is used to measure the same thing is referred to as (p. 128)

   a.   reliability.

   b.   validity.

   c.   useability.

   d.   consistency.

9. The extent to which a measuring instrument actually measures what it is supposed to measure is referred to as (p. 128)

   a.   reliability.

   b.   validity.

   c.   useability.

   d.   measurability.

10. Good reliability in diagnostic classification does not in itself guarantee (p. 128)

   a.   usefulness.

   b.   validity.

   c.   concreteness.

   d.   all of the above.

PRACTICE TEST NUMBER 3

1. The psychiatric classification system widely used in Europe is the (p. 129)

   a.   ICD-10.

   b.   DSM.

   c.   UCS.

   d.   TAT.

2. The psychiatric classification system used in the United States is the (p. 129)

   a.   ICD-10.

   b.   DSM.

   c.   UCS.

   d.   TAT.

3. Although purporting to be a categorical model of classification, the authors of the book say the DSM is, in fact, a (p. 129)

   a. prototypal.

   b. dimensional.

   c. category within itself.

   d. b and c.

4. A diagnostic interview that follows no preexisting plan is called a(n) (p. 134)

   a. structured interview.

   b. unstructured interview.

   c. spontaneous interview.

   d. organized interview.

5. A diagnostic interview that follows a sort of master plan is called a(n) (p. 134)

   a. structured interview.

   b. unstructured interview.

   c. spontaneous interview.

   d. organized interview.

6. A neurological diagnostic aid that reveals how an organ is functioning by measuring metabolic processes is the (p. 109)

   a. PET scan.

   b. CAT scan.

   c. EEG.

   d. angiogram.

7. Which of the following is the most highly regarded six-hour neuropsychological test? (p. 110)

   a. Halstead-Reitan

   b. Luria-Nebraska

   c. Stanford-Binet

   d. Wechsler Adult Intelligence Scale

8. According to the text, the rating scale specifically targeted for depression that has almost become the standard for selecting clinically depressed research subjects is the (p. 113)

   a. Beck Depression Inventory.

   b. Schedule for Rating Depressive Temperament.

   c. Leeds Depression Rating Scale.

   d. Hamilton Rating Scale for Depression.

9. Which of the following is a structured personality test? (p. 119)

    a. MMPI
    b. Rorschach
    c. Sentence Completion Test
    d. TAT

10. Which of the following personality tests would most likely be used for personnel screening for a dangerous job? (p. 119)

    a. California Psychological Inventory
    b. MMPI
    c. 16 PF
    d. Strong Vocational Inventory

COMPREHENSIVE PRACTICE TEST

The following tests are designed to give you an idea of how well you understood the entire chapter. There are three different types of tests: multiple-choice, true-false, and essay.

MULTIPLE-CHOICE

1. The initial clinical assessment is used to (p. 106)

    a. identify the main dimensions of the problem.
    b. predict the likely course of events.
    c. establish a baseline.
    d. all of the above.

2. When assessing an individual, the clinician integrates information concerning the person's personality traits, behavior patterns, environmental demands, etc. into a consistent, meaningful picture often called a(n) (p. 107)

    a. Rorschach.
    b. TAT
    c. dynamic formulation.
    d. hypothesis.

3. _____ testing provides a clinician with behavioral information on how organic brain damage affects a person's functions. (p. 110)

    a. TAT
    b. Rorschach
    c. MMPI
    d. Neuropsychological

4.   A classification system's usefulness depends upon its (p. 128)

   a.   reliability
   b.   validity
   c.   a and b.
   d.   none of the above.

5.   A _____ approach for classifying abnormal behavior assumes that human behavior can be divided into either healthy or disordered, and that within the disordered category, there are non-overlapping types with a high degree of homogeneity in both symptoms displayed and underlying organization of the disorder. (p. 128)

   a.   dimensional
   b.   prototyped
   c.   behavioral
   d.   categorical

6.   A _____ approach for classifying abnormal behavior assumes that a person's typical behavior is the product of different strengths of behaviors along several definable dimensions. (p. 128)

   a.   dimensional
   b.   prototypal
   c.   behavioral
   d.   categorical

7.   A _____ approach to classifying abnormal behavior is a conceptual entity depicting an idealized combination of characteristics that access together in a standard way at the level of actual observation. (p. 128)

   a.   dimensional
   b.   prototypal
   c.   behavioral
   d.   categorical

8.   A limitation of the DSM classification system is that (p. 130)

   a.   the differentiation of disorders is too wide.
   b.   it contains too few disorders.
   c.   real patients often don't fit into the precise lists of signs and symptoms.
   d.   a and b.

9.   Individuals are evaluated according to five axes. The first three deal with (p. 130)

   a.   psychosocial stresses.
   b.   global assessment of functioning.
   c.   assessing an individual's present clinical status.
   d.   b and c.

10.   The fourth and fifth axes of the DSM-IV-TR deal with (pp. 130-31)

     a.   psychosocial stresses.

     b.   global assessment of functioning.

     c.   assessing an individual's present clinical status.

     d.   b and c.

11.   Clinical interviews have been criticized as unreliable, and evidence of this unreliability includes the finding that different clinicians often arrive at different formal diagnoses. For this reason, recent versions of the DSM have emphasized an approach that   (p. 112)

     a.   employs a hierarchical structure.

     b.   employs multidimensional assessments.

     c.   requires confirmation by convergent information.

     d.   employs "operational" assessment.

12.   Two general categories of psychological tests used in clinical practice are   (p. 114)

     a.   intelligence and personality.

     b.   philosophy and religion.

     c.   speech perception and reaction time.

     d.   tactual performance and auditory perception.

13.   Personality tests are often grouped into two categories: (p. 114)

     a.   behavioral and psychodynamic.

     b.   conscious and unconscious.

     c.   projective and objective.

     d.   verbal and performance.

14.   The aim of a projective test is to   (p. 114)

     a.   predict a patient's future behavior.

     b.   compare a patient's responses to those of persons who are known to have mental disorders.

     c.   assess the way a patient perceives ambiguous stimuli.

     d.   assess the role of organic factors in a patient's thinking.

15.   Behaviorists have criticized the MMPI for being too   (p. 120)

     a.   action-oriented.

     b.   "mentalistic."

     c.   objective.

     d.   superficial.

TRUE - FALSE

1.   In cases of severe disorders, decisions regarding treatment may be made about a client with his or her consent or consultation with family members. T / F (p. 107)

2. Assessment of an individual may involve coordinated use of physical, psychological, and environmental assessment procedures. (T) F (p. 107)

3. Confidentiality is not an important issue for clients, because they want as many people as possible to know about their problems. T /(F) (p. 108)

4. Rating scales, when used in clinical observation and self-reports, encourages reliability, objectivity, and allows the rater to indicate the presence, absence, or prominence of a behavior. T / F (p. 113)

5. Two general categories of psychological tests used for clinical practice are general medical exams and intelligence tests. T / F   (p. 114)

6. An agreed-upon classification system allows clinicians to be confident of communicating clearly. (T) F (p. 127)

7. The classification of mental disorders is intended to give direct insight into a person's problems. (T)/ F (p. 127)

8. A classification system, once completed, is not changed. T /(F) (p. 127)

9. Validity presupposes reliability. (T)/ F (p. 128)

10. The number of recognized mental disorders has remained constant from the first DSM-I to the DSM-IV. T /(F) (pp. 129-30)

11. Acute mental disorders are relatively short in duration. (T) F (p. 133)

12. Chronic mental disorders are relatively short in duration. T /(F) (p. 133)

ESSAY QUESTIONS

1. What assessment techniques would be favored by the following? (p. 112)

   a. Biologically oriented clinician

   b. Psychoanalytically oriented clinician

   c. Behaviorally oriented clinician

   d. Cognitively oriented behaviorist

   e. Humanistically oriented clinician

   f. Interpersonally oriented clinician

2. What are the elements of psychological assessment? (p. 112)

WEB LINKS TO ITEMS OR CONCEPTS DISCUSSED IN THIS CHAPTER

Clinical assessment

www.ncaa.nhs.uk/

www.sci.sdsu.edu/CAL/CAL.html

www.mcc.ca/pdf/RD_EN.pdf (pdf from Medical Council of Canada)

Esteban

esteban.polymtl.ca/

www.ecis.org/esteban

CRISS-CROSS

Now that you know all there is to know about this chapter, here's your opportunity to put that knowledge to work.

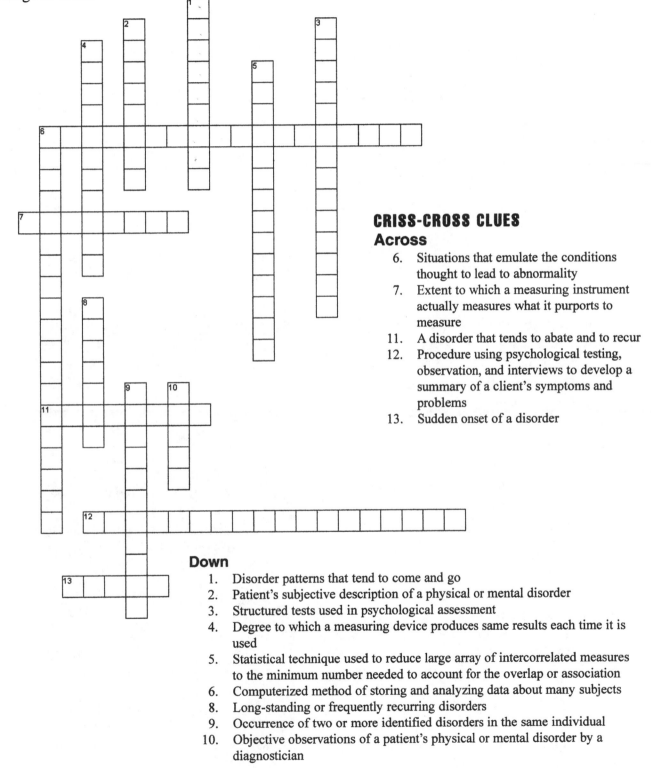

CRISS-CROSS CLUES
Across

6. Situations that emulate the conditions thought to lead to abnormality
7. Extent to which a measuring instrument actually measures what it purports to measure
11. A disorder that tends to abate and to recur
12. Procedure using psychological testing, observation, and interviews to develop a summary of a client's symptoms and problems
13. Sudden onset of a disorder

Down

1. Disorder patterns that tend to come and go
2. Patient's subjective description of a physical or mental disorder
3. Structured tests used in psychological assessment
4. Degree to which a measuring device produces same results each time it is used
5. Statistical technique used to reduce large array of intercorrelated measures to the minimum number needed to account for the overlap or association
6. Computerized method of storing and analyzing data about many subjects
8. Long-standing or frequently recurring disorders
9. Occurrence of two or more identified disorders in the same individual
10. Objective observations of a patient's physical or mental disorder by a diagnostician

Puzzle created with Puzzlemaker at DiscoverySchool.com

CHAPTER FIVE

Stress and Adjustment Disorders

BEFORE YOU READ

Chapter 5 begins with a detailed discussion of stress, a topic of increasing concern as modern life becomes more and more pressured. The text discusses the potential sources of stress, the functional equivalence of biological, psychological, and sociocultural sources of stress, and the general strategies for coping with stressful demands. Reactions of individuals to war, concentration camps, and civilian disasters are described and can be viewed as case studies of human functioning under levels of severe stress.

The chapter describes: 1) the coping techniques used by individuals in these situations; and 2) the symptoms that arise when coping techniques fail to eliminate the stress—leading, in many cases, to adjustment disorders. In some of the incidents you will read about, it may seem unbelievable that any person could cope without developing severely abnormal behavior.

The practical implications of this chapter are seen in applications, such as preparing people to cope more effectively when they face stressful situations.

OBJECTIVES

After reading this chapter, you should be able to:

1. Define the concepts of stressor, stress, and coping, describe the basic categories of stressors, and discuss factors that increase or decrease a person's vulnerability to stress.

2. Contrast the two major categories of coping responses and outline the numerous negative consequences of a failure to cope successfully.

3. Characterize the DSM-IV diagnosis of adjustment disorder and describe three major stressors and the consequences that increase the risk of adjustment disorder.

4. List the diagnostic criteria for acute stress disorder and post-traumatic stress disorder (PTSD), and compare and contrast the two disorders.

5. Summarize what is known about the major features of reactions to catastrophic events.

6. Identify the factors that influence the effects of rape on the victim and describe the typical immediate and long-term consequences of rape.

7. Characterize the phenomenon of combat-related stress and of PTSD in connection with battlefield stress.

8. List and illustrate the long-term effects of being a prisoner of war or in a concentration camp, and note the methodological problems associated with biased sampling.

9. Outline the factors that appear to influence combat-related stress problems, and describe the long-term effects of PTSD.

10. Describe the psychological problems associated with being tortured, with being a refugee, and with being held hostage.

11. Summarize the approaches that have been used to treat or to prevent stress disorders and evaluate their effectiveness.

12. Discuss the issue of using psychotropic medications to treat PTSD.

AS YOU READ

Answers can be found in the Answer Key at the end of the book.

KEY WORDS

Each of the words below is important in understanding the concepts presented in this chapter. Write the definition next to each of the words.

eustress (p. 140)

stress (p. 140)

stressor (p. 140)

coping strategies (p. 140)

distress (p. 140)

crisis (p. 142)

crisis intervention (p. 143)

stress tolerance (p. 144)

task-oriented response (p. 145)

defense-oriented response (p. 145)

personality or psychological decompensation   (p. 146)

general adaptation syndrome (p. 147)

psychoneuroimmunology (p. 149)

adjustment disorder (p. 150)

acute distress disorder (p. 153)

post-traumatic stress disorder (p. 152)

disaster syndrome (p. 153)

stress inoculation training (p. 166)

debriefing (p. 167)

WHO'S WHO AND WHAT'S WHAT—MATCHING

Match the following terms with their definitions.

Term		Definition
_____ Post-Traumatic Stress Disorder	A	a maladaptive response within three months of a stressor
_____ psychoneuroimmunology	B	one's ability to withstand stress
_____ adjustment disorder	C.	an adjustment demand
_____ crisis	D.	severe psychological and physical symptoms as a reaction to unexpected environmental crises
_____ stress	E.	preventative strategy, prepares people to meet stressful situations
_____ stressor	F.	a by-product of poor or inadequate coping
_____ eustress	G.	new field of study which focuses on the effects of stress on the immune system
_____ stress tolerance	H.	when a stressful situation exceeds one's adoptive capacities
_____ stress-inoculation training	I.	positive stress

SHORT ANSWERS
Provide brief answers to the following questions.

1. Explain the Social Readjustment Rating Scale and what it predicts. (p. 143)

2. Name the three interactional levels in coping with stress and give examples of each. (p. 145)

3. Selye (1956, 1976b) found that the body's reaction to sustained and excessive stress typically occurs in three major phases. Name and briefly explain each. (p. 147)

4. Explain how the sympathetic nervous system (SNS) reacts when an organism is faced with danger—the fight-or-flight response. Also, explain why there may be a danger connected to this. (p. 147)

5. Following a disaster, a victim's initial responses typically follow three stages. Name and briefly explain these. (p. 153)

6. Name and explain five areas of life functioning that may be affected by a rape. (p. 156)

7. The trauma of military combat was called "shell shock" in World War II, "operational fatigue," or "combat exhaustion" in the Korean and Vietnam wars, and, currently, "acute stress disorder." Discuss its causes and effects. (pp. 157-59)

FILL IN THE BLANKS

Read the following and fill in the blanks. These questions are designed to help you focus on specific details.

1. Three Axis 1 categories are ___*adjustment disorder*___, ___*acute stress disorder*___, and ___*PTSD*___. (p. 140)

2. Although a particular ___*stressor*___ may predominate in a situation, we usually confront a continuously changing pattern of interrelated and sometimes contradictory demands. (p. 142)

3. ___*Distress*___ can exact a high cost in terms of lowered efficiency, depletion of adaptive resources, wear and tear on the biological system, and, in extreme cases, severe personality and physical deterioration—even death. (p. 146)

4. When trauma victims were exposed to trauma-related cues (an audio recording of an event similar to the one they experienced), they showed ___*increased distress*___ and a ___*heightened reactivity*___ even years after the event. (p. 148)

THE DOCTOR IS IN...PSYCHIATRIC HELP—5¢

Read the following scenarios and diagnose the client. Remember to look carefully at the criteria for the disorder before you make a decision as to the diagnosis. Make a list of other information you might need to help you understand the causal factors.

1. Becky came to your office because she had been sexually assaulted six months ago and is having difficulty. She tells you that she feels anxious and depressed. The rapist was an acquaintance of hers and she has been questioning her ability to judge people and trust is very difficult to develop. Her self-esteem is really low and she is having a problem concentrating at school because she keeps having thoughts about the rape. Becky has been having nightmares and feeling has started to drink a lot to help her sleep. Her friends have been supported but they seem to be getting tired of her mood swings and angry outbursts. Becky feels like she is going crazy.

    How would you diagnose Becky and why? What treatment would you recommend for her? (pp. 156-57, 166)

PICTURE THIS

Below are pictures that represent key people or concepts from the book. Write the answers on the line to the right of the clues.

1. **STRESS**  **R** _____

2.  _____

3.  **ST(-D)** _____

4. **   ESS D** _____

AFTER YOU READ

Answers can be found in the Answer Key at the end of the book.

PRACTICE TESTS

Take the following three multiple-choice tests to see how much you have comprehended from the chapter. Each represents roughly one-third of the chapter. As you study the chapter, use these to check your progress.

PRACTICE TEST NUMBER 1

1. A wide range of obstacles, such as prejudice and discrimination, loneliness, inadequate self-control, the death of a loved one, fall into the category of (p. 140)

    a. adjustments.

    b. acutes.

    c. frustrations.

    d. pressures.

2. The simultaneous occurrence of two or more incompatible needs or motives, such as career versus family needs, is described as (p. 140)

    a.   pressure.
    b.   conflict.
    c.   frustration.
    d.   adjustment.

3. Feeling the need to achieve goals or behave in particular ways—internal or external—is known as (p. 141)

    a.   pressure.
    b.   frustration.
    c.   conflict.
    d.   post-traumatic.

4. The term, "_____," is used to refer to times when a stressful situation approaches or exceeds the adaptive capacities of a person or group. (p. 142)

    a.   crisis
    b.   traumatic
    c.   frustrating
    d.   acute

5. A crisis or trauma may occur as a result of (p. 143)

    a.   a disaster, such as a flood.
    b.   a nasty divorce.
    c.   an injury or disease.
    d.   all of the above.

6. The faster the changes, the greater the (p. 143)

    a.   frustration.
    b.   stress.
    c.   excitement.
    d.   LCU.

7. A person's _____ of the stressor has an impact—one person's stressor is another person's thrill. (p. 144)

    a.   perception
    b.   use
    c.   level
    d.   accumulation

8. The term, "_____," refers to a person's ability to withstand stress without becoming seriously impaired. (p. 144)

    a. frustration
    b. intervention
    c. stress tolerance
    d. vulnerability

9. _____ can moderate the effects of stress on a person, and can even reduce illness and early death (p. 144)

    a. Lack of support
    b. Positive social and family relationships
    c. Bureaucracy
    d. Understanding national politics

10. _____ can make a stressor more potent and weaken a person's capacity to cope with it. (p. 144)

    a. Lack of support
    b. Positive social and family relationships
    c. Bureaucracy
    d. Understanding national politics

PRACTICE TEST NUMBER 2

1. When confronting stress, a challenge is (p. 145)

    a. to meet the requirements of the stressor.
    b. to protect oneself from psychological damage and disorganization.
    c. to remain calm and in control.
    d. a and b.

2. Severe stress may result in alterations that can impair the body's ability to fight off (p. 146)

    a. family relatives.
    b. invading bacteria and viruses.
    c. coping resources.
    d. biological adaptation.

3. In using its resources to meet one severe stressor, an organism may _____ tolerance for other stressors. (p. 146)

    a. suffer a lowering of
    b. experience greater
    c. be better prepared with
    d. not develop a

4. Five years after the nuclear accident at Three Mile Island, people exposed to the incident showed (p. 148)

    a. a high tolerance for radioactivity.
    b. a high level of radioactivity.
    c. symptoms of high stress.
    d. a dislike of islands.

5. One extremely stressful situation is loss of (p. 150)

    a. direction.
    b. gainful employment.
    c. the car keys.
    d. all of the above.

6. The sudden unexpected death of a loved one accounts for about _____ of all PTSD cases seen in a community. (p. 150)

    a. one-third
    b. 1.732 percent
    c. three-quarters
    d. 10 percent

7. A normal grieving process typically lasts up to _____ and may involve negative health effects, such as high blood pressure, changes in eating habits, and even thoughts of suicide. (p. 151)

    a. a week or two
    b. a month
    c. about a year
    d. decades

8. In the U.S., Post-Traumatic Stress Disorder (PTSD) appears to occur in about _____ adults at some time in their lives, but the reported rates are lower in national populations with fewer natural disasters and a lower crime rate. (p. 152)

    a. 1 in 12
    b. 1 in 100
    c. 1 in 1,000
    d. 1 in 1,000,000

9. There is a _____ ratio of female to male prevalence of PTSD, due largely to the occurrence of assaultive violence against women. (p. 152)

    a. 1:1
    b. 2:1
    c. 1:2
    d. 10:1

10.   The symptoms of PTSD may vary greatly, depending on the (p. 152)

     a.   nature and severity of the terrifying experience.

     b.   degree of surprise.

     c.   personality make-up of the person.

     d.   all of the above.

PRACTICE TEST NUMBER 3

1.   Regarding PTSD causal factors, (p. 155)

     a.   personality seems to play a role.

     b.   the nature of the event itself appears to account for most of the stress-response variance.

     c.   appears to be a greater likelihood of post-traumatic disorder among women than men.

     d.   all of the above.

2.   An extensive survey of college health behavior reported that _____ percent of female students acknowledged having been forced to have sexual intercourse. (p. 156)

     a.   2

     b.   5

     c.   10

     d.   20

3.   _____ is the most frequent cause of PTSD in women. (p. 156)

     a.   Childbirth

     b.   Rape

     c.   Being in a traffic accident

     d.   a and c

4.   In stranger rape, initially the victim is likely to have a strong fear of (p. 156)

     a.   the consequences of the rape.

     b.   physical harm or death.

     c.   betrayal.

     d.   guilt.

5.   In acquaintance rape, the reaction may be (p. 156)

     a.   physical harm or death.

     b.   betrayal.

     c.   guilt.

     d.   b and c.

6. Survivors of POW camps commonly showed (pp. 159-60)

    a. impaired resistance to physical illness.
    b. low frustration tolerance.
    c. frequent dependence on alcohol and drugs.
    d. all of the above.

7. Many adults who emigrate—especially those forced to leave their homes—experience a high degree of stress and psychological adjustment problems. However, even greater degrees of stress can occur with (p. 162)

    a. those left behind.
    b. their children.
    c. their spouses.
    d. their new neighbors.

8. Torture induces psychological effects independent of other stressors, but the impact of torture could be lessened if victims were able to (p. 164)

    a. escape.
    b. predict and ready themselves for the pain they were about to experience.
    c. meditate and place themselves into a higher plane.
    d. none of the above.

9. A process of stress-inoculation training prepares people to tolerate an anticipated threat by (p. 166)

    a. providing information about the situation and ways people can deal with such dangers.
    b. providing self-statements that promote effective adaptation are rehearsed.
    c. having the person practice making such self-statements while being exposed to stressors.
    d. all of the above.

10. A study found that brief therapy treatment _____ the traumatic event significantly reduced PTSD symptoms. (p. 169)

    a. occurring before
    b. immediately following
    c. anytime within the first year or two after
    d. none of the above

COMPREHENSIVE PRACTICE TEST
The following tests are designed to give you an idea of how well you understood the entire chapter. There are three different types of tests: multiple-choice, true-false, and essay.

MULTIPLE-CHOICE

1. The term, "stress," has typically been used to refer to the _____ placed on an organism, and the organism's internal biological and psychological responses to such demands. (p. 140)

    a. conflicts
    b. adjustive demands
    c. pressures
    d. crisis

2. The symptoms of stress _____ when a person is more closely involved in an immediately traumatic situation. (p. 142)

    a. go away
    b. intensify
    c. remain constant
    d. cause acne

3. The longer a stressor operates, the _____ its effects. (p. 142)

    a. more acute
    b. less frustrating
    c. more severe
    d. less severe

4. Encountering a number of stressors at the same time will make these _____ than when occurring separately. (p. 142)

    a. less acute
    b. more exciting
    c. more severe
    d. less severe

5. Stress operating through the hypothalamic-pituitary-adrenal system can result in a _____, making persons vulnerable to diseases to which they would normally be immune. (p. 149)

    a. raising of blood pressure
    b. lowering of blood levels
    c. higher perspiration output
    d. suppression of the immune system

6.   What seems to push a normal reaction into the category of post-traumatic stress disorder is (p. 150)

    a.   higher perspiration output.

    b.   suppression of the immune system.

    (c.)   the inability to function as usual.

    d.   rising blood pressure.

7.   Acute stress disorder occurs (p. 153)

    a.   at least four weeks after the traumatic event and lasts longer than four weeks.

    (b.)   within four weeks and last from two days to four weeks.

    c.   early and is long-lasting and late-arising.

    d.   none of the above.

8.   Post-traumatic stress disorder differs from acute stress disorder in that it (p. 153)

    a.   lasts longer than four weeks.

    b.   occurs within four weeks of the traumatic event and lasts from two days to four weeks.

    c.   may be long-lasting or late-arising.

    d.   a and c.

9.   _____ following a traumatic experience is considered important in preventing conditioned fear from establishing itself and becoming resistant to change. (p. 156)

    a.   Obtaining medical attention

    b.   Applying a tourniquet

    (c.)   Prompt psychotherapy

    d.   Getting back into a regular routine

10.   After suffering a rape (female or male), a victim is very likely to (p. 156)

    a.   suffer anxiousness.

    b.   experience disturbed concentration and intrusive thoughts.

    c.   behave atypically, such as aggressively, or through substance abuse.

    (d.)   all of the above.

11.   Most physically wounded soldiers have shown _____ symptoms than non-physically wounded soldiers (except in cases of permanent mutilation). (p. 159)

    a.   more anxiety

    b.   less anxiety or less combat exhaustion

    c.   extreme anxiety or combat exhaustion

    d.   more mental exhaustion

12. A study of a large sample of former POWs found that half reported symptoms of PTSD in the year following their releases, and _____ met PTSD criteria 40 to 50 years after their wartime experiences. (p. 160)

    a. none
    b. a few
    c. nearly a third
    d. only six

13. Among returning WW II POWs, within the first six years, (p. 160)

    a. nine times as many died from tuberculosis as would have been expected in civilian life.
    b. four times as many died from gastrointestinal disorders, over twice as many from cancer, heart disease, and suicide as the norm.
    c. three times as many from accidents.
    d. all of the above.

14. A causal factor in combat stress problems is (pp. 160-61)

    a. temperament—a soldier's emotional and physical stamina.
    b. psychosocial—personal freedom frustrations, stresses from combat, personality.
    c. sociocultural—esprit de corps, acceptability of war goals, quality of leadership.
    d. all of the above.

15. Psychological symptoms experienced after having been tortured include (p. 163)

    a. pain, nervousness, insomnia, tremors, weakness, fainting, sweating, and diarrhea.
    b. night terrors and nightmares, depression, suspiciousness, social withdrawal and alienation, irritability, and aggressiveness.
    c. concentration problems, disorientation, confusion, memory deficits, aggressiveness, impulsivity, and suicide attempts.
    d. all of the above.

TRUE - FALSE

1. All situations, positive and negative, that require adjustment can be stressful. T / F (p. 140)

2. Stresses can be damaging if these are too severe for our coping resources—or if we believe as if these are. T / F (p. 146)

3. Severe and sustained stress on any level has very little effect on an organism's overall adaptive capacity. T / F (p. 146)

4. People who are recently divorced or separated are markedly overrepresented among people with psychological problems. T / F (p. 151)

5. Even though PTSD can have a large impact on a person, young persons, in particular, don't feel the need to avoid social situations or excitable stimuli.   T (F) (p. 152)

6. Training and preparation can insulate persons from PTSD. This is why police officers never suffer from it.   T (F) (p. 152)

7. PTSD can result in the traumatic event being persistently re-experienced by the person, or, conversely, deliberate avoidance of any stimuli associated with the trauma, such as cars, if the event were a car crash. (T / F   (p. 153)

8. Everyone has a breaking point, and at sufficiently high levels of stress, the average person can be expected to develop some psychological difficulties following a traumatic event. (T/ F   (p. 155)

9. Being held hostage can produce disabling psychological symptoms in victims for months following the incident. (T/ F   (p. 162)

ESSAY QUESTIONS

1. Explain the three responses of personality decompensation. (p. 149)

2. Coping with rape: Describe the feelings and problems women experience at different points during their traumas. (pp. 156-57)

3.   Identify and briefly explain the approaches to treating the symptoms of PTSD. (pp. 166-69)

WEB LINKS TO ITEMS OR CONCEPTS DISCUSSED IN THIS CHAPTER

Crisis intervention

    www.nasponline.org/NEAT/crisis_0911.html

    www.crisisinterventionnetwork.com/

Adjustment Disorder

    www.mentalhealth.com/dis/p20-aj01.html

    www.mftsource.com/Treatment.Adjust.htm

Stress Inoculation

    mentalhelp.net/psyhelp/chap5/chap5n.htm

    www.prevention.psu.edu/SIT2.htm

psychoneuroimmunology

    hometown.aol.com/AAAPNI/

    www.mc.vanderbilt.edu/adl/pathfinders/ psychoneuroimmuno/research.html

    digilander.libero.it/danielefocosi/ psychoneuroimmunology.html

    ctoc.osu.edu/PNI.html

CRISS-CROSS

Now that you know all there is to know about this chapter, here's your opportunity to put that knowledge to work.

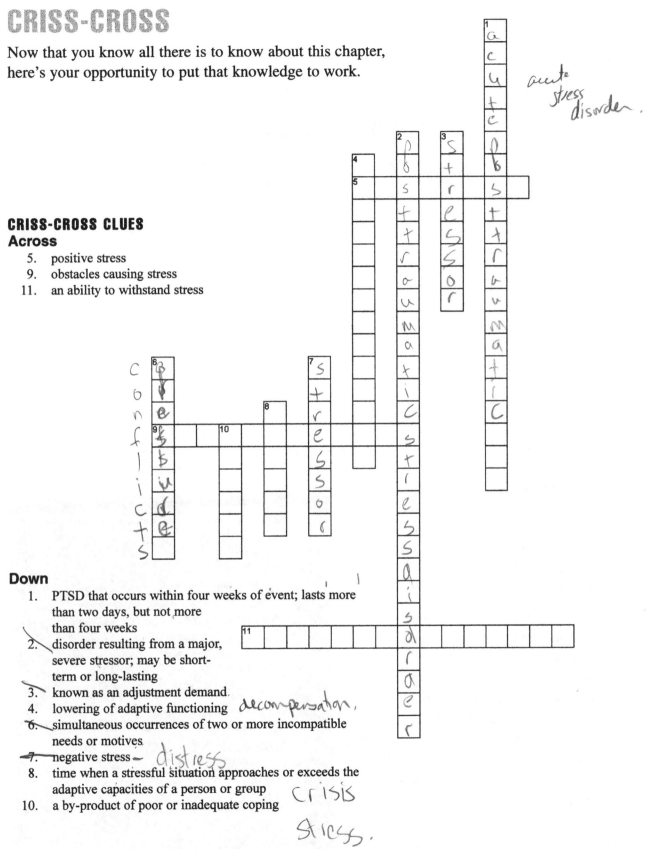

CRISS-CROSS CLUES
Across

5. positive stress
9. obstacles causing stress
11. an ability to withstand stress

Down

1. PTSD that occurs within four weeks of event; lasts more than two days, but not more than four weeks
2. disorder resulting from a major, severe stressor; may be short-term or long-lasting
3. known as an adjustment demand
4. lowering of adaptive functioning *decompensation*
6. simultaneous occurrences of two or more incompatible needs or motives
7. negative stress — *distress*
8. time when a stressful situation approaches or exceeds the adaptive capacities of a person or group *crisis*
10. a by-product of poor or inadequate coping *stress*

Puzzle created with Puzzlemaker at DiscoverySchool.com

Panic, Anxiety, and Their Disorders

BEFORE YOU READ

"Worry wart!" "What, me worry?" "Don't worry, be happy." We have all heard these phrases and, for most of us, these serve to remind us that we can, indeed, become too anxious and need to step back. However, for the more than 23 million Americans who each year are coping with an anxiety disorder, these trivial sayings can serve to remind them of this often debilitating disorder.

Chapter 6, provides you with an overview and understanding of panic, anxiety and their disorders. You will learn there are many different types of anxiety disorders, from phobias (specific and social) to panic disorders, that literally can keep people afflicted with them from venturing out of their homes. Also, you will be introduced to generalized anxiety and obsessive-compulsive disorders.

The authors give you a thorough look at the prevalence rates, causes, and treatment methods available for each of the five anxiety disorders dealt *(next page)* with in this chapter. Since anxiety disorders seem to occur in all cultures around the world, there is a section on sociocultural causal factors and several different examples of cultural differences in sources of worry.

Remember, as you read this chapter, chances are you know someone who has an anxiety disorder. This chapter will give you greater insight into these disorders and why they are so difficult to treat.

OBJECTIVES

After reading this chapter, you should be able to:

1. Compare and evaluate the merits of Freud's use of the concept of anxiety in the etiology of the neuroses versus the descriptive approach used in DSM since 1980.

2. Distinguish between fear and anxiety.

3. Describe the major features of phobias, identify and differentiate different subtypes of phobia, explicate the major etiological hypotheses, and discuss the most effective treatment approaches.

4. List the diagnostic criteria for panic disorder, contrast panic attacks and other types of anxiety, explain the association with agoraphobia. Summarize prevalence, age of onset, and comorbidity.

5. Describe recent findings on biological, behavioral, and cognitive influence for anxiety proneness. Summarize the evidence that anxiety sensitivity constitutes a diathesis for development of panic attacks.

6. Describe how safety behaviors and cognitive biases help to maintain panic.

7. Compare and contrast the major treatment approaches for panic disorder and agoraphobia.

8.   Summarize the central features of generalized anxiety disorder, and distinguish among psychoanalytic, conditioning, and cognitive theories of etiology.

9.   Identify the central nervous system processes and structures associated with generalized anxiety disorder, and evaluate treatments for the disorder.

10. Describe the defining features of obsessive-compulsive disorder, summarize theories of etiology along with supporting evidence (or the lack thereof), and outline the treatment of OCD.

11. Provide several examples of sociocultural effects on anxiety disorders.

AS YOU READ

KEY WORDS

Each of the words below is important in understanding the concepts presented in this Chapter. Write the definition next to each of the words.

neurotic behavior (p. 174)

neurosis (p. 174)

anxiety (p. 175)

fear (p. 174)

anxiety disorder (p. 176)

phobia (p. 176)

specific phobia (p. 176)

blood-injection injury phobia (p. 177)

social phobia (p. 182)

agoraphobia (p. 188)

panic provocation agents (p. 190)

interoceptive fears (p. 196)

anxiety sensitivity (p. 194)

generalized anxiety disorder (p. 197)

immunization (p. 199)

obsessive-compulsive disorder (pp. 202-03)

obsessions (p. 203)

compulsions (p. 203)

WHO'S WHO AND WHAT'S WHAT—MATCHING

Match the following psychological tests with the appropriate description of each test's purpose.

Psychological Test

_D_ Phobia
_G_ Neuroticism
_F_ Neurotic behavior
_I_ Inflation effect
_A_ Vicarious conditioning
_C_ Nocturnal panic
_E_ Introceptive avoidance
_J_ Anxious apprehension
_M_ CRH
_L_ Bed nucleus of the stria terminali
_K_ TKS
_H_ Aaron Beck
_B_ O. H. Mowrer

Definition

A. the transmission of a phobia from one person or animal to another by observing a person or animal behaving fearfully
B. credited with devising a two-process theory of avoidance learning in OCD   Mowrer
C. panic attack that occurs during sleep
D. persistent and disproportionate fear of some specific object or situation that presents little or no actual danger
E. avoidance of activities that create arousal sensations
F. exaggerated use of avoidance behaviors or defense mechanisms
G. basic personality trait—aproneness to experience negative mood states
H. cognitive psychologist who coined the phrase, "automatic thoughts," which are associated with panic triggers   BECK
I. when a person is exposed to a more intense traumatic experience (not paired with the conditioned stimulus) after a first traumatic experience, thus becoming more fearful of the conditioned stimulus
J. future-oriented mood state in which a person attempts to be constantly ready to deal with negative upcoming events
K. anxiety disorder found in Japan related to Western social phobia
L. extension of the amygdala believed to be important brain area mediating generalized anxiety
M. anxiety producing hormone recently implicated as playing a role in GAD

SHORT ANSWERS

Provide brief answers to the following questions.

1. List the five subtypes of specific phobia and give examples of each. (p. 176)

Animal   Atypical
Blood-Injection
Natural Environmental
Situational

2. Discuss methods used to treat social phobias. (p. 182)

3. You are a psychoanalyst and a client comes to see you with GAD. How would explain the causal factors for this disorder? (pp. 202-03)

4. Describe the different types of obsessive thoughts and compulsions. (p. 212)

FILL IN THE BLANKS

Read the following and fill in the blanks. These questions are designed to help you focus on specific details.

1. The DSM-IV-TR recognizes _____seven_____ primary types of anxiety disorders. (p. 176)

2. The National Cormorbidity Survey found that anxiety disorders affect approximately _____30_____ percent of the female population and _____19_____ percent of men at some point in their lives. (p. 176)

3. The three main categories of phobia are _____specific_____ phobia, _____social_____ phobia, and _____agoraphobia_____. (p. 176)

4. _____Blood-injection injury_____ and _____environmental_____ phobias begin in childhood, but _____claustrophobia_____ and _____agoraphobia_____ tend to begin in adolescence and early adulthood. (p. 177)

5. The experiments by Mineka and Cook showed that laboratory-reared monkeys could learn to be afraid of snakes by observing a _____ monkey behaving fearfully with snakes. It was also found that the monkeys could learn fear by watching a _____ of wild monkeys responding fearfully to snakes. This suggests that _____media_____ may play a role in _____vicarious_____ conditioning of fears and phobias in people. (p. 181)

6. The _____preparedness_____ theory says that humans and animals are more likely to have phobias for snakes, water, heights and enclosed places because of our evolutionary history of these things being associated with trauma. (p. 181)

7. An uncued panic attack that occurs during sleep is known as _____nocturnal panic_____. (p. 187)

8. Current estimates are that 30 to 50 percent of persons with panic disorder will experience a serious _____depression_____ at some point in their life and meet the criteria for _____dependent_____ or _____avoidant_____ personality disorder. (p. 190)

9. Currently, two neurotransmitters systems are most implicated in panic attacks. These are the ___*NE*___ and ___*serotonin*___ systems. (p. 191)

10. The ___*behavioral*___ *comprehensive learning* theory of panic proposes that initial panic attacks become associated with initially neutral interoceptive and exteroceptive cues through a conditioning process. (p. 192)

11. Experience with controlling aspects of one's life may ___*immunize*___ us from developing generalized anxiety disorder. (p. 199)

12. Fear and panic involve the activation of the ___*fight or flight*___ response, while generalized anxiety is a more ___*diffuse*___ emotional state involving ___*AROUSAL*___ and a ___*preparation*___ for possible impending threat. (p. 202)

13. The behavioral model has been useful in helping to understand what ___*factors*___ may help to ___*maintain*___ obsessive-compulsive behavior and in generating an effective form of ___*treatment*___. However, it has not been as helpful in explaining why people with OCD develop ___*obsessions*___ in the first place. (p. 206)

14. People with OCD seem to have an overactivation of the ___*frontal cortex*___, which delivers the "stuff of obsession," and a dysfunction of the ___*cortic-basal ganglia-thalamic circuit*___ circuit, which leads to inappropriate behavioral responses. (p. 210)

THE DOCTOR IS IN...PSYCHIATRIC HELP—5¢

Read the following scenarios and diagnose the client. Remember to look carefully at the criteria for the disorder before you make a decision as to the diagnosis. Make a list of other information you might need to help you understand the causal factors.

1. Teresa comes to your office. She has been referred to you by her primary care doctor who, after doing a complete work-up, could find nothing wrong with her. She tells you she feels as if she is losing control and going crazy. You ask her to explain. She says that for the last two months, she has been unexpectedly having shortness of breath, heart palpitations, dizziness, and sweating. These experiences seem to come out of the blue and make her so afraid of having other feelings like these, that she is afraid leave her house.

   How would you diagnose her and why? Also create a treatment plan for her. (pp. 186-89, 195-96)

2. Ned visits your office. He is has made an appointment because his family says he needs to see you. His constant worrying is concerning them and becoming difficult to deal with. Ned tells you he has been feeling anxious about the future and says that he needs to be ready to deal with any negative thing that might come up—like his car breaking down or getting lost when trying to get to a new area. Both of these would affect his work, thus, his financial well-being, and, ultimately, his family. He tells you he can't seem to control the constant state of apprehension and always feels tense and overaroused. He hasn't been sleeping well and has had difficulty concentrating at work (which is also worrying him, as he thinks is may affect his employment). His family says he is constantly irritable and he has felt a lot of muscle tension, especially in his neck and shoulders.

How would you diagnose Ned and what would be the most effective treatment for him? (pp. 197-98, 202)

3. Jean has over the last few months, been washing her hands 50 to 75 times a day. Her hands are now cracked and bleeding and she is unable to work. In addition to hand washing she has to constantly check her stove and door locks and she must do this in a particular way or she has to start all over again. She has come to see you because she is about to lose her marriage as a result of her behavior. Jean knows her behaviors are senseless and excessive but she can't control them. How would you diagnose Jean and what treatment plan would you create?   (pp. 202-04, 210-12)

PICTURE THIS

Below are pictures that represent key people or concepts from the book. Write the answers on the line to the right of the clues.

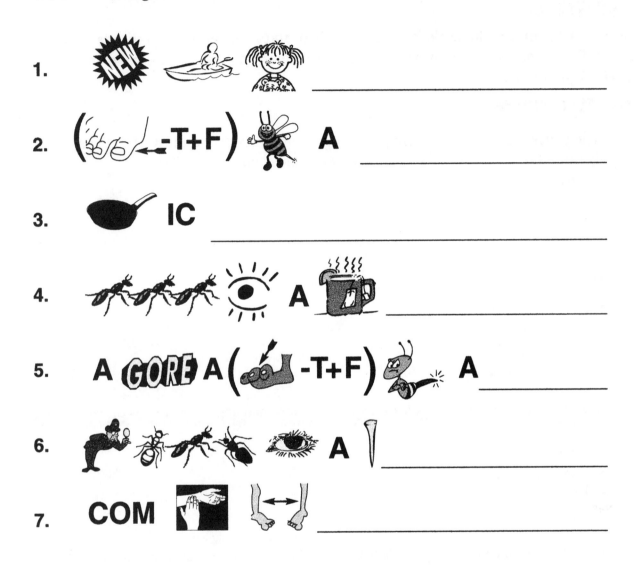

1. _____

2. A _____

3. _____

4. _____

5. A _____

6. A _____

7. _____

AFTER YOU READ

PRACTICE TESTS

Take the following three multiple-choice tests to see how much you have comprehended from the chapter. Each represents roughly one-third of the chapter. As you study the chapter, use these to check your progress.

PRACTICE TEST NUMBER 1

1. Who believed that neuroses were psychological disorders that resulted when there was significant anxiety that was a result of intrapsychic conflict? (p. 174)

   a. Pavlov

   b. Ellis

   c. Freud

   d. Beck

2. The components of fear and panic are (p. 174)

   a. cognitive/subjective.

   b. physiological.

   c. behavioral.

   d. all of the above.

3. Anxiety, unlike fear, is a complex blend of emotions and cognitions that is oriented to the (p. 175)

   a. object of fear.

   b. past experience.

   c. future.

   d. all of the above.

4. Many human and animal experiments have established that the basic fear and anxiety response patterns are highly (p. 175)

   a. predictable.

   b. conditionable.

   c. inevitable.

   d. a and c.

5. Phobic behavior tends to be reinforced by the reduction in anxiety that occurs when a feared situation is (p. 177)

    a. faced.
    b. faced and dealt with.
    c. avoided.
    d. understood.

6. _____ percent of people with blood-injury phobia have a history of fainting when confronted with the sight of blood or injury. (p. 178)

    a. Seventy-five
    b. Fifty
    c. Twenty-five
    d. Ten

7. Which viewpoint believes that phobias represent a defense against anxiety? (p. 178)

    a. behavioral
    b. cognitive
    c. psychodynamic
    d. humanistic

8. By watching her older sister react in a fearful way to spiders, Keri learned to also be afraid of spiders. This is called (p. 179)

    a. aping conditioning.
    b. mimicking conditioning.
    c. vicarious conditioning.
    d. none of the above.

9. John had dogs all of his life and was quite comfortable being around dogs. When John was bitten by a dog, he did not develop a phobia. Why? (p. 180)

    a. He didn't care.
    b. It didn't hurt.
    c. The dog didn't mean it.
    d. His experiences had immunized him.

10. Steve watches as his therapist goes up and down an elevator in a calm and nonchalant way. Later, he is walking into the elevator with his therapist and going up one floor. This is an example of (p. 182)

    a. participant modeling.
    b. specific phobia modeling.
    c. reality modeling.
    d. none of the above.

PRACTICE TEST NUMBER 2

1. Social phobias usually begin in (p. 183)

    a. early childhood.

    b. mid-life.

    c. adolescence or early adulthood.

    d. old age.

2. Which of the famous performers below suffer from social phobia? (p. 183)

    a. Barbara Streisand

    b. Carly Simon

    c. Michael Jackson

    d. a and b.

3. Like other phobias, social phobias are often (p. 184)

    a. evolving.

    b. learned.

    c. easily ignored.

    d. none of the above.

4. Unlike specific phobias, social phobia can sometimes be treated with (p. 186)

    a. cognitive therapy.

    b. behavioral therapy.

    c. medication.

    d. none of the above.

5. What distinguishes panic attacks from other types of anxiety? (p. 187)

    a. brevity

    b. intensity

    c. physiological symptoms

    d. a and b

6. Panic attacks are about twice as prevalent in women as in men. This is thought to be a result of _____ factors. (p. 189)

    a. behavioral

    b. gender

    c. sociocultural

    d. unconscious

7. In family and twin studies, panic disorders have a _____ heritable component. (p. 190)

    a. high

    b. low

    c. moderate

    d. predictable

8. The _____ is the central area involved in what has been called a "fear network" with connections to lower (locus coeruleus) and higher (prefrontal cortex) areas of the brain. (p. 191)

    a. hippocampus
    b. amygdala
    c. limbic system
    d. all of the above

9. Beck and Emery (1985) and Clark (1986, 1988, 1997) proposed a model of panic that says clients are hypersensitive to their bodily sensations and prone to giving them the direst possible interpretations. What is this theory called? (p. 192)

    a. fear of fear theory
    b. comprehensive learning theory
    c. cognitive theory
    d. biological readiness theory

10. Ken often has an upset stomach. He is very anxious about this condition. Although Ken does not have any panic attacks, his preexisting high level of _____ makes him more prone to developing a panic disorder. (p. 194)

    a. awareness
    b. cognition
    c. a and b
    d. anxiety sensitivity

PRACTICE TEST NUMBER 3

1. It is estimated that GAD is experienced by approximately _____ percent of the population in any one-year period and _____ percent at some point in their lives. (p. 198)

    a. 10, 70
    b. 2, 4
    c. 8, 11
    d. 3, 5

2. The role of worry for people with GAD (p. 200)

    a. has positive and negative consequences.
    b. has minor and major consequences.
    c. is unknown at this time.
    d. is not of interest to researchers because GAD has so many other aspects to study.

3. A(n) _____ is a overt repetitive behavior or more covert mental act. (p. 203)

    a. compulsion
    b. obsession
    c. behavior
    d. GAD

4. Cognitive factors that contribute to OCD behavior are (p. 209)
    a. attention drawn to disturbing material relevant to obsession.
    b. difficulty blocking out negative irrelevant input.
    c. low confidence in memory skills.
    d. all of the above.

5. Biological causal factors are _____ implicated in the causes of OCD. (p. 209)
    a. strongly
    b. mildly
    c. superficially
    d. somewhat

6. According to biological psychiatrists, panic disorder is qualitatively different from generalized anxiety because of an apparent finding that a _____ drug appeared to block panic attacks in agoraphobics without affecting their anticipatory anxiety. (p. 195)
    a. minor tranquilizer
    b. tricyclic antidepressant
    c. barbiturate
    d. monoamine oxidase inhibitor

7. Which of the following is not typically a part of cognitive-behavior therapy for panic disorder? (p. 195)
    a. exposure to feared situations and/or feared bodily sensations
    b. deep muscle relaxation and breathing retraining
    c. identification and modification of logical errors and automatic thoughts
    d. carbon dioxide inhalation and/or lactate infusion

8. The benzodiazepines, minor tranquilizers that reduce generalized anxiety, probably exert their effects through stimulating the action of (p. 201)
    a. acetylcholine.
    b. GABA.
    c. serotonin.
    d. norepinephrine.

9. An impulse the person cannot seem to control is called a(n) (p. 203)
    a. compulsion.
    b. delusion.
    c. hallucination.
    d. focal phobia.

10. The personality disorders with which OCD most often occurs are (p. 205)
    a. narcissistic and antisocial.
    b. borderline and histrionic.
    c. schizoid and schizotypal.
    d. avoidant and dependent.

COMPREHENSIVE PRACTICE TEST

The following tests are designed to give you an idea of how well you understood the entire chapter. There are three different types of tests: multiple-choice, true-false, and essay.

MULTIPLE-CHOICE

1. The term, "neurosis," was dropped in the DSM–III in the year (p. 174)
    a. 1969.
    b. 1980.
    c. 1975.
    d. 1990.

2. The most common way of distinguishing between <u>fear</u> and <u>anxiety</u> is that fear involves a(n) (p. 174)
    a. increase in heart rate.
    b. unpleasant interstate of something dreadful going to happen.
    c. inability to specify a clear danger.
    d. obvious source of danger.

3. Paula has extreme irrational fear. She feels anxious and has physical responses, such as a racing heart and dizziness. Paula will probably first be seen by her (p. 176)
    a. primary care doctor.
    b. therapist.
    c. psychiatrist.
    d. dentist.

4. Specific phobias were formerly known as _____ phobias. (p. 176)
    a. objective
    b. complicated
    c. subjective
    d. simple

5. At the age of 21 months, Karen was a very timid and shy child. She hid behind her mother and rarely ventured over to play with other children in her play group. Based on the study done by Kagan and his colleagues, what can you predict about the risk of Karen developing multiple specific phobias by the age of seven or eight? It is (p. 181)
    a. about the same as other children in her play group.
    b. less then uninhibited children in general.
    c. higher because of temperamental factors.
    d. higher because her play group has more boys than girls.

6. The most common specific social phobia is fear of (p. 183)

   a. public speaking.

   b. crowds.

   c. urinating in public restrooms.

   d. public affection.

7. From an evolutionary perspective, social phobia are a by-product of (p. 184)

   a. dominance hierarchies.

   b. learning.

   c. observing.

   d. modeling.

8. Billy, who is 25 months old, is behaviorally inhibited. What can you predict, based on the Hayward et. al. and Kagan research, will be the likelihood of Billy developing a social phobia by the age of 13? He (p. 184)

   a. has increased risk.

   b. has no increased risk.

   c. will develop a social phobia.

   d. none of the above.

9. An early hypothesis about the origins of agoraphobia was that it was a (p. 192)

   a. fear of fear.

   b. fear of going shopping.

   c. fear of commitment.

   d. none of the above.

10. Unlike other anxiety disorders that usually have an acute onset, people with GAD report (p. 198)

   a. being anxious most of their lives.

   b. a slow and insidious onset.

   c. sudden onset.

   d. a and b.

11. Something that may account for why people with GAD feel constantly tense and vigilant for possible threats is their relative lack of (p. 199)

   a. interest in their surroundings.

   b. understanding.

   c. safety signals.

   d. something to be really worried about.

12. GAD seems to share a common genetic diathesis with (p. 201)

　　a. personality disorders.

　　b. PTSD.

　　c. major depressive disorder.

　　d. eating disorders.

13. A(n) _____ is a persistent and recurrent intrusive thought, image or impulse that is experienced as disturbing and inappropriate. (p. 203)

　　a. compulsion

　　b. obsession

　　c. behavior

　　d. GAD

14. With OCD, what factors seem consistent in almost all the different clinical presentations? (p. 205)

　　a. Anxiety is the affective symptom.

　　b. Compulsions usually reduce the anxiety.

　　c. Nearly all people afflicted with OCD fear they will be responsible for something terrible. happening to themselves or others.

　　d. All of the above.

15. OCD may be characterized by excessively high levels of (p. 210)

　　a. GABA.

　　b. fluoxetine.

　　c. serotonin.

　　d. none of the above.

TRUE - FALSE

1. Fear or panic is a basic emotion that involves activation of the "flight or fight" response. T / F (p. 174)

2. Anxiety involves a positive mood, worry about the future and the ability to predict the future threat. T / F (p. 175)

3. It has been proven that classical conditioning does not produce fears and phobias. T / F (p. 178)

4. Life experiences influence a person's likelihood of developing a phobia. T / F (p. 180)

5. The best treatment for specific phobia is cognitive therapy. T / F (p. 182)

6. The treatment of choice for specific phobias is exposure therapy. T / F (p. 182)

7. The term, "social anxiety disorder," is increasingly preferred by researchers and clinicians, instead of social phobias. T / F (p. 183)

8. Social phobics have a deep sense of control over events in their lives. T / F (p. 185)

9. Agoraphobia can occur in the absence of full-blown panic attacks. T / F (p. 189)

10. Seven to 30 percent of adults who have experienced panic attacks will go on to develop panic disorder. T / F (p. 190)

11. The learning theory model is better able to explain why panic attacks often occur without any preceding negative automatic thoughts or during sleep at night than the cognitive model. T / F (p. 194)

12. People with panic disorder have their attention automatically drawn to pleasant information in their environment. T / F (p. 194)

13. Most people with GAD manage to function in spite of their high levels of worry and anxiety. T / F (p. 198)

14. People with GAD have a history of experiencing many important events in their lives in which they feel are predictable and controllable. T / F (p. 199)

15. GABA, a neurotransmitter, is now strongly implicated in generalized anxiety. T / F (p. 201)

16. OCD is different from other anxiety disorders in that there is a large gender difference in adults. T / F (p. 204)

17. When OCD clients were asked to suppress intrusive thoughts, they reported twice as many intrusive thoughts on those days as opposed to the days they were given no instructions. T / F (p. 209)

ESSAY QUESTIONS

1. Discuss the criteria for diagnosing generalized anxiety disorder (GAD). (pp. 198-99)

2.   Give examples of cultural differences in sources of worry. (p. 212)

WEB LINKS TO ITEMS OR CONCEPTS DISCUSSED IN THIS CHAPTER

Anxiety, panic

    www.nimh.nih.gov/anxiety/anxietymenu.cfm
    www.adaa.org/
    www.anxietynetwork.com/
    www.med.nyu.edu/Psych/screens/anx.html
    www.algy.com/anxiety/
    www.apa.org/pubinfo/panic.html

CRISS-CROSS

Now that you know all there is to know about this chapter, here's your opportunity to put that knowledge to work.

CRISS-CROSS CLUES
Across
1. the experienced emotion when the source of danger is obvious
3. clearly excessive ritualistic overt repetitive behaviors *neurosis*
5. the exaggerated use of avoidance behaviors or defense mechanisms
7. involves fears of situations in which a person is exposed to the scrutiny of others
8. the experienced emotion when the source of danger is not obvious
9. a collection of nuclei critical involved in the emotion of fear
Down
2. a blend of emotions that is more oriented to the future and much more diffuse than fear
4. may involve fears of things (animals, water, heights, tunnels, spiders)
6. disturbing persistent, recurrent, intrusive thoughts, images, or impulses

Puzzle created with Puzzlemaker at DiscoverySchool.com

CHAPTER SEVEN

Mood Disorders and Suicide

BEFORE YOU READ

Chances are you know someone with a mood disorder. Mood disorders are ranked fourth of society's 150 "disease-burdens." Everybody gets sad at some time, but not everybody who is sad has a mood disorder. Also, what may be seen as depression or mania in one culture may not be considered so in another. Why that is, and why some people developing prolonged, maladaptive and persistent mood disorders will be found in chapter seven.

This chapter presents you with insights into the prevalence and causal factors of mood disorders. In addition, you will have an opportunity to study the differences and similarities between the unipolar and bipolar disorders and explore various treatment possibilities.

Look at the case studies and information boxes. These examples will help you conceptualize the information being presented.

Lastly, unlike other disorders, people who suffer from mood disorders are quite vulnerable to suicide attempts and completions. The final portion of this chapter gives you an overview of suicide, a picture of who is likely to commit suicide, and some ideas on suicide prevention and intervention programs.

OBJECTIVES

After reading this chapter, you should be able to:

1. Define the characteristics of mood disorders

2. Explain the prevalence of mood disorders

3. Describe unipolar mood disorders

4. Differentiate depressions that are not mood disorders from those that are

5. Identify the mild to moderate depressive disorders

6. Describe criteria for diagnosing major depressive disorder and the subtypes

7. Discuss biological and psychosocial causal factors in unipolar and bipolar mood disorders

8. Describe various types of bipolar disorders

9. Explain how various sociocultural factors affect unipolar and bipolar disorders

10. Assess treatments and outcomes of mood disorders

11. Explain prevalence rates of suicide among people with mood disorders

12. Describe who is likely to attempt suicide and who is likely to complete suicide

13. Describe the various motives for why someone takes his or her own life

14. Explain the sociocultural and biological variables that affect suicide

15. Evaluate the ethical issues involved in the right to die

AS YOU READ

Answers can be found in the Answer Key at the end of the book.

Who's Who and What's What—Match each of the following people with her/his accomplishment or theory.

_____ Martin Seligman	A. depressogenic schemas/negative automatic thoughts
_____ Emile Durkheim	B. "Mourning and Melancholia"
_____ Aaron Beck	C. learned helplessness theory
_____ Sigmund Freud	D. hopelessness theory
_____ Emil Kraepelin	E. introduced the term, "manic-depressive insanity"
_____ Abramson et al., 1989	F. French sociologist who studied the sociocultural factors in suicide

KEY WORDS

Each of the words below is important in understanding the concepts presented in this chapter. Write the definition next to each of the words. The page numbers are provided in case you need to refer to the book.

depression (p. 216)

mood disorders (p. 216)

unipolar (p. 216)

dysthymic (p. 220)

major depressive disorder (p. 220)

specifiers (p. 222)

reccurence (p. 223)

relapse (p. 223)

attributions (p. 234)

learned helplessness (p. 234)

positive affect (p. 238)

bipolar disorder (p. 243)

manic episode (p. 241)

hypomanic episode   (p. 241)

cyclothymiac (p. 241)

rapid cycling (p. 244)

schizoaffective disorder (p. 244)

ECT (p. 251)

suicide (p. 254)

Death with Dignity Act (p. 261)

SHORT ANSWERS

Provide brief answers to the following questions.

1. A friend of yours recently lost a grandparent. You have just finished studying mood disorders in your Abnormal Psychology class. What could you tell him about the normal response phases to the loss? (p. 218)

2.   In the Brown and Harris 1978 study, what factors were associated with the women who experienced stressful life events but did not become depressed? (p. 230)

3.   Discuss the ways interpersonal problems can play a causal role in depression and how depression affects others. (pp. 236-37)

4.   Explain the emphasis suicide prevention centers have when working with someone who is contemplating suicide. (p. 260)

FILL IN THE BLANKS

Read the following and fill in the blanks. These questions are designed to help you focus on specific details.

1.   The lifetime prevalence for dysthymia is nearly ___5___ percent for men and ___8___ percent for women. (p. 220)

2.   Three specifiers connected with major depression are major depressive episode with _melancholic_ features, severe major depressive episode with _psychotic_ features, and major depressive episode with _typical_ features. (p. 222)

3. When delusions or hallucinations with psychotic features are present during a major depressive episode, these must be _mood-congruent_, with content portraying a negative tone. (p. 222)

4. Depression may _recur_ at sometime following a period of remission, or it may _relapse_, which refers to the return of symptoms within a short period of time. (p. 223)

5. Whybrow et. al. suggested that psychosocial stressors may play a role in the development of mood disorders by causing long-term changes in _brain_ functioning. (p. 246)

6. The reformulated helplessness theory proposes three critical dimensions on which attributions are made: _internal/external_, _global/specific_, and _stable/unstable_. (pp. 234-35)

7. _Bipolar_ disorders are distinguished from _depressive/unipolar_ disorders by the presence of manic or hypomanic symptoms. (p. 216)

8. Although the symptoms listed are the same for manic and _depressive_ episodes, there is much less impairment in social and occupational functioning in _hypomania_ and, to qualify, hospitalization must not be required. (p. 241)

9. _Adjustment disorder w/depressed mood_ and _dysthymia_ are considered the mild-to-moderately-severe main categories of depressive disorders. (p. 220)

10. _Cyclothymia_ is considered the mild-to-moderately-severe category of bipolar disorders. (p. 241)

11. A person who experiences a _manic episode_ has markedly elevated euphoric and expansive moods, often interrupted by occasional outbursts of intense irritability, or even violence. (p. 241)

12. Someone who meets the criteria for a major mood disorder and at least two major symptoms of schizophrenia is diagnosed with _schizoaffective disorder_. (p. 244)

13. "_Mood stabilizer_" is used to describe lithium and related drugs, because these have anti-manic and anti-depressant effects. (p. 251)

14. Electroconvulsive therapy is often used with severely depressed, suicidal patients because antidepressants often take _3_ to _4_ weeks to produce significant improvement. ECT is also used with patients who have not responded to other forms of _psychological_ treatment. When selection criteria are carefully observed, a complete remission of symptoms occurs after about six to 12 treatments. (p. 244)

15. Fill in the missing information in the following questions about the risk of suicide. (p. 254)

   a. The vast majority of those who commit suicide do so during the _recovery_ phase of depression.

   b. The risk of suicide is just __1__ percent during the year a depressive episode occurs but rises to __15__ percent over the entire lifetime of an individual who experiences recurrent episodes.

   c. Experts agree that the actual number of suicides is probably _2to4_ times as high as the official number.

THE DOCTOR IS IN...PSYCHIATRIC HELP—5¢

Read the following scenarios and diagnose the client. Remember to look carefully at the criteria for the disorder before you make a decision as to the diagnosis. Make a list of other information you might need to help you understand the causal factors.

1. Helen comes into your office asking for help. She is a 29-year-old woman, married with no children. She would like to have children at some point. Helen reports that she has been feeling sad for a long time—almost three years now. Although she does have periods of feeling normal, these don't last. There is nothing she can remember that triggered her feeling bad. Recently her husband has been making comments about how little she has been eating. Helen says that she has no energy and can't seem to sleep through the night. She is starting to think of herself as a worthless person for not being able to just snap out of it. (p. 220-21)

2. As a leading expert on adolescent suicide, you have been asked to give a talk on known risk factors. What would you include in your speech? (pp. 254-60)

3. Winter is coming, and Miles is feeling incredibly sad. He moved to Minnesota three years ago to take a new job. He likes his job and finds it very rewarding. When he finally comes to see you, he reports that it takes a lot of effort for him to get out of bed. He tells you that the last two years were about the same; he felt a similar way but figured that it was just the newness of his surroundings. Now he isn't sure. He tells you that he feels much better, even normal, when spring comes around. (p. 223)

4. Ed was brought to the hospital by the police. His wife had called them when he had become aggressive. She had refused to give him a credit card. He had been awake for almost three days straight, working on a very big plan to buy a city and become the mayor. He had been spending money that they didn't have, and his wife was worried. Ed's scheme had been gaining momentum for almost a week. When he was admitted to the hospital, he talked non-stop about needing a phone, because the deal was about to go through. He kept telling the hospital staff he was going to become famous and be able to save the city from ruin.

    After talking to his wife, you discover that not too long ago, Ed had been very depressed. Before he became so "crazy," as she put it, she thought that maybe he was getting better. How would you diagnose Ed? Why? (p. 241)

PICTURE THIS

Below are pictures that represent key people or concepts from the book. Write the answers on the line to the right of the clues.

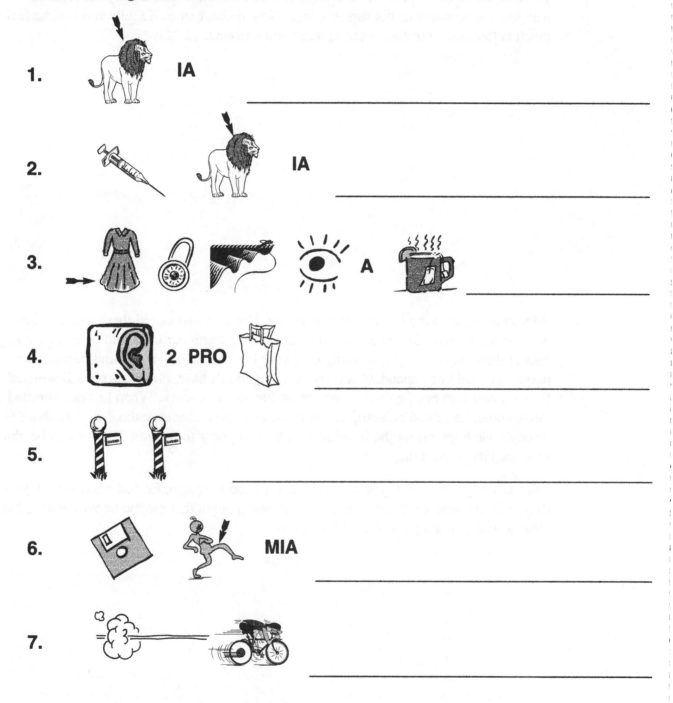

1. **IA** _____

2. **IA** _____

3. **A** _____

4. **2 PRO** _____

5. _____

6. **MIA** _____

7. _____

AFTER YOU READ

PRACTICE TESTS

Take the following three multiple-choice tests to see how much you have comprehended from the chapter. Each represents roughly one-third of the chapter. As you study the chapter, use these to check your progress.

PRACTICE TEST NUMBER 1

1. In 1990, out of the 150 health conditions that were considered to be a "disease-burden" to society, depression ranked (p. 216)

   a.   tenth.

   (b) fourth.

   c.   first.

   d.   twenty-fifth.

2. Mania is characterized by (p. 216)

   a.   sadness and dejection.

   b.   shame and confusion.

   (c) excitement and euphoria.

   d.   frustration and anxiety.

3. Depression is characterized by (p. 216)

   (a) sadness and dejection.

   b,   shame and confusion.

   c.   excitement and euphoria.

   d.   frustration and anxiety.

4. Mood disorders are differentiated by (p. 216)

   a.   severity.

   b.   frequency.

   c.   duration.

   (d) a and c.

5. A person who has been diagnosed with dysthymia may experience normal mood periods that may last (p. 220)

   (a) a few days or weeks, up to a maximum of two months.

   b.   six months or more.

   c.   several days but no more than one month.

   d.   none of the above.

6. Sue meets the criteria for being diagnosed with major depressive disorder. However, her therapist also notes some patterns of symptoms that she feels are important for understanding the disorder and treating Sue effectively. These additional patterns are called (p. 222)

    a. equalizers.
    b. identifiers.
    c. noteworthy.
    d. specifiers.

7. Mood disorders were previously called (p. 216)

    a. affective disorders.
    b. selective disorders.
    c. affective disorders.
    d. defective disorders.

8. Twin studies have provided evidence that there may be a _____ genetic component to unipolar depression. (p. 224)

    a. significant
    b. minimal
    c. moderate
    d. overwhelming

9. In the 1960s and 70s, research was focused on the following neurotransmitters and their effect on depression: (p. 225)

    a. norepinephrine, dopamine and serotonin.
    b. serotonin and epinephrine.
    c. coritsol, norephinephrine and DST.
    d. none of the above.

10. Originally, diathesis-stress models assumed that diatheses were biological. Recently, depression researchers have begun to propose diatheses that are (p. 230)

    a. cognitive.
    b. social.
    c. subconscious.
    d. a and b.

PRACTICE TEST NUMBER 2

1. Two personality variables that may contribute to a diathesis for depression are (p. 230)

    a. extrovert and introvert.
    b. neuroticism and low positive affectivity.
    c. vulnerable and anger.
    d. none of the above.

2. The cognitive diatheses that have been studied for depression focus on _____ patterns of thinking. (p. 238)

   a. positive

   b. inconsistent

   c. negative

   d. a and b

3. Research has found that a person may have a vulnerability to depression if he/she experiences an early childhood loss of a parent and (p. 230)

   a. poor parental care.

   b. support of siblings.

   c. involvement with an extended family.

   d. all of the above.

4. One of the most important contributions of the psychodynamic approach to depression has been to point out the (p. 231)

   a. importance of dreams.

   b. importance of the id.

   c. importance of early loss (real or imagined).

   d. creation of defense mechanisms.

5. According to the behavioral theories of depression, people become depressed when their responses no longer produce positive reinforcement or when (p. 232)

   a. they learn depression is good.

   b. their rate of negative reinforcement increases.

   c. they generalize.

   d. none of the above.

6. A psychological theory on reasons why these are sex differences in unipolar depression proposes that women are more prone to experience   (p. 236)

   a. a lack of control over negative life events.

   b. discrimination in the workplace.

   c. poverty.

   d. all of the above.

7. The mild-to-moderate range of bipolar disorder is known as (p. 241)

   a. dysthymia.

   b. cyclothymia.

   c. hyperemania.

   d. unipolar.

8. Who introduced the term, "manic-depressive," insanity to describe a series of attacks of elation and depression? (p. 242)

    a.   Freud

    b.   Hippocrates

    c.   Kraepelin

    d.   Charcot

9. Even without formal therapy, the great majority of manic and depressed patients recover from a given episode within less than (p. 250)

    a.   two weeks.

    b.   one year.

    c.   one month.

    d.   two years.

10. In suicides associated with depression, suicide is committed most often during the _____ phase of a depressive episode. (p. 254)

    a.   early onset

    c.   peak of depression

    b.   late onset

    d.   recovery

PRACTICE TEST NUMBER 3

1. A disorder that involves mood swings between subclinical levels of depression and mania is (p. 241)

    a.   bipolar disorder.

    b.   manic depression.

    c.   dysthymic disorder.

    d.   cyclothymic disorder.

2. Bipolar mood disorder is distinguished from major depression by (p. 243)

    a.   at least one episode of mania.

    b.   disturbance of circadian rhythms.

    c.   evidence of earlier cyclothymia.

    d.   evidence of earlier dysthymia.

3. The original learned helplessness theory refers to the depressed patient's perception that (p. 234)

    a.   accustomed reinforcement is no longer forthcoming.

    b.   there is no control over aversive events.

    c.   reinforcement is inadequate.

    d.   the world is a negative place.

4. Since about 1990, the type of antidepressants increasingly prescribed because of fewer side effects are (p. 257)

    a. tricyclics.

    b. selective serotonim re-uptake inhibitors (SSRIs).

    c. imipramine.

    d. ECT.

5. _____ is a brief form of treatment for unipolar depression that is highly structured and attempts to each people to evaluate their beliefs and negative automatic thoughts. (p. 252)

    a. CBT

    b. ECT

    c. IPT

    d. none of the above

6. This treatment for unipolar depression focuses on current relationships issues, trying to help the person understand and change maladaptive interaction patterns. (p. 253)

    a. CBT

    b. ECT

    c. IPT

    d. none of the above

7. Two main thrusts of suicide prevention efforts are the treatment of the person's mental disorders and   (p. 260)

    a. cognitive therapy.

    b. family therapy.

    c. crisis intervention.

    d. psychotherapy.

8. A disorder that involves mood swings between subclinical levels of depression and mania is (p. 220)

    a. bipolar disorder.

    b. manic depression.

    c. dysthymic disorder.

    d. cyclothymic disorder.

9. Bipolar mood disorder is distinguished from major depression by (p. 243)

    a. at least one episode of mania.

    b. disturbance of circadian rhythms.

    c. evidence of earlier cyclothymia.

    d. evidence of earlier dysthymia.

10. All of the following are symptoms of the manic phase of bipolar mood disorder, **except** (p. 241)

   a. a notable increase in activity.
   b. euphoria.
   c. high levels of verbal output.
   d. deflated self-esteem.

COMPREHENSIVE PRACTICE TEST

The following tests are designed to give you an idea of how well you understood the entire chapter. There are three different types of tests—Multiple-choice, true-false, and essay.

MULTIPLE-CHOICE

1. Simultaneous symptoms of mania and depression is referred to as (p. 216)

   a. trouble.
   b. overwhelming.
   c. mixed episode.
   d. unipolar.

2. Unipolar and bipolar mood disorders, while not completely separate, are different in (p. 216)

   a. symptoms.
   b. causal factors.
   c. treatment.
   d. all of the above.

3. Which of the following mood disorders is more common and has actually increased in recent years? (p. 218)

   a. cyclothymia
   b. major depression
   c. dysthymia
   d. adjustment disorder with depressed mood

4. Mild depression may be seen as "normal and adaptive" if (p. 218)

   a. it is brief and mild.
   b. involves looking at issues that would normally be avoided.
   c. keeps us from using energy to obtain futile goals.
   d. all of the above.

5. A diagnosis of major depressive disorder ***cannot*** be made if the person has experienced (p. 220)

   a. hypersomnia.

   b. psychomotor agitation.

   c. hypomania.

   d. diminished ability to concentrate.

6. Depression occurs during which of the following life cycle stages? (pp. 221-22)

   a. infancy.

   b. adolescence.

   c. middle adulthood.

   d. all of the above.

7. Depression in infants is known as (p. 221)

   a. baby blues.

   b. anaclitic depression.

   c. infant unipolar disorder.

   d. none of the above.

8. When major depression and dysthymia coexist in an individual, it is referred to as (p. 222)

   a. double trouble.

   b. double depression.

   c. two depressive disorders.

   d. depressive subtypes.

9. Because depressive episodes are time-limited, these are usually specified as (p. 223)

   a. starting and stopping.

   b. first and second.

   c. single and recurrent.

   d. a. and b.

10. A neurophysiological finding that damage to the _____ but not the _____ anterior cortex often results in depression. (p. 225)

   a. right, left

   b. left, right

   c. frontal, middle

   d. middle, frontal

11. Circudian rhythms, which may play a causal role in depression, are controlled by strong and weak   (p. 227)

    a. links.

    b. beats.

    c. oscillators.

    d. kentilators.

12. John is not looking forward to the fall. This is the time when his appetite increases and he experiences hypersomnia. He also starts to feel pretty low. John suffers from seasonal affective disorder. Treatment for John will include (p. 227)

    a. behavioral therapy.

    b. psychotherapy.

    c. R.E.T.

    d. light therapy.

13. Gary has fallen further and further behind in his rent. His roommates are threatening to kick him out. This stressful life event is known as a(n) (p. 229)

    a. independent life event.

    b. dependent life event.

    c. secondary life event.

    d. primary life event.

14. Women who are at a genetic risk for depression will experience more (p. 229)

    a. good days that bad.

    b. likelihood of hearing starched shorts.

    c. stressful life events.

    d. none of the above.

15. In the brains of depressed patients, abnormalities have been detected in the (p. 227)

    a. anterior cingulate cortex.

    b. hippocampus.

    c. amygdala.

    d. all of the above.

TRUE – FALSE

1. Major depression is more common in men (21% lifetime prevalence rate) than women (13% lifetime prevalence rate). T / F (p. 218)

2. It is normal to feel depressed as a result of a recent loss or stress. T / F (p. 218)

3. Postpartum blues and postpartum depression are the same thing and very common in women who have recently given birth. T / F   (p. 219)

4. Dysthymia and major depression sufferers have periods of normal moods. T / F (p. 220)

5. When a person suffers from double depression, recovery is very likely to occur and not reoccur, once a person has been treated. T / F   (p. 222)

6. Seasonal affective disorders are an example of recurrent depressive episodes. T / F (p. 223)

7. Findings for genetic contribution to mild forms of unipolar depressions are not as consistent as for major depression. T / F   (p. 224)

8. Hormones play a significant role in causing depression in women. T / F (p. 236)

9. Bipolar is distinguished from major depression by at least one episode of mania or a mixed episode. T / F   (p. 242)

10. A recent survey documented that more than 75% of people with depression don't receive treatment or receive inappropriate care. T / F   (p. 250)

11. Tricyclies have been the antidepressants most commonly prescribed since about 1990. T / F (p. 250)

12. Discontinuing antidepressants when symptoms have remitted may cause relapse. T / F (p. 251)

13. Women are about three times as likely to attempt suicide as are men, but three times more men than women die by suicide each year. T / F   (p. 254)

14. Marital therapy has not been shown to be as effective as cognitive therapy for people who have unipolar depression and marital discord.   T / F (p. 253)

15. Children are at increased risk for suicide if they have lost a parent or have been abused. T / F   (p. 255)

16. Genetic factors, as well as alterations in serotonia functioning can, contribute to causal factors for suicide.   T / F (p. 255)

17. Suicidal ambivalence means the person wants to die.   T / F (p. 259)

18. Those who threaten suicide seldom do.   T / F (p. 259)

ESSAY QUESTIONS

1. Describe Aaron Beck's cognitive theory of depression. (pp. 232-34)

2. Discuss the issues associated with the controversy regarding a person's right to die. (p. 261)

3.   Discuss the causal factors in bipolar disorder. (pp. 245-47)

4.   Explain the sociocultural factors affecting unipolar and bipolar disorders. (pp. 247-49)

WEB LINKS TO ITEMS OR CONCEPTS DISCUSSED IN THIS CHAPTER

Bipolar disorder

       www.pendulum.org/   (Pendulum Resources)

       bipolar.about.com/mbody.htm

       www.frii.com/~parrot/bip.html

Unipolar disorder

       www.mooddisordersinfo.com/html/ unipolar_or_bipolar.html

       www.tcd.ie/Psychiatry/Neuropsychiatry/unidep.htm

Suicide treatment

       cebmh.warne.ox.ac.uk/cebmh/elmh/nelmh/ suicide/treatment/pst1.html

       suicidecrisiscenter.com/treatment.html

CRISS-CROSS

Now that you know all there is to know about this chapter, here's your opportunity to put that knowledge to work.

CRISS-CROSS CLUES
Across
6.   severe alterations in mood for a long period of time
11. depression recurs at some point after remission
13. a markedly elevated, euphoric, and expansive mood

Down
1.   being persistently depressed for at least two years
2.   ending one's own life
3.   cyclical mood changes less severe than in bipolar disorder
4.   experiencing depressive and manic episodes
5.   positive affect
7.   as recurrence, except in a fairly short time
8.   different patterns of symptoms or features
9.   elevated or euphoric episode
10. major mood disorder **and** exhibiting two symptoms of schizophrenia
12. experiencing only depressive episodes
14. answers humans give to "Why?" (as in "Why does everything happen to me?")

Puzzle created with Puzzlemaker at DiscoverySchool.com

CHAPTER EIGHT

Somatoform and Dissociative Disorders

BEFORE YOU READ

You will find in Chapter 8 a detailed description of the clinical picture, causal pattern, and treatment of somatoform and dissociative disorders. In the somatoform disorders, the central presenting problem is physical complaints or physical disabilities in the absence of any physical pathology, presumably reflecting underlying psychological difficulties. In the dissociative disorders, the central problem is a failure of certain aspects of memory due to an active process of dissociation, such as in dissociative amnesia, in which individuals cannot remember their names, do not know how old they are, where they live, etc. According to the text, both types of disorders appear to be ways of avoiding psychological stress while denying personal responsibility for doing so. There are suggestions, as well, that both may be associated with traumatic childhood experiences. Whereas our personal experience with anxiety and depression in everyday life aids our understanding of the extreme deviations of those emotions, these disorders will likely seem less familiar and less readily grasped as exaggerated forms of everyday psychological phenomena.

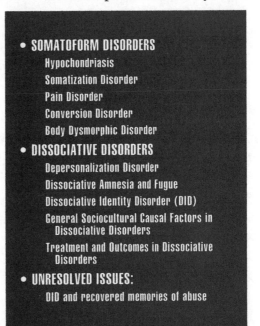

- SOMATOFORM DISORDERS
    Hypochondriasis
    Somatization Disorder
    Pain Disorder
    Conversion Disorder
    Body Dysmorphic Disorder
- DISSOCIATIVE DISORDERS
    Depersonalization Disorder
    Dissociative Amnesia and Fugue
    Dissociative Identity Disorder (DID)
    General Sociocultural Causal Factors in
        Dissociative Disorders
    Treatment and Outcomes in Dissociative
        Disorders
- UNRESOLVED ISSUES:
    DID and recovered memories of abuse

OBJECTIVES

After reading this chapter, you should be able to:

1. Describe the major manifestations of somatoform disorders.

2. List the primary presenting symptoms of somatization disorder and hypochondriasis and note the similarities and differences between these closely related disorders.

3. Explain what is meant by a pain disorder. Discuss the difficulties of determining that pain is of psychological, rather than physical, origin and of reliably assessing an entirely subjective phenomenon.

4. Characterize the symptoms of conversion disorder, trace the history of the concept of "conversion," and describe the likely cause and chain of events in the development of a conversion disorder.

5. Discuss the etiological contributions of biological, psychosocial, and sociocultural factors to the somatoform disorders.

6. Compare and contrast the treatments for the somatoform disorders. What is known regarding their effectiveness, as compared to no treatment at all?

7. Compare the major features of dissociative amnesia and fugue, dissociative identity disorder, and depersonalization disorder.

8. Discuss the causal factors that contribute to the dissociative disorders, and note the critical difficulty caused by the fallibility of memory in determining the contribution of childhood abuse to these disorders.

9. Describe the most appropriate treatments for the dissociative disorders, as well as the limitations of biological and psychological treatments.

10. Describe the issues related to DID and recovered memories.

AS YOU READ

Answers can be found in the Answer Key at the end of the book.

KEY WORDS

Each of the words below is important in understanding the concepts presented in this chapter. Write the definition next to each of the words.

somatoform disorders (p. 266)   pain disorder (p. 270)

dissociative disorders (p. 266)   conversion disorder (p. 271)

hypochondriasis (p. 266)   hysteria (p. 272)

somatization disorder (p. 268)   secondary gain (p. 272) malingering (p. 274)

factitious disorder (p. 274)

body dysmorphic disorder (p. 275)

derealization (p. 278)

depersonalization (p. 278)

depersonalization disorder (p. 278)

dissociative amnesia (p. 279)

dissociative fugue (p. 280)

dissociative identity disorder (p. 281)

host identity (p. 282)

alter identities (p. 282)

WHO'S WHO AND WHAT'S WHAT—MATCHING

Match the following psychological disorders with their descriptions.

Disorder

_____ somatoform disorder

_____ hypochoncriasis disorder

_____ somatization disorder

_____ pain disorder

_____ conversion disorder

_____ body dysmorphic disorder

_____ dissociative disorders

_____ depersonalization disorder

_____ dissociative fugue

_____ dissociative identity disorder

_____ dissociative amnesia

Description

A. severe pain but no medical pathology to explain it

B. anxious preoccupation with having a disease based on a misinterpretation of bodily signs or symptoms

C. patterns of symptoms affecting sensory or voluntary motor functions, even though medical examination reveals no physical basis for these

D. psychological problems are manifested in physical disorders that often mimic medical conditions, for which no medical evidence can be found

E. many different complaints of physical ailments in four symptom categories spreading over several years

F. inability to recall previously sorted information that cannot be accounted for by ordinary forgetting; common initial reaction to severe stress

G. person manifests two or more distinct identities or personality states that alternate in some way in taking control of behavior

H. normal processes regulating awareness and multichannel capacities of the mind apparently become disorganized, leading to various anomalies

I. a person not only goes into an amnesic state, but also leaves home surroundings and becomes confused about his or her identity

J. an obsessive preoccupation with some perceived flaw in one's appearance

SHORT ANSWERS
Provide brief answers to the following questions.

1. Four criteria must be met for somatization disorder to be present. Briefly explain. (p. 269)

   a.

   b.

   c.

   d.

2. List conversion disorder's four categories of symptoms. (pp. 273-74)

   a.

   b.

   c.

   d.

3. Describe a way of telling the difference between people with malingering/factitious disorders and other somatoform disorders. (p. 274)

4. Name four types of psychologenic amnesia that are recognized and give a brief description of each. (p. 280)

   1.

   2.

   3.

   4.

5. In very rare cases of DID, called dissociative fugue, a person is not only amnesic for some or all aspects of his or her past, but also... Discuss this further. (pp. 280-81)

FILL IN THE BLANKS

Read the following and fill in the blanks. These questions are designed to help you focus on specific details.

1. People with hypochondriasis are most often anxious and preoccupied with _____, other minor physical abnormalities or with _____ physical sensations. (p. 266)

2. There seems to be a familial linkage between _____ in men and _____ in women. (p. 269).

3. To persons suffering pain disorder, the pain experienced is _____and it can hurt as much as pain with _____. (p. 270)

4. A symptom, such as partial paralysis or a pseudoseizure, which may appear to have a medical or neurological basis until medical examination reveals these cannot be fully explained by any known medical condition, is known as _____. (p. 271)

5. People with body dysmorphic disorder frequently will engage in excessive grooming behavior, often trying to _____ through their hair style, clothing, or makeup. (p. 275)

6. Often persons suffering from depersonalization disorder report feeling like they are living in _____—quite unpleasant and aversive—and the person may feel as if he or she is _____, even though insight into what is happening is retained. (p. 278)

7. Dissociative identity disorder (DID) is a dramatic dissociative disorder in which a patient manifests at least _____ or personality states that alternate in some way _____. (p. 281)

8. In DID, _____ identities is usually the case, but a large series of cases showed an average of _____with some claiming as many as _____. (p. 282)

THE DOCTOR IS IN...PSYCHIATRIC HELP—5¢

Read the following scenarios and diagnose the client. Remember to look carefully at the criteria for the disorder before you make a decision as to the diagnosis. Make a list of other information you might need to help you understand the causal factors.

1. As the psychiatrist in a large hospital, you have been called in to evaluate a patient who had been admitted two days before. The patient, Cathy, had awakened in the morning and had been unable to see. She was blind. After being admitted to the hospital and the doctors determining there had been no accident, a complete medical and neurological exam was done. The results turned up nothing that would cause the blindness. You were called in to see if there could be a psychological cause. After talking to her for a while, you find out that husband had died unexpectedly about three months ago, leaving her with financial problems. She was going to have to get a job and she was worried about her employability. You ask if she has a picture of her husband. She says, "Yes," and walks to the shelf skirting a chair that is in her way.

    How would you diagnose Cathy and why. How would you treat her?

2. Frank comes to see you because he has been urged him to talk to somebody. He is wearing sunglasses, even though he is in your office, and it is dark outside. When you ask him about the glasses, he tells you that his eyelids are horrible and ugly. He doesn't want anyone to see them—ever. Frank tells you that he spends much of the day checking his eyelids and trying to make them look better. He is saving for another surgery, his third, because he just can't stand the way his eyes look. You ask if he dates, has friends or a job. Frank says that he doesn't date (Who would want to be with someone as ugly as he is?), so he has started to withdraw even from his few friends. He recently lost his job because he was unable to meet clients, looking the way he does.

    How would you diagnose Frank and why? How would you treat him?

3. Jackie comes to see you because she has been feeling rather odd lately. She tells you that she is feeling "unreal"—like she is not a part of her body. Jackie says that she is beginning to see her life as a movie because she feels so isolated from herself. She explains that when this experience occurs, it is like looking at the world through someone else's eyes. Her friends and even herself are viewed through these eyes as "automatons." These experiences are now happening two or three times per week and last for several hours.

What would be your diagnosis for Jackie and why? How would you treat her and what would you expect treatment outcomes to be?

PICTURE THIS

Below are pictures that represent key people or concepts from the book. Write the answers on the line to the right of the clues.

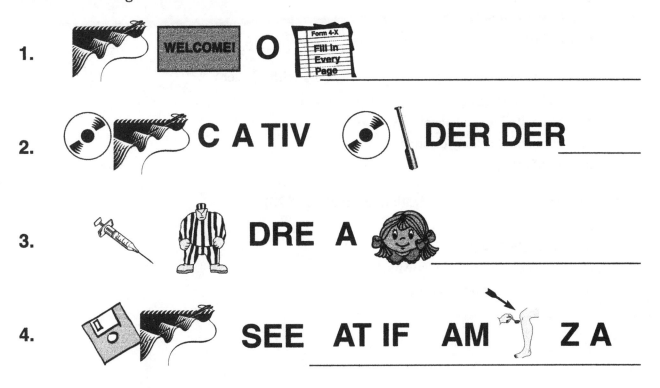

1.

2.

3.

4.

AFTER YOU READ

Answers can be found in the Answer Key at the end of the book.

PRACTICE TESTS

Take the following three multiple-choice tests to see how much you have comprehended from the chapter. Each represents roughly one-third of the chapter. As you study the chapter, use these to check your progress.

PRACTICE TEST NUMBER 1

1. Dissociative disorders are some of the more dramatic phenomena to be observed in the entire domain of psychopathology, for example, (p. 266)

    a. people who cannot recall who they are or where they may have come from.

    b. people who have two or more distinct identities or personality states that alternatively take control of the individual's behavior.

    c. people who have intense pain for which no medical symptoms can be found.

    d. a and b.

2. People with _____ are preoccupied with fears of having a serious disease, based on misinterpretation of one or more bodily signs or symptoms, and is not reassured when medical examination can find no physical problem. (p. 266)

    a. depersonalization disorder

    b. dissociative fugue

    c. hypochondriasis

    d. halitosis

3. Somatization disorder very commonly occurs with (p. 266)

    a. major depression.

    b. panic disorder and phobic disorders.

    c. generalized anxiety disorder.

    d. all of the above.

4. Evidence exists that somatization disorder (p. 270)

    a. runs in families.

    b. is racially based.

    c. seems concentrated in individual communities.

    d. occurs mostly near oceans.

5. Patients with somatization disorder tend to think of themselves as (p. 270)

    a. physically weak.

    b. unable to tolerate stress.

    c. unable to tolerate physical activity.

    d. all of the above.

6. All of the following are part of a chain of events in the development of a conversion disorder, **except** (p. 271)

    a. a conscious plan to use illness as an escape.

    b. a desire to escape from an unpleasant situation.

    c. a fleeting wish to be sick in order to avoid the situation.

    d. the appearance of the symptoms of some physical ailment.

7. A typical example of symptoms of conversion disorder would be (p. 271)

    a. partial paralysis.

    b. blindness or deafness.

    c. pseudoseizures.

    d. all of the above.

8. Freud used the term, "conversion hysteria," because he believed the symptoms were an expression of (p. 272)

    a. widespread anger.

    b. built-up hostility.

    c. repressed sexual energy.

    d. being a parent.

9. Conversion disorder occurs _____ often in women than in men. (pp. 272)

    a. much less

    b. two-10 times more

    c. about as

    d. a little less

10. Although it can develop at any age, conversion disorder most commonly occurs (pp. 272-73)

    a. between early adolescence and early adulthood.

    b. during middle age.

    c. during infancy or early childhood.

    d. about eight weeks before death.

PRACTICE TEST NUMBER 2

1. Early studies showed that perhaps _____ of patients diagnosed with conversion disorders were later diagnosed with an organic illness. (p. 274)

   a. 1%

   b. 10%

   c. 25-50%

   d. 77%

2. People with _____ disorders are intentionally producing or grossly exaggerating psychological or physical symptoms for external reasons, such as avoiding work or military service. (p. 274)

   a. malingering and formfactitious

   b. conversion

   c. pain

   d. somatoform

3. A person with _____ disorder is obsessed with a perceived or imagined flaw or flaws in his or her appearance. It is so intense that it causes clinically significant distress and/or impairment in social or occupational functioning. (p. 275)

   a. conversion

   b. pain

   c. factitious

   d. body dysmorphic

4. People with body dysmorphic disorder (BDD) may think (p. 276)

   a. their skin has ugly blemishes.

   b. their breasts are too small.

   c. their face is too thin.

   d. all of the above.

5. Dissociative disorders are methods in which individuals avoid stress by (p. 278)

   a. escaping from their personal identities.

   b. projecting blame for their "sins" on others.

   c. separating themselves from significant others.

   d. withdrawing from stressful situations.

6. It is likely that some people may have certain _____ that make them more susceptible to developing dissociative symptoms than others. (p. 278)

   a. ineffective genes

   b. mystical properties

   c. lack of self control

   d. personality traits

7. In _____, one's sense of one's own self and one's own reality is temporarily lost, usually occurring during or after periods of severe stress. (p. 278)

    a. psychogenic pain disorder

    b. retrograde measles

    c. depersonalization

    d. hypochondriasis

8. When episodes of depersonalization become persistent and recurrent and interfere with normal functioning, _____ may be diagnosed. (p. 278)

    a. psychogenic pain disorder

    b. depersonalization disorder

    c. dissociative amnesia

    d. hypochondriasis

9. If _____ is caused by brain pathology, it most often involves failure to retain new information and experiences, that is, the information contained in the experience is not registered and does not enter memory storage. (p. 279)

    a. hypochondriasis

    b. psychogenic pain disorder

    c. retrograde amnesia

    d. retrograde measles

10. _____ is a fairly common initial reaction to intolerably stressful circumstances. (pp. 279-80)

    a. Dissociative amnesia

    b. Brain pathology

    c. Hypochondriasis

    d. Retrograde measles

PRACTICE TEST NUMBER 3

1. In very rare cases, called _____, a person is not only amnesic for some or all aspects of his or her past, but also departs from home surroundings. (p. 280)

    a. retrograde measles

    b. dissociative fugue

    c. disappropriate stressful symnabulolism

    d. multiple personality disorder

2. Dissociative identity disorder (DID) was formerly known as (p. 281)

    a. Scarlett O'Hara fever.

    b. dissociative fugue.

    c. multiple personality disorder.

    d. depersonalization disorder.

3. The identity switches in DID typically occur (p. 282)

    a. very quickly (in a matter of seconds).

    b. over a period of several hours.

    c. during a full moon.

    d. just prior to taking a test.

4. DID's alter identities may differ in (p. 282)

    a. gender, age,and sexual orientation.

    b. handedness, handwriting, and prescription for eyeglasses.

    c. foreign languages spoken and general knowledge.

    d. all of the above.

5. _____ may or may not be aware of each other, or may attempt to take over control from the host identity. (p. 282)

    a. Escapists

    b. Malingerers

    c. Alter identities

    d. Localized amnesiacs

6. DID was rare until around _____, but now thousands of cases have been reported. (p. 283)

    a. 1800

    b. World War I

    c. 1979

    d. September 11, 2001

7. DID has now been identified throughout the world. It has been found (p. 283)

    a. in all racial groups.

    b. in all cultures.

    c. in countries ranging from Nigeria and Ethiopia, to Turkey, Australia, and the Carribean.

    d. all of the above.

8. A major cause of DID appears to be (p. 283)

    a. the rise of individual anger and inner rage.

    b. childhood sexual abuse.

    c. air and water pollution.

    d. broken families and the fast pace of modern society.

9. For _____ patients, most therapists set integration of the previously separate alters, together with their collective merging into the host personality, as the ultimate goal of treatment. (p. 289)

   a. conversion disorder

   b. BDD

   c. DID

   d. JPG

10. A controversy exists concerning DID, including (p. 290)

    a. how it develops.

    b. whether it is real or faked.

    c. whether memories of childhood abuse are real, and if the memories are real whether the abuse played a causal role.

    d. all of the above.

COMPREHENSIVE PRACTICE TEST

The following tests are designed to give you an idea of how well you understood the entire chapter. There are three different types of tests: multiple-choice, true-false, and essay.

MULTIPLE-CHOICE

1. Body dysmorphic disorder (BDD) age of onset is usually in adolescence when many people start to become preoccupied with their appearance and appears to be (p. 277)

   a. more prevalent in men than women.

   b. approximately equal in men and women.

   c. more prevalent in women than men.

   d. unheard of in Canada.

2. Treatment approaches for BDD focus on (p. 277)

   a. getting patients to identify and change distorted perceptions of their body.

   b. exposure to anxiety-provoking situations (e.g., wearing something that highlights, rather than disguises, their defect).

   c. prevention of checking responses (e.g., mirror checking, reassurance seeking, and repeatedly examining their imaginary defect).

   d. all of the above.

3. Only in the past _____ has the concept of dissociation become a major research area in the field of cognitive psychology. (p. 278)

   a. few months

   b. few years

   c. quarter-century

   d. 150 years

4. Like somatoform disorders, _____ disorders appear mainly to be ways of avoiding anxiety and stress and of managing life problems that threaten to overwhelm the person's usual coping resources. (p. 278)

    a. dissociative

    b. generalized

    c. hypochondriasis

    d. low-esteem

5. In _____ people may feel they are floating above their physical bodies, which may suddenly feel very different—as if drastically changed or unreal. (p. 278)

    a. depersonalization disorder

    b. psychogenic pain disorder

    c. hypochondriasis

    d. cognitive psychology

6. Circumstances, for example those occurring during wartime combat conditions or immediately after a catastrophic event, such as a serious car wreck, may cause failure to recall previously stored personal information that cannot be accounted for by ordinary forgetting. This is called   (pp. 279-80)

    a. psychogenic pain disorder.

    b. dissociative amnesia.

    c. hypochondriasis.

    d. alter ego.

7. In DID, the primary or host identity is most frequently encountered, but alter identities may (p. 282)

    a. be more concerned with personal-identity issues.

    b. take control at different points in time.

    c. become moody and refuse to cooperate.

    d. become an alter ego.

8. People with DID often show (p. 282)

    a. moodiness and erratic behavior.

    b. headaches, hallucination, and substance abuse.

    c. post-traumatic symptoms, and other amnesic and fugue symptoms.

    d. all of the above.

9. In _____ amnesia, the individual forgets his/her entire life history. (p. 280)

    a. localized

    b. selective

    c. generalized

    d. continuous

10. Approximately _____ more females than males are diagnosed as having the DID, believed by some to be due to the greater proportion of abuse among females than males. (p. 283)

    a. 25%

    b. 75%

    c. 3-9 times

    d. The numbers for females and males are about the same.

11. One of the primary techniques used in most treatments of DID is (p. 289)

    a. esteem exercise.

    b. hypnosis.

    c. projection.

    d. withdrawing stress.

12. DID patients who recover memories of abuse (often in therapy) have sued _____ for inflicting abuse. (p. 290)

    a. each other

    b. their parents

    c. schools and teachers

    d. anyone who seems to have a lot of money

13. DID patients have also sued _____ for implanting memories or abuse they later came to believe had actually not occurred. (p.290)

    a. their parents

    b. schools and teachers

    c. therapists and institutions

    d. everyone who seems to have any money at all

14. Some parents, asserting they had been falsely accused, formed an international support organization called _____ and have sometimes sued therapists for damages, alleging the therapists induced false memories of parental abuse in their child. (p. 290)

    a. The False Memory Syndrome Foundation

    b. Parents Against False Memories

    c. The International Order of Falsely Accused Parents

    d. The International Support Organization

15. Alter personalities would be expected in cases of (p. 282)

    a. psychogenic pain disorder.

    b. conversion disorder.

    c. hypochondriasis.

    d. dissociative identity disorder.

TRUE – FALSE

1. Somatoform disorders share one key feature: all are expressions of psychological difficulties in the "body language" of medical problems that, on careful examination, cannot be documented to exist.   T / F (p. 266)

2. Somatization disorder is not extremely difficult to treat because much systematic research has been conducted.   T / F   (p. 270)

3. Indications exist that people with hypochondriasis often had an excessive amount of illness in their families while growing up. T / F   (p. 268)

4. Contemporary views of conversion disorder see it as serving the function of providing a plausible excuse, enabling the individual to escape or avoid an intolerably stressful situation without having to take responsibility for doing so. T / F   (p. 272)

5. Conversion disorder was not very common in the past and and hardly ever occurred prior to World War II. T / F   (p. 272)

6. Normally, conversion disorder involved men who would ordinarily be considered unstable. T / F (p. 272)

7. Most of us have concerns about our appearance; but people with body dysmorphic disorder are far more extreme, leading, in many cases, to complete preoccupation and significant emotional pain.   T / F (p. 276)

8. We all dissociate to a degree, occasionally.   T / F   (p. 278)

9. Like somatoform disorders, dissociative disorders appear mainly to be ways of avoiding anxiety and stress and of managing life problems that threaten to overwhelm the person's usual coping resources.   T / F (p. 278)

10. Some have proposed that both eating disorders and BDD are variants of a "body image disorder" (not an official category). People with both BDD and eating disorders are preoccupied with their appearance and overemphasize their importance for relationships. T / F (p. 277)

ESSAY QUESTIONS

1. Discuss pain disorder. (pp. 270-71)

2. Describe the criteria commonly used for distinguishing between conversion disorders and true organic disturbances. (pp. 273-74)

3. At least four serious controversies exist concerning DID. Explain. (pp. 285-87, 290-91)

WEB LINKS TO ITEMS OR CONCEPTS DISCUSSED IN THIS CHAPTER

Somatoform and Dissociative Disorders

     www.merck.com/pubs/mmanual/section15/ chapter186/186d.htm

     www.psyweb.com/Mdisord/somatd.html

     wasp.canberra.edu.au/uc/lectures/scides/sem961/ Unit4316/Psy302_Lecture_Notes_Week_3.txt

     www.byu.edu/~psychweb/bnc/ab/ab-n13.htm

     www.nlm.nih.gov/medlineplus/ency/article/000954.htm

     www.psychiatry.ox.ac.uk/cebmh/whoguidemhpcuk/ disorders/f44.html

     www.merck.com/pubs/mmanual/section15/ chapter186/186c.htm

     www.sidran.org/didbr.html

     www.issd.org/indexpage/isdguide.htm

     www.multiple-personality.com/

CRISS-CROSS

Now that you know all there is to know about this chapter, here's your opportunity to put that knowledge to work.

CRISS-CROSS CLUES
Across
7. new term for "multiple personality disorder"

Down
1. seemingly medical conditions without evidence of physical pathology to account for these
2. not only amnesic but leaves home and may assume a new identity
3. the human mind's capacity to engage in complex activity independent of conscious awareness
4. presence of persistent and severe pain without a purely medical cause
5. may include partial paralysis, blindness, pseudoseizures, but without any known medical condition
6. intentionally over-exaggerating physical symptoms to avoid work
7. when one's sense of the reality of the outside world is temporarily lost
8. failure to recall when that failure cannot be accounted for by ordinary forgetting

Puzzle created with Puzzlemaker at DiscoverySchool.com

CHAPTER NINE

Eating Disorders and Obesity

BEFORE YOU READ

What makes people like Karen Carpenter and so many others look into a mirror and see a fat person instead of someone so thin her bones are showing? Or Princess Diana, who would binge eat and then purge, running the risk of doing irreparable harm to her body? Chapter 9 provides insight into the world of eating disorders. The first portion looks at the clinical aspects of eating disorders and describes the different types—anorexia nervosa, bulima nervosa and other forms. Prevalence and the ways in which Western culture is having an impact on the development of eating disorders in other cultures is also addressed. Case studies give you an opportunity to further understand the problems related to these disorders.

What influences people to develop eating disorders is the subject of the next section. Several areas are explored, including the role of serotonin and a concept called the set-point theory.

The difficulties in treating eating disorders are discussed, including the many different facets necessary to help the patient. A discussion of obesity follows; the worldwide epidemic of this problem makes it important to address, even though it is not considered an eating disorder.

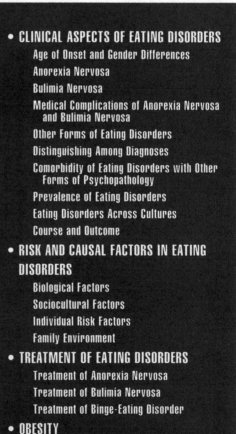

- **CLINICAL ASPECTS OF EATING DISORDERS**
    Age of Onset and Gender Differences
    Anorexia Nervosa
    Bulimia Nervosa
    Medical Complications of Anorexia Nervosa and Bulimia Nervosa
    Other Forms of Eating Disorders
    Distinguishing Among Diagnoses
    Comorbidity of Eating Disorders with Other Forms of Psychopathology
    Prevalence of Eating Disorders
    Eating Disorders Across Cultures
    Course and Outcome
- **RISK AND CAUSAL FACTORS IN EATING DISORDERS**
    Biological Factors
    Sociocultural Factors
    Individual Risk Factors
    Family Environment
- **TREATMENT OF EATING DISORDERS**
    Treatment of Anorexia Nervosa
    Treatment of Bulimia Nervosa
    Treatment of Binge-Eating Disorder
- **OBESITY**
    Biological Factors
    Psychological Factors
    Learning Perspective
    Sociocultural Factors
    Treatment of Obesity
    The Importance of Prevention

OBJECTIVES

After reading this chapter, you should be able to:

1. Discuss the clinical aspects of eating disorders, such as age of onset and gender differences.
2. Define anorexia nervosa and bulima nervosa and the subtypes.
3. Describe the medical complications of the various eating disorders.
4. Identify other forms of eating disorders, such as EDNOS and BED.
5. Explain the comorbidity of eating disorders with other forms of psychopathologies.
6. Discuss prevalence rates of eating disorders in this culture and across cultures.
7. Describe the biological, sociocultural, individual, and family risk and causal factors associated with eating disorders.
8. Explain the various methods used for treating eating disorders and be able to evaluate each.
9. Define obesity and identify risk and causal factors.
10. Discuss prevention and treatment methods for obesity.

AS YOU READ

Answers can be found in the Answer Key at the end of the book.

WHO'S WHO AND WHAT'S WHAT—MATCHING

Match the names in the left column with the proper definition from the right.

Name/Term	Definition
_____ Princess Diana	A. published the first medical account of anorexia nervosa in 1689
_____ Karen Carpenter	B. comes from the Greek words meaning "ox" and "hunger"
_____ Richard Morton	C. suffered from bulima nervosa
_____ Charles Lasegue and Sir William Gull	D. instrumental in naming the eating disorder, anorexia nervosa, in 1873.
_____ Anorexia nervosa—restricting type	E. suffered from anorexia nervosa which ultimately lead to her death
_____ Anorexia nervosa—binge-eating purging type	F. low weight is maintained by tightly controlling how much food is eaten
_____ Bulima nervosa	G. proposed the term, "bulima nervosa," in 1979
_____ Russell, a British psychiatrist	H. breakdown of eating restraint, resulting in periods of binge-eating and efforts to purge

KEY WORDS
Each of the words below is important in understanding the concepts presented in this chapter. Write the definition next to each of the words.

anorexia nervosa (p. 295)

anorexia nervosa—restricting type (p. 296)

anorexia nervosa—binge-eating/purge type (p. 296)

bulima nervosa—purging and nonpurging types (p. 298)

eating disorders not otherwise specified (EDNOS) (pp. 300-01)

binge-eating disorder (p. 301)

meta-analysis (p. 303)

serotonin (p. 304)

set-point theory (p. 304)

negative affect (p. 308)

perfectionism (p. 308)

cognitive-behavioral therapy (CBT) (p. 310)

body mass index (BMI) (p. 313)

obesity (p. 313)

randomized controlled trials (p. 311)

SHORT ANSWERS
Provide brief answers to the following questions.

1. Describe the risk factors for eating disorders in males. (p. 295)

2. What are the DSM-IV-TR criteria for bulima nervosa? (p. 298)

3. Mary was diagnosed with an eating disorder—anorexia nervosa. She sought treatment for the disorder. Based on the research done by Lowe in 2001, what can you say about her recovery possibilities? (p. 303)

4. Explain how the study done by Anne Becker of the women in Fiji illustrates the impact the media has on thinness. (pp. 305-06)

FILL IN THE BLANKS

Read the following and fill in the blanks. These questions are designed to help you focus on specific details.

1. At the heart of anorexia nervosa is an intense fear of _____, a refusal to maintain a body weight that is _____, a distorted perception of body _____ and _____, and an absence of at least three consecutive _____. (p. 296)

2. Unlike patients with anorexia nervosa, bulimic patients are typically of _____ weight and may even be slightly _____. (p. 298)

3. A 21-year follow-up of patients with anorexia nervosa suggests that patients tend not to maintain a _____ form of the disorder but tend to make a progression to _____ and _____ over time. (p. 301)

4. Research suggests that some personality traits in eating disordered patients might _____ the onset of the disorder and _____ when the eating disorder remits and the patient has recovered. (p. 302)

5. Research is now suggesting that even _____ going on a diet can itself be a _____ for overeating. (p. 309)

6. When treatment for anorexia nervosa does not address the _____ issues that fuel the behavior, any weight gain will be _____. (p. 310)

7. Unlike patients with anorexia or bulima, most binge-eating disorder patients do not overvalue _____, although they do _____ their own bodies. (p. 312)

THE DOCTOR IS IN...PSYCHIATRIC HELP—5¢

Read the following scenarios and diagnose the client. Remember to look carefully at the criteria for the disorder before you make a decision as to the diagnosis. Make a list of other information you might need to help you understand the causal factors.

1. Mary is 5'6" tall and weighs 96 pounds. She tells you that whenever she looks in the mirror, all she sees is a fat person. Mary has restricted her eating to just a few pieces of celery and carrots each day. There is a ritual to her eating pattern. Mary's hair is thin and her nails are brittle. She is still having regular menstrual periods.

   How would you diagnose Mary and why? (p. 301)

2. Glenn, a 45-year-old male, comes to your office. His wife insisted that he come in to see you. Glenn is 5'8" tall and weight 350 pounds. Even though his health is in jeopardy, he finds himself binging on all kinds of food from cakes and cookies to pizzas, fried chicken and hamburgers. He feels disgusted with his behavior. You ask if he purges and he tells you that he does not. He says that sometimes he will exercise excessively after binging but not every time.

   How would you diagnose Glenn and why? (p. 301)

3. Diane, a 14-year-old girl, is referred to you because she has anorexia nervosa. Her parents are very concerned but a bit shocked when you suggest that you would like to see the whole family in therapy, not just Diane. What would you expect to see as family characteristics when you talk to Diane's family? How would you proceed with treatment? (pp. 309-11)

AFTER YOU READ

Answers can be found in the Answer Key at the end of the book.

PRACTICE TESTS

Take the following three multiple-choice tests to see how much you have comprehended from the chapter. Each represents roughly one-third of the chapter. As you study the chapter, use these to check your progress.

PRACTICE TEST NUMBER 1

1. One eating disorder that is found almost exclusively in men is (p. 295)
   a. anorexia nervosa.
   b. bulima nervosa.
   c. male pattern eating disorder.
   d. reverse anorexia.

2. In this type of anorexia nervosa, every effort is made to limit how much food is eaten and caloric intake is tightly controlled. (p. 296)
   a. binge-eating purging type
   b. binge-eating disorder type
   c. restricting type
   d. bulima nervosa

3. This type of anorexia nervosa involves a breakdown of restraint that results in periods of binge eating. (p. 296)
   a. binge-eating purging type
   b. binge-eating disorder type
   c. restrictive type
   d. bulima nervosa

4. Karen has the eating disorder, bulima nervosa. During her average binge, she could consume as much as _____ calories. (p. 298)
   a. 2,000
   b. 10,000
   c. 4,800
   d. 1,200

5. The DSM-IV distinguishes between two types of bulima nervosa. These are (p. 298)
   a. purging and nonpurging.
   b. starving and nonstarving.
   c. binging and nonbinging.
   d. none of the above.

6. The difference between a person with bulima nervosa and a person with the binge-eating/purging type of anorexia nervosa is (p. 298)

    a.   the type of binging.

    b.   the type of purging.

    c.   weight.

    d.   all of the above.

7. A newer eating disorder diagnosis that is currently not found in the DSM but is listed in the Appendix and warrants further study is (p. 301)

    a.   BED.

    b.   EDNOS.

    c.   OCD.

    d.   TNT.

8. Sally has an eating disorder. She also engages in self-harming behavior. Sally's behavior is similar to how many other people with eating disorders? (p. 302)

    a.   more than one-half

    b.   about three-quarters

    c.   less than one-third

    d.   over 90 %

9. A common disorder found in relatives of patients with eating disorders is (p. 304)

    a.   schizophrenia.

    b.   mood disorders.

    c.   anxiety disorders.

    d.   none of the above.

10. This neurotransmitter, in addition to being linked with mood disorders and impulsivity, also modulates appetite and feeding behavior. (p. 304)

    a.   Serotonin

    b.   dopamine

    c.   GABA

    d.   al of the above

PRACTICE TEST NUMBER 2

1. The majority of girls and women who have anorexia seem to come from a (p. 305)

    a.   single-parent home.

    b.   middle-class background.

    c.   higher social class background.

    d.   a and b.

2. The first model to exemplify the current sociocultural ideal of extreme thinness was (p. 305)

    a. Marilyn.

    b. Brittany.

    c. Sandra.

    d. Twiggy.

3. Internalizing the _____ is associated with a range of problems that are thought to be risk factors for eating disorders. (p. 306)

    a. over-weight ideal

    b. Sleeping Beauty ideal

    c. Monroe ideal

    d. thin-ideal

4. There seems to be a perceptual discrepancy between how young girls and women regard their own bodies and the media representation of the (p. 306)

    a. "ideal" female form.

    b. natural looking woman.

    c. older woman.

    d. none of the above.

5. The average age that young women start to diet is now between (p. 308)

    a. 7 and 9.

    b. 15 and 18.

    c. 12 and 13.

    d. 18 and 19.

6. This is a causal risk factor for body dissatisfaction. (p. 308)

    a. negative affect

    b. upbeat attitude

    c. high self-esteem

    d. social support

7. Until her death in 1984, who was considered the the world's leading authority on the psychotherapy of anorexic disorders? (p. 310)

    a. Anna Freud

    b. Hilde Bruch

    c. Jean Miller

    d. Carla Rogers

8. The phenomenon of eating disorder patients learning from other patients about how to deceive hospital staff into thinking they are complying with treatment is known as (p. 310)

     a. contamination.

     b. controlling behavior.

     c. contagion.

     d. cognitive manipulation.

9. With many young women seeing anorexia as a lifestyle choice and not recognizing the danger involved, they are turning to _____ Web sites for validation. (p. 311)

     a. pro-ana

     b. pro-choice

     c. pro-life

     d. pro-food

10. This type of treatment has proven to be effective in treating anorexia and bulima by helping to modify distorted beliefs about weight, food and self. (p. 310)

     a. EDT

     b. CNT

     c. behavioral

     d. CBT

PRACTICE TEST NUMBER 3

1. The _____ component of CBT for bulima is focused on normalizing eating patterns. (p. 312)

     a. behavioral

     b. cognitive

     c. cathartic

     d. all of the above

2. The _____ component of CBT for bulima challenges the dysfunctional thought patterns that perpetuate a binge cycle. (p. 312)

     a. behavioral

     b. cognitive

     c. cathartic

     d. all of the above

3. When patients with bulima stop trying so hard to restrain their eating, they seem to (p. 312)

     a. get worse by eating more.

     b. stay about the same.

     c. improve.

     d. get better, then get worse.

4. Significant depression is a comorbid condition for binge-eaters, affecting around
    _____during their lifetime. (p. 312)
    a.   25%
    b.   37%
    c.   76%
    d.   60%

5. Obesity is defined based on a statistic called the (p. 313)
    a.   CBT.
    b.   BMI.
    c.   GABA.
    d.   MMPI.

6. From a diagnostic perspective, obesity is not a(n) (p. 314)
    a.   problem if the person recognizes it.
    b.   treatable problem like other eating disorders.
    c.   eating disorder.
    d.   health risk.

7. Adult obesity is related to the number and size of the _____ in the body. (p. 314)
    a.   hormones
    b.   T-cells
    c.   adipose cells
    d.   lymphocites

8. A key influence on excessive eating and obesity is (p. 314)
    a.   television.
    b.   family behavior patterns.
    c.   magazines.
    d.   peers.

9. If you were a psychoanalyst and were treating a patient who was obsessed, you would
    view him or her as fixated in what stage of psychosexual development? (p. 314)
    a.   oral
    b.   anal
    c.   phallic
    d.   latency

10. This type of obesity was defined by Bruch as obesity that occurs in adults as a response
    to trauma or stress. (p. 315)
    a.   overwhelming
    b.   traumatic
    c.   acute stress
    d.   reactive

COMPREHENSIVE PRACTICE TEST
The following tests are designed to give you an idea of how well you understood the entire chapter. There are three different types of tests: multiple-choice, true-false, and essay.

MULTIPLE-CHOICE

1. At the heart of anorexia nervosa and bulimia nervosa is an intense and pathological fear of becoming (p. 294)

    a. too thin.

    b. overweight and fat.

    c. under nourished.

    d. all of the above.

2. Another component of anorexia and bulima is a pursuit of _____ that is relentless and sometimes deadly. (p. 294)

    a. muscle

    b. obesity

    c. thinness

    d. a career

3. Although people of all different ages have been known to develop eating disorders, the period of greatest risk is in the (p. 294)

    a. teenage years.

    b. early adulthood.

    c. middle age.

    d. a and b.

4. The clinical picture of the binge-eating/purging type of anorexia give it much in common with (p. 297)

    a. EDNOS.

    b. BED.

    c. Bulima nervosa.

    d. none of the above.

5. If a person meets the criteria for anorexia nervosa he/she can't be diagnosed with bulima nervosa because (p. 298)

    a. the two are very similar.

    b. there is a greater mortality associated with anorexia than with bulima.

    c. you can only have one diagnosis.

    d. none of the above.

6. Eating disorders are no longer confined to industrialized Western countries but can be found in (p. 302)

    a. India.

    b. Africa.

    c. Asia.

    d. all of the above.

7. The long-term mortality rate for bulimia nervosa is around (p. 303)

    a. 10%

    b. 6%

    c. 0.5%

    d. 1%

8. People with anorexia and bulima often show a long-standing pattern of excessive (p. 308)

    a. upbeat attitude.

    b. high self-esteem.

    c. social support.

    d. perfectionism.

9. Although implicated in the development of eating disorders, currently there is not enough empirical evidence that _____ is a risk factor for eating disorders. (p. 309)

    a. overly indulgent grandmother

    b. single parent family

    c. childhood sexual abuse

    d. being an only child

10. Family therapy has been found to be most effective when it is used to treat this group, whose eating disorder has a fairly recent onset. (p. 311)

    a. adolescents

    b. mid-twenties

    c. young adults

    d. none of the above

11. Because many patients with bulima also suffer from mood disorders, they are often treated with (p. 312)

    a. psychotherapy.

    b. behavioral therapy.

    c. antidepressants.

    d. hospitalization.

12. On average, how many patients with bulima who were treated with cognitive behavioral therapy stopped binging and purging after treatment? (p. 312)

  a. 100%

  b. 75%

  c. 50%

  d. none

13. Obesity can result in (p. 314)

  a. diabetes.

  b. high blood pressure.

  c. musculoskeletal problems.

  d. all of the above.

14. The rates of obesity are rising too quickly to be only a result of genetics. This rise implies what has become a significant influence? (p. 314)

  a. old age

  b. increase in activity

  c. unhealthy lifestyles

  d. all of the above.

15. Being obese is defined as having a body mass index of _____ or above. (p. 313)

  a. 30

  b. 10

  c. 25

  d. 35

16. An extreme method for treating obesity involves (p. 316)

  a. antidepressants.

  b. psychotherapy.

  c. psychosurgery.

  d. gastric bypass surgery.

TRUE – FALSE

1. Eating disorders in the elderly are easily diagnosed because doctors are aware of the problem.   T / F (p. 294)

2. Patients with anorexia nervosa, even if they are painfully thin or emaciated, often deny having any problems.   T / F (p. 296)

3. Thirty to fifty percent of patients transition from the restricting type to the binge-eating purging type of anorexia nervosa during the course of their disorder.   T / F (p. 296)

4. Death is often a direct outcome of the eating disorder bulima nervosa.   T / F   (p. 298)

5. There is a great deal of comorbidity associated with eating disorders and other diagnosable psychiatric conditions.   T / F   (p. 301)

6. Recent work has proven, and it has been widely accepted, that the restrictive type of anorexia has a genetic base.   T / F   (p. 304)

7. Body dissatisfaction is an important risk factor for pathological eating.   T / F   (p. 307)

8. Dieting is not regarded as a risk factor for the development of eating disorders in young women.   T / F   (p. 307)

9. About 17% of patients with severe eating disorders have to be committed to a hospital for treatment against their will.   T / F   (p. 310)

10. The most immediate concern with patients with anorexia is to restore their weight to a level that is not life-threatening.   T / F   (p. 310)

11. Obesity tends to persist over time.   T / F   (p. 314)

ESSAY QUESTIONS

1. Discuss the medical complications of anorexia nervosa and bulima nervosa. (p. 300)

    Anorexia

    Bulima

2.   Describe Garner's set-point theory and its relation to eating disorders. (p. 304)

WEB LINKS TO ITEMS OR CONCEPTS DISCUSSED IN THIS CHAPTER

Anorexia

    www.anad.org/

    www.findinfo.com/anorexia.htm

    familydoctor.org/handouts/063.html

Bulima

    define.ansme.com/words/b/bulima_nervosa.html

Bing-eating Disorder

    www.niddk.nih.gov/health/nutrit/pubs/binge.htm

    www.athealth.com/Consumer/disorders/Bingeeating.html

    www.anred.com/

CRISS-CROSS

Now that you know all there is to know about this chapter, here's your opportunity to put that knowledge to work.

CRISS-CROSS CLUES

Across
5. having a BMI above 30
7. A neurotransmitter that has been implicated in modulating appetite and feeding behavior
8. may cause people to be much more likely to subscribe to the thin ideal; may help maintain bulimic pathology

Down
1. frequent occurrence of episodes of out-of-control binge-eating, followed by recurrent inappropriate behavior that is intended to prevent weight gain.
2. a causal risk factor; focusing on one's limitations and short-comings
3. physiologically regulated weight the body tries to defend or maintain
4. means lack of appetite induced by nervousness
6. a statistic used to define obesity

Puzzle created with Puzzlemaker at DiscoverySchool.com

CHAPTER TEN

Health Problems and Behavior

BEFORE YOU READ

The realization is beginning to set in that, in health terms, the body and the mind work together in concert and that to treat the maladies of the human race means to care for the physical and the psychological. What in the past may have been considered to be a purely physical problem may have roots in psychology and vice versa. Indeed, it is becoming clear that psychological factors can have a profound effect on not only the length and effectiveness of the recuperative period of an illness or surgical procedure, but also a significant hand in causing the problem in the first place.

It is also apparent that negative affects, such as anger, anxiety, and depression, can have a great—even devastating—effect on a person's health, physical and psychological.

New fields of study, such as positive psychology, are emerging to probe how and why these events happen.

OBJECTIVES

After reading this chapter, you should be able to:

1. Explain how psychological problems can cause or affect medical problems, and how medical problems can cause or affect psychological problems.

2. Discuss how and why behavioral medicine extends our conception of disease beyond the traditional medical focus on physical breakdown of organs and organs systems.

3. Explain the role cortisol and other hormones play in stress reaction, and why extended contact can be problematic over the longer term.

4. Describe the function of the immune system, and the specialized roles by B-cells, T-cells and macrophages.

5. Explain the interactions between the nervous system, the immune system, and behavior, and psychoneuroimmunology's relationship to these.

6. Explain what cytokines are, how they work, and why researchers are so excited about these.

7. Explain why negative emotional states can impair the function of the immune system and the cardiovascular system.

8. Discuss damaging habits and lifestyles—such as smoking—and how these enhance risk for physical disease.

9. Explain the relationships between chronic negative emotions—such as anger, hostility, anxiety, and depression—and physical illness.

10. Discuss positive psychology as an emerging field associated with health and well-being.

11. Explain why a patient's physical factors—such as genetic vulnerabilities and possible organ weaknesses—need to be considered during treatment regardless of strong evidence of psychological contributions to its development.

12. Explain cognitive-behavior therapy's promise in helping an individual's coping resources for managing stressful life circumstances.

AS YOU READ

Answers can be found in the Answer Key at the end of the book.

KEY WORDS

Each of the words below is important in understanding the concepts presented in this chapter. Write the definition next to each of the words.

behavioral medicine (p. 322)   T-cells and B-cells (p. 327)

health psychology (p. 322)   cortisol (p. 325)

HPA Axis (p. 326)   antigen (p. 327) immunosuppression (p. 328)   placebo effect (p. 332)

cytokines (p. 328)   essential hypertension (p. 334)

psychoneuroimmunology (p. 328)   Type A behavior pattern (p. 335)

positive psychology (p. 331)   biofeedback (pp. 343-44)

negative affect (p. 331)   chronic fatigue syndrome (p. 345)

MATCHING
Match the following terms with their appropriate definitions.

Terms	**Definition**
_____ psychoneuroimmunology	A. a focus on human traits and resources that might have direct implications for our physical and mental well-being
_____ health psychology	B. broad interdisciplinary approach involving many disciplines
_____ behavioral medicine	C. focus on altering physiological states
_____ positive psychology	D. relaxed, more laid-back, and less time-pressured people
_____ biofeedback	E. the study of the interactions between behavior, the nervous system, and the immune system
_____ Type A behavior pattern	F. excessive competitive drive, extreme commitment to work, impatience or time urgency, and hostility
_____ Type B behavior pattern	G. subspecialty deals with psychology's contributions to diagnosis, treatment, and prevention of psychological components of physical problems

SHORT ANSWERS
Provide brief answers to the following questions.

1. Cortisol is a good hormone to have around in an emergency. But there is also a down side to cortisol. Explain. (pp. 325-26)

2. Optimism and its opposite, hopelessness, can have a significant impact on one's health. Explain. (pp. 330-33)

3. Explain the prevalence of hypertension in the African-American community in the United States. (p. 334)

4. What is the importance of asking yourself, "In the past month, have I felt so sad, discouraged, hopeless or had so many problems that I wondered if anything was worthwhile?" (p. 337)

5. Why should depression and CHD be linked? (p. 337)

FILL IN THE BLANKS

Read the following and fill in the blanks. These questions are designed to help you focus on specific details.

1. Organic malfunctions causing hypertension account for only a small percentage; the large majority of hypertension cases is called _____. (p. 334)

2. Key factors in work-related stress seem to be _____ and _____. (p. 338)

3. It appears that any sociocultural conditions that markedly increase life stress tend to play havoc with the biological human organism and lead to _____, as well as _____. (p. 342)

4. It may turn out that the greatest contribution of _____ will be in the area of altering self-injurious habits, such as smoking and excessive alcohol use. (p. 344)

AFTER YOU READ

Answers can be found in the Answer Key at the end of the book.

PRACTICE TESTS

Take the following three multiple-choice tests to see how much you have comprehended from the chapter. Each represents roughly one-third of the chapter. As you study the chapter, use these to check your progress.

PRACTICE TEST NUMBER 1

1. The emphasis of _____ is on the role that psychological factors play in the occurrence, maintenance and prevention of physical illness. (p. 322)

    a.   health attitude

    b.   behavioral medicine

    c.   psychoneuroimmunology

    d.   biofeedback

2. Antigens in the blood stream are searched out and destroyed by (p. 327)

    a.   B-cells.

    b.   T-cells.

    c.   macrophages.

    d.   all of the above.

3. Gastric ulcers (p. 324)

    a.   are caused by purely psychological origins.

    b.   are caused by the Helicobacter pylori bacterium.

    c.   may have psychological or physical, as well as common lifestyle factors.

    d.   are one of the great mysteries of life.

4. A person who is depressed due to having an underactive thyroid would be a victim of (p. 324)

    a.   Mental Disorder Due to a General Medical Condition.

    b.   Psychological Factor Affecting a General Medical Condition.

    c.   extreme bad luck.

    d.   negative affects.

5. Cortisol (p. 325)

    a.   is necessary in an emergency, as it prepares the body for a fight or flight response.

    b.   can damage brain cells, especially in the hippocampus, if not shut off.

    c.   may cause an allergic reaction if allowed to accumulate.

    d.   a and b.

6. Long-term stress (p. 326)

    a. might compromise the body's ability to heal and fight infections.

    b. is being linked to diminished immune reactivity.

    c. proves to be a good thing, as the body becomes stronger by dealing with it.

    d. a and b.

7. The immune system has been likened to a police force, in that   (pp. 326-27)

    a. if it is too weak, it cannot function effectively, and the body succumbs to damage from invading viruses and bacteria.

    b. if it is too strong and not selective, it can turn on its own normal cells.

    c. it protects and serves.

    d. a. and b.

8. In an experiment where self-evaluations of the subjects were manipulated negatively, the power of the killer cell cytotoxicity to eradicate an antigen was (p. 328)

    a. unaffected.

    b. greatly increased.

    c. significantly diminished.

    d. difficult to determine.

9. Unexpectedly, it was found that just as Pavlov's dogs learned to salivate to a tone, immunosuppression can be (p. 328)

    a. easily turned on or off at will.

    b. classically conditioned.

    c. controlled with music.

    d. associated with a period of intense grieving.

10. Conditions demonstrated to be associated with diminished immune function include (p. 330)

    a. sleep deprivation.

    b. space flight.

    c. death of a spouse.

    d. all of the above.

PRACTICE TEST NUMBER 2

1. Lifestyle factors—habits or behavior patterns presumable under our own control—play _____ role in three of the leading causes of death in this country: coronary heart disease, automobile accidents, and alcohol-related deaths. (p. 330)

    a. no significant

    b. a major

    c. a small, but growing

    d. a cameo

2. It is widely known that use of the latex condom is an effective measure for preventing transmission of the HIV-1 retrovirus, (p. 330)

    a. yet very large numbers of sexually active persons do not use these.

    b. it is not necessary in your town, because HIV-1 has not reached there yet.

    c. and most sexually active persons carry and always use these.

    d. but, although these are effective, these are not cool.

3. Considering optimism as it affects health, (pp. 330-31)

    a. many surgeons will delay a major operation until they are convinced that a patient is reasonably optimistic about the outcome.

    b. in an everyday sense, it seems to serve as a buffer against disease.

    c. people with too little optimism experience a psychological sense of helplessness.

    d. all of the above.

4. Chronic anger and hostility in a person (p. 331)

    a. can be risk factors for coronary heart disease and death.

    b. have very little effect on that person's health.

    c. identify him as a type B personality.

    d. identify him as a taxi driver.

5. Neuroticism, anxiety, and depression are known as _____ emotions. (p. 331)

    a. difficult

    b. negative

    c. hurtful

    d. powerful

6. Positive psychology has shown the health benefits of (p. 331)

    a. humor and laughter.

    b. positive affectivity.

    c. forgiving people as opposed to harboring a grudge.

    d. all of the above.

7. With stress, the normal heartbeat, regular pulse, and relatively low blood pressure (pp. 333-34)

    a. all become greater, faster, and higher for a short period and then return to normal.

    b. become part of the "flight-or-fight" pattern and must work harder.

    c. increase and usually return to normal when the crisis passes, although under continuing emotional strain, high blood pressure may become chronic.

    d. b and c.

8. High blood pressure is insidious and dangerous, due to the fact that (p. 334)

    a. its regulation is so complex that when it goes awry, identifying the causal factors can be extremely difficult.

    b. it often increases, only to recede when the patient enters a doctor's office.

    c. no one really knows what causes it or how to treat it.

    d. sprinkling less salt on French fries seems to help some people, but not others.

9. Studying the relationship between anger and blood pressure showed that participants who _____ had the lowest blood pressure. (p. 335)

    a. expressed their anger

    b. suppressed their anger

    c. used constructive anger

    d. both a and b.

10. Investigating patients who had had heart attacks, researchers found that clinically depressed patients were _____ more likely to die in the next six months than were their nondepressed counterparts. (p. 337)

    a. no

    b. two times

    c. five times

    d. forty-two times

PRACTICE TEST NUMBER 3

1. Another study that followed 1,500 men and women with no prior history of heart disease for 14 years found that persons who had suffered major depression were _____ more likely to have had a heart attack. (p. 337)

    a. one and one-half times

    b. two times

    c. four times

    d. not

2. People with low levels of emotional support (unmarried, small social network, lack of friends) are _____ likely to develop CHD, _____ likely to have another cardiac event, and _____ likely to die over the next five years. (p. 337)

    a. more, three times more, three times more

    b. less, not, not

    c. just as, twice as, more

    d. not, not, less

3. Mental stress is known to (p. 338)

    a. raise systolic blood pressure.

    b. cause an elevation in epinephrine.

    c. reduce the oxygen supply to the heart muscle.

    d. all of the above.

4. In a study of twins where only one had CHD, it was found that the twin suffering from heart disease was _____ work-oriented, took _____ leisure time, had _____ home problems and, in general, experienced greater _____ in his lives than his healthier twin brother. (p. 339)

    a.   equally, less, equal amount of, dissatisfactions

    b.   more, less, more, dissatisfactions

    c.   less, more, fewer, satisfactions

    d.   less, less, fewer, satisfactions

5. Death rates from varied causes, including physical disease, are _____ in people who have recently undergone marital problems or divorce than in the general population. (p. 340)

    a.   about the same

    b.   markedly higher

    c.   lower

    d.   statistically unimportant

6. People who have a good social support system (p. 340)

    a.   have lower blood pressure.

    b.   have higher natural killer cell activity in the blood.

    c.   hardly ever get sick.

    d.   a and b.

7. For patients with CHD, appropriate treatment might include (p. 342)

    a.   lipid lowering medications.

    b.   anxiolytic (anxiety reducing) medications.

    c.   anticoagulants.

    d.   all of the above.

8. In the first study of emotional disclosure in people with rheumatoid arthritis, it was found that those who had engaged in emotional disclosure had _____ physical dysfunction than people in the control condition. (p. 343)

    a.   no difference in

    b.   much more

    c.   significantly less

    d.   slightly less

9. Why emotional disclosure provides clinical benefits is not clear. Possibly it is because (p. 343)

    a.   patients are given an opportunity for emotional catharsis or "blowing off steam."

    b.   writing provides an opportunity for people to re-think and re-appraise their problems.

    c.   exercise of any type is a benefit.

    d.   a and b.

10. Biofeedback (pp. 343-44)

  a. has been a glowing success in the treatment of negative events.

  b. generally has failed to live up to the enthusiasm it originally generated.

  c. may prove to be effective in the control of musculoskeletal pain.

  d. b and c.

COMPREHENSIVE PRACTICE TEST

The following tests are designed to give you an idea of how well you understood the entire chapter. There are three different types of tests: multiple-choice, true-false, and essay.

MULTIPLE-CHOICE

1. It is becoming more apparent that a disorder (p. 322)

  a. may be entirely physical in origin.

  b. may be entirely psychological in origin.

  c. may be primarily physical or psychological but is always a disorder of the whole person.

  d. a and b.

2. Studies examining the association between stress and immune functioning established an association between the occurrence of stressful circumstances and (p. 326)

  a. acne.

  b. diminished immune reactivity.

  c. maladaptive behavior.

  d. negative affects.

3. A man hearing voices telling him to refuse dialysis for his kidney disease is an example of (p. 324)

  a. alien abduction.

  b. a man who is going to die.

  c. a major new DSM-IV category called Mental Disorder Due to a General Medical Condition.

  d. what DSM-IV references as Psychological Factor Affecting a General Medical Condition.

4. A stress response involves biological responses, including (pp. 325-26)

  a. the hypothalamus, which stimulates the sympathetic nervous system, which stimulates the adrenal glands to secrete adrenaline and noradrenaline.

  b. an increase in heart rate and a preparation to metabolize glucose more rapidly.

  c. the pituitary gland secretes adrenocorticotropic hormone, which activates the adrenal cortex into producing the stress hormone called cortisol.

  d. all of the above.

5. While stress has not been found to cause specific physical diseases, it (p. 326)

    a.   is becoming a key underlying theme in our understanding of the development and course of virtually all organic illness.

    b.   may serve as a predisposing, precipitating, or reinforcing factor in the causal pattern.

    c.   may interfere with the body's normal defensive forces or immunological system.

    d.   all of the above.

6. In studies of groups of uninfected high-risk and early stage HIV-infected gay men, it was found that (p. 328)

    a.   behavioral interventions, such as aerobic exercise, had positive psychological and immunocompetence effects.

    b.   depressed mood was associated with enhanced HIV-1 activity.

    c.   psychological depression compromised immune function.

    d.   all of the above.

7. Psychoneuroimmunology, the study of the interactions between behavior, the nervous system, and the immune system (pp. 328-29)

    a.   has shown that, unlike previously thought, the immune system is not "closed" and responsive only to external challenges.

    b.   the nervous system and the immune system communicate.

    c.   the brain influences the immune system and the immune system influences the brain.

    d.   all of the above.

8. Research has shown that depression (or negative affect) shows (p. 330)

    a.   a strong association between dysphoric mood and compromised immune function.

    b.   the state of being depressed in itself adds something beyond any negative effects of the stressors precipitating this mood.

    c.   that depressive affect reliably associated with lowered numbers of white cells following foreign protein challenge lowered natural killer cell activity and lowered quantities of several varieties of circulating white cells.

    d.   all of the above.

9. Concerning negative emotions—the negative affect—it has been shown that (p. 331)

    a.   negative emotions can be damaging to our health.

    b.   depression is associated with measurable and undesirable changes in immune functioning and even seems to increase mortality from all causes in medical inpatients.

    c.   anxiety seems to be associated with the development of coronary heart disease, in men and women and to delay recovery from surgery.

    d.   all of the above.

10. In 1996, the number of sudden cardiac deaths in the United States in people ages 15 to 34 was (p. 332)

    a.   9.

    b.   77.

    c.   467.

    d.   3,000.

11. A group of men identified as either Type A or Type B was followed for eight and a half years. Compared to Type B personality, Type A personality was associated with _____ coronary artery disease and risk of recurrent myocardial infarction. (p. 335)

    a. much less
    b. about the same
    c. much more
    d. a and c.

12. In a two-year study of 34,000 male professionals with panic disorder, agoraphobia, and generalized anxiety, men with the highest levels of phobic anxiety were _____ likely to have a fatal heart attack and _____ likely to suffer sudden cardiac death than were men with the lowest levels. (p. 337)

    a. not, less
    b. three times more, six times more
    c. 1.414 times more, 1.732 times more
    d. 1.414 times less, 1.732 times less

13. Genetic contributions to disease may involve (p. 338)

    a. an underlying physical vulnerability for acquiring a disease.
    b. the psychological make-up of the individual and his/her stress tolerance.
    c. an interaction between a and b.
    d. all of the above.

14. If a particular environmental stressor may have been a key causal factor in the development of a physical illness, removal of this stressor (p. 342)

    a. will bring about recovery.
    b. will bring about recovery only if combined with learning more effective coping techniques.
    c. may not be enough to bring about recovery if organic changes have already taken place.
    d. may cause the patient to die.

15. _____ is based on the assumption that because autonomic responses can be learned, these can be unlearned. (p. 344)

    a. Biofeedback
    b. Meditation
    c. Behavior therapy
    d. Emotional disclosure

TRUE – FALSE

1. The ailments to which people are most vulnerable—whether physical, psychological, or both—are determined in no small part by who we are, where we live, and how we live. T / F (p. 322)

2. The "fight-or-flight response" involves primarily the sympathetic division of the autonomic nervous system. T / F (p. 325)

3. Stress appears to speed up the onset or increase the severity of a disorder, and to interfere with the body's immunological defenses and other homeostatic repair functions. T / F (p. 326)

4. The immune system and the nervous system are separate, closed systems that operate independently of each other. T / F (pp. 328-29)

5. Depression has little or no effect on the immune system. T / F (p. 330)

6. Stress has been shown to slow down the healing of wounds by as much as 24-40%. T / F (p. 330)

7. Usually, if shown a clear relationship between lifestyle and health risk, people can make lasting lifestyle changes. T / F (p. 330)

8. Had it not been for the placebo effect, the medical profession, as we know it, might not have survived to the twentieth century, because until the early 1900s, medical practitioners had little else to offer disease sufferers. T / F (p. 332)

9. Heart attack patients who are depressed at the time of their heart attacks or shortly afterward show a greatly increased risk for future coronary events and cardiac deaths. T / F (p. 336)

10. Stress does not have to be extreme or severe in order to have potentially lethal consequences down the road. T / F (p. 338)

11. Some physical disorders may be acquired, maintained, or both in much the same way as other behavior patterns. T / F (p. 342)

ESSAY QUESTIONS

1. In "Developments in Research 10.1 Cytokines: The Link Between the Brain and the Immune System," these newly discovered small protein molecules allow the immune system to communicate with itself and with the brain. Discuss cytokines, what these are, what these do, and what their promise is. (p. 329)

2.   Chronic fatigue syndrome can leave a person physically exhausted for months or even
      years. Discuss this disorder. (p. 345)

3.   Discuss the behavioral medicine approach to physical illness. (p. 322)

WEB LINKS TO ITEMS OR CONCEPTS DISCUSSED IN THIS CHAPTER

Clinical assessment

    www.lmb.uni-muenchen.de/groups/ ibelgaufts/cytokines.html

    bioinformatics.weizmann.ac.il/cytokine/

    health.yahoo.com/health/encyclopedia/000818/0.html

    www.uth.tmc.edu/schools/med/surgery/organ_transplant/ Frames/historyofimmunosuppression.html

    www.ash-us.org/

    www.jhypertension.com/

    www.phassociation.org/

    www.mco.edu/whl/

    www.cdc.gov/nchs/fastats/hyprtens.htm

CRISS-CROSS

Now that you know all there is to know about this chapter, here's your opportunity to put that knowledge to work.

CRISS-CROSS CLUES
Across
9. hypertension for which there is no known cause
Down
1. study of interactions among behavior, the nervous system, and the immune system
2. a compromising of the body's immune system to the possible detriment of one's health
3. a field that deals with psychology's contributions to diagnosis, treatment, and prevention
4. a patient who believes a treatment is going to be effective and is likely to improve, even if the treatment has no effect
5. foreign bodies (viruses, bacteria, and others) in one's body
6. a treatment based on altering physiological states
7. broad, interdisciplinary approach of physical disorders thought to have psychosocial factors as a partial cause
8. chemical messengers in the blood that appear to be of crucial importance for health
10. a leucocyte that matures in the thymus

Puzzle created with Puzzlemaker at DiscoverySchool.com

Personality Disorders

BEFORE YOU READ

In this chapter, several specific disorders of personality are discussed. With these disorders we encounter for the first time, behavior is not episodic and, generally, is not exacerbated by stress. Rather, the personality disorders represent ingrained "lifestyles" or characteristic patterns that are maladaptive of meeting the individual's needs. Usually, these maladaptive approaches significantly impair at least some aspect of functioning. Often, the person with a personality disorder ends up imposing on other people's rights in order to obtain his or her goals.

Chapter 11 includes descriptions of the various types of personality disorders (which vary considerably in form and severity), their causal patterns, and their treatment. Special attention is given to one particular personality disorder—antisocial personality and psychopathy—because of the extensive research on this topic.

OBJECTIVES

After reading this chapter, you should be able to:

1. List the clinical features of the personality disorders and the problems associated with diagnosis.

2. Compare and contrast the different types of personality disorders and identify the three clusters into which most personality disorders are grouped.

3. Summarize what is known about the biological, psychological, and sociocultural causal factors of personality disorders.

4. Discuss the difficulties of treating individuals with personality disorders and describe the approaches to treatment that have been tried.

5. Compare and contrast the DSM-IV concept of antisocial personality and Cleckley's concept of psychopathy.

6. List the clinical features of psychopathy and antisocial personality.

7. Summarize the biological, psychosocial, and sociocultural causal factors in psychopathy and antisocial personality and the integrated developmental perspective.

8. Explain why it is difficult to treat psychopathy and antisocial personality and describe the most promising of the as yet unproven approaches to treatment.

AS YOU READ

Answers can be found in the Answer Key at the end of the book.

KEY WORDS

Each of the words below is important in understanding the concepts presented in this Chapter. Write the definition next to each of the words.

personality disorder or character disorder (p. 350)

temperament (p. 352)

paranoid personality disorder (p. 353)

schizoid personality disorder (p. 354)

schizotypal personality disorder (p. 356)

histrionic personality disorder (p. 357)

narcissistic personality disorder (p. 358)

antisocial personality disorder (ASPD) (p. 359)

borderline personality disorder (BPD) (p. 360)

avoidant personality disorder (p. 362)

dependent personality disorder (p. 363)

obsessive-compulsive personality disorder (OCPD) (p. 364)

passive-aggressive personality disorder (p. 365)

depressive personality disorder (p. 365)

psychopathy or sociopathy (p. 370)

WHO'S WHO AND WHAT'S WHAT—MATCHING
Match the following personality disorders with the appropriate description.

Personality Disorder	Description
_____ Paranoid	A. hypersensitivity to rejection, shyness, insecurity
_____ Schizoid	B. overconcern with attractiveness; self-dramatization
_____ Schizotypal	C. impulsive, drastic mood shifts, self-mutilation
_____ Histrionic	D. suspicious and mistrustful; blames others
_____ Narcissistic	E. persistent unhappiness or dejection; feelings of inadequacy, guilt, and self-criticism
_____ Antisocial	F. lacks desire to form attachments; poor relationships
_____ Borderline	G. negative attitudes, passive resistance; complaining, sullen, and argumentative
_____ Avoidant	H. grand preoccupation with self, lack of empathy
_____ Dependent	I. excessive concern with order, rules; perfectionistic
_____ Obsessive-Compulsive	J. peculiar thought patterns; odd perception & speech
_____ Passive Aggressive	K. lacking morals or ethics, deceitful, manipulative
_____ Depressive	L. discomfort being alone, indecisive, difficulty ending relationships

SHORT ANSWERS
Provide brief answers to the following questions.

1. Give the five criteria in the DSM-IV-TR definition of personality disorder. (p. 351)

2. Discuss the possible biological and psychological causal factors for personality disorders. (pp. 352-53)

Short Answers continue on page 188

PERSONALITY DISORDER

Personality disorders discussed in the text cover a lot of ground and can leave you confused. As you discover items while studying

CLUSTER A
Characteristics of Cluster A disorders:

Paranoid personality disorder

Characteristics:

Causal Factors:

Treatment or hope for treatment:

Miscellaneous points or terms:

Schizoid personality disorder

Characteristics:

Causal Factors:

Treatment or hope for treatment:

Miscellaneous points or terms:

Schizotypal personality disorder

Characteristics:

Causal Factors:

Treatment or hope for treatment:

Miscellaneous points or terms

CLUSTER B
Characteristics of Cluster B disorders:

Histrionic personality disorder

Characteristics:

Causal Factors:

Treatment or hope for treatment:

Miscellaneous points or terms:

Narcissistic personality disorder

Characteristics:

Causal Factors:

Treatment or hope for treatment:

Miscellaneous points or terms:

Antisocial personality disorder

Characteristics:

Causal Factors:

Treatment or hope for treatment:

Miscellaneous points or terms:

Borderline personality disorder

Characteristics:

Causal Factors:

Treatment or hope for treatment:

Miscellaneous points or terms:

CLUSTERS ARE ARRANGED BY SIMILARITY OF DISORDERS.

DATA BASE

this chapter, use this section to jot down facts and descriptive words or make notes for later comparison or reference.

CLUSTER C
Characteristics of Cluster C disorders:

Avoidant personality disorder
Characteristics:

Causal Factors:

Treatment or hope for treatment:

Miscellaneous points or terms:

Dependent personality disorder
Characteristics:

Causal Factors:

Treatment or hope for treatment:

Miscellaneous points or terms:

Obsessive-compulsive personality disorder
Characteristics:

Causal Factors:

Treatment or hope for treatment:

Miscellaneous points or terms:

> **PASSIVE-AGGRESSIVE AND DEPRESSIVE DISORDERS REMAIN IN A PROVISIONAL CATEGORY**
> ---
> **ANTISOCIAL PERSONALITY AND PSYCHOPATHY:**
> Their tendency is to disregard and violate the rights of others through deceit and antisocial behavior

PROVISIONAL CATEGORY

Passive-aggressive personality disorder
Characteristics:

Causal Factors:

Treatment or hope for treatment:

Miscellaneous points or terms:

Depressive personality disorder
Characteristics:

Causal Factors:

Treatment or hope for treatment:

Miscellaneous points or terms:

ANTISOCIAL PERSONALITY AND PSYCHOPATHY

Antisocial personality
Characteristics:

Causal Factors:

Treatment or hope for treatment:

Miscellaneous points or terms:

Psychopathy
Characteristics:

Causal Factors:

Treatment or hope for treatment:

Miscellaneous points or terms:

3. Many studies have found that people with borderline personality disorder report a large number of negative, even traumatic, events in childhood, including abuse and neglect, separation and loss, and parental psychopathology. However, it is difficult to say childhood trauma plays a causal role. Why? (p. 361)

4. Discuss the difference between a loner with schizoid personality disorder and the loner who is avoidant. (p. 362-63)

FILL IN THE BLANKS

Read the following and fill in the blanks. These questions are designed to help you focus on specific details.

1. Two of the general features characterizing most personality disorders are _____ and _____. (p. 350)

2. People who tend to see themselves as blameless, finding fault for their own mistakes and failures in others, even to the point of ascribing evil motives to others, suffer from _____. (p. 353)

3. Teenagers who have a_____ personality disorder have been shown to be at increased risk for developing schizophrenia and schizophrenia-spectrum disorders in adulthood. (p. 356)

4.   Those with _____ personality disorder tend to overestimate their abilities and accomplishments and behave in stereotypical ways to gain acclaim and recognition and feed their fantasies of unlimited success, power, beauty, or brilliance. (p. 358)

5.   Those with _____ personality disorder tend to be impulsive, irritable, and aggressive, and sow a pattern of generally irresponsible behavior. (p. 359)

6.   There is substantial co-occurrence of borderline personality disorder with other personality disorders—especially _____. _____, _____, and _____. (p. 361)

7.   Histrionic and dependent personalities have strong needs for reassurance and approval, but the _____ personality is gregarious, flamboyant, and actively demanding of attention, whereas the _____ personality is more docile and self-effacing. (p. 364)

8.   Borderline and dependent personalities fear abandonment, but the _____ personality, who usually has intense and stormy relationships, reacts with feelings of emptiness or rage if abandonment occurs, where the _____ personality reacts initially with submissiveness and appeasement, but finally with an urgent seeking of a new relationship. (p. 364)

9.   Persons with _____ personality disorder have difficulty in interpersonal relationships, because of excessive devotion to work and because of difficulty expressing emotions. (p. 364)

10. The person who is pessimistic, prone to worry, with an emphasis on distorted cognitions and interpersonal traits, may be a _____ personality. (p. 365)

11. The primary goal of treatment for _____ personalities is seen as strengthening the weak egos of these individuals, with a particular focus on their primary primitive defense mechanism of splitting, which leads them to see other people as "all good" or "all bad." (p. 367)

12. People with _____ personality disorder have a lifelong pattern of unsocialized and irresponsible behavior, with little regard for safety—either their own or that of others. (p. 368)

13. Psychopathic personalities exhibit the antisocial and aggressive behaviors of antisocial personalities, and, in addition, are selfish, callous, exploitative, and lacking in _____ or _____. (p. 369)

THE DOCTOR IS IN...PSYCHIATRIC HELP—5¢

Read the following scenarios and diagnose the client. Remember to look carefully at the criteria for the disorder before you make a decision as to the diagnosis. Make a list of other information you might need to help you understand the causal factors.

1. Helen, a 31-year-old waitress, comes to the office of a male therapist, seeking help trying to understand why she doesn't have a relationship. She tells him about her life in a very dramatic and lively manner and makes flirtaous comments like, "I can't understand why no one likes me—what I wouldn't do to have some cute guy like you just sweep me off my feet." She then looks at the therapist and smiles seductively. Helen told the therapist that she feels so comfortable with him after just five minutes, that she is sure they will become friends. Although Helen presents her life in a very dramatic way, she does not tell the therapist many details.

    How would Helen be diagnosed and why? (p. 357)

2. Jack, a computer software engineer, comes to your office because he is having problems at work and possibly is going to lose his job if things don't change. You ask him what has happened. He looks at you suspiciously, and asks you who else you have been talking to. You assure him you haven't talked to anyone. He tells you that others at work are talking about him behind his back, and he knows they are responsible for his having to see a therapist. Jack tells you he has no friends at work or any place else. He had two friends once, but he stopped seeing them when they couldn't go out to dinner with him once, because of "other commitments." Jack believed that the two of them plotted together against him. Jack was coherent and seemed in contact with reality—as he saw it.

    How would you diagnose Jack and why? (p. 353)

3. Pam sits in your office not saying much and having a difficulty talking about herself. She manages to tell you that she is alone much of the time—something she doesn't like—and would like to feel comfortable meeting people. Pam tells you that she is so afraid of people not liking her or criticizing her, that she hardly ever goes out. She is extremely self–conscious and avoids situations in which she might be criticized or rejected.

    How would you diagnose Pam and why? (p. 362)

4. As a therapist, what issues will you face in treating the three patients above? (pp. 366-68)

AFTER YOU READ

Answers can be found in the Answer Key at the end of the book.

PRACTICE TESTS

Take the following three multiple-choice tests to see how much you have comprehended from the chapter. Each represents roughly one-third of the chapter. As you study the chapter, use thse to check your progress.

PRACTICE TEST NUMBER 1

1. Personality disorders were formerly known as (p. 350)

   a. fatal flaws.

   b. character disorders.

   c. personality patterns.

   d. none of the above.

2. Studies estimate that _____ persons meet criteria for at least one personality disorder at some point in their lifetime. (p. 350)

   a. about 9 out of 10

   b. fewer than 1% of

   c. about 13% of

   d. 42

3. Most personality traits have been found to be (p. 353)

   a. difficult to maintain.

   b. moderately heritable.

   c. difficult to explain.

   d. all of the above.

4. Many studies have suggested that _____ may be an important factor in a subset of causes for several different personality disorders. (p. 353)

   a. genes

   b. private schooling

   c. early emotional, physical, and sexual abuse

   d. understanding the psychobiological substrate

5. Persons with _____ personality disorder commonly bear grudges, are unwilling to forgive perceived insults and slightest, and are quick to react with anger. (p. 353)

   a. schizoid

   b. paranoid

   c. narcissistic

   d. antisocial

6. Persons with _____ personality disorder rarely experience strong positive or negative emotions, are unable to express their feelings, appear as cold and distant, and can be classified as loners or introverts. (p. 355)

    a. schizoid
    b. paranoid
    c. narcissistic
    d. antisocial

7. Persons with _____ personality disorder are excessively introverted with pervasive social and interpersonal deficits, as in question 6, but, in addition, they have cognitive and perceptual distortions and eccentricities in their communication and behavior. (p. 356)

    a. schizoid
    b. schizotypal
    c. borderline
    d. antisocial

8. Persons with _____ personality disorder exhibit excessive attention-seeking behavior, using their lively, dramatic, and often excessively extroverted styles, and tend to feel unappreciated if not the center of attention. (p. 357).

    a. histrionic
    b. narcissistic
    c. borderline
    d. antisocial

9. Persons with _____ personality disorder show an exaggerated sense of self-importance, a preoccupation with being admired, and a lack of empathy for the feelings of others. (p. 358)

    a. histrionic
    b. narcissistic
    c. borderline
    d. schizoid

10. Narcissistic personality disorder may be more frequently observed in (p. 358)

    a. older persons.
    b. men than in women.
    c. women than in men.
    d. television news anchors.

PRACTICE TEST NUMBER 2

1. Persons with _____ personality disorder continually violate and show disregard for the rights of others through deceitful, aggressive, or antisocial behavior, typically without remorse or loyalty to anyone. (p. 359)

    a. schizoid
    b. schizotypal
    c. borderline
    d. antisocial

2. Persons with _____ personality disorder show a pattern of behavior characterized by impulsivity and instability in interpersonal relationships, self-image, and moods. (p. 360)

    a. schizoid
    b. schizotypal
    c. borderline
    d. histrionic

3. Persons with _____ personality disorder display extreme affective instability, which often leads to erratic self-destructive behaviors, such as binges of gambling, sexual promiscuity, and suicide attempts. (p. 360)

    a. schizoid
    b. schizotypal
    c. borderline
    d. histrionic

4. Overall, about _____ of patients with borderline personality disorder reported some type of childhood abuse or neglect. (p. 361)

    a. 1.732%
    b. 20%
    c. half
    d. 90%

5. A study (Paris, 1999) suggests that borderline personality disorder may be more prevalent in our society today than in the past and in many other cultures, because of (p. 362)

    a. global warming.
    b. the weakening of the family structure in our society.
    c. the increase of violence in entertainment and the media.
    d. all of the above.

6. Persons with _____ personality disorder have a pattern of extreme social inhibition and introversion, leading to lifelong patterns of limited social relationships. (p. 362)

    a. avoidant
    b. schizotypal
    c. borderline
    d. antisocial

7. Persons with _____ personality disorder show an extreme need to be taken care of, which leads to clinging and submissive behavior. (p. 363)

    a. avoidant
    b. dependent
    c. borderline
    d. obsessive-compulsive

8. Dependent personality disorder occurs in about 2-4% of the population and is (p. 364)

    a. usually found east of the Mississippi.
    b. found mostly in older men.
    c. more common in women than men.
    d. a product of domineering grandparents.

9. Persons with _____ personality disorder are characterized by the need for perfectionism and an excessive concern with maintaining order and control. (p. 364)

    a. schizoid
    b. schizotypal
    c. obsessive-compulsive
    d. histrionic

10. The obsessive-compulsive personality (p. 364)

    a. believes that "I am completely helpless."
    b. is quite rigid and stubborn.
    c. has difficulty delegating tasks to others.
    d. b and c.

PRACTICE TEST NUMBER 3

1. Persons diagnosed with _____ personality disorder show a pervasive pattern of passive resistance to demands in social or work situations, sometimes being highly critical or scornful of authority. (p. 365)

    a. schizoid
    b. passive-aggressive
    c. obsessive-compulsive
    d. histrionic

2. Persons diagnosed with _____ personality disorder show a usual mood state of unhappiness, gloominess, or dejection. (p. 365)

    a. avoidant
    b. depressive
    c. obsessive-compulsive
    d. borderline

3. Treatment of borderline personality disorder using drugs is controversial because (p. 367)

    a. victims become addicted rapidly.

    b. it is so frequently associated with suicidal behavior.

    c. drugs tend to cause them to "cross the border" and not return.

    d. drugs tend to cause them to develop other disorders.

4. Persons diagnosed with _____ personality disorder persistently disregard and violate the rights of others through a combination of deceitful, aggressive, or antisocial behavior. (p. 368)

    a. psychopathy

    b. antisocial

    c. obsessive-compulsive

    d. borderline

5. The prevalence of antisocial personality disorder in the general population is estimated to be about _____% for males and _____% for females. (p. 368)

    a. 3, 1

    b. 33, 3

    c. 3, 10

    d. 50, 0

6. Persons diagnosed with _____ are characterized by callousness, selfishness, and an exploitative use of others, as well as being antisocial, impulsive, and socially deviant lifestyle. (p. 369).

    a. psychopathy

    b. antisocial

    c. obsessive-compulsive

    d. borderline

7. Released prison inmates who were diagnosed as psychopaths were estimated to be _____ than those without a psychopathy diagnosis. (p. 369)

    a. three times more likely to reoffend

    b. four times to reoffend violently

    c. less likely to reoffend

    d. a and b.

8. An important factor in the probability that a child with a genetic or constitutional liability will develop conduct disorder, and later adult psychopathy or ASPD is (p. 375)

    a. poor and ineffective parenting skills, especially ineffective discipline, monitoring, and supervision.

    b. parents' own antisocial behavior.

    c. divorce and other parental transitions.

    d. all of the above.

9. A "burned-out psychopath" is one who (p. 377)

    a.   died in the electric chair.

    b.   had a bad reaction to electroshock therapy.

    c.   is an older, wiser person whose criminal activities have lessened after age 40.

    d.   had a bad reaction to drugs.

10. The best multifaceted cognitive-behaviorally oriented treatment programs (p. 377)

    a.   can cure 77% of antisocial personalties and 34% of psychopaths.

    b.   generally produce changes of only modest magnitude.

    c.   greatly help at least half of the patients.

    d.   have proven to only make things worse in the long run.

COMPREHENSIVE PRACTICE TEST

The following tests are designed to give you an idea of how well you understood the entire chapter. There are three different types of tests: multiple-choice, true-false, and essay.

MULTIPLE-CHOICE

1. In their study, Widiger and colleagues found that _____ patients who qualified for for one or more personality disorder diagnosis also qualified for at least one more. (p. 352)

    a.   42

    b.   22.6% of

    c.   85% or

    d.   only a few

2. The ultimate goal would be to achieve a biopsychosocial perspective on the origins of each personality disorder, (p. 352)

    a.   and it was reached last month.

    b.   but we are far from that goal today.

    c.   and it is expected that will happen soon.

    d.   but it will probably never happen.

3. Cluster A personality disorders are described as (p. 366)

    a.   odd/eccentric.

    b.   anxious/fearful.

    c.   erratic/dramatic.

    d.   all of the above.

4. People with narcissistic personality disorder do not, as a rule, seek psychological treatment because (p. 358)

    a.   they are afraid of what they might learn.

    b.   they view themselves as nearly perfect and in no need of change.

    c.   they claim they never have the time.

    d.   they are extremely suspicious.

5. To be considered an antisocial personality disorder, the pattern of behavior must have been occurring since the age of 15, and before age 15, the person must have shown (p. 359)

    a.   destruction of property, deceitfulness or theft.

    b.   persistent patterns of aggression toward people or animals.

    c.   serious violation of rules at home or in school.

    d.   all of the above.

6. Approximately 20-40% of borderline personalities have cognitive symptoms that include (p. 360)

    a.   relatively short or transient episodes in which they appear to out of contact with reality.

    b.   experiencing delusions or other psychotic-like symptoms, such as hallucinations, paranoid ideas, body image distortions, or dissociative symptoms.

    c.   complaints about personal misfortunes or of being misunderstood and unappreciated.

    d.   a and b.

7. People with avoidant personality disorder (p. 362)

    a.   do not seek out other people but do not enjoy their aloneness.

    b.   have great anxiety due to their inability to relate comfortable to other people.

    c.   tend to be hypersensitive and may see ridicule or disparagement where none was intended.

    d.   all of the above.

8. A person with dependent personality disorder (p. 363)

    a.   may remain in an abusive relationship due to a fear that defending herself might cause her to lose her partner.

    b.   may not function well on his own.

    c.   has great difficulty making even simple everyday decisions due to a lack of self-confidence.

    d.   all of the above.

9. A person with passive-aggressive personality disorder (p. 365)

    a.   may not function well on her own.

    b.   commonly complains about personal misfortunes or of being misunderstood or unappreciated.

    c.   believes that "I am completely helpless."

    d.   views himself as nearly perfect and in no need of change.

10. Personality disorders are generally very difficult to treat, in part, because (p. 366)

    a. people suffering from these disorders view themselves as nearly perfect and in no need of change.

    b. these are, by definition, enduring, pervasive, and inflexible patterns of behavior.

    c. it is very difficult to get and keep the attention of persons suffering these disorders.

    d. all of the above.

11. People who suffer from _____ personality disorder may experience transient psychotic symptoms, believe that they have magical powers, and may engage in magical rituals. (p. 356)

    a. schizoid

    b. paranoid

    c. schizotypal

    d. antisocial

12. Psychopaths are (p. 370)

    a. often charming, spontaneous, and likeable on first acquaintance.

    b. deceitful and manipulative, callously using others to achieve their own ends.

    c. prone to acting out impulses in remorseless and often senseless violence.

    d. all of the above.

13. Psychopaths (p. 370)

    a. seem to have good insight into other people's needs and weaknesses and are adept at exploiting them.

    b. are irresponsible and unfaithful mates, being manipulative and exploitative in sexual relationships.

    c. have learned to take, rather than earn, what they want and seldom forgo immediate pleasure for future gains and long-range goals.

    d. all of the above.

14. _____ in childhood is the single best predictor of who develops an adult diagnosis of psychopathy or antisocial personality. (p. 374)

    a. An absorption in computer games

    b. Excess access to television, particularly violent television

    c. The number of antisocial behaviors exhibited

    d. Heavy metal and other violent and antisocial forms of music

15. The criminal activities of many psychopathic and antisocial personalities declines after the age of _____, but the egocentric, callous, and exploitative dimension does not. (p. 377)

    a. 25

    b. 40

    c. 60

    d. 92

TRUE – FALSE

1. Rather than stemming from debilitating reactions to stress, personality disorders seem largely to come from gradual development of inflexible and distorted personality and behavioral patterns. T/ F (p. 350)

2. In milder cases of these disorders, we find people who generally function adequately, but who would be described by their relatives, friends, or associates as troublesome, eccentric, or difficult to get to know. T/ F   (p. 350)

3. People with personality disorders do not usually learn from previous mistakes and troubles. T/ F (p. 351)

4. Although many patients have a mix of personality disorders, it is not uncommon to find individuals to fit the "ideal" descriptions in the textbook. T / F (p. 353)

5. The prevalence in the general population of histrionic personality disorder is estimated at 20-30% and never occurs in women. T / F (p. 357)

6. In a sense, all children begin life as narcissists and only gradually acquire a perspective-taking ability. T/ F   (p. 358)

7. Self-mutilation is one of the most characteristic features of borderline personality. T/ F (p. 360)

8. Approximately 75% of individuals diagnosed as borderline personalities are women. T/ F (p. 361)

9. There are cases of generalized social phobia without avoidant personality disorder, but very few cases of avoidant personality disorder without generalized social phobia. T/ F (p. 363)

10. A person with dependent personality disorder may fail to get appropriately angry with others because of a fear of losing their support. T/ F   (p. 363)

11. People with obsessive-compulsive personality disorder have lifestyles characterized by overconscientiousness, inflexibility, and perfectionism. T / F   (p. 364)

12. No systematic studies of treating people yet exist for paranoid, schizoid, narcissistic, or histrionic disorders. T/ F   (p. 368)

13. The psychopath's conscience seems to be severely retarded or nonexistent. T/ F (p. 370)

ESSAY QUESTIONS

1. Perhaps more misdiagnoses occur in diagnosing personality disorders than any other category. Why is this? Explain. (pp. 351-52)

2. Antisocial personality disorder can be an extremely serious affliction, and persons suffering from it can be a danger to society. Name and explain the criteria that need to be met before a diagnosis can be made. (p. 368)

3. People with psychopathic and antisocial personalities are extremely difficult to treat.
    Why is this so? (pp. 376-77)

WEB LINKS TO ITEMS OR CONCEPTS DISCUSSED IN THIS CHAPTER

Antisocial Personality Disorder

  www.mentalhealth.com/dis/p20-pe04.html

  faculty.ncwc.edu/toconnor/401/401lect16.htm

  www.geocities.com/ptypes/antisocialpd.html

Borderline Personality Disorder

  www.bpdcentral.com/

  www.mentalhealth.com/dis/p20-pe05.html

  www.psycom.net/depression.central.borderline.html

Narcissistic Personality Disorder

  www.mentalhealth.com/dis/p20-pe07.html

  www.mental-health-today.com/narcissistic/

  www.geocities.com/ptypes/narcissisticpd.html

Paranoid Personality Disorder

  www.geocities.com/ptypes/paranoidpd.html

CRISS-CROSS

Now that you know all there is to know about this chapter, here's your opportunity to put that knowledge to work.

CRISS-CROSS CLUES

Across

2. impulsiveness, mood shifts
6. mistrust of others, sees self as blameless
8. self-dramatization, overconcern with attractiveness
9. disregards and violates the rights of others
10. antisocial, impulsive, socially deviant lifestyle
11. perfectionist, excessive concern with order, rules

Down

1. peculiar; oddities of perception and speech
3. hypersensitivity to rejection
4. grandiosity, self-promoting
5. impaired social relationships, no desire for relationships
7. subordination of needs to keep others involved in relationships

Puzzle created with Puzzlemaker at DiscoverySchool.com

Substance-Related Disorders

BEFORE YOU READ

Many of America's health problems are due to self-injurious practices, such as excessive drinking, smoking, and overeating. Such behaviors are considered addictive when these substances or activities, as well as others, are needed and used pathologically.

Chapter 12 covers the major addictive disorders, focusing primarily on alcohol and drug abuse and dependence. Then it turns to drug categories (narcotics, stimulants, sedatives, hallucinogens), all of which can lead to an additive behavior, and which can cause destructive effects to the body. Additionally, it discusses Ecstasy, a new chic drug that has recently emerged.

A great deal of background information is presented to help document the extent of the various addictive behaviors and their costs to society. Treatment approaches that have been developed for each addiction are then described.

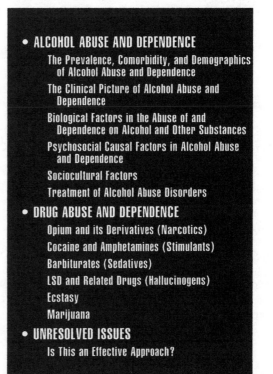

- ALCOHOL ABUSE AND DEPENDENCE

    The Prevalence, Comorbidity, and Demographics of Alcohol Abuse and Dependence

    The Clinical Picture of Alcohol Abuse and Dependence

    Biological Factors in the Abuse of and Dependence on Alcohol and Other Substances

    Psychosocial Causal Factors in Alcohol Abuse and Dependence

    Sociocultural Factors

    Treatment of Alcohol Abuse Disorders

- DRUG ABUSE AND DEPENDENCE

    Opium and its Derivatives (Narcotics)

    Cocaine and Amphetamines (Stimulants)

    Barbiturates (Sedatives)

    LSD and Related Drugs (Hallucinogens)

    Ecstasy

    Marijuana

- UNRESOLVED ISSUES

    Is This an Effective Approach?

OBJECTIVES

After reading this chapter, you should be able to:

1. Outline the major divisions of psychoactive substance-related disorders, define alcohol abuse and alcohol dependence, summarize the many negative consequences of alcohol for both the individual and society, and indicate the prevalence and gender ratio of excessive drinking.

2. Describe the clinical picture of alcohol abuse, including the biological and psychological effects of chronic consumption of alcohol.

3. Review the biological, psychosocial, and sociocultural contributors to alcohol abuse and dependence.

4. Summarize the research findings on the results of treatment and relapse prevention for alcohol-dependent persons.

5. List the specific drugs and their effects, summarize theories of causal factors, and review treatments for the following drugs of abuse: opium and its derivatives, cocaine and amphetamines, barbiturates, LSD and other hallucinogens, marijuana, and caffeine and nicotine.

6. Discuss the controversy surrounding controlled drinking versus abstinence.

AS YOU READ

Answers can be found in the Answer Key at the end of the book.

KEY WORDS

Each of the words below is important in understanding the concepts presented in this chapter. Write the definition next to each of the words.

addictive behavior (p. 384)

psychoactive drugs (p. 384)

toxicity (p. 384)

substance abuse (p. 384)

substance dependence (p. 384)

tolerance (p. 384)

withdrawal symptoms (p. 384)

alcoholism (p. 385)

alcoholic (p. 385)

mesocorticolimbic dopamine pathway (MCLP) (p. 391)

caffeine (p. 403)

nicotine (p. 403)

opium (p. 406)

morphine (p. 406)

heroin (p. 406)

endorphins (p. 408)

methadone (p. 409)

cocaine (p. 409)

amphetamine (p. 410)

barbiturates (p. 411)

hallucinogens (p. 413)

LSD (p. 413)

Ecstasy (p. 414)

mescaline (p. 414)

methamphetamine (p. 414)

psilocybin (p. 414)

marijuana (p. 415)

hashish (p. 415)

pathological gambling (p. 416)

WHO'S WHO AND WHAT'S WHAT—MATCHING
Match the following drugs with their effects.

Drug	Effects
_____ Alcohol	A. intoxicant found in coffee and chocolate
_____ Caffeine	B. mild hallucinogen from a plant; can produce mild euphoria or unpleasant experiences depending upon the mood of the user
_____ Nicotine	C. synthesized drug first used in inhalant for stuffy noses; recalled when discovered that customers were chewing the wicks for "kicks;" newer, more powerful preparation is methedrine, also known as speed
_____ Ecstasy	D. a hallucinogen and a stimulant; popular among young adults
_____ Opium	E. poisonous alkaloid associated with 14% of all deaths in the U.S.
_____ Morphine	F. hallucinogen distorts sensory images, causing users to see or hear things differently and unusually
_____ Heroin	G. the major problem drug in the U.S.; associated with over half of highway deaths, 50% of all rapes, 40-50% of murders, 40% of all assaults
_____ Methadone	H. drug from a plant, costly, a "high" for the affluent
_____ Cocaine	I. a mixture of about 18 alkaloids; morphine and heroin made from this
_____ Amphetamine	J. derived from peyote cactus; hallucinogen used for centuries
_____ Barbiturates	K. derived from opium; was used during Civil War as pain killer; legal as prescription only
_____ LSD	L. derived from opium; first used in cough syrup around 1900; highly addictive; illegal in U.S.
_____ Mescaline	M. addictive drug used as substitute for heroin during treatment
_____ Marijuana	N. sedatives, depressants that slow down the nervous system; large doses produce immediate sleep or death

SHORT ANSWERS

Provide brief answers to the following questions.

1. Discuss the relationship between being pregnant and drinking alcohol. (p. 388)

2. Discuss the two factors apparently involved in the overpowering hold that occurs in some people after only a few uses of a drug, such as opium, cocaine, or alcohol. (pp. 390-91)

3. Discuss the neurochemical process underlying addiction in the role the drug plays in activating the "pleasure pathway."   (p. 391)

4. The development of alcohol-related problems includes living in an environment that promotes use of the substance. Explain. (p. 393)

5. Is there an "alcoholic personality"—a type of character organization that predisposes a person to use alcohol, rather than some other defensive pattern of coping with stress? Explain.   (p. 394)

6. Discuss the immediate effects of mainlined or snorted heroin. (p. 407)

7. The view that cocaine users did not develop physiological dependence has changed over the past 20 years. Explore this change of view. (p. 409)

FILL IN THE BLANKS

Read the following and fill in the blanks. These questions are designed to help you focus on specific details.

1. _____ occurs when an individual develops a tolerance for a substance or exhibits _____ when it is not available. (p. 384)

2   Two major diagnostic classifications of addictive or substance-related disorders are those that involve _____ from prolonged and excessive ingestion of psychoactive substances and _____. (p. 384)

3. Two major categories of substance abuse disorders are substance _____ disorders and substance _____ disorders. (p. 384)

4. Alcohol abuse is associated with more than _____% the deaths and major injuries suffered in automobile accidents each year, with about _____% of all murders, _____% of all assaults, and more than _____% of all rapes. (p. 385)

5. People who abuse alcohol following periods of sobriety are known as _____. (p. 384)

6. Organic impairment, including brain shrinkage, occurs in a high proportion of people with alcohol dependency, especially among _____. (p. 385)

7.   Associated with a lower incidence of alcoholism are _____, _____, and _____. (p. 387)

8.   Not only do alcoholics become physiologically dependent on alcohol, they develop a powerful _____ as well. (p. 393)

9.   In acute intoxication, the initial focus is on _____, _____, and _____. (p. 398)

10. After a physiological craving for opium or one of its derivatives has been established, users find that they have become physiologically dependent on the drug in the sense that they _____ when they don't take. (p. 407)

11. In our society, a narcotics subculture exists in which addicts can obtain drugs and protect themselves against society's sanctions. Once young addicts join, they become _____, indifferent to their friends, and become _____, seeing drugs as a means of _____ and conventional values. (p. 408)

12. A person going through barbiturate withdrawal becomes _____ and manifests coarse tremors of the hands and face. Also _____, weakness, _____, vomiting, _____, rapid heart rate, _____, and loss of weight. An acute _____ may develop. (p. 413)

13. Ecstasy (MDMA) is both a _____ and a _____, and is considered to be a "_____" drug. (p. 414)

THE DOCTOR IS IN...PSYCHIATRIC HELP—5¢

Read the following scenarios and diagnose the client. Remember to look carefully at the criteria for the disorder before you make a decision as to the diagnosis. Make a list of other information you might need to help you understand the causal factors.

1.   You have been working with Tony, who is dependent on alcohol. He has had several problems with the law and has lost his job as a result of his drinking. His wife has told him that if he doesn't get help, she is going to leave. As Tony's therapist, how would you treat him? (pp. 398-403)

2.   Lupe brings her father, Martin, into to see you. She had gone to his house and found him asleep on the kitchen table, a bottle of pills and an alcoholic drink sitting near by. He is an older gentleman who about a year ago lost his wife to cancer. As you are talking, he tells you that he had been having difficulty sleeping until his doctor had given him something. These helped, but he found that having a drink made these work faster, and, since he was on a fixed income, the pills lasted longer even though the label said not to drink. Lupe tells you that her father has become very sluggish and is having sudden mood shifts. Lately, it seems that she is finding him this state more often.

What do you think Martin is taking and why? What are the potential dangers involved if something isn't done to help Martin? (pp. 411-413)

PICTURE THIS

Below are pictures that represent key people or concepts from the book. Write the answers on the line to the right of the clues.

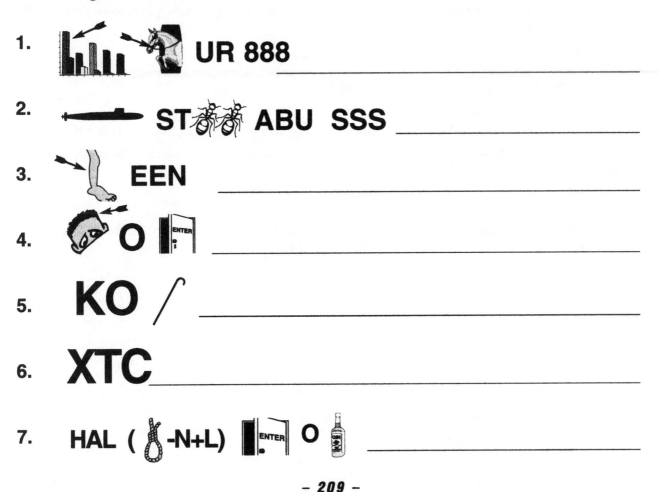

1.   ▪▪▪ 🐴 **UR 888** _____

2.   ▬ **ST** 🐜🐜 **ABU SSS** _____

3.   🦵 **EEN** _____

4.   😀 **O** [ENTER] _____

5.   **KO / ** _____

6.   **XTC** _____

7.   **HAL (🪢 -N+L)** [ENTER] **O** 🍾 _____

AFTER YOU READ

Answers can be found in the Answer Key at the end of the book.

PRACTICE TESTS

Take the following three multiple-choice tests to see how much you have comprehended from the chapter. Each represents roughly one-third of the chapter. As you study the chapter, use these to check your progress.

PRACTICE TEST NUMBER 1

1. As a problem facing our society today, addictive behavior is (p. 384)

    a.   just beginning to be understood and controlled.

    b.   one of the most pervasive and intransigent mental health problems.

    c.   overrated and over blown.

    d.   a severe problem only in lower income neighborhoods.

2. Substance abuse generally involves (p. 384)

    a.   use of a substance, resulting in potentially hazardous behavior.

    b.   a continued use, despite persistent social, psychological, occupational, or health problems.

    c.   a marked psychological need for increasing amounts of a substance to achieve the desired effects.

    d.   a and b.

3. Substance dependence involves (p. 384)

    a.   use of a substance, resulting in potentially hazardous behavior.

    b.   a continued use, despite persistent social, psychological, occupational, or health problems.

    c.   a marked psychological need for increasing amounts of a substance to achieve the desired effects.

    d.   b and c.

4. The need for increased amounts of a substance to achieve the desired effects, resulting from biological changes in the body, is (p. 384)

    a.   abuse.

    b.   dependence.

    c.   tolerance.

    d.   withdrawal.

5. Depression ranks high among the mental disorders often comorbid with alcoholism, not surprisingly, since alcohol (p. 385)

    a. speeds one up.

    b. activates the dancing gene.

    c. is a depressant.

    d. causes many problems, which is depressing.

6. When the blood-alcohol level reaches approximately 0.5 percent, the individual passes out, which is a good thing, because (p. 387)

    a. any more drinking would just be a waste of money.

    b. both dancing and driving at that level are pretty much out of the question.

    c. concentrations above 0.55 percent are usually lethal.

    d. all of the above.

7. The effects of alcohol vary for different drinkers, depending on (p. 387)

    a. their physical condition.

    b. the amount of food in their stomach.

    c. the duration of their drinking.

    d. all of the above.

8. A physiological effect of alcohol is (p. 387)

    a. a tendency toward decreased sexual inhibition, but lowered sexual performance.

    b. a lapse of memory—a blackout.

    c. headache, nausea, and fatigue of a hangover.

    d. all of the above.

9. Researchers believe that genetics may have a role in one's susceptibility to alcoholism because (p. 391)

    a. almost one-third of alcoholics in a study had at least one parent with an alcohol problem.

    b. females in a study were five times more likely to be alcoholic if both of their parents were alcoholic.

    c. children of alcoholic parents who had been adopted by nonalcoholic foster parents had nearly twice the number of alcohol problems by their late 20s as did a control group.

    d. all of the above.

10. Certain ethnic groups, particularly Asians and Native Americans, have abnormal physiological reactions to alcohol, known as "_____," including flushing of the skin, a drop in blood pressure, heart palpitations, and nausea. (p. 392)

    a. the fatal flaw

    b. alcohol flush reaction

    c. hypnotic effect

    d. pressure-and-palpitation flush reaction

PRACTICE TEST NUMBER 2

1. Stable family relationships and parental guidance are extremely important molding influences for children, and this stability is often _____ in families of substance abusers. (p. 393)

    a. lacking
    b. very strong
    c. inconsistent
    d. not discussed

2. About _____% of persons with schizophrenia have either alcohol or drug abuse dependency as well. (p. 394)

    a. 10
    b. 25
    c. 50
    d. 99.44

3. About _____ people die each year in the United States of alcohol poisoning. (p. 396)

    a. 42
    b. 650
    c. 4,000
    d. all of the above.

4. In cultures whose religious values restrict or prohibit the use of alcohol, the incidence of alcoholism is (p. 396)

    a. about the same as other groups.
    b. minimal.
    c. actually higher.
    d. unknown, as they refuse to discuss it.

5. In the Alcoholics Anonymous (AA) view (p. 401)

    a. one's alcoholism can be cured through group meetings and the understanding of peers.
    b. one is never cured but an alcoholic for life, whether or not one is drinking.
    c. the alcoholic is weak-willed and lacking in moral strength.
    d. having a drink or occasionally "falling off the wagon" is nothing to worry about.

6. Drug abuse and dependence are most common during (p. 403)

    a. adolescence and young adulthood.
    b. finals week.
    c. middle and pre-retirement age.
    d. all of the above.

7. A study of job satisfaction found that multiple drug use (polydrug), predicted impaired work functioning and job dissatisfaction (p. 404)

    a. up to three weeks.
    b. six months.
    c. a year.
    d. four years later.

8. Because morphine is so addictive, a chemical, called acetic anhydride, was added to it around the turn of the 20th century in hopes of converting it into a more controllable substance. This new mix was called (p. 406)

    a. aspirin.
    b. heroin.
    c. acetydride.
    d. the Whopper.

9. Opium and its derivatives, morphine, codeine, and heroin were outlawed in 1914 by (p. 406)

    a. President Woodrow Wilson.
    b. World War I.
    c. the Harrison Act.
    d. the Mann Act.

10. In a recent survey, about _____ Americans acknowledged having tried heroin and almost _____ people admitted using it withing the past 12 months. (p. 407)

    a. 120,000, 42
    b. one million, 77,000
    c. half a million, 6,500
    d. 2.4 million, 250,000

PRACTICE TEST NUMBER 3

1. Typically the life of a narcotic addict becomes increasingly centered on obtaining and using the drugs, so the addiction usually (p. 408)

    a. leads to socially maladaptive behavior.
    b. forces the addict to lie, steal, and associate with undesirable contacts.
    c. causes females to turn to prostitution as a means to finance their addiction.
    d. all of the above.

2. The most frequently cited reason for beginning to use heroin was (p. 408)

    a. pleasure.
    b. curiosity.
    c. peer pressure.
    d. all of the above.

3. In contrast to opiate derivatives, cocaine, which depress the action of the central nervous system, (p. 409)

    a. speeds it up.

    b. causes it to open.

    c. is very expensive.

    d. causes the dancing gene to increase its performance.

4. In 2000 about _____% of emergency room visits were cocaine related. (p. 409)

    a. 1.732

    b. 4

    c. 13

    d. 29

5. Many life problems experienced by cocaine abusers result, in part, from (p. 410)

    a. the low quality of people they are forced to deal with.

    b. the considerable amounts of money required to support their habits.

    c. disfunction and disinterest in sexual performance.

    d. fetal crack syndrome.

6. The earliest amphetamine—benzedrine—was first synthesized in 1927 and soon available in drugstores as an inhalant to relieve stuffy noses. However, it was soon withdrawn because (p. 410)

    a. it was so powerful that stuffy noses ceased to be a problem.

    b. some customers were chewing the wicks in the inhalers for "kicks."

    c. it didn't work.

    d. it was discovered that nutmeg worked just as well.

7. Curiously, amphetamines have _____ effect on many youngsters. (p. 411)

    a. a stimulating

    b. a calming

    c. an invigorating

    d. no

8. Methedrine, used in large amounts, can raise blood pressure (p. 411)

    a. enough to cause immediate death.

    b. slightly.

    c. over a period of time.

    d. none of the above. It does not raise blood pressure in any amount.

9. A common effect of barbiturates is (p. 411)

    a. slow speech.

    b. impaired decision making and problem solving.

    c. sudden mood shifts.

    d. all of the above.

10. Psychedelic drugs do not, in fact, "create" sensory images, but (p. 413)

    a. increase the effects.

    b. distort these, so that a person sees or hears things in different and unusual ways.

    c. categorizes odd events.

    d. none of the above.

COMPREHENSIVE PRACTICE TEST

The following tests are designed to give you an idea of how well you understood the entire chapter. There are three different types of tests: multiple-choice, true-false, and essay.

MULTIPLE-CHOICE

1. Alcohol abuse and dependency are _____ in the United States. (p. 385)

    a. problematical, but certainly not serious

    b. one of the most destructive and psychiatric disorders

    c. required at some Fraternities

    d. usually receding as a problem for adults and elders

2. The life expectancy with alcohol dependency is about _____ than that of the average citizen. (p. 385)

    a. 12 years shorter

    b. 12 years longer

    c. a couple of years shorter

    d. about the same, but it seems longer

3. In addition to various physical problems, an excessive drinker usually suffers from (p. 388)

    a. chronic fatigue, oversensitivity, and depression.

    b. lowered feelings of adequacy and worth, impaired reasoning and judgement, and gradual personality deterioration.

    c. coarse and inappropriate behavior, lowered pride and personal appearance, and becoming generally touchy and irritable,

    d. all of the above.

4. A number of investigators have pointed out that the typical alcohol abuser is (p. 394)

    a. unable or unwilling to tolerate tension and stress.

    b. discontented with his or her life.

    c. misunderstood and just looking for a good time.

    d. a and b.

5. Many young people begin to use alcohol, because they expect that it will (p. 395)

    a. lower tension and anxiety.

    b. increase their popularity.

    c. increase sexual desire and pleasure in life.

    d. all of the above.

6. Alcohol abuse and dependence are difficult to treat because (p. 398)

    a. many alcoholics refuse to admit they have a problem.

    b. they refuse to seek assistance before they "hit bottom."

    c. many leave treatment before therapy is completed.

    d. all of the above.

7. A multidisciplinary approach to the treatment of drinking problems appears to be most effective because (p. 398)

    a. the problems are often complex.

    b. researchers really aren't sure what works yet.

    c. a substance abuser's needs change as treatment progresses.

    d. a\ and b.

8. Caffeine and nicotine are (p. 403)

    a. drugs of dependence.

    b. mild stimulants.

    c. mild depressants.

    d. harmless pastimes.

9. In 2000, heroin overdose accounted for _____% of all drug episodes of emergency room admissions. (p. 407)

    a. 1.723

    b. 4

    c. 11

    d. 16

10. The use of opium derivatives over a period of time usually results in a physiological craving for the drug. The time required varies, but it has been estimated that continual use over a period of _____ is sufficient. (p. 407)

    a. 42 minutes

    b. two weeks

    c. 30 days

    d. a year

11. Strong doses of barbiturates cause sleep almost immediately. Excessive doses (p. 411)

    a. are lethal.

    b. are extremely enlightening.

    c. cause the dance gene to take control, and the user will not be able to sit still.

    d. none of the above.

12. A person undergoing a "bad trip" on LSD may (p. 414)

    a. ask for a ticket refund.

    b. set himself afire.

    c. jump off a building.

    d. b and c.

13. Ecstasy users have been found to be more likely to (p. 414)

    a. use marijuana.

    b. engage in binge drinking.

    c. have multiple sexual partners.

    d. all of the above.

14. Until the late 1960s, marijuana use in the United States was confined largely to (p. 415)

    a. members of lower socioeconomic minority groups.

    b. people in the entertainment and related fields.

    c. British rock groups.

    d. a and b.

15. Continued use of high dosages of marijuana over time tends to produce (p. 416)

    a. art.

    b. junk mistaken as art.

    c. lethargy and passivity.

    d. none of the above.

TRUE – FALSE

1. Tolerance for a substance is the need for less and less to achieve the desired effect. T / F (p. 384)

2. Substance dependence means that an individual will show tolerance for a drug and/or withdrawal symptoms when the drug is unavailable. T / F (p. 384)

3. One in seven people meet the criteria for alcohol abuse. T / F (p. 385)

4. Men are about five times more likely to have an alcohol problem then women. T / F (p. 386)

5. In a study, college freshmen from families with alcohol abusing parents viewed their families as less healthy and had more problematic family relationships than those with nonalcohol abusing parents. T / F (p. 393)

6. There is a strong association between antisocial personality disorder and alcohol, aggression, and high rates of substance abuse. T / F (p. 394)

7. Excessive use of alcohol is one of the most frequent causes of divorce in the United States. T / F (p. 395)

8. Users of opium derivatives gradually build up a tolerance to the drug, so that increasingly larger amounts are needed to achieve the desired effects. T / F (p. 407)

9. The ill health and general personality deterioration often found in opium addiction do not result directly from the pharmacological effects of the drug, but are usually products of the sacrifice of money, proper diet, social position, and self-respect as an addict becomes more desperate to procure the required daily dosage. T / F (p. 408)

10. Opiate addicts were found to be highly impulsive and showed an inability to delay gratification. T / F (p. 408)

11. Addicts often dread the discomfort of withdrawal, but in a hospital setting, it is less abrupt and usually involves the administration of a medication that eases the distress. T / F (p. 408)

12. Amphetamines were initially considered to be "wonder pills" that helped people stay alert, and were used by both the Allied and German soldiers to ward off fatigue during World War II. T / F (p. 410)

ESSAY QUESTIONS

1. Alcohol has complex and seemingly contradictory effects on the brain from the activation of the brain's "pleasure areas" to the health risks and degradation that can result from heavy and long-term usage. Discuss this, particularly in relation to the items below.   (pp. 387-91)

   a.   physiological effects

   b.   mood and realities

   c.   pregnancy

   d.   chronic use

   e.   dependence

   f.   organic damage

   g.   physical and mental decline

2. A controversy exists between whether alcoholics need to give up drinking altogether or whether they can learn to drink moderately, with some new research on one side and groups like AA on the other. Discuss this. (pp. 400-01)

3. Withdrawal from heroin can be agonizing or not even very painful. It does appear to be an interesting experience, at the very least. Explain this. (pp. 407-08)

WEB LINKS TO ITEMS OR CONCEPTS DISCUSSED IN THIS CHAPTER

Substance abuse

www.samhsa.gov/

www.samhsa.gov/centers/csap/csap.html

www.icpsr.umich.edu/SAMHDA/

Ecstasy

www.nida.nih.gov/Infofax/ecstasy.html

Alcoholism

www.niaaa.nih.gov/

www.ncadd.org

alcoholism.about.com/

CRISS-CROSS

Now that you know all there is to know about this chapter, here's your opportunity to put that knowledge to work.

CRISS-CROSS CLUES

Across

3. involves marked physiological need for a substance and produces withdrawal symptoms, if unavailable
5. opium derivative; removed from medical practice
7. the need for increasing amounts of a substance
9. widely used poisonous alkaloid; very addictive; difficult withdrawal; causes many deaths annually
10. drug used as replacement for heroin during treatment
11. the poisonous nature of a substance
12. grows as a plant, highly addictive; morphine and heroin are derived from it

Down

1. pathological use resulting in potentially hazardous behavior, or persistent social or health problems
2. behavior based on the pathological need for a substance
4. thought to be a mild pick-me-up, has intoxicating and/or withdrawal potential
6. hallucinogen and stimulant popular as a party drug currently
8. a person with a serious drinking problem

Puzzle created with Puzzlemaker at DiscoverySchool.com

Sexual Variants, Abuse, And Dysfunctions

BEFORE YOU READ

"Sexuality is a central concern of our lives, influencing with whom we fall in love and mate, and how happy we are with them and with ourselves." This quote from your textbook sets the stage for Chapter 13. Sexuality is a often a difficult issue to deal with, because it is something that is very private, as in a couple dealing with a sexual dysfunction, and at the same time, very public, as in child abuse and rape.

Chapter 13 opens with an introduction discussing the enormous variability within and between cultures in sexual practices and attitudes, particularly homosexuality, which is not viewed in DSM-IV as a mental disorder. The chapter then covers three separate sections that are related to sexual behavior: sexual variants, sexual abuse, and sexual dysfunctions.

The first discusses paraphilias, in which unusual objects, rituals, or situations have become centrally important to the person's full sexual satisfaction. It also deals with gender-identity disorders, in which the person strongly rejects his or her biological sex and wishes to be of the opposite sex. Some of these behaviors are considered minor criminal offenses, e.g., exhibitionism or voyeurism, as well as being included as mental disorders in DSM-IV. The next section treats the major crimes of sexual abuse: childhood sexual abuse, pedophilia, incest, and rape. Only one of these (pedophilia) is listed as a mental disorder in DSM-IV, though the victims of the crimes are, of course, at increased risk for mental disorders.

The third section concerns sexual dysfunctions—problems that may interfere with an individual's full enjoyment of sexual relations. The sexual dysfunctions are not mental disorders but are simply problems that interfere with full sexual enjoyment and are readily treated.

- **SOCIOCULTURAL INFLUENCES ON SEXUAL PRACTICES AND STANDARDS**
    - Case 1: Degeneracy and Abstinence Theory
    - Case 2: Ritualized Homosexuality in Melanesia
    - Case 3: Homosexuality and American Psychiatry
- **SEXUAL AND GENDER VARIANTS**
    - The Paraphilias
    - Causal Factors and Treatments for Paraphilias
    - Gender Identity Disorders
- **SEXUAL ABUSE**
    - Childhood Sexual Abuse
    - Pedophilia
    - Incest
    - Rape
    - Treatment and Recidivism of Sex Offenders
- **SEXUAL DYSFUNCTIONS**
    - Dysfunction of Sexual Desire
    - Dysfunctions of Sexual Arousal
    - Orgasmic Disorders
    - Dysfunctions Involving Sexual Pain
- **UNRESOLVED ISSUES**
    - How Harmful is Child Sexual Abuse?

OBJECTIVES

After reading this chapter, you should be able to:

1. Provide a number of examples of sociocultural influences in sexual practices and cultural standards and values.

2. Define, give examples of, and describe the clinical features of the following paraphilias: fetishism, transvestic fetishism, voyeurism, exhibitionism, sadism, and masochism.

3. Discuss the most effective treatments for paraphilias, and summarize causal factors implicated in their etiology.

4. Define and describe the clinical features and treatment of the gender identity disorders (gender identity disorder of childhood, transsexualism).

5. Review what is known about the frequency and nature of childhood sexual abuse. Discuss the controversies surrounding childhood testimony regarding sexual abuse and adult "recovered memories" of childhood sexual abuse.

6. Define pedophilia and summarize what is known about pedophiles.

7. Review what is known about the frequency and nature of incest.

8. Summarize what is known about rape and rapists, and discuss the issues regarding the frequency of rape and the motivation of rapists. Describe attempts to treat sex offenders.

9. Define the sexual dysfunctions, describe their general features, review etiological theories, and summarize the major approaches to treatment.

10. Knowledgeably discuss the difficulty of deciding the extent of the harm caused by childhood sexual abuse.

AS YOU READ

Answers can be found in the Answer Key at the end of the book.

KEY WORDS

Each of the words below is important in understanding the concepts presented in this Chapter. Write the definition next to each of the words.

abstinence theory (p. 423)

degeneracy theory (p. 423)

fetishism (p. 428)

paraphilias (p. 428)

transvestic fetish (pp. 428-29)

autogynephilia (p. 429)

exhibitionism (p. 430)

voyeurism (p. 430)

sadism (p. 431)

masochism (pp. 431-32)

gender dysphoria (p. 433)

gender identity disorder (p. 433)

transsexualism (p. 434)

sexual abuse (p. 436)

pedophilia (p. 440)

incest (p. 441)

rape (p. 441)

desire phase (p. 447)

resolution (p. 447)

sexual dysfunction (p. 447)

sexual aversion disorder (p. 448)

excitement phase (p. 447)

orgasm (p. 447)

hypoactive sexual desire disorder (p. 448)

male erectile disorder (pp. 448-49)

female sexual arousal disorder (p. 450)

female orgasmic disorder (p. 451)

male orgasmic disorder (p. 451)

premature ejaculation (p. 451)

dyspreunia (p. 452)

vaginismus (p. 452)

WHO'S WHO AND WHAT'S WHAT—MATCHING

Match the following person or term with the appropriate answer.

Person/Term	Answer
_____ Simon Tissot	A. sexual activity with a person who is legally defined to be under the age of consent
_____ Reverend Sylvester Graham	B. dangerous form of masochism that involves self-strangulation to the point of oxygen deprivation
_____ Dr. John Harvey Kellogg	C. anonymously published book in London that started the hypothesis that masturbation caused insanity
_____ Onania, or the Heinous Sin of Self Pollution	D. advocated the abstinence theory during the 1830s
_____ Havelock Ellis and Magnus Hirschfeld	E. said, during the late nineteenth and early twentieth centuries, that homosexuality was natural and nonpathological
_____ Evelyn Hooker	F. erectile problem in young men where erection will not diminish, even after a couple of hours
_____ autoerotic asphyxia	G. Swiss physician who developed the "degeneracy theory"
_____ statutory rape	H. wrote about the 39 signs of the "secret vice" (masturbation) and made a fortune publishing books discouraging masturbation; also urged people to eat more cereal
_____ priapism	I. demonstrated that psychologists could not tell the difference between psychological test results of homosexuals and heterosexuals

Match the dysfunction with its characteristic.

Dysfunction

of Sexual Desire

_____ Hypoactive sexual desire disorder

_____ Sexual aversion disorder

of Sexual Arousal

_____ Male erectile disorder

_____ Female sexual arousal disorder

of Orgasm

_____ Premature ejaculation

_____ Male orgasmic disorder

_____ Female orgasmic disorder

Sexual Pain Disorders

_____ Vaginismus

_____ Dyspareunia

Characteristics

A. inability to achieve or maintain an erection

B. difficulty in achieving orgasm, either manually or during sexual intercourse

C. painful coitus; may have either organic or psychological basis

D. little or no sexual drive or interest

E. nonresponsiveness to erotic stimulation, physically and emotionally

F. inability to ejaculate during intercourse

G. involuntary muscle spasm at the entrance to the vagina preventing penetration

H. total lack of interest in sex and avoidance of sexual contact

I. unsatisfactorally brief period between the beginning of sexual stimulation and ejaculation

SHORT ANSWERS

Provide brief answers to the following questions.

1. Why has research about childhood sexual abuse increased in the past decade? (p. 436)

2. What are the differences between intrafamilial and extrafamilial child molesters? (p. 441)

FILL IN THE BLANKS

Read the following and fill in the blanks. These questions are designed to help you focus on specific details.

1. Despite the substantial _____ in sexual _____ and _____ in different times and places, people typically behave as though the sexual _____ of their time and place were the only correct approach, and they tend to be _____ of sexual _____. (p. 423)

2. Many people probably have some _____ inclinations, which are checked by practical considerations, such as the possibility of being _____, and by the _____ attitudes concerning the right to _____. (p. 430)

3. Paraphilic _____ and _____, including activities, such as pinching, biting, whipping, sticking with a needle, or slashing with a razor, are the _____ or _____ means to _____ gratification seem to be rare. (p. 431)

4. Two etiological facts, which are important concerning paraphilia, are that nearly all persons with paraphilias are _____, and that people with paraphilias often have _____. (pp. 432-33)

5. Many researchers believe that male vulnerability to forming _____ associations with _____ stimuli is a result of _____ and _____ conditioning and/or social learning through _____ and _____. (p. 433)

6. The research by Ceci and colleagues on what influences children's testimony concluded: "_____thinking about a _____ event can lead some preschool children to produce _____, _____ reports that _____ are unable to discern from their reports of actual events." (p. 438)

7. Perhaps the most common type of pedophile is someone who is _____, _____, and _____ and may be drawn to children because he feels in _____ only relative to them. (p. 440)

8. Incest is more common than is generally believed, in part, because many _____ are reluctant to report it or do not consider themselves _____. (p. 441)

9. Feminist scholars have challenged the view that the rapist is motivated by _____ and believe that rape is motivated by the need to _____, assert _____, and to _____ the victim. (p. 442)

10. What characterizes both date rapists and incarcerated rapist is _____ and an _____. (p. 443)

11. Barlow and colleagues believe that sexually dysfunctional men and women get distracted by _____ _____ about their _____ performance, not _____ per se. (p. 449)

THE DOCTOR IS IN...PSYCHIATRIC HELP—5¢

Read the following scenarios and diagnose the client. Remember to look carefully at the criteria for the disorder before you make a decision as to the diagnosis. Make a list of other information you might need to help you understand the causal factors.

1. Jim was referred to you by the courts. He was caught after breaking into a woman's house to steal her underwear. Jim says that he is almost relieved at being caught as his problem was getting worse. He used the underwear to fantasize while he masturbated. You ask him how long this behavior has been going on and he tells you that he has had these feelings since as an adolescent, he found one of his sister's girlfriend's underwear in the bathroom (he had a crush on her).

    How would you diagnosis Jim and why? (p. 428)

2. Darla comes to your office. She is an attractive female in her late 40s. She begins by telling you that she was born a boy but always felt like a girl. She never wanted to play boy games, preferred to be with girls, and often wished she would wake up in the morning and find that she had become a girl. She began cross-dressing almost 20 years ago and has lived full-time as a female for the last 10 years. Darla has been on hormones for several years and is looking to have surgery. She is employed as a secretary and has passed as a woman for many years.

    How would you diagnose Darla? Why and what would you recommend as treatment? (p. 433-436)

3. Susan and Ben come to your office seeking couple's counseling. They are both frustrated with their sexual relations. Susan experiences involuntary spasms around her vagina when they attempt to have intercourse. It is very painful and she can't go on. This has begun to affect Ben and he has started to have erectile dysfunctions. They love each other very much and want to work this out.

    How would diagnose the problem and what else would you want to know about the couple? (p. 452)

PICTURE THIS

Below are pictures that represent key people or concepts from the book. Write the answers on the line to the right of the clues.

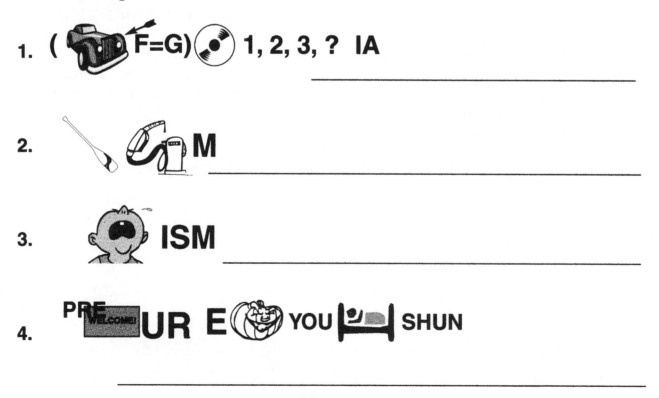

1. (🚗↗F=G) 💿 1, 2, 3, ? IA
    _____

2. 🥄 ⛽ M
    _____

3. 👶 ISM
    _____

4. PRE⬛UR E🎃 YOU 🛏 SHUN
    _____

AFTER YOU READ

PRACTICE TESTS

Take the following three multiple-choice tests to see how much you have comprehended from the chapter. Each represents roughly one-third of the chapter. As you study the chapter, use these to check your progress.

PRACTICE TEST NUMBER 1

1. This society in the South Pacific holds two beliefs that are reflected in their sexual practices: semen conservation and female pollution. (p. 424)
   a. Bali
   b. Melanesia
   c. Sambia
   d. Jamacian

2. Homosexuality was removed as a sexual deviation from the DSM in (p. 424)
   a. 1966.
   b. 1973.
   c. 1981.
   d. 1977.

3. Glenn is a 35-year-old married man who cross-dresses. He becomes sexually aroused while looking at himself dressed as a woman. His wife is aware of his cross-dressing and doesn't have a problem with it. Glenn is considered to have a (pp. 428-29)
   a. transvestic fetish.
   b. exhibitionistic fetish.
   c. voyeuristic fetish.
   d. fetish fetish.

4. A Peeping Tom is another name for someone who is a(n) (p. 430)
   a. exhibitionist.
   b. transvestite.
   c. erotophilia.
   d. voyeur.

5. The legal term for _____ is "indecent exposure." (p. 430)
   a. exhibitionism
   b. transvestism
   c. erotophilism
   d. voyeurism

6. Steve finds great sexual pleasure in being bound by his lover and humiliated—and sometimes whipped. He has participated in this behavior for over two years now. Steve would be considered a(n) (pp. 431-32)
   a. sadist.
   b. transvestite.
   c. exhibitionist.
   d. masochist.

7. The most common outcome of boys with gender identity disorder appears to be (p. 433)
   a. transsexualism.
   b. gender confusion.
   c. heterosexualism.
   d. homosexuality.

8. _____ appears in genetic males and is a paraphilia characterized by sexual arousal at the thought or fantasy of being a woman. (p. 435)
   a. Autoerotic
   b. Autogynephilic
   c. Gynoplasty
   d. None of the above

9. The accuracy of children's testimony is an issue, because children (p. 437)
   a. are susceptible to the influence of others.
   b. can't always distinguish fact from fantasy.
   c. are not called on to testify all that often.
   d. a and b.

10. _____ is one of the most important and interesting contemporary controversies in the domain of psychopathology and mental health. (p. 440)
   a. Recovered memory
   b. Homosexuality
   c. Gender identity disorder
   d. b and c

PRACTICE TEST NUMBER 2

1. _____ is diagnosed when an adult has recurrent, intense sexual urges or fantasies about sexual activity with a prepubertal child. (p. 440)
   a. Paraphilia
   b. Pedophilia
   c. Erotophilia
   d. Fetishism

2. The typical victim of a pedophile is a girl between the ages of (p. 440)
   a. 5 and 8.
   b. 15 and 18.
   c. 12 and 15.
   d. 8 and 11.

3. _____ is sexual activity that occurs under actual or threatened forcible coercion of one person by another. (p. 441)
   a. Incest
   b. Rape
   c. Sadism
   d. Masochism

4. According to the figure 13.1 on page 441, who of the following was most likely to force a woman to perform a sexual act? (p. 441)

    a. someone she knew well
    b. acquaintance
    c. stranger
    d. someone she was in love with

5. What percentage of rapes are committed in the rapist's neighborhood? (p. 442)

    a. 50
    b. 80
    c. 45
    d. 38

6. About how many rapes are single-offender rapes in which the victim may know the offender? (p. 442)

    a. one-third
    b. one-half
    c. two-thirds
    d. one-quarter

7. The psychological impact of rape was first called (p. 442)

    a. post-traumatic stress disorder.
    b. rape stress disorder.
    c. acute trauma syndrome.
    d. rape trauma syndrome.

8. The psychological impact of rape is now called (p. 442)

    a. post-traumatic stress disorder.
    b. rape stress disorder.
    c. acute trauma syndrome.
    d. rape trauma syndrome.

9. _____ rape is a favorite tactic of defense attorneys, which some police and court jurisdictions still believe, even though it is a myth. (p. 442)

    a. Victim-credibility
    b. Victim-consent
    c. Victim-precipitated
    d. None of the above

10. Rapists show some deficits in their cognitive appraisals of women's (p. 444)

    a. feelings.
    b. intentions.
    c. boundaries.
    d. a and b.

PRACTICE TEST NUMBER 3

1. Recently, both explanations and treatments of sexual dysfunction have become increasingly (p. 447)

    a. psychological.
    b. behavioral.
    c. physiological.
    d. less obvious.

2. The DSM-IV-TR says that sexual dysfunction can occur in which phase? (p. 447)

    a. desire
    b. excitement
    c. orgasm
    d. all of the above

3. Hypoactive sexual desire disorder seems to have a very strong _____ component, especially for women. (p. 448)

    a. psychological
    b. physiological
    c. behavioral
    d. none of the above

4. In this type of sexual desire dysfunction, the person shows extreme avoidance of all genital sexual contact with a partner. (p. 448)

    a. hypoactive sexual desire disorder
    b. sexual aversion disorder
    c. erectile insufficiency
    d. sexual repulsion disorder

5. Sexual interest in men and women depends on (p. 448)

    a. estrogen.
    b. dopamine.
    c. seratonin.
    d. testosterone.

6. The general neglect of research and treatment of female sexual dysfunction is an implicit attitude that women don't care about (p. 448)

    a. their bodies.
    b. their relationships.
    c. sex.
    d. the NFL.

7. _____ was formerly called impotence. (p. 448)

    a. Erectile contraction disorder
    b. Male erectile disorder
    c. Priapism
    d. all of the above

8. Masters, Johnson and Kaplan, believed that erectile dysfunction was primarily a function of _____ about sexual performance. (p. 449)

    a. excitement
    b. interest
    c. anxiety
    e. fantasizing

9. Viagra will promote an erection only if _____ is present. (p. 450)

    a. a partner
    b. sexual desire
    c. an opportunity
    d. all of the above

10. Female sexual arousal depends on the neurotransmitter known as (pp. 450-51)

    a. GABA.
    b. Dopamine.
    c. VIP.
    d. SEX.

COMPREHENSIVE PRACTICE TEST

The following tests are designed to give you an idea of how well you understood the entire chapter. There are three different types of tests: multiple-choice, true-false, and essay.

MULTIPLE-CHOICE

1. The major reason that there are fewer sex researchers than other researchers is (p. 422)

    a. sexual taboos.
    b. sexual issues are controversial.
    c. nobody is interested in sexual issues.
    d. a and b.

2. The _____ theory, developed in the 1750s, had the central belief that semen was necessary for masculine characteristics and physical and sexual vigor in men, thus masturbation and patronizing prostitutes were considered harmful. (p. 423)

    a. degeneracy
    b. abstinence
    c. onanistic
    d. semen conservation

3. During what decade did the American Medical Association declare that masturbation was a normal part of adolescent behavior, and the Boy Scouts do away with their antimasturbation warnings? (p. 424)

    a. 1960s
    b. 1950s
    c. 1980s
    d. 1970s

4. The DSM-IV-TR criteria for this group of disorders is a persistent pattern, lasting at least six months, that causes significant distress or impairment, in which unusual objects, rituals, or situations are required for full sexual satisfaction. (p. 428)

    a. pedophilias
    b. paraphilias
    c. erotophilias
    d. all of the above

5. Ted Bundy and Jeffrey Dahmer were cited in your text book as extreme examples of this paraphilia. (p. 431)

    a. masochism
    b. sadism
    c. voyeurism
    d. frotteurism

6. Sexual abuse includes (p. 436)

    a. pedophilia.
    b. rape.
    c. incest.
    d. All of the above.

7. Although short-term consequences of childhood sexual abuse include fears, PTSD, sexual inappropriateness, and poor self-esteem, approximately _____ of sexually abused children show no symptoms. (p. 436)

    a. one-half
    b. a quarter
    c. two-thirds
    d. one-third

8. Long-term consequences of childhood sexual abuse may include (p. 436)

    a. dissociative symptoms.
    b. somatization disorder.
    c. borderline personality disorder.
    d. all of the above.

9. Culturally prohibited relations between family members, such as brother and sister or a parent and child, are known as (p. 441)

    a. rape.
    b. acquaintance rape.
    c. incest.
    d. paraphilia.

10. This is the most common form of incest but it is rarely reported. (p. 441)

    a. father-daughter
    b. mother-son
    c. uncle-niece
    d. brother-sister

11. According to the FBI Uniform Crime Reports, the greatest concentration of rapists arrested are between _____ years old. (p. 443)

    a. 18 and 24

    b. 25 and 35

    c. 15 and 20

    d. 16 and 23

12. It is difficult to establish the prevalence rates for rape, because studies may (p. 442)

    a. vary in the definitions used.

    b. vary in the way information is gathered.

    c. not have enough subjects.

    d. a and b.

13. Studies done by Raymond Knight and Robert Prentky have shown that all rapists actually have _____ motives. (p. 442)

    a. empathetic

    b. aggressive

    c. sexual

    d. b and c

14. _____ is most likely to occur after a lengthy abstinence and is the most common male sexual dysfunction. (p. 451)

    a. impotence

    b. male erectile disorder

    c. male orgasmic disorder

    d. premature ejaculation

15. When treating female orgasmic disorder, it is important to distinguish between a _____ and a _____ dysfunction. (p. 452)

    a. past, present

    b. subjective, objective

    c. lifelong, situational

    d. interest, disinterest

16. _____ in women is more likely to have an obvious organic basis. (p. 452)

    a. Female orgasmic disorder

    b. Female sexual arousal disorder

    c. Vaginismus

    d. Dyspareunia

TRUE – FALSE

1. Special caution must be taken when classifying sexual practices as "abnormal" or "deviant."   T / F (p. 422)

2. The belief that homosexuality is a mental illness has been associated with people's discomfort conceerning the sexual behaviors of homosexual people. T / F (p. 427)

3.   Nearly all of the people with paraphilias are female.   T / F   (p. 428)

4.   Fetishes only cause overt harm to others when accompanied by illegal acts like theft or destruction of property.   T / F   (p. 430)

5.   Voyeurism is the most common sexual offense reported to the police in the United States, Canada, and Europe.   T / F   (p. 430)

6.   The vast majority of the studies concerning paraphilias have been with men who have not committed any offense, but have come into clinics to participate in research.   T / F (p. 433)

7.   Sexual abuse is sexual contact that involves physical or psychological coercion or at least one individual who cannot reasonably consent to the contact.   T / F   (p. 436)

8.   Research has shown that the use of anatomically correct dolls greatly increases the accuracy of three- or four-year olds' reports of what happened to them.   T / F   (p. 439)

9.   The incest taboo is virtually universal among human societies.   T / F   (p. 441)

10.   If the partner is under 18, but consents, it can't be considered statutory rape.   T / F   (p. 442)

11.   Women who are repeat victims of rape tend to be victims in situations other than rape. T / F   (p. 443)

12.   Conviction rates for rape are low.   T / F   (p. 444)

13.   Megan's Law, intended to protect potential victims, has also encouraged harassment of sex offenders.   T / F   (p. 445)

14.   A high percentage of people will never experience a sexual dysfunction in their life time. T / F   (p. 448)

ESSAY QUESTIONS

1.   Discuss the types of treatment that are used with sex offenders (psychological, biological, surgical), the goals and effectiveness. (pp. 444-46)
     Goals:

     Therapies:

2.   What were some of the conclusions of Bruce Rind's research on the association between early sexual experiences and mental health in young adulthood? (p. 453)

WEB LINKS TO ITEMS OR CONCEPTS DISCUSSED IN THIS CHAPTER

Pedophilia

www.geocities.com/ericw_970/

www.time.com/time/magazine/article/ 0,9171,1101020429-232584,00.html

www.usnews.com/usnews/issue/020422/opinion/22john.htm

Gender identity disorder

www.athealth.com/Consumer/disorders/GenderIden.html

www.mental-health-today.com/gender/

www.behavenet.com/capsules/disorders/genderiddis.htm

CRISS-CROSS

Now that you know all there is to know about this
chapter, here's your opportunity to put that
knowledge to work.

CRISS-CROSS CLUES

Across

3. culturally prohibited sexual relations between family members
4. third sexual phase, resulting in the release of sexual tension and peak of sexual pleasure
6. obtaining sexual gratification involving the use of some inanimate object (shoes, for instance)
7. experiencing sexual gratification by inflicting pain and cruelty
9. when an adult has sexual urges, fantasies, or activity with a prepubertal child
10. persons with gender identity disorder wishing to change their sex
11. sexual arousal by the thought of being a woman (males only)
12. behaviors involving exposure of genitals to others in inappropriate circumstances

Down

1. involuntary spasm of the muscles at the entrance to the vagina, preventing penetration
2. receiving sexual fantasies and behavior while observing unsuspecting females undressing or couples having sex
5. experiencing sexual stimulation from pain and degradation
8. sexual contact that involves physical or psychological coercion

Puzzle created with Puzzlemaker at DiscoverySchool.com

CHAPTER FOURTEEN

Schizophrenia and Other Psychotic Disorders

BEFORE YOU READ

The schizophrenias include some of the most extreme deviations of psychopathology possible. For this reason, this condition fascinates many people, including psychologists. Because schizophrenia involves disorders in thought, and perception, and affect motor behavior and social relationships, researchers have hoped that the study of schizophrenia—where the processes have broken down—might, in turn, lead to a better understanding of unimpaired psychological functioning.

Several different types of schizophrenia are described in Chapter 14, and then the biopsychosocial causal factors of the whole group are discussed. Evidence for biological causal factors, in particular, are emphasized in this chapter. Overall, the causes of schizophrenia have been more thoroughly researched than many of the other conditions studied so far. Finally, the treatment of schizophrenia—with antipsychotic drugs and psychosocial approaches—is described and evaluated. The chapter continues with a short discussion of the clinical picture and etiology of delusional disorders, and concludes with a discussion of whether schizophrenia can be prevented and what it might take to do so.

OBJECTIVES

After reading this chapter, you should be able to:

1. Explain the epidemiology of schizophrenia, as well as the origins of its construct.

2. Describe the clinical picture of schizophrenia, including the diagnostic signs of the positive and negative symptoms.

3. Compare and contrast the subtypes of schizophrenia.

4. Describe the clinical features of other psychotic disorders.

5. Summarize the biological, psychosocial, and sociocultural causal influences in schizophrenia.

6. Evaluate the various biological and psychosocial treatments for schizophrenia.

7. Discuss current issues in treating schizophrenia, including limitations of antipsychotics and the need for expanded psychsocial intervention.

8. Explain the difficulties associated with trying to prevent schizophrenia.

AS YOU READ

Answers can be found in the Answer Key at the end of the book.

KEY WORDS

Each of the words below is important in understanding the concepts presented in this Chapter. Write the definition next to each of the words.

psychosis (p. 458)   positive symptoms (p. 463)

delusion (p. 460)   Type I schizophrenia (p. 463)

delusional disorder (p. 460)   Type II schizophrenia (p. 463)

dementia praecox (p. 460)   paranoid schizophrenia (p. 464)

demence precoce (p. 460)   disorganized schizophrenia (p. 464)

hallucination (p. 461)   catatonic schizophrenia (p. 465)

negative symptoms (p. 463)   undifferentiated schizophrenia (p. 466) residual schizophrenia (p. 466)

schizoaffective disorder (p. 466)

schizophreniform disorder (p. 466)

shared psychotic disorder (p. 467)

brief psychotic disorder (p. 467)

dopamine (p. 479)

receptor supersensitivity (p. 479)

glutamate (p. 480)

expressed emotion (EE) (p. 483)

antipsychotics (neuroleptics) (p. 486)

cognitive remediation (p. 488

WHO'S WHO AND WHAT'S WHAT—MATCHING

Match the following names and terms with their correct definitions or descriptions.

Name/Term	Description/Definition
_____ Genain quadruplets	A. imitation of the act of others
_____ John Haslam	B. Swiss psychiatrist who in 1911 used the term, "schizophrenia," to characterize a split within the intellect and between the intellect and emotion and external reality
_____ John Tilly Matthews	C. completely new made-up words by a patient with schizophrenia
_____ Benedict Morel	D. Studied by David Rosenthal at NIMH in the mid-1950s, because all developed schizophrenia but were discordant with severity
_____ Emil Kraepelin	E. theory that schizophrenic individuals find themselves unable to maintain a job or maintaining relationships; thus, they are likely to to end up at the lower end of the socioeconomic ladder
_____ Eugen Bleuler	F. An apothecary in London who in 1810 gave the first detailed clinical description of schizophrenia
_____ Neologisms	G. theory that the lower the SES, the higher the prevalence of schizophrenia, because the conditions of lower-class existence are stressful, increasing the risk for schizophrenia
_____ echopraxia	H. The first person described in detail in 1810 with schizophrenia
_____ echolalia	I. measure of how understandable and "easy to follow" the speech of a family member is
_____ communication deviance	J. German psychiatrist who used the term, "dementia praecox," to refer to a group of conditions that feature mental deterioration beginning early in life
_____ sociogenic hypothesis	K. mimicking of another's phases
_____ social drift hypothesis	L. Used the term, "demence precoce," to describe the symptoms of a 13-year-old boy in 1860

WHO'S WHO AND WHAT'S WHAT—MATCHING

Match the following types of schizophrenia with their definitions.

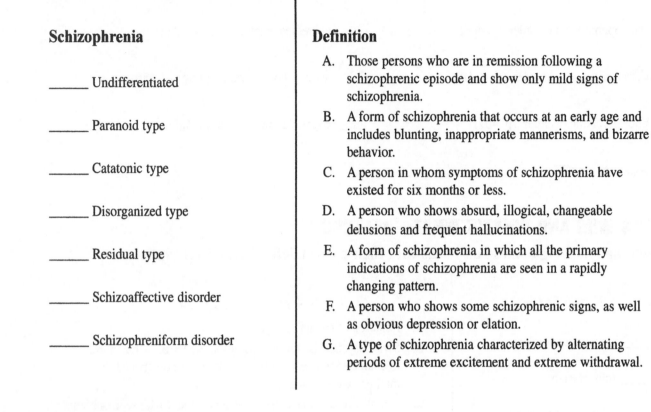

Schizophrenia

_____ Undifferentiated

_____ Paranoid type

_____ Catatonic type

_____ Disorganized type

_____ Residual type

_____ Schizoaffective disorder

_____ Schizophreniform disorder

Definition

A. Those persons who are in remission following a schizophrenic episode and show only mild signs of schizophrenia.

B. A form of schizophrenia that occurs at an early age and includes blunting, inappropriate mannerisms, and bizarre behavior.

C. A person in whom symptoms of schizophrenia have existed for six months or less.

D. A person who shows absurd, illogical, changeable delusions and frequent hallucinations.

E. A form of schizophrenia in which all the primary indications of schizophrenia are seen in a rapidly changing pattern.

F. A person who shows some schizophrenic signs, as well as obvious depression or elation.

G. A type of schizophrenia characterized by alternating periods of extreme excitement and extreme withdrawal.

SHORT ANSWERS

Provide brief answers to the following questions.

1. Describe the types of delusions common in schizophrenia. (p. 461)

2. Give examples of the prenatal factors that could trigger or cause schizophrenia. (pp. 473-74)

3. List examples of the positive and negative symptoms of schizophrenia. (p. 461)
    Positive:

    Negative:

4. Discuss the three types of prevention programs with relation to schizophrenia.
    (pp. 490-91)

FILL IN THE BLANKS

Read the following and fill in the blanks. These questions are designed to help you focus on specific details.

1. The vast majority of schizophrenia cases begin in late _____ or early _____. (p. 459)

2. A delusion involves a disturbance in the _____ of thought. (p. 460)

3. Patients with auditory hallucinations show an increase of activity in the _____ area of the brain involved with speech _____, not the _____ area of the brain involved with speech _____. (p. 462)

4. _____ involves the sudden onset of _____ symptoms or of grossly _____ or _____ behavior that cause great turmoil, but the episodes are usually quite brief. This disorder is often triggered by _____. (p. 467)

5. According to Torrey et al. (1994), the overall pairwise concordance rates for schizophrenia are ____ % in MZ twins and ____ % in DZ twins. Thus, a reduction in shared genes from 100% to 50%, reduces the risk of schizophrenia nearly ____%. Also, ____ % gene-sharing with a schizophrenic proband is associated with a lifetime risk of ____ %. In absolute terms, though this is low, it is still markedly higher than that of the general population. (p. 468)

6. The Danish adoption study found a preponderance of schizophrenia in _____ relatives, as compared to _____ relatives, of schizophrenic adoptees. (p. 471)

7. The Danish adoption study, however, did not include independent assessments of the _____ of the _____ into which index (those who became schizophrenic) and control (those who did not) youngsters had been placed. (p. 471)

8. The Wahlberg and colleagues study raises the possibility that certain kinds of _____ may protect people with _____. (p. 472)

9. Schizophrenia is a genetically _____, not a genetically _____ disorder. (p. 474)

10. Recent research efforts have moved toward exploring the idea that the problem of schizophrenia lies not in overall dopamine levels but in _____. (p. 479)

11. When the diagnostic criteria for schizophrenia changed in 1980 and became more _____, some of the _____ trends in recovery were _____. (p. 479)

12. The best predictor of long-term outcome for patients with schizophrenia is the percentage of time they spend experiencing _____ symptoms in the _____ years of their illness. (p. 485)

13. _____ training is an emphasis on helping patients deal with their neurocognitive deficits. (p. 488)

THE DOCTOR IS IN...PSYCHIATRIC HELP—5¢

Read the following scenarios and diagnose the client. Remember to look carefully at the criteria for the disorder before you make a decision as to the diagnosis. Make a list of other information you might need to help you understand the causal factors.

1. Sharon comes to visit you. She has been referred by her sister. Sharon had been picked up by the police outside of Tom Hanks' house. She told the police that she and Tom were getting married and that she was the love of his life. Sharon said that his latest movie was dedicated to her, and that he conveyed it through a secret message on the screen that only she could pick up. With Sharon's permission, you talk to her sister and discover that other than this behavior, Sharon seems normal. How would you diagnosis Sharon and why? (pp. 466-67)

2. You are a family therapist. A family comes to see you, bringing their 23-year-old son who suffers from schizophrenia. How would you treat this family, and, based on studies, what would you expect the son's outcome to be? (p. 487)

    Treatment:

    Outcome:

PICTURE THIS

Below are pictures that represent key people or concepts from the book. Write the answers on the line to the right of the clues.

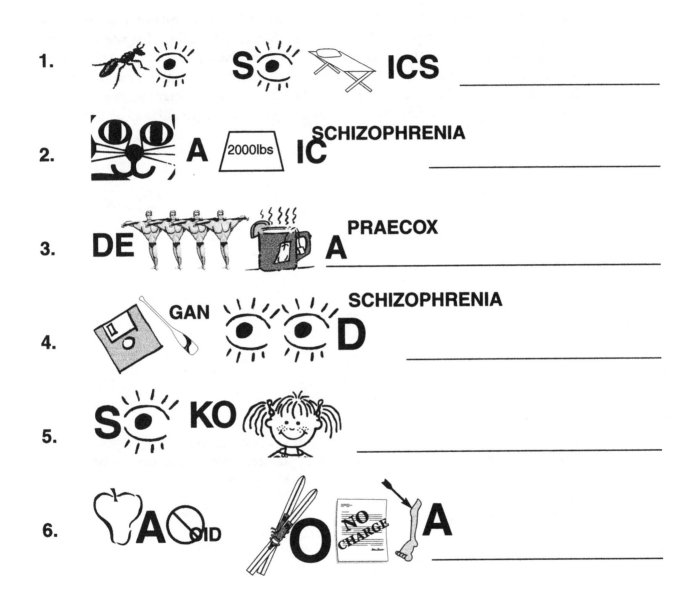

1. [ant] [eye] S[eye] [cot] ICS _____

2. [cat] A [2000lbs] IC SCHIZOPHRENIA _____

3. DE [4 chorus dancers] [coffee mug] A PRAECOX _____

4. [floppy disk with oar] GAN [eye] [eye] D SCHIZOPHRENIA _____

5. S[eye] KO [girl] _____

6. [pear] A [no circle] OID [skis] O [no charge] [foot with arrow] A _____

AFTER YOU READ

Answers can be found in the Answer Key at the end of the book.

PRACTICE TESTS

Take the following three multiple-choice tests to see how much you have comprehended from the chapter. Each represents roughly one-third of the chapter. As you study the chapter, use these to check your progress.

PRACTICE TEST NUMBER 1

1. The hallmark of schizophrenia is a significant loss of contact with reality, referred to as (p. 458)

    a. hallucinations.

    a. delusions.

    b. psychosis.

    c. manic reaction.

2. Symptoms of schizophrenia include oddities in (p. 458)

    a. perception.

    b. thinking.

    c. sense of self.

    d. all of the above.

3. Schizophrenia is about as prevalent as (p. 458)

    a. epilepsy.

    b. heart disease.

    c. stroke.

    d. none of the above.

4. Schizophrenia tends to develop earlier in _____ than in _____. (p. 459)

    a. women, men

    b. men, women

    c. old age, adulthood

    d. pre-schoolers, elementary-age children

5. Schizophrenia is becoming more common and severe in males than females. This could be a result of female hormones playing a (p. 459)

    a. destructive role.

    b. constructive role.

    c. passive role.

    d. protective role.

6. Late-onset schizophrenia is much more likely to strike women than men around (p. 459)

    a.   retirement age.

    b.   menopause.

    c.   35-40 years of age.

    d.   none of the above.

7. _____ is an erroneous belief that is fixed and firmly held despite clear and contradictory evidence. (p. 460)

    a.   Hallucination

    b.   Delusion

    c.   Differentiation

    d.   Dementia

8. _____ is a sensory experience that occurs in the absence of any external perceptual stimulus. (p. 461)

    a.   Hallucination

    b.   Delusion

    c.   Differentiation

    d.   Dementia

9. Disorganized speech is the external manifestation of a disorder in thought (p. 462)

    a.   form.

    b.   content.

    b.   interpretation.

    c.   all of the above.

10. _____ symptoms reflect behavioral excesses or distortions in schizophrenic patients. (p. 463)

    a.   Catatonic

    b.   Negative

    c.   Positive

    d.   Alogia

PRACTICE TEST NUMBER 2

1. _____ symptoms reflect behavioral deficits in schizophrenic patients. (p. 463)

    a.   Catatonic

    b.   Negative

    c.   Positive

    d.   Alogia

SCHIZOPHRENIA AND OTHER PSYCHOTIC DISORDERS   CHAPTER **FOURTEEN**

2. Delusions of grandeur are common in _____ schizophrenia. (p. 464)

    a. disorganized
    b. catatonic
    c. residual
    d. paranoid

3. In the past, _____ schizophrenia was called hebephrenic. One of its
    characteristics is flat or inappropriate affect. (p. 464)

    a. disorganized
    b. catatonic
    c. residual
    d. paranoid

4. _____ schizophrenia was once common in Europe and North America but has
    become less prevalent in recent years. It is still found in less industrialized regions of the
    world. (p. 465)

    a. Disorganized
    b. Catatonic
    c. Residual
    d. Paranoid

5. _____ schizophrenia is considered by the authors as something of a wastebasket
    category, because a patient may meet the the criteria for schizophrenia but not fit into one
    of the other types. (p. 466)

    a. Undifferentiated
    b. Residual
    c. Disorganized
    d. Paranoid

6. The category used for people who have suffered at least one episode of schizophrenia,
    and now don't have positive symptoms but clinically show negative symptoms, is
    (p. 466)

    a. undifferentiated.
    b. residual.
    c. disorganize.
    d. paranoid.

7. Most instances of acute, reactive schizophrenic breakdown occurring for the first time
    appear to be (p. 466)

    a. undifferentiated.
    b. paranoid.
    c. catatonic.
    d. disorganized.

8. The central feature of _____ schizophrenia is pronounced motor symptoms. (p. 465)

    a. undifferentiated
    b. catatonic
    c. disorganized
    d. paranoid

9. In the attempt to overcome the difficulty of separating hereditary from environmental influences, researchers have used the (p. 469)

    a. adoption strategy.
    b. wait and see strategy.
    c. sibling closeness strategy.
    d. None of the above.

10. Something that was not included in the Danish adoption studies, which proved to be significant in future studies done by Tienari and colleagues and Wahlberg, was an independent assessment of (p. 471)

    a. individuals in the study.
    b. diagnostic techniques.
    c. statistical techniques.
    d. child-rearing adequacy of the adoptive families.

PRACTICE TEST NUMBER 3

1. As a genetic researcher, you have decided to move away from the family, twin, and adoption schizophrenia studies you had been focusing on and become involved in a new paradigm. This paradigm shift would probably be a study of (p. 472)

    a. behaviors.
    b. the unconscious thoughts of schizophrenic.
    c. treatment methods.
    d. molecular genetics.

2. In addition to prenatal viral infections, researchers are looking at _____ as a factor that could cause or trigger schizophrenia. (p. 473)

    a. rhesus incompatibility
    b. early nutritional deficiency
    c. perinatal birth complications
    d. all of the above.

3. Researchers now accept that schizophrenia is a _____ disorder, wherein vulnerability to schizophrenia stems from a brain lesion that lies dormant until normal maturation of the brain occurs. (p. 475)

    a. cognitive

    b. defense mechanism

    c. simple

    d. neurodevelopmental

4. Studies by Elaine Walker and her colleagues found what differences between preschizophrenic children and their healthy siblings? (p. 475)

    a. motor abnormalities

    b. less positive facial emotions

    c. more negative facial emotions

    d. All of the above.

5. Because the brain normally occupies the skull fully, the enlarged ventricles of some schizophrenics imply a(n) (p. 476)

    a. decreased pressure on the brain.

    b. loss of brain tissue mass.

    c. increased amount of spinal fluid.

    d. predisposition to hydrocephaly.

6. Postmortem studies show that there are more _____ receptors in the brains of patients with schizophrenia than in controls. (p. 479)

    a. C4

    b. G3

    c. D1

    d. D2

7. _____ is an excitatory neurotransmitter that researchers suspect might be involved in schizophrenia. (p. 480)

    a. GABA

    b. Dopamine

    c. Glutamate

    d. None of the above

8. A significant percentage of patients with schizophrenia are deficient in their ability to track a moving target. The skill required to do this task is called (p. 481)

    a. rapid eye movement.

    b. smooth-pursuit eye movement.

    c. tracking eye movement.

    d. following ability eye movement.

9. Theories on the causes of schizophrenia that no longer are applicable because of the lack of empirical support are (p. 481)

    a. double-bind hypothesis.

    b. schizophrenogenic mother.

    c. gross parental ineptitude.

    d. all of the above.

10. _____ help patients find the services they need in order to function in the community. (p. 487)

    a. Psychotherapists

    b. Case managers

    c. Psychiatrists

    d. Nurses

COMPREHENSIVE PRACTICE TEST

The following tests are designed to give you an idea of how well you understood the entire chapter. There are three different types of tests: multiple-choice, true-false, and essay.

MULTIPLE-CHOICE

1. The most common form of hallucination is (p. 461)

    a. tactile.

    b. visual.

    c. auditory.

    d. olfactory.

2. Modern research has found support for the idea that auditory hallucinations are really misperceived (p. 462)

    a. external stimuli.

    b. radio signals.

    c. thought insertions.

    d. self-talk.

3. Type I schizophrenia is associated with this subsyndrome. (p. 463)

    a. apathy

    b. poverty of speech

    c. positive

    d. negative

4. Type II schizophrenia is associated with this subsyndrome. (p. 463)

    a. delusions

    b. sudden onset

    c. positive

    d. negative

5. Carlos is referred to you with psychotic symptoms that meet the criteria for schizophrenia. However, he also exhibits clear mood changes. What would your diagnosis of Carlos be? (p. 466)

    a. schizophreniform
    b. catatonic
    c. undifferentiated
    d. schizoaffective

6. Jennifer comes into your office for an appointment. For the past two months she has been experiencing schizophrenia-like psychoses but really not severe enough yet for her to be diagnosed with schizophrenia. How would you diagnose Jennifer? (p. 466)

    a. schizophreniform
    b. catatonic
    c. undifferentiated
    d. schizoaffective

7. A person in whom symptoms of schizophrenia have existed for six months or less would be diagnosed as the (p. 466)

    a. undifferentiated type.
    b. catatonic type.
    c. disorganized type.
    d. schizophreniform disorder.

8. Shared psychotic disorder, in which one person passes on or shares a delusion with someone he or she is close to, is also known as (p. 467)

    a. sibling rivalry.
    b. cyclical psychotic disorder.
    c. undifferentiated disorder.
    d. folie á deus.

9. An assumption that can create some problems when interpreting the findings of twin studies is (p. 469)

    a. these all have the same genetic make-up.
    b. MZ and DZ twins will develop schizophrenia.
    c. MZ and DZ twins have equally similar environments.
    d. all of the above.

10. If schizophrenia were exclusively genetic, the concordance rate for identical twins would be _____ percent. (p. 480)

    a. 1
    b. 25
    c. 50
    d. 100

11. The prevalence of schizophrenia in the first-degree relatives of a proband with schizophrenia is about what percent? (p. 468)

  a. 25

  b. 10

  c. 3

  d. 2

12. Wahlberg and colleagues found that children who were at genetic risk and lived with families that had high _____ showed high levels of thought disorder. (p. 472).

  a. levels of affection

  b. communication deviance

  c. number of siblings

  d. a and c

13. The Finnish Adoption Study has provided strong confirmation of what model for the origins of schizophrenia? (p. 472)

  a. psychoanalytical

  b. cognitive

  c. diathesis-stress

  d. behavioral

14. Focusing on MZ concordance rates has perhaps caused an overestimation of the heritability of schizophrenia because MZ and DZ twins do not have equally similar _____ environments. (p. 474)

  a. prenatal

  b. home

  c. community

  d. none of the above

15. In 1995 Davis, Phelps and Bracha, found that MZ twins who were monochorionic, as opposed the MZ twins who were dichorionic, had about what percent concordance rate with schizophrenia? (p. 474)

  a. 11

  b. 24

  c. 60

  d. 82

16. Negative symptoms of schizophrenia seem to be linked to which part of the brain? (p. 478)

  a. frontal lobe

  b. temporal lobe

  c. medial

  d. amygdala

17. Positive symptoms of schizophrenia seem to be linked to which part of the brain, especially on the left side? (p. 478)

    a. temporal lobe
    b. hippocampus
    c. amygdala
    d. all of the above.

18. The overall organization of the cells in the brain is called the brain's (p. 478)

    a. wave.
    b. structure.
    c. cytoarchitecture.
    d. pattern.

19. Some evidence points to patients with schizophrenia as missing particular types of neurons known as (p. 478)

    a. inhibitory interneurons.
    b. micro neurons.
    c. macro neurons.
    d. excitatory neurons.

20. The first antipsychotics, developed over 50 years ago to treat schizophrenia, are called (p. 486)

    a. conventional antipsychotics.
    b. typical antipsychotics.
    c. unconventional antipsychotics.
    d. a and b.

21. The newer class of antipsychotics is referred to as (p. 486)

    a. nouveau antipsychotics.
    b. novel antipsychotics.
    c. atypical antipsychotics.
    d. b and c.

22. Betty, who is schizophrenic, goes to a group everyday where she learns employment skills, relationship skills, and skills in managing medication. This type of training is referred to as (p. 487)

    a. real life.
    b. case management.
    c. social-skills.
    d. family.

23. The goal of cognitive-behavioral therapy when treating schizophrenia is to (p. 488)

    a.   decrease the intensity of positive symptoms.

    b.   reduce relapse.

    c.   decrease social disability.

    d.   all of the above.

24. _____ therapy is staged, which means that it comprises different components that are administered at different points in the patient's recovery. (p. 490)

    a.   Personal therapy

    b.   Cognitive therapy

    c.   Psychodynamic

    d.   Behavioral

TRUE – FALSE

1. Schizophrenia is a single, discrete illness.   T / F (p. 458)

2. People who have a parent with schizophrenia have a statistically higher risk of developing the disorder than those who do not.   T / F   (p. 458)

3. Delusions reflect a disorder of thought content.   T / F   (p. 462)

4. A preponderance of negative symptoms in the clinical picture is considered a good sign for the patient's future outcome.   T / F   (p. 463)

5. The prognosis for someone diagnosed with schizophreniform disorder is better than for established forms of schizophrenia.   T / F   (p.466)

6. The terms, "familial" and "genetic," are synonymous.   T / F   (p. 468)

7. Schizophrenia probably involves several, or perhaps many, genes working together to make a person susceptible.   T / F   (p. 472)

8. The first signs of schizophrenia may be found in the way that children move. T / F (p. 476)

9. Schizophrenics are very sensitive to pain.   T / F   (p. 477)

10. Schizophrenia manifests itself more in defective cognition than in defective biology.   T / F (p. 480)

11. Patients living in more industrialized countries do better than patients living in less industrialized countries. T / F   (p. 485)

12. Patients who were treated with a "befriending" intervention in the Sensky and colleagues study did unexpectedly well. T / F   (p. 489)

ESSAY QUESTIONS

1. Discuss how dopamine became implicated in schizophrenia. (p. 479)

2. Define and explain expressed emotion (EE) and its connection to patient relapse. (p. 483)

3. Compare the conventional antipsychotics with the newer, novel ones in terms of effectiveness and side effects. (p. 486)

    Conventional: Haldol and Thorazine

    Novel: Clozal, Risperday, Zyprexa, Seroquel, Geodon

WEB LINKS TO ITEMS OR CONCEPTS DISCUSSED IN THIS CHAPTER

Psychosis

     www.aacap.org/about/glossary/Psychos.htm

     www.psyspiritstory.co.uk/

     www.eppic.org.au/

Schezophrenia

     www.schizophrenia.com/

     www.narsad.org/

     www.mentalhealth.com/dis/p20-ps01.html

CRISS-CROSS

Now that you know all there is to know about this chapter, here's your opportunity to put that knowledge to work.

CRISS-CROSS CLUES

Across

1. an excitatory neurotransmitter that is widespread in the brain
3. a wide variety of disordered processes of varied etiology, developmental pattern, and outcome
4. the most important neurotransmitter implicated in schizophrenia
8. pronounced motor signs, either of an excited or stuporous type of schizophrenia
9. an erroneous belief that is fixed and firmly held
10. a class of drugs introduced in the mid-1950s that transformed the environment in mental hospitals

Down

2. a measure of the family environment
5. the hallmark of schizophrenia, a significant loss of contact with reality
6. a sensory experience occurring without any external perceptual stimulus
7. an absence or deficit of behaviors normally present in schizophrenia

Puzzle created with Puzzlemaker at DiscoverySchool.com

CHAPTER FIFTEEN

Cognitive Disorders

BEFORE YOU READ

You can think, breath, dream, feel, and do all those other things you do, because you have a brain. The brain is involved in everything we are capable of doing. However, many things can go wrong. Chapter 15 covers several types of brain impairments. The first part of the chapter discusses diagnostic issues, clinical signs of brain damage, and neuropsychological brain disorders. Then follows a more in-depth look at delirium, dementia (with particular attention paid to Alzheimer's disease), dementia from HIV infection, vascular dementia and amnestic syndrome.

The next portion of the chapter deals with disorders involving head injury. A clinical picture of mild and severe traumatic brain injury is presented. Treatments and outcomes complete the section.

Unresolved issues presents interesting insights concerning the question of whether or not dietary supplements enhance brain functioning.

OBJECTIVES

After reading this chapter, you should be able to:

1. Explain why the DSM-IV dropped the terms, "functional mental disorders" and "organic mental disorders."

2. Discuss diagnostic issues and clinical signs of brain damage.

3. Explain the diffuse versus focal damage as it relates to brain impairment.

4. Describe how neuropsychology and psychopathology interact with each other.

5. Define delirium in terms of clinical presentation and discuss clinical treatments and outcomes.

6. Define dementia and describe the three disorders presented, Alzheimer's, dementia from HIV-1 infection and vascular dementia, in terms of clinical picture, prevalence, any genetic or environmental aspects, treatment outcomes and effects on caregivers.

7. Explain amnetic syndrome.

8. Explain traumatic brain injury (TBI), describe the clinical picture and discuss treatment outcomes.

9. Discuss the research on the benefits of dietary supplements on brain functioning.

AS YOU READ

Answers can be found in the Answer Key at the end of the book.

KEY WORDS

Each of the words below is important in understanding the concepts presented in this Chapter. Write the definition next to each of the words.

functional mental disorders (p. 495)

late-onset Alzheimer's disease (p. 505)

delirium (p. 499)

neurofibrillary tangles (p. 502)

dementia (p. 500)

organic mental disorders (p. 495)

early-onset Alzheimer's disease (p. 504)

plaques (p. 502)

APOE-4 allele (p. 505)

retrograde amnesia (p. 511)

AIDS-related dementia (p. 508)

traumatic brain injury (p. 509)

amnestic syndrome (p. 509)

vascular dementia (p. 508)

anterograde amnesia (p. 511)

WHO'S WHO AND WHAT'S WHAT—MATCHING

Name the brain structures using the terms in bold in the top of the box.
Match the term with its proper answer.

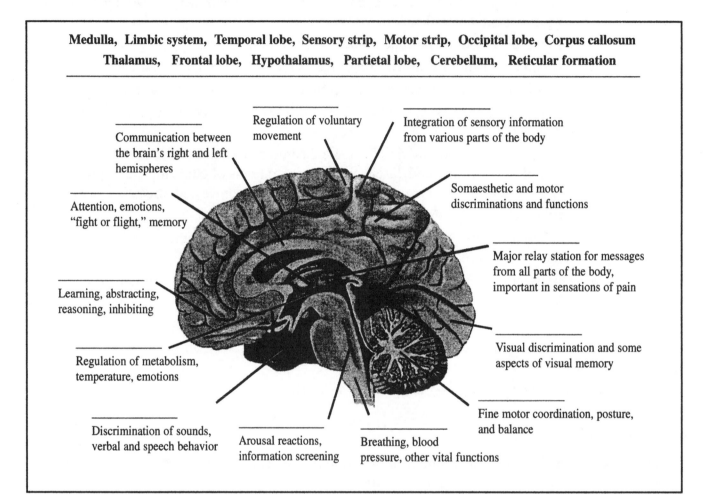

Medulla, Limbic system, Temporal lobe, Sensory strip, Motor strip, Occipital lobe, Corpus callosum
Thalamus, Frontal lobe, Hypothalamus, Partietal lobe, Cerebellum, Reticular formation

Regulation of voluntary movement

Integration of sensory information from various parts of the body

Communication between the brain's right and left hemispheres

Somaesthetic and motor discriminations and functions

Attention, emotions, "fight or flight," memory

Major relay station for messages from all parts of the body, important in sensations of pain

Learning, abstracting, reasoning, inhibiting

Visual discrimination and some aspects of visual memory

Regulation of metabolism, temperature, emotions

Fine motor coordination, posture, and balance

Discrimination of sounds, verbal and speech behavior

Arousal reactions, information screening

Breathing, blood pressure, other vital functions

Match the term with its proper answer.

Term/Name	Answer
_____ Anosognosia	A. genes on chromosome 14 and 1 that are associated with very early onset Alzheimer's disease
_____ Alois Alzheimer	B. famous historical victim of a traumatic brain injury
_____ Presenilin 1 and presenilin 2	C. German neuropathologist who first described AD
_____ Apolipoprotein (APOE)	D. inability for realistic self-appraisal
_____ Phineas Gage	E. gene on chromosome 19 that plays a great role in late onset Alzheimer's

SHORT ANSWERS

Provide brief answers to the following questions.

1. Why are cognitive disorders discussed in the textbook? (p. 494)

2. What determines the extent and magnitude of behavioral deficits or psychological impairments in persons with damage to brain tissue? (p. 495)

FILL IN THE BLANKS

Read the following and fill in the blanks. These questions are designed to help you focus on specific details.

1. The brain is the only organ capable of _____ and _____ about itself. (p. 494)

2. _____, _____, _____ active people have enhanced _____ to mental and behavioral _____ following significant brain injury. (p. 499)

3. _____, _____ and overall brain _____ are physical evidence of Alzheimer's. (p. 503)

4. Contrary to initial assumptions, the organic brain effects associated with AIDS patients was not due to secondary infections, but due to the presence of the _____ itself.

5. AIDS-related dementia damage appears to be concentrated in _____ regions, notably the _____, the tissue surrounding the _____, and deeper gray matter structures, such as the _____ and _____. (p. 508)

6. The later phases of AIDS dementia include _____ regression, _____, _____ thinking, _____, and marked _____. (p. 508)

7. A sudden interruption of the blood supply to parts of the brain is a _____. (p. 508)

8. The characteristics between VAD and AD are similar, but the decline in VAD is not as smooth, because a) the discrete character of an _____, b) variations over time in the volume of blood delivered by a _____, and c) a tendency for VAD to be associated with more severe _____. (p. 508)

9. Disorders that result from traumatic injuries to the brain are more common than any other forms of _____ disease, except _____. (p. 509)

THE DOCTOR IS IN...PSYCHIATRIC HELP—5¢

Read the following scenarios and diagnose the client. Remember to look carefully at the criteria for the disorder before you make a decision as to the diagnosis. Make a list of other information you might need to help you understand the causal factors.

1. Glen is an 82-year-old man who suddenly became very confused, not able to remember things and very agitated—pacing his room endlessly at night. In addition, he was unable to stay on tasks long enough to even complete dressing himself. The morning would find him cooperative, but that could change quickly to anger. Glen had been taking several medications and was recently given another.

    How would you diagnose Glen and why. Also, what treatment would you use? (pp. 499-500)

2. Terry is a 44-year-old man who has a long history of alcohol abuse. He has come to see you at the insistence of his sister with whom he is staying. In your interview with Terry, he is very capable of telling you about his life and past experiences working on oil rigs around the world. You had asked him to look a picture in a magazine and tell you what he saw. He was able to do this as he looked at the picture. However, when you asked him to recall what the picture was about a few minutes later, he had no idea what you were talking about and made up a story that seemed to him a reasonable explanation as to why he didn't recall the picture.

    How would you diagnose Terry and why? (p. 509)

3. What six factors in the case below suggest that your patient has an unfavorable prognosis? (p. 513)

> "*An 18-year-old male who had several run-ins with the law during high school received a serious head injury in a motorcycle accident. He was in a coma for almost a month. He is currently suffering some paralysis, and is very angry and depressed. He refuses to cooperate with his physical therapist. His parents, who live in a remote rural area where no rehabilitation facilities are available, will take him back home, but are rather unenthusiastic about the prospect.*"

a.

b.

c.

d.

e.

f.

PICTURE THIS

Below are pictures that represent key people or concepts from the book. Write the answers on the line to the right of the clues.

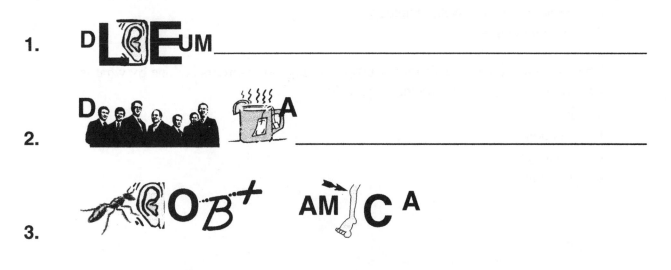

1.

2.

3.

AFTER YOU READ

Answers can be found in the Answer Key at the end of the book.

PRACTICE TESTS

Take the following three multiple-choice tests to see how much you have comprehended from the chapter. Each represents roughly one-third of the chapter. As you study the chapter, use these to check your progress.

PRACTICE TEST NUMBER 1

1. Before the DSM-IV was published, delirium, dementia, and other amnestic and cognitive disorders, were considered (p. 495)

    a. functional mental disorders.

    b. dysfunctional mental disorders.

    c. organic mental disorders.

    d. brain injury disorders.

2. When structural defects in the brain occur before birth or at a very early age, the typical result is (p. 494)

    a. mental retardation.

    b. delirium.

    c. dementia.

    d. progressive.

3. To distinguish the possibility of a brain disorder from mood disorder, the clinician will look to see if the client has (p. 494)

    a. headaches.

    b. a major change in behavior.

    c. a prior history of psychopathology.

    d. all of the above.

4. The diagnostic coding of various neuropsychological disorders is done by what is causing the _____ problem. (p. 495)

    a. medical

    b. emotional

    c. cognitive

    d. functional

5. The screening test that clinicians often use to determine the possibility of cognitive impairment is the (p. 496)

    a.   MMPI.

    b.   TAT.

    c.   MMSE.

    d.   MAAPT.

6. The _____ hemisphere of the brain is mostly responsible for language and solving mathematical equations. (p. 497)

    a.   right

    b.   left

    c.   center

    d.   remote

7. The study by LoSasso et. al. (2001) found that nail salon technicians had significantly more cognitive and neurological impairments, probably due to an exposure to (p. 497)

    a.   so many people.

    b.   long work hours.

    c.   neurotoxic substances.

    d.   dietary restrictions.

8. After a traumatic brain injury caused by an accident or a fall, for example, around _____ percent of patients make a suicide attempt. (p. 499)

    a.   10

    b.   18

    c.   8

    d.   5

9. Most people who have neuropsychological disorders do not develop _____ symptoms. (p. 499)

    a.   any further

    b.   any permanent

    c.   other

    d.   psychopathological

10. A rapid and widespread disorganization of complex mental processes caused by a generalized disturbance in brain metabolism is called (p. 499)

    a.   amnestis syndrome.

    b.   hallucinosis.

    c.   dementia.

    d.   delirium.

PRACTICE TEST NUMBER 2

1. Delirium is treated with (p. 500)

    a. neuroleptic medications.

    b. benzodiazines.

    c. Aricept.

    d. a and b.

2. What is the correct order for the continuum of level of consciousness? (p. 500)

    a. coma, delirium, stupor, alert awake

    b. alert awake, stupor, delirium, coma

    c. alert awake, delirium, stupor, coma

    d. stupor, delirium, coma, alert awake

3. Children are at high risk of delirium, because their brains are not yet fully (p. 500)

    a. organized.

    b. developed.

    c. integrated.

    d. active.

4. At least _____ different disorders are known to cause dementia. (p. 501)

    a. 35

    b. 28

    c. 50

    d. 65

5. Alzheimer's cannot be absolutely confirmed until the patient's (p. 502)

    a. complete physical exam.

    b. complete neurological exam.

    c. behavior has deteriorated sufficiently.

    d. death.

6. Which of the following is the most common behavioral manifestation of Alzheimer's disease? (p. 503)

    a. slow mental deterioration

    b. jealousy delusions

    c. paranoid delusions

    d. psychopathological symptoms

7. Since there is no cure for Alzheimer's, _____ care seems to help with diminishing the patient's and caregiver's distress and some of the complications that come with the disorder. (p. 506)

    a. family

    b. palliative

    c. hospital

    d. nursing home

8. These drugs have been shown to slow the rate at which patients with Alzheimer's deteriorate. (p. 506)

    a. placebos

    b. tacrine

    c. donepezil

    d. b and c

9. Environmental factors that could contribute to Alzheimer's include (p. 505)

    a. diet.

    b. aluminum.

    c. head trauma.

    d. all of the above.

10. Most people with Alzheimer's live (p. 507)

    a. with family members in the community.

    b. in nursing homes.

    c. on the streets.

    d. on their own.

PRACTICE TEST NUMBER 3

1. Vascular dementia involves a(n) (p. 508)

    a. appearance of senile plaques.

    b. continuing recurrence of small strokes.

    c. increase in neurofibrillary tangles.

    d. loss of neurons in the basal forbrain.

2. Laura has been diagnosed with VAD and AD. As a clinician, you would refer to this condition as (p. 508)

    a. unfortunate dementia.

    b. mixed dementia.

    c. double dementia.

    d. twin dementia.

3. Patients with VAD are more likely to suffer from _____ disorders than patients with Alzheimer's. (p. 508)

    a. anxiety

    b. cognitive

    c. stress

    d. mood

4. A person with VAD is vulnerable to sudden death from a (p. 508)

    a. stroke.

    b. cardiovascular disease.

    c. head injury.

    d. a and b.

5. Traumatic brain injury affects more than _____ people each year in the United States. (p. 509)

    a. 42

    b. 2 million

    c. 42,000

    d. 150,000

6. The general types of TBI recognized by clinicians are (p. 510)

    a. closed-head injuries.

    b. penetrating head injuries.

    c. skull fractures.

    d. all of the above.

7. If a head injury is sufficiently severe to result in unconsciousness, the person may experience retrograde amnesia or an inability to recall (p. 511)

    a. events immediately following the injury.

    b. events immediately preceding and following the injury.

    c. events immediately preceding the injury.

    d. names or faces of friends.

8. In a study of TBI in boxers, it was found that the presence of the _____ genetic-risk factor was associated with more chronic neurological deficits. (p. 511)

    a. granulovacuoles

    b. APOE-4

    c. PS1

    d. PS2

9. A recent study has shown that older individuals and individuals who have TBI share several changes in (p. 511)

    a. how they see the world.

    b. their rates of speaking.

    c. information-processing speed.

    d. all of the above.

10. Common after effects of moderate brain injury are (p. 513)

    a. chronic headaches.

    b. anxiety.

    c. impaired memory.

    d. All of the above.

COMPREHENSIVE PRACTICE TEST

The following tests are designed to give you an idea of how well you understood the entire chapter. There are three different types of tests: multiple-choice, truefalse, and essay.

MULTIPLE-CHOICE

1. The thick outer membrane that protects the brain and literally means "hard mother" is called the (p. 494)

    a. corpus callosum.

    b. medulla.

    c. cerebellum.

    d. dura mater.

2. When the brain is damaged or brain functioning is in some way compromised, _____ changes result and are the most obvious signs of a damaged brain. (p. 494)

    a. cognitive

    b. mood

    c. personality

    d. movement

3. The _____ hemisphere of the brain is mostly responsible for grasping overall meanings in novel situations, reasoning on a nonverbal, intuitive level, and appreciation of spatial relations. (p. 497)

    a. right

    b. left

    c. center

    d. remote

4. In contrast to diffuse damage that results indementia, focal lesions are _____ areas of abnormal change in brain structure. (p. 496)

   a. deep
   b. circumscribed
   c. large
   d. progressive

5. The most common cause of delirium is (p. 500)

   a. stoke.
   b. HIV/AIDS.
   c. drug intoxication.
   d. syphilis.

6. _____ has a gradual onset, but even in the early stages, memory for recent events is affected. (p. 501)

   a. Dementia
   b. Delirium
   c. TBI
   d. all of the above

7. Data from a large Canadian study suggest that, after the first contact with a doctor for memory problems, a person with AD may live as little as (p. 504)

   a. 9-1/2 weeks.
   b. 1 day.
   c. 3.3 years.
   d. 7 years.

8. Cases of early on-set AD appear to be caused by rare (p. 504)

   a. brain cell mutations.
   b. environmental factors.
   c. genetic mutations.
   d. neurological mutations.

9. The widespread use of antiviral therapy has reduced the prevalence of dementia due to HIV to around _____ percent. (p. 508)

   a. 42
   b. 50
   c. 20
   d. 1.732

10. Cerebral arteriosclerosis can be medically managed by decreasing the likelihood of further (p. 508)

    a. contact with hazardous waste.

    b. medical problems.

    c. strokes.

    d. none of the above.

11. Amnestic syndrome is most commonly caused by chronic (p. 509)

    a. reckless driving.

    b. poor eating habits.

    c. problems with personal hygiene.

    d. alcohol use.

12. Post-trauma epilepsy is common in (p. 510)

    a. closed-head injuries.

    b. penetrating head injuries.

    c. skull fractures.

    d. b and c.

13. The TBI that could result from a roller coaster ride is (p. 510)

    a. closed-head injury.

    b. penetrating head injury.

    c. skull fracture.

    d. none of the above.

14. The _____ a child, who has a significant traumatic brain injury, the more likely to be adversely affected they are. (p. 513)

    a. older

    b. younger

    c. more mature

    d. a and c

15. Oken and colleagues concluded in 1998 that patients with Alzheimer's who took _____ performed better cognitively. (p. 514)

    a. ginkgo

    b. placebo

    c. phosphatatidylserine

    d. choline

TRUE – FALSE

1. Alzheimer's disease is the most common cause of dementia.   T / F (p. 502)

2. Alzheimer's disease usually begins after about age 65.   T / F (p. 503)

3. AD is not an inevitable consequence of aging.   T / F   (p. 504)

4. People who are the caregivers for Alzheimer's patients are at high risk for depression.
    T / F   (p. 507)

5. Brain damage is the root cause of amnestic disorders.   T / F (p. 509)

6. Sports injuries are the most common cause of TBI.   T / F   (p. 509)

7. In a majority of brain injury cases, notable personality changes occur.   T / F   (p. 513)

ESSAY QUESTIONS

1. Discuss the progressively diffuse damage that may occur when a brain disorder has a
    mainly focal origin but gradually spreads over a greater area to become diffuse. (p. 499)

2.   List and describe the brain abnormalities that are characteristic of Alzheimer's disease. (p. 505)

WEB LINKS TO ITEMS OR CONCEPTS DISCUSSED IN THIS CHAPTER

Dementia

     dementia.ion.ucl.ac.uk/

     www.nlm.nih.gov/medlineplus/dementia.html

     www.alz.uci.edu/

Delirium

     www.mentalhealth.com/dis/p20-or01.html

Alzheimer's Disease

     www.alz.org/

     www.alzheimers.org/

     www.alzheimers.org/pubs/adfact.html

     www.ninds.nih.gov/health_and_medical/ disorders/alzheimersdisease_doc.htm

     www.nlm.nih.gov/medlineplus/alzheimersdisease.html

CRISS-CROSS

Now that you know all there is to know about this
chapter, here's your opportunity to put that
knowledge to work.

CRISS-CROSS CLUES

Across

5. a form of amnesia in which a person cannot recall events after an injury
7. an acute confusional state lying between normal wakefulness and stupor
8. a syndrome in which short-term memory is so impaired that the person is unable to
   recall events from a few minutes previously

Down

1. dementia similar to progressive, but caused by a series of circumscribed cerebral infarcts
2. gradual, permanent decline from a previously attained level of functioning
3. a form of amnesia where person cannot recall the events preceding the injury
4. brain abnormalities characteristic of Alzheimer's disease
5. the man who first described Alzheimer's disease
6. dementia producing general deterioration of the brain; observed in AIDS patients

Puzzle created with Puzzlemaker at DiscoverySchool.com

CHAPTER SIXTEEN

Disorders of Childhood And Adolescence

BEFORE YOU READ

Many of the mental disorders described in previous chapters do not develop until early or middle adulthood. There are some problems, however, that develop in childhood and adolescence. Some of these are unique to childhood, such as hyperactivity, and other problems, such as withdrawal, may be forerunners of serious adult psychopathology like depression or schizoid behavior. Thus, it is ill-advised to assume that children are simply "mini-adults." This chapter discusses the types of problems seen in children and adolescents, including attention-deficit hyperactivity disorder, oppositional defiant disorder, conduct disorder, anxiety disorders, childhood depression, enuresis, encopresis, sleepwalking, and tics—as well as delinquency. In each instance, there is an attempt to indicate the clinical picture, causal factors, and the long-range outcome for the problem.

Learning disorders, such as dyslexia, their clinical picture, causal factors, and treatment, are disscussed next. Also noted is an emphasis on the lack of awareness and options available to the children suffering from learning disorders.

Following learning disorders is information on mental retardation, its different levels or degrees, and characteristic behaviors associated with each level. Causal factors and treatment for this disorder is also presented, along with explanations of various forms of mental retardation.

The chapter concludes with a discussion of the difficulties in planning better programs and treatments to help children and adolescents. This leads to the question, "Can Society Deal with Deliquent Behavior?"

OBJECTIVES

After reading this chapter, you should be able to:

1. List special features of childhood disorders that make these different from adult disorders, and describe how young children are especially vulnerable to develop psychological problems.

2. Discuss general issues in the classification of childhood and adolescent disorders.

3. Describe the clinical features, list several of the multiple causes, and summarize approaches to treatment of attention-deficit hyperactivity disorder.

4. Describe the clinical features, causal factors, and treatment of conduct disorder and oppositional defiant disorder.

5. Describe the clinical features, causal factors, and treatment of the anxiety disorders of childhood.

6. Describe the clinical features, causal factors, and treatment of childhood depression.

7. Summarize what is known about the symptom disorders of functional enuresis, functional encopresis, sleepwalking, and tics as these occur in children and adolescents.

8. Describe the clinical features, causal factors, and treatment of autism.

9. Review treatments approaches, outcomes and prevention with regard to mental retardation.

10. Describe the clinical features, causal factors, and treatment of learning disorders.

11. Explain the four levels of mental retardation and describe the functioning associated with each level.

12. Discuss the types of brain defects associated with mental retardation.

13. List and explain mental retardation stemming from biological causes, especially Down syndrome, PKU, and cranial anomalies.

14. List and explain six special factors that must be considered in relation to treatment for children.

15. Outline the findings regarding the prevalence of child abuse, list the deficits seen among abused children, discuss potential causal factors in child abuse, and summarize efforts to prevent child abuse.

16. Describe the need for mental health services for children, and review the difficulties with recent efforts to increase the available resources.

17. Discuss delinquency as a major societal problem, summarize the many causal factors involved in delinquency, and describe different ways that society deals with delinquency.

AS YOU READ

Answers can be found in the Answer Key at the end of the book.

KEY WORDS

Each of the words below is important in understanding the concepts presented in this Chapter. Write the definition next to each of the words.

developmental psychopathology (p. 518)

attention-deficit/hyperactivity disorder (ADHD) (p. 520)

Pemoline (p. 521)

Ritalin (p. 521)

oppositional defiant disorder (p. 522)

juvenile delinquency (p. 522)

conduct disorder (p. 523)

separation anxiety disorder (p. 525)

selective mutism (p. 526)

enuresis (p. 530)

encopresis (p. 531)

sleepwalking disorder (p. 532)

tic (p. 532)

autism (p. 533)

Asberger's disorder (p. 533)

pervasive developmental disorders (PDDs) (p. 533)

Tourette's syndrome (p. 533)

echolalia (p. 534)

dyslexia (p. 538)

learning disorders (p. 538)

mental retardation (p. 540)

Down syndrome (p. 543)

macrocephaly (p. 545)

hydrocephaly (p. 546)

microcephaly (p. 546)

mainstreaming (p. 547)

phenylketonuria (PKU) (p. 545)

WHO'S WHO AND WHAT'S WHAT—MATCHING

Match the following with the appropriate description.

_____ Imipramine

_____ intranasal hormone replacement used to treat enuresis

_____ somnambulism

_____ NREM

_____ Asberger's disorder

_____ Tourette's syndrome

_____ Kanner

_____ autistic-savant

_____ Siegel

_____ "Eden Model"

_____ Integrative Strategy Instruction

_____ hypoxia

_____ Langdon Down

_____ Children's Defense Fund

A. the first to describe autism in infancy and childhood

B. author of the book, *The World of the Autistic Child*

C. an approach to assisting people with autism over the course of their lifespan

D. an extreme tic disorder invloving multiple motor and vocal patterns

E. a public-interest group based in Washington D.C. that advocates for children

F. sleepwalking

G. medication used to treat enuresis

H. DDAVP

I. a period during sleep when sleepwalking takes place

J. a comprehensive intervention model to facilitate learning in LD children offered by Ellis

K. autistic children who show markedly discrepant and relatively isolated abilities

L. pervasive developmental disorder that appears later than autism

M. lack of sufficient oxygen to the brain

N. the first person to describe the best known clinical conditions associated with moderate and severe mental retardation

SHORT ANSWERS

Provide brief answers to the following questions.

1. What are the three subtypes of ADHD now recognized in the DSM-IV-TR? (p. 521)

2. What are the clinical signs of separation anxiety? (p. 525)

3. Describe the clinical picture of a child with autism. (pp. 534-536)

4. What two groups do children who are institutionalized fall into? (p. 546)

FILL IN THE BLANKS
Read the following and fill in the blanks. These questions are designed to help you focus on specific details.

1. Zill and Schoenborn in 1990, reported that boys have a higher rate of _____ problems over the _____ and _____ years but _____ rates are higher for girls. (p. 518)

2. Hyperactive children are highly _____ and often _____ to _____instructions or _____ to demands placed on them. (p. 520)

3. Pelham and colleagues (1993) found that _____ _____ and _____ _____ significantly reduced ADHD. (p. 522)

4. The essential feature of oppositional defiance disorder is a recurrent pattern of _____, _____, _____, and _____ behavior toward _____ figures that persist for at least _____ months. (p. 522)

5. Children who develop a conduct disorder at an _____ age are much _____ likely to develop _____ personality disorder as adults than are _____ who develop coduct disorders suddenly in _____. (p. 523)

6. _____ treatment of anxiety disorders in children and adolescents is becoming more _____ today, although the _____ of drugs in treating these disorders is _____. (p. 527)

7. Before _____ rates of depression are somewhat _____ in boys, but depression occurs at about _____ the rate for _____ girls as boys. (p. 528)

8.   Children who have _____ _____enuresis have never been _____;
     children who have _____ _____ enuresis have been _____ for at
     least a year but have regressed. (p. 531)

9.   The term, "functional enuresis," refers to the habitual involuntary discharge of urine after the
     age of expected continence, which is age ___, that is not _____ caused. (p. 531)

10. In a review of the treatment of bedwetting, Houts, Berman, and Abramson (1994)
     concluded that treated children were _____ at follow-up than nontreated
     children and that learning-based procedures were _____ effective than were
     medications. (p. 531)

11. Sleepwalking involves repeated episodes in which a person leaves his or her bed and
     walks around without _____ or
     _____. (p. 532)

12. The diagnosis of learning disorder is restricted to those cases in which there is a clear
     _____ in _____ performance, or if the person is not a student, in
     _____ activities, and impairment is not due to _____
     _____ or to a pervasive _____. (p. 538)

13. Mild mental retardation, where IQ range is _____ to _____ is considered
     _____. Moderate mental retardation, where IQ range is _____ to
     _____ is considered _____. In severe mental retardation, where IQ range is
     _____ to _____, is considered _____ and profound mental retardation
     where IQ range is _____, is considered _____. (pp. 540-41)

THE DOCTOR IS IN...PSYCHIATRIC HELP—5¢

**Read the following scenarios and diagnose the client. Remember to look carefully at the criteria
for the disorder before you make a decision as to the diagnosis. Make a list of other information
you might need to help you understand the causal factors.**

1.   Mark, who is seven years old, is referred to your office by his school. He comes to the
     session with his mother. The school report says that Mark is defiant, disobedient, and has
     tried to punch his teacher and the principal on more than one occasion. This behavior has
     been getting worse for the last year. In fact, Mark was suspended last year for spitting at
     his teacher. You note that the mother is also hostile and believes that coming to see you is
     a waste of time. You find out that the household is in turmoil, as the parents are always
     fighting, and get the feeling that the children are often the reason for the fighting.

     How would you diagnose Mark, and what treatment would you recommend?   (pp. 522-25).

2. Gary is a four-year-old boy who has started wetting the bed. Up until his new sister arrived, this hadn't been a problem. However, for the last two months since the new baby came home from the hospital, he has been wetting the bed and occasionally his pants. His parents are troubled and don't know what to do.

    How would you diagnose Gary and what would you do to treat him? (p. 531)

AFTER YOU READ

Answers can be found in the Answer Key at the end of the book.

PRACTICE TESTS

Take the following three multiple-choice tests to see how much you have comprehended from the chapter. Each represents roughly one-third of the chapter. As you study the chapter, use these to check your progress.

PRACTICE TEST NUMBER 1

1. Until the twentieth century, children were seen as being (p. 518)

    a. unique in their psychopathology.
    b. miniature adults.
    c. unable to have any mental illness.
    d. All of the above.

2. Clinicians now realize that to understand childhood disorders, they must take into account (p. 518)

    a. developmental processes.
    b. play time.
    c. siblings.
    d. unconscious motivations.

3. Cindy is two years old, has temper tantrums, and puts everything she finds into her mouth. This behavior, for her age, is (p. 518)

    a. appropriate.
    b. inappropriate.
    c. a sign of anxiety.
    d. something to watch as it may lead to future psychopathology.

4. The DSM-I, which provided the first limited classification system to include childhood disorders, was published in (p. 519)

    a.   1962.

    b.   1974.

    c.   1952.

    d.   1949.

5. A problem with the early classification system for childhood disorders is that it was (p. 519)

    a.   not updated.

    b.   the same one used for adults.

    c.   not incluclusive of the disorders that were important at the time.

    d.   Inclusive of too many disorders.

6. Attention-deficit/hyperactivity disorder, conduct disorder, anxiety disorders of childhood, depressive disorders, symptom disorders, and autism are coded on which axis? (p. 520)

    a.   Axis I

    b.   Axis II

    c.   Axis III

    d.   Axis IV

7. Learning disabilities and mental retardation are coded on which axis? (p. 520)

    a.   Axis I

    b.   Axis II

    c.   Axis III

    d.   Axis IV

8. Perhaps because of their behavioral problems, children with ADHD are often lower in intelligence by about _____IQ points. (p. 520)

    a.   3 to 5

    b.   15 to 20

    c.   7 to 15

    d.   2 to 8

9. ADHD is thought to occur in about _____ percent of the school-aged children. (p. 520)

    a.   3 to 5

    b.   15 to 20

    c.   7 to 15

    d.   20 to 80

10.   ADHD is more frequently found in boys before the age of (p. 520)

    a.   10.

    b.   11.

    c.   12.

    d.   8.

PRACTICE TEST NUMBER 2

1.   ADHD first appeared in the DSM-II in (p. 521)

    a.   1952.

    b.   1975.

    c.   1968.

    d.   1959.

2.   Oppositional defiant disorder is apparent by about the age of (p. 522)

    a.   8.

    b.   9.

    c.   15.

    d.   18.

3.   Conduct disorder is apparent by about the age of (p. 522)

    a.   8.

    b.   9.

    c.   15.

    d.   18.

4.   Risk factors that oppositional defiant and conduct disorders have in common include (p. 523)

    a.   family discord.

    b.   socioeconomic disadvantage.

    c.   antisocial behavior in parents.

    d.   all of the above.

5.   Conduct disordered children and adolescents are frequently comorbid for (p. 523)

    a.   depressive symptoms.

    b.   substance abuse disorder.

    c.   conversion disorder.

    d.   a and b.

6.   An effective treatment strategy for conduct disorder is the (p. 524)

    a.   juvenile justice system model.

    b.   cohesive family model.

    c.   punitive model.

    d.   IP model.

7. The goal of teaching behavior therapy techniques to the parent or parents of children with conduct disorder is so they can (p. 525)

    a. function as therapists in reinforcing desirable behavior.

    b. function as disciplinarians.

    c. increase their child's behavior.

    d. decrease their interaction with the child.

8. _____ is the most common childhood anxiety disorder. (p. 525)

    a. Selective mutism

    b. Post-traumatic stress

    c. Separation anxiety

    d. OCD

9. Selective mutism is rare in clinical populations and is seen most typically at what age? (p. 526)

    a. within the first year of life

    b. elementary school age

    c. kindergarten

    d. preschool

10. Although childhood and adult depression essentially use the same DSM diagnostic criteria, a recent modification to the childhood diagnosis is (p. 528)

    a. sadness.

    b. loss of appetite.

    c. irritability.

    d. withdrawal.

PRACTICE TEST NUMBER 3

1. Depression in children has been related to depression in (p. 530)

    a. their siblings.

    b. their mothers.

    c. their fathers.

    d. b and c.

2. Andrea is five years old has been diagnosed with childhood depression. She could benefit from what type of therapy? (p. 530)

    a. antidepressants

    b. play therapy

    c. cognitive-behavioral therapy

    d. psychoanalytical therapy

3. A tic is a persistent, intermittent muscle twitch or spasm, usually limited to a (p. 532)

    a. particular movement.
    b. particular time of day.
    c. generalized pattern.
    d. localized muscle group.

4. Tommy has been diagnosed with Tourette's syndrome. He is typical of other children with Tourette's. Tommy is probably how old? (p. 533)

    a. 15
    b. 2
    c. 42
    d. 7

5. _____ was a pioneer in the development of behavioral treatment for autistic children. (p. 537)

    a. Sigmund Freud
    b. Ivar Lovaas
    c. Albert Ellis
    d. Eric Erikson

6. Many famous and successful people have overcome their learning disabilities. Which of the following people had a learning disability? (p. 539)

    a. Sir Winston Churchill
    b. Woodrow Wilson
    c. Nelson Rockerfeller
    d. all of the above

7. Ionizing radiation may harm a child by acting directly on the _____ or may damage the sex chromosomes of either parent. (p. 542)

    a. fertilized egg
    b. womb
    c. brain tissue
    d. unfertilized egg

8. Research has shown that a person with Down syndrome have the greatest deficits in (p. 544)

    a. math skills.
    b. spatial relationships.
    c. verbal and language-related skills.
    d. visual-motor coordination.

9. Treatment without parental consent is permitted in all of the following cases, **except** (p. 548)

    a. immature minors.

    b. emancipated minors.

    c. emergency situations.

    d. court-ordered situations.

10. Haney and Gold found that most delinquent acts were committed (p. 553)

    a. alone, without any help.

    b. in association with one or two other persons.

    c. with three or four other persons.

    d. as part of a gang of at least a dozen.

COMPREHENSIVE PRACTICE TEST

The following tests are designed to give you an idea of how well you understood the entire chapter. There are three different types of tests: multiple-choice, true-false, and essay.

MULTIPLE-CHOICE

1. Children are vulnerable to psychological problems because they (p. 519)

    a. have less self-understanding.

    b. haven't developed a stable sense of identity.

    c. haven't a clear understanding of what is expected of them.

    d. All of the above.

2. _____ is devoted to studying the origins and course of individual maladaptation in the context of normal growth processes. (p. 518)

    a. Behavioral psychopathology

    b. Cognitive psychopathology

    c. Aging psychopathology

    d. Developmental psychopathology

3. Recent research, although inconclusive, has pointed to ADHD being a result of (p. 521)

    a. biological factors.

    b. social environmental factors.

    c. cognitive behavioral factors.

    d. a and b.

4. The medication Ritalin is often used to decrease overactivity and distractibility in children with ADHD. Side effects of this medication include (p. 521)

    a. decreased blood flow to brain.

    b. disruption of growth hormone.

    c. psychotic symptoms.

    d. all of the above.

5. Which of the following is the most common developmental sequence for conduct disorder (CD), antisocial personality (ASP), delinquency, and/or oppositional defiant disorder (ODD)? (p. 522)

   a. CD, ODD, ASP
   b. ODD, CD, ASP
   c. CD, ASP, ODD
   d. CD, ODD, delinquency

6. Anxiety disorders are more common in which group? (p. 525)

   a. boys
   b. girls
   c. teenagers
   d. middle-school children

7. Causal factors for childhood depression are also implicated in (p. 529)

   a. childhood anxiety disorders.
   b. autism.
   c. mental retardation.
   d. b and c.

8. Children's exposure to early _____ events can increase their risk for developing depression. (p. 529)

   a. happy
   b. traumatic
   c. unplanned
   d. all of the above

9. Enuresis and encopresis are known as (p. 530)

   a. elimination disorders.
   b. anal fixation disorders.
   c. anxiety disorders.
   d. none of the above.

10. The onset of sleepwalking disorder is usually between the ages of six and 12. It is classified under _____ in the DSM-IV-TR, rather than disorders of infancy, childhood, and adolescence. (p. 532)

   a. mood disorders
   b. anxiety disorders
   c. sleep disorders
   d. dissociative disorders, particularly fugue

11. Causal factors in autism include (p. 536)

   a. genetic factors.

   b. disturbance in the central nervous system.

   c. chromosome abnormalities.

   d. all of the above.

12. All of the following are true of infantile autism, **except** (p. 534)

   a. it afflicts about 6.5 out of every 10,000.

   b. it is usually identified before the child is 30 months old.

   c. it occurs much more frequently in boys than in girls.

   d. most cases are found in the upper classes.

13. The drug(s) used most often in autism is/are _____; however, the effects have not been very impressive. (p. 536)

   a. haloperidol

   b. barbiturates

   c. caffeine

   d. anti-anxiety

14. Dana has trouble in school. He has difficulty spelling and in word recognition. Often Dana will omit, add, or distort words. Dana probably has (p. 538)

   a. autism.

   b. dyslexia.

   c. mental retardation.

   d. ADHD.

15. Mental retardation is coded on (p. 540)

   a. Axis I.

   b. Axis II.

   c. Axis III.

   d. Axis IV.

16. Which of the following degrees of retardation is, by far, the most common? (p. 540)

   a. profound

   b. moderate

   c. severe

   d. mild

17. One of the major factors that needs to be taken into account when studying or treating children is (p. 548)

   a. child advocacy programs are always available.

   b. children are dependent on those around them.

   c. drug therapy is usually warranted.

   d. children are small adults.

18. The goal of early intervention programs for children is to (p. 551)

    a.   reduce the stressors in the child's life.

    b.   strengthen the child's coping mechanisms.

    c.   not have the problem repeat itself.

    d.   a and b.

19. Many habitual delinquents share the traits typical of the _____ personality. (p. 553)

    a.   antisocial

    b.   obsessive-compulsive

    c.   narcissistic

    d.   passive-aggressive

20. Alienation from family and the broader society causes juveniles to become more vulnerable to (p. 553)

    a.   incest and related sexual crimes.

    b.   negative influences of TV and other media.

    c.   the psychological support afforded by membership in a delinquent gang.

    d.   solitary acts of violence.

TRUE – FALSE

1. Progress in child psychopathology has caught up with that in adult psychopathology. T / F (p. 518)

2. Young children, if they attempt suicide or act violently toward another person, probably do so without any understanding of the finality of death.   T / F (p. 519)

3. Hyperactive children are not anxious.   T / F (p. 520)

4. Pemoline, when used to treat children with ADHD, has as many side effects as Ritalin. T / F (p. 521)

5. Not all children with conduct disorder will go on to become antisocial personalities. T / F (p. 522)

6. Kazdin (1995) said that family and social context factors are not as important causal factors in conduct disorders as genetics. T / F (p. 524)

7. Selective mutism should be diagnosed only if the child actually has the ability to speak and knows the language. T / F (p. 526)

8. Typically, children with anxiety disorders grow up to be adults who don't fit in.   T / F (p. 527)

9. Depression in children and adolescents occurs with high frequency. T   T / F (p. 528)

10.   Children can learn to be depressed.   T / F (p. 529)

11.   The average age of children with encopresis is three years.   T / F (p. 532)

12.   If a baby is to inherit PKU, both parents must carry the recessive gene.   T / F (p. 545)

13.   The treatment of children has come to mean family therapy for all members, including both parents, the child, and his or her siblings.   T / F (p. 549)

14.   Play therapy, when used with children, is an effective tool that can be used to reduce problems and promote adjustment.   T / F (p. 549)

ESSAY QUESTIONS

1.   Explain the causal factors in childhood anxiety disorders. (p. 526)

2. Discuss the causal effects of mental retardation. (pp. 542-43)

WEB LINKS TO ITEMS OR CONCEPTS DISCUSSED IN THIS CHAPTER

Autism

        www.autism-society.org/

        www.autism.org/contents.html

        www.autism.com/

        www.autism-resources.com/

Dyslexia

        www.dyslexia.com/

        www.interdys.org/

        www.interdys.org/index.jsp

Down Syndrome

        www.ndss.org/

        www.nas.com/downsyn/

        www.ds-health.com/

        www.nads.org/

        www.ndsccenter.org/

CRISS-CROSS

Now that you know all there is to know about this chapter, here's your opportunity to put that knowledge to work.

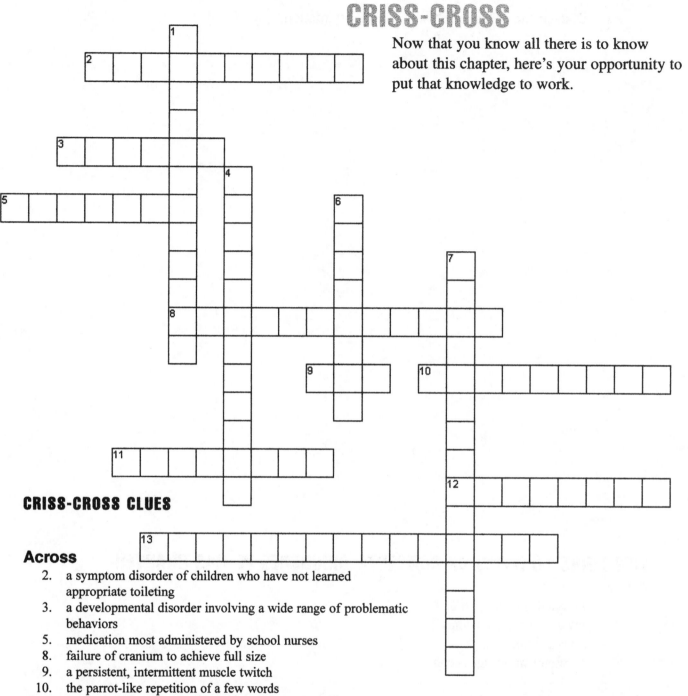

CRISS-CROSS CLUES

Across

2. a symptom disorder of children who have not learned appropriate toileting
3. a developmental disorder involving a wide range of problematic behaviors
5. medication most administered by school nurses
8. failure of cranium to achieve full size
9. a persistent, intermittent muscle twitch
10. the parrot-like repetition of a few words
11. another medication used in the treatment of ADHD
12. habitual, involuntary discharge of urine after the age of expected continence
13. a liver-based disorder, leading to brain damage if not diagnosed early

Down

1. irreversible limitations on survivability, achievement, and competence; 1 in every 1,000 babies
4. damage caused by accumulation of an abnormal amount of cerebrospinal fluid in the cranium
6. problems in word recognition and reading comprehension; routinely timo, dda, and trotsid words; often resulting in slow reading   *(Can't read those words? Maybe you have dyslexia. !yllaeR)*
7. anxiety-based condition involving persistent failure to speak in certain situations

Puzzle created with Puzzlemaker at DiscoverySchool.com

CHAPTER SEVENTEEN

Therapy

BEFORE YOU READ

Why do people seek therapy, and whom can they see for help? How do we know if therapy is effective, and under what conditions can it actually be harmful? And how do we assess what therapuetic approach—medication, psychotherapy, or both—should be considered and used? Chapter 17 deals with these questions.

A discussion follows on biological methods for the treatment of mental disorders, focusing on four major classes of psychotropic medications: antipsychotics (or neuroleptics), antidepressants, antianxiety medications, and mood-stabilizers for bipolar disorders. The authors analyse the history, major effects, side effects, modes of action, and effectiveness of each class. Other biological treatments, such as electroconvulsive therapy and neurosurgery, are also described. Potentially divisive issues, such as "cosmetic psychopharmacology," are mentioned, as well as the liability clinicians face when dispensing medications.

The major psychological therapies—psychodynamic therapies, behavior therapy, cognitive and cognitive-behavior therapies, humanistic-experiential therapies, couples, and family therapies—are covered. No single approach to psychotherapy has yet proven capable of handling the entire range of problems seen clinically. Consequently, the inclination to identify strongly with one approach or another is decreasing. Today, many therapists are familiar with a variety of techniques chosen from several therapeutic approaches and use these depending on the type of problems the client is having.

The chapter closes with discussions on the influences of social values and cultural diversity of psychotherapy.

OBJECTIVES

After reading this chapter, you should be able to:

1. Provide a general overview of the a) the assumptions and goals of psychotherapy, b) varied types of individuals who receive psychotherapy, c) various categories of providers of psychotherapeutic services and their specialized training, d) critical elements of the therapeutic relationship, and e) qualities that enhance therapy.

2. Discuss the many difficulties associated with attempting to evaluate the effectiveness of psychotherapy.

3. Explain what is meant by negative process, and describe potential deteriorative effects in psychotherapy.

4. Discuss the methodology, as well as the value and limitations, of efficacy psychotherapy outcome studies, and the other issues related to determining a therapeutic approach.

5. Summarize the major psychopharmacological treatments currently in use (antipsychotics, antidepressants, antianxiety drugs, and lithium and other mood-stabilizers), discussing their history, major effects, side effects, modes of action, and effectiveness.

6. Outline the issues associated with the widespread possibility of "cosmetic psychopharmacology" drugs, such as Prozac.

7. Describe early attempts at biological intervention, including coma and convulsive therapies and neurosurgery, and indicate which are currently believed to be effective.

8. Discuss the advantages of combining the biological and psychological forms of treatment.

9. List and describe the basic goals and techniques of the behavior therapies. Summarize recent developments in the behavior therapies, and evaluate their effectiveness in the treatment of maladaptive behavior.

10. List and describe the basic goals and techniques of the cognitive and the cognitive-behavior therapies. Summarize recent developments, and evaluate their effectiveness in the treatment of maladaptive behavior.

11. List and describe the basic goals and techniques of the humanistic-experiential therapies. Summarize recent developments in the humanistic-experiential therapies, and evaluate their effectiveness in the treatment of maladaptive behavior.

12. List and describe the basic goals and techniques of psychoanalysis, as well as developments in psychodynamic therapy since Freud. Evaluate the effectiveness of the psychodynamic approach to the treatment of maladaptive behavior.

13. Describe the basic goals and techniques of couples counseling, family therapy, and group therapy. Summarize recent developments in these therapies, and evaluate their effectiveness in the treatment of maladaptive relationships.

14. Review the issues and evidence surrounding the matching or mismatching of ethnicity in client-therapy pairings, and its potential effects on the therapeutic process.

AS YOU READ

Answers and page numbers can be found in the Answer Key at the end of the book.

KEY WORDS

Each of the words below is important in understanding the concepts presented in this Chapter. Write the definition next to each of the words.

psychotherapy (p. 558)

efficacy (p. 563)

double-blind (p. 563)

placebo (p. 563)

psychopharmacology (p. 563)

randomized clinical trial (p. 563)

antipsychotic drugs (p. 565)

half-life (p. 565)

tardive dyskinesia (p. 566)

antidepressant drugs (p. 568)

antianxiety drugs (p. 571)

electroconvulsive therapy (ECT) (p. 574)

neurosurgery (p. 576)

behavior therapy (p. 577)

systematic desensitization (p. 577)

imaginal exposure (p. 578)

in vivo exposure (p. 578)

modeling (p. 579)

token economy (p. 580)

response shaping (p. 580)

cognitive/cognitive-behavioral therapy (p. 581)

manualized therapy (p. 581)

stress-inoculation therapy (p. 582)

rational emotive behavior therapy (REBT) (p. 583)

client-centered therapy (p. 584)

psychodynamic therapy (p. 586)

free association (p. 587)

latent content (p. 587)

manifest content (p. 587)

resistance (p. 587)

transference (p. 587)

counter-transference (p. 588)

marital therapy (p. 589)

traditional behavioral couple therapy (p. 589)

family systems therapy (p. 590)

integrative behavioral couple therapy (p. 590)

structural family therapy (p. 590)

WHO'S WHO AND WHAT'S WHAT—MATCHING
Match the following psychological tests with the appropriate description of each test's purpose.

Psychological Test

_____ John Cade

_____ Albert Ellie

_____ psychoactive

_____ Carl Rogers

_____ Ugo Cerletti and Lucio Bini

_____ team approach

_____ negative process

_____ working alliance

_____ Aaron Beck

_____ Peter Kramer

_____ Virginia Satir

_____ Antonio Moniz

_____ Ladislas von Meduna

_____ randomized clinical trials

_____ depot neuroleptics

Purpose

A. involves coordinated efforts of medical, psychological, social work, and other mental health personnel working together as each case warrants.

B. a relationship between client and therapist that is essential to psychotherapuetic gain

C. what Binder and Strupp refer to as a rupture in the therapeutic alliance

D. efficacy trials

E. mind-altering

F. antipsychotic medications administered in a long-acting injectable form

G. author of *Listening to Prozac*

H. discovered that lithium salts were effective in treating manic disorders

I. regarded as the modern originator of inducing convulsions to treat mental disorders

J. Italian physicians who after visiting a slaughter house and seeing electric shock used on animals, passed electric current through a patient's head, a method which became known as ECT

K. introduced the frontal lobotomy in 1935

L. founder of REBT

M. his cognitive therapy assumes that client's problems stem from illogical thinking

N. founder of client-centered therapy

O. founder of conjoint family therapy

SHORT ANSWERS
Provide brief answers to the following questions.

1. What are the elements of a therapeutic alliance? (p. 560)

2. When evaluating treatment success, what sources of information are important? (p. 561)

3. Discuss the advantages and disadvantages of Buspirone in treating anxiety. (p. 572)

4. Compared with some other forms of therapy, behavior therapy has some distinct advantages. Briefly explain. (p. 580)

5. According to cognitive therapies, clients' errors in the logic behind their thinking leads them to problems like depression. Briefly explore this. (p. 582)

6. Briefly explain why the humanistic-experiential therapies have been criticized. (pp. 585-86)

FILL IN THE BLANKS

Read the following and fill in the blanks. These questions are designed to help you focus on specific details.

1. The belief that people with _____ problems can learn more _____ ways of _____, _____ and _____ is the conviction underlying all _____. (p. 558)

2. The half-life is the time it takes for the _____ of _____ drug in the body to be _____ by _____ percent. (p. 565)

3. Patients taking SSRIs tend to improve after about _____ to _____ weeks of treatment and are considered to have had a _____ response to treatment if they show at least a _____ percent improvement in their symptoms. (p. 568)

4. If a patient remains symptom free for _____ to _____ months or more, they are considered to have _____. (p. 570)

5. In spite of their side effects, MAO inhibitors are still used in certain cases of _____ _____ that are characterized by _____, and _____, and do not respond well to other classes of antidepressants. (p. 570)

6. Side effects of lithium include increased _____, _____, _____ _____, _____, and _____. It can also be _____ if the recommended dose is exceeded. (p. 573)

7. Instead of exploring past traumatic events or inner conflicts, the _____ focuses on the problem or symptom that is causing the distress. (p. 577)

8. The suppression of problematic behavior may be as simple as _____, provided, of course, _____. (p. 579)

9. One basic assumption underlying Beck's cognitive therapy approach is that problems like _____ result from clients' _____ about _____, the _____, and _____. (p. 581)

10. Many of us have learned _____ beliefs and _____ values that cause us to expect too much of ourselves, leading us to _____ and then to feel that we are _____. (p. 581)

11. Existential therapists do not follow any rigidly prescribed procedures but, rather, emphasize the _____ and his or her "_____." (p. 585)

12. Although gestalt therapy is commonly used in a _____, the emphasis is on _____. (p. 585)

13. Analytic interpretation involves a therapist's tying together a client's often _____ into a _____ to help the client _____ into the relationship between his or her _____ and the _____ that drive it. (p. 587)

THE DOCTOR IS IN...PSYCHIATRIC HELP—5¢

Read the following scenario and diagnose the client. Remember to look carefully at the criteria for the disorder before you make a decision as to the diagnosis. Make a list of other information you might need to help you understand the casual factors.

1. Bernice is a 47-year-old woman who recently lost her job in an auto factory. She is depressed and very concerned about how she is going to make ends meet when her unemployment insurance runs out. All she has ever done was to work factory jobs. She married right out of high school and supported her husband through school, as did her parents. Her husband was killed in an auto accident seven years ago. She has two children, 22 and 15 years old. Bernice tells you that she is concerned about her drinking. Her father was an alcoholic and her mother was always sad and withdrawn. She believed this was the reason her father drank, but wasn't certain, since he drank for as long as she could remember. Right now she finds herself wanting to drink, but trying not to give in to it, because she feels it might be bad for her. Her self-esteem is very low as she feels that she is not smart enough—since she only has a high school diploma—to do anything but work in a factory. Her kids are supportive and doing well, but she still feels like a bad mother, because she can't give them all the things she sees other kids have. She feels this way in spite of her children telling her they don't need or want those things.

    After reading the above scenario, pretend that you are a therapist and decide what aspects of the scenario would be emphasized/important for each of the following approaches. Also, discuss one aspect of treatment from each approach you would use with Bernice.

Pharmacological (pp. 563, 567)

      Treatment:

Behavior (p. 579)

      Treatment:

Cognitive and Cognitive-Behavioral (pp. 581-83)

      Treatment:

Humanisitic—Experiential (p. 584)

      Treatment:

Psychodynamic (pp. 586-88)

      Treatment:

AFTER YOU READ

Answers can be found in the Answer Key at the end of the book.

PRACTICE TESTS

Take the following three multiple-choice tests to see how much you have comprehended from the chapter. Each represents roughly one-third of the chapter. As you study the chapter, use these to check your progress.

PRACTICE TEST NUMBER 1

1.   Who are the most obvious candidates for psychological treatment? (p. 558)

    a.   Susan, whose husband left her

    b.   Andre, who lost his job

    c.   Carlos, whose wife just died from cancer

    d.   all of the above

2.   A new drug developed by a pharmaceutical company must obtain approval from what agency before it can be marketed? (p. 563)

    a.   NIMH

    b.   DEA

    c.   FDA

    d.   CCM

3. In the case of *Osherhoff vs. Chestnut Lodge,* Osherhoff received a settlement out of court because Chestnut Lodge (p. 564)

    a. put him on a waitlist for six months, during which time he continued to suffer major depression.

    b. had not administered drug therapy.

    c. had administered the wrong drug therapy.

    d. had provided psychotherapy by a minimally-trained psychotherapist.

4. The unique quality of antipsychotic drugs is their ability to (p. 565)

    a. calm patients.

    b. put patients to sleep.

    c. reduce patients' anxiety.

    d. reduce the intensity of delusions and hallucinations.

5. Virtually all of the antipsychotic drugs accomplish the same biochemical effect, which is (p. 565)

    a. blocking dopamine receptors.

    b. blocking the production of noradrenalin.

    c. stimulating the production of endorphins.

    d. stimulating the production of glutamic acid.

6. Tardive dyskinesia is a side effect of taking conventional (p. 566)

    a. antipsychotic medication.

    b. antidepressant medication.

    c. ECT.

    d. none of the above.

7. In 1988, this became the first SSRI to be released in the United States. (p. 567)

    a. Zoloft

    b. Haldol

    c. Prozac

    d. Paxil

8. The immediate short-term effects of the tricycic antidepressants serve to (p. 567-68)

    a. reduce central nervous system arousal.

    b. reduce intracranial pressure by absorbing cerebral spinal fluid.

    c. increase the availability of lithium in the central nervous system for absorption.

    d. increase the availability of serotonin and norepinephrine in the synapses.

9. The first antidepressant medications to be developed in the 1950s were (p. 570)

    a. SSRIs

    b. SNRIs

    c. MAO inhibitors

    d. tricyclics

10. Antidepressants are also being widely used to treat (p. 571)

    a. bulimia.

    b. panic disorders.

    c. GAD.

    d. all of the above.

PRACTICE TEST NUMBER 2

1. Benzidiazepines are used to treat (p. 571)

    a. depression.

    b. anxiety.

    c. bipolar.

    d. none of the above.

2. Lithium compounds are used in the treatment of (p. 573)

    a. anxiety.

    b. hyperactivity and specific learning disabilities.

    c. bipolar mood disorders.

    d. hallucinations and delusions.

3. Which of the following caused an immediate decrease in the widespread use of psychosurgical procedures in this country? (p. 576)

    a. a 1951 law banning all such operations

    b. the advent of electroconvulsive therapy (ECT)

    c. the advent of the major antipsychotic drugs

    d. the unusually high mortality rate

4. Psychosurgery is sometimes used for patients with debilitating (p. 576)

    a. obsessive-compulsive disorders.

    b. severe self-mutilation.

    c. schizophrenia.

    d. a and b.

5. In _____, positive reinforcement is often used to establish, by gradual approximation, a response that was initially resisted. (p. 580)

    a. response shaping
    b. token economy.
    c. modeling.
    d. avoidance therapy.

6. Systematic desensitization is aimed at teaching a person in the presence of an anxiety-producing stimulus to relax, because (p. 596)

    a. avoidance therapy makes one extremely tense.
    b. it is difficult, if not impossible, to feel pleasant and anxious at the same time.
    c. resistance is futile.
    d. sooner or later, one will have to confront one's fatal flaw.

7. In systematic desensitization, a patient confronting a feared real stimulus, as opposed to an imaginal one, is called (p. 578)

    a. desensitized exposure.
    b. unimaginative exposure.
    c. in vivo exposure.
    d. indecent exposure.

8. Using a form of the old-fashioned method of punishment to modify undesirable behavior is called (p. 578)

    a. aversion therapy.
    b. avoidance therapy.
    c. abhorrence therapy.
    d. subversion therapy.

9. Aversion therapy has been used successfully in the treatment of (p. 578)

    a. bizarre psychotic behavior.
    b. sexual deviance.
    c. smoking, drinking, overeating, drug dependence, and gambling.
    d. all of the above.

10. A therapist who believes it possible to take away something without putting something in its place is likely to be (p. 579)

    a. canonized.
    b. ineffective.
    c. treated like a thief.
    d. very effective.

PRACTICE TEST NUMBER 3

1. In 1964, Bandura found that the most effective treatment for snake phobia was   (p. 579)

    a. avoidance therapy.

    b. live modeling of fearlessness, combined with instruction and guided exposure.

    c. having patients crawl through snake pits.

    d. suppressing problematic behavior.

2. Generally, behavioral therapy has been found to be less useful for (p. 580)

    a. responses not initially in an individual's behavioral repertoire.

    b. the more pervasive and vaguely defined the client's problem is.

    c. older female patients.

    d. shy, withdrawn adolescents.

3. Behavioral techniques are the backbone of modern approaches to treating (p. 580)

    a. sexual dysfunctions.

    b. racism.

    c. psychopathy.

    d. eustice.

4. Albert Ellis' _____ posits that a well-functioning individual behaves rationally and in tune with empirical reality. (p. 581)

    a. cognitive therapy

    b. rational emotive behavior therapy (REBT)

    c. classical psychotherapy

    d. response shaping

5. Stress-inoculation therapy is a type of self-instructional training focused on (p. 582)

    a. avoidance training.

    b. altering the self-statements an individual routinely makes in stress-producing situations.

    c. reinforcers for socially appropriate behavior.

    d. all of the above.

6. During therapy, a gestalt therapist is likely to ask, (p. 585)

    a. "What are you aware of in your body now?"

    b. "When you close your eyes, do you see the light?"

    c. "What does it feel like in your gut when you think of that?"

    d. a and c.

7. Therapists must constantly beware of developing negative feelings toward the client, which is known as (p. 588)

    a. negative affect analysis.

    b. psychosis psychoanalysis.

    c. counter-transference.

    d. cognitive transcounterysis.

8. In integrative behavioral couple therapy (IBCT), _____ are integrated with change strategies to provide a form a therapy that is more tailored to individual characteristics and the needs of the couple. (p. 590)

    a. acceptance strategies
    b. fighting stances
    c. "flight-or-fight" strategies
    d. kugnitive fu

9. Most family therapists believe that _____—not just the designated "client"—must be directly involved in the therapy if lasting improvement is to be achieved. (p. 590)

    a. a teacher
    b. the family dog
    c. the family
    d. a minister

10. The _____ are based on the assumption that we have the freedom and the responsibility to control our own behavior. (p. 584)

    a. existential therapies
    b. humanistic-experiential therapies
    c. avoidance technology
    d. Democratic Party doctrines

COMPREHENSIVE PRACTICE TEST
The following tests are designed to give you an idea of how well you understood the entire chapter. There are three different types of tests: multiple-choice, true-false, and essay.

MULTIPLE-CHOICE

1. It is estimated that _____ percent of patients receive medications and psychotherapy. (p. 564)

    a. 55
    b. 75
    c. 25
    d. 65

2. Patients who received both had an overall positive response rate of _____ percent. (p. 563)

    a. 55
    b. 75
    c. 85
    d. 65

3. Which of the following would you see as making substantial gains in personal growth as a result of therapy? (p. 558)

    a. Louis, who feels he would like to go back to school to finish his degree.
    b. Meagan, who is depressed and suicidal.
    c. Tommy, who has a drinking problem that has affected his entire life.
    d. Paula, who has severe GAD.

4. Research suggests that about _____ percent of patients show clinically significant change after 21 therapy sessions. (p. 562)

    a. 75
    b. 50
    c. 25
    d. 28

5. A particularly harmful unethical behavior on the part of the therapist towards his or her client is (p. 562)

    a. going over the allotted hour for the therapy session.
    b. canceling an appointment.
    c. engaging in a sexual relationship.
    d. referring the client when it is apparent that the two of them can't work together.

6. A new drug that seems to be more effective in treating major depression, is (p. 568)

    a. Effexor, a SSRI.
    b. Effexor, a SNRI.
    c. Prozac, a SSRI.
    d. Prozac, a SNRI.

7. Carl Rogers client-centered therapy focuses on (p. 584)

    a. placing the client at the center of therapy sessions and answering his/her questions.
    b. natural power of the organism to heal itself.
    c. removing the constraints and restrictions that grow out of unrealistic demands that people tend to place on themselves.
    d. b and c.

8. The view of the existential therapist is that human beings, being aware of their own existence, are responsible for (p. 585)

    a. deciding what kind of person to become.
    b. establishing their own values.
    c. actualizing their own potentialities.
    d. all of the above.

9. The main two basic forms of psychodynamic therapy are (p. 586)

    a. transference and counter-transference.

    b. negative affect analysis and manifest analysis.

    c. manifest psychosis and latent oriented psychoanalytical.

    d. classical psychoanalysis and psychoanalytically oriented psychotherapy.

10. According to psychoanalysis, a dream has two kinds of content: (p. 587)

    a. transference and dream transference.

    b. cognitive content and dreary content.

    c. manifest content and latent content.

    d. big, hairy spider content and sexual content.

11. In _____, the therapist is careful to maintain a neutral manner, to allow the client to "work though" the conflict. (p. 587)

    a. dreams

    b. negative affect analysis

    c. psychoanalysis

    d. all of the above.

12. The original version of Freud's psychoanalysis is practiced only rarely today, because it (p. 588)

    a. is arduous.

    b. is costly in time, money, and emotional commitment.

    c. may take several years before all major issues have been resolved.

    d. all of the above.

13. The interpersonal therapy model developed by Klerman and associates, originally targeted for the problem of depression, has since been shown to be a promising treatment for (p. 589)

    a. avoidance recession.

    b. bulimia nervosa.

    c. avoidable stress.

    d. antisocial personality disorder.

14. Structural family therapy's approach is that family members will have altered experiences in the family and behave differently if (p. 590)

    a. they pack up and move to a different town.

    b. they change the organization of the family in such a way that members will behave more supportively and less pathogenically toward each other.

    c. the family context can be changed.

    d. b and c.

15. Today, clinical practice is characterized by a relaxation of the boundaries previously found between disciplines, and most psychotherapists (pp. 590-91)

    a. do pretty much what they want, striking out in whatever direction seems appropriate.

    b. try to borrow and combine concepts and techniques from various schools.

    c. don't really want to talk about it.

    d. all of the above.

TRUE – FALSE

1. Therapy can offer magical transformations.   T / F   (p. 558)

2. A client's motivation and the seriousness of the problem are important to the outcome of therapy. T / F (p. 559)

3. Effective therapy depends, to some extent, on a good match between the client and therapist.   T / F (p. 561)

4. Whites metabolize antidepressants and antipsychotic medications more slowly than African Americans.   T / F (p. 565)

5. Atypical antipsychotics may effectively treat the positive and negative symptoms of schizophrenia.   T / F (p. 567)

6. SSRIs are chemically related to the older tricyclic antidepressants.   T / T (p. 567)

7. A patient is in remission when treatment removes all symptoms.   T / T (p. 568)

8. Prozac, Paxil, and Zoloft are now among the drugs most often prescribed by physicians. T / F (p. 569)

9. Benzodiazepines are widely prescribed, because these aren't addictive.   T / F   (p. 571)

10. A variety of behavioral techniques have developed to help patients unlearn maladaptive behaviors. T / F (p. 577)

11. In token economy programs, patients earn tokens good for privileges by demonstrating appropriate ward behavior. T / F (p. 580)

12. Psychoanalysis is not easy to describe, and the problem is complicated because of inaccurate conceptions based on cartoons and other forms of caricature. T / F (p. 586)

13. The greatest contribution of the interpersonal approach may be its role in the developing movement toward "integration" of the various forms of therapy.   T / F (p. 588)

14. Although it is quite routine at the start of couples therapy for each partner to secretly harbor the idea that only the other will have to do the changing, it is nearly always necessary for both do so. T / F   (p. 589)

15. Often wives can see clearly what is "wrong" with their husbands, but not what attitudes and behaviors of their own are contributing to the marital impasse.   T / F (p. 589)

16. Husbands tend to have remarkable "insight" into their wives' flaws, but not their own. T / F (p. 589)

17. The criticism has been raised that psychotherapy can be viewed as an attempt to get people adjusted to a "sick" society, rather than to encourage them to work toward its improvement.   T / F (p. 591)

18. Even though there is little or no solid evidence that psychotherapeutic outcomes are diminished when client and therapist differ in race or ethnicity, most members of minority groups state a strong preference for therapists who share their ethnic background.   T / F (p. 592)

ESSAY QUESTIONS

1. Explain current views of ECT from the public view and a therapeutic view. Also discuss the types and the effectiveness. (pp. 574-75)

2. Evaluate cognitive-behavioral therapies. (pp. 583-84)

3. Name and discuss the four basic techniques of Freud's psychoanalysis. (pp. 586-88)

WEB LINKS TO ITEMS OR CONCEPTS DISCUSSED IN THIS CHAPTER

Behavior Therapy

       www.aabt.org/

       www.vanderbilt.edu/AnS/psychology/ health_psychology/BI_Therapy.htm

Cognitive therapy

       www.cognitivetherapy.com/

Rational Emotive Behavior Therapy (REBT)

       www.rebt.org/

       www.iret.org/

       panicdisorder.about.com/cs/therapyrebt/

Sigmund Freud

       www.freud.org.uk/

       www.psychoanalysis.org

       freud.t0.or.at/

CRISS-CROSS

Now that you know all there is to know about this chapter, here's your opportunity to put that knowledge to work.

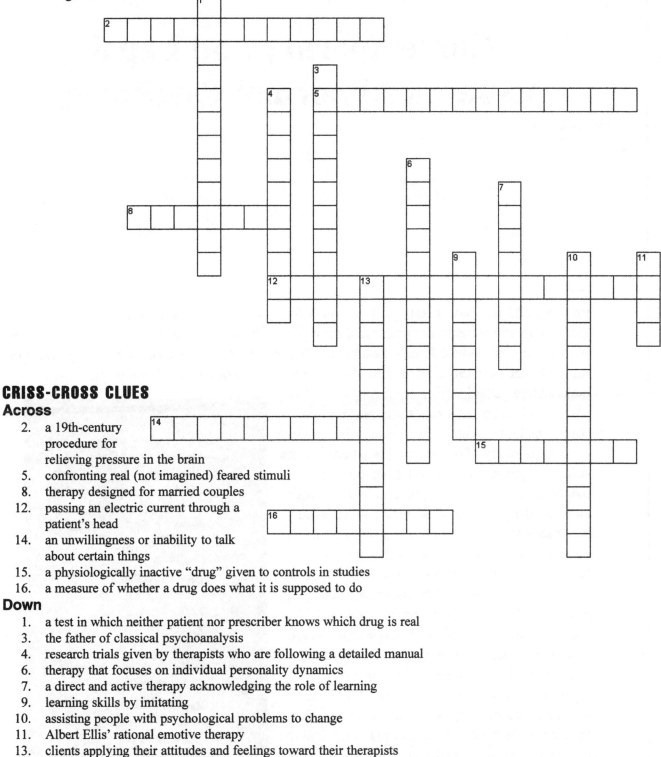

CRISS-CROSS CLUES

Across

2. a 19th-century procedure for relieving pressure in the brain
5. confronting real (not imagined) feared stimuli
8. therapy designed for married couples
12. passing an electric current through a patient's head
14. an unwillingness or inability to talk about certain things
15. a physiologically inactive "drug" given to controls in studies
16. a measure of whether a drug does what it is supposed to do

Down

1. a test in which neither patient nor prescriber knows which drug is real
3. the father of classical psychoanalysis
4. research trials given by therapists who are following a detailed manual
6. therapy that focuses on individual personality dynamics
7. a direct and active therapy acknowledging the role of learning
9. learning skills by imitating
10. assisting people with psychological problems to change
11. Albert Ellis' rational emotive therapy
13. clients applying their attitudes and feelings toward their therapists

Puzzle created with Puzzlemaker at DiscoverySchool.com

CHAPTER EIGHTEEN

Contemporary and Legal Issues in Abnormal Psychology

BEFORE YOU READ

Previous chapters have catalogued the many forms of mental disorders and have briefly described various treatment programs, most of which focus either directly on the patient or involve only immediate family members. Chapter 18, by contrast, describes programs and research that are focused at the broader societal level in order to attempt to prevent maladaptive behavior from occurring in the first place. This chapter tackles some of the more controversial legal and ethical issues surrounding psychopathology. For example, what constitutes sufficient grounds to commit a person to a mental institution? What are a patient's rights? How is "dangerousness" defined and assessed? What should a therapist do when told that a patient is planning to harm another person? Does insanity at the time of a crime preclude or absolve guilty intent? The chapter also discusses how the U.S. government, professional and volunteer agencies, and world organizations are involved in improving mental health. Finally, Chapter 18 discusses the neglect of patients' needs associated with managed healthcare and deinstitutionalization, as well as challenges for the future, the need for societal planning, and the importance of individual contributions.

OBJECTIVES

After reading this chapter, you should be able to:

1. Define "universal intervention," and explain how universal intervention includes biological, psychosocial, and sociocultural efforts.

2. Define "selective intervention," and describe and illustrate selective intervention programs, using the example of teen alcohol and drug abuse prevention.

3. Define "indicated intervention," describe two types of crisis intervention, and describe and illustrate three types of indicated intervention, using the example of an airplane crash or other major disaster.

4. Describe efforts to resocialize patients in mental hospitals and aftercare programs, including methods for making a mental hospital a therapeutic community. Compare the effectiveness of these approaches.

5. Outline the procedures involved in civil commitment and the safeguards for patients' rights and due process in involuntary commitment.

6. Discuss the problems of assessing and predicting "dangerousness" and explain the obligations of the clinician under the "duty-to-warn" legal doctrine.

7. Review the various legal rulings relevant to the insanity defense and discuss the problems and controversies associated with this concept.

AS YOU READ

Answers can be found in the Answer Key at the end of the book.

KEY WORDS

Each of the words below is important in understanding the concepts presented in this Chapter. Write the definition next to each of the words.

indicated interventions (p. 596)   Tarasoff decision (p. 610)

selective interventions (p. 596)   NGRI plea (p. 611)

universal interventions (p. 596)   insanity defense (p. 611)

milieu therapy (p. 602)   guilty but mentally ill (GBMI) (p. 615)

social-learning programs (p. 602)   health maintenance organization (HMO) (p. 620)

deinstitutionalization (p. 604)   managed health care (p. 620)

forensic psychology (forensic psychiatry) (p. 606)

WHO'S WHO AND WHAT'S WHAT—MATCHING

Alphabet Soup. The acronyms in column one are all related to mental health. Name these in the second column and describe what each does in the third. (pp. 615-17—textbook, only)

Acronym	What it means...	What it is...
AABT		
APA		
APA		
APS		
NAMI		
NIMH		
NIOSH		
WHO		

SHORT ANSWERS

Provide brief answers to the following questions.

1. Briefly discuss the three requirements for psychosocial "health." (p. 597)

    a.

    b.

    c.

2. Our government has approached the drug abuse problem with three broad strategies, all of which have proven insufficient. Name these and discuss. (p. 599)

    a.

    b.

    c.

3. Discuss the three general therapeutic principles that guide the "milieu therapy" approach. (p. 602)

    a.

    b.

    c.

4. A large study compared the relative effectiveness of three treatment approaches. Discuss what was discovered. (pp. 602-03)

    a. Milieu therapy

    b. Social-learning treatment program

    c. Traditional mental hospital treatments

5. An overcontrolled hostile person can become dangerous. Explain. (p. 609)

FILL IN THE BLANKS

Read the following and fill in the blanks. These questions are designed to help you focus on specific details.

1. Without a supportive community, individual development is _____. (p. 598)

2. Prominent social forces promoting the early use of alcohol in young people are attractive _____, the influence of _____, negative _____, and the ready _____. (p. 598)

3. Attempts to effect psychologically desirable social change are likely to involve ideological and political issues that may inspire _____, including _____. (p. 598)

4. Recent estimates suggest that there are some _____ chronically mentally ill individuals in America, of whom _____ reside in mental hospitals, with the remainder living in nursing homes. (p. 602)

5. The Tarasoff decision spelled out a therapist's _____ in situations where there has been an explicit threat on a specific person's life. (p. 610)

6. An important contribution of the World Health Organization (WHO) is its _____, which enables clinicians and researchers in different countries to use a uniform set of diagnostic categories. (p. 617)

7. Job dissatisfaction and poor mental health have been associated with work assignments involving _____ tasks that allow for _____ and give the worker _____ of having contributed to the ultimate product. (p. 617)

THE DOCTOR IS IN...PSYCHIATRIC HELP—5¢

Read the following scenarios and diagnose the client. Remember to look carefully at the criteria for the disorder before you make a decision as to the diagnosis. Make a list of other information you might need to help you understand the causal factors.

1. Stuart, a 26-year-old man you had been seeing for several years comes, into your office demanding to see you immediately, even though he doesn't have an appointment. He hasn't seen you for more than a month, because he had a job and was trying to go to school. Stuart is diagnosed with schizophrenia and is fine as long as he takes his medications; his behavior indicates he is not taking his medication. You try explaining to him that you have other appointments, but he becomes more and more agitated, talking about the people at work who are out to get him—but that he is going to get them first. Stuart is dishelved and looks like he hasn't bathed in several days. He tells you that you have to help him or he will do something awful.

    As Stuart's therapist, what would you do and why? (p. 606)

2.   Jack had been friends with Jill for two years. He was madly in love with her although, she had made it clear that she liked him only as a friend and didn't want a romantic relationship. About five months ago, Jill met Brian and they dating. Jack felt jealous and left out. He had been through other "boyfriends" and always managed to wait them out until Jill stopped seeing them. This time is different, and Jill is talking about possibly marrying Brian. Jack is beside himself and is consumed with anger and jealousy. He is talking about killing Brian and making it look like an accident. He reasons that Jill will then have to seek him out again for comfort. When asked how he would make it look like an accident, Jack replies that he would fix the breaks on Brian's car. Jack has the knowledge to do such a thing.

As Jacks' therapist, how would you respond, and what are your legal responsibilities? (p. 610)

AFTER YOU READ

Answers can be found in the Answer Key at the end of the book.

PRACTICE TESTS

Take the following three multiple-choice tests to see how much you have comprehended from the chapter. Each represents roughly one-third of the chapter. As you study the chapter, use these to check your progress.

PRACTICE TEST NUMBER 1

1.   Universal interventions are concerned with (p. 596)

   a.   altering conditions that can cause or contribute to mental disorders.

   b.   establishing conditions that foster positive mental health.

   c.   early detection and prompt treatment of maladaptive behavior.

   d.   a and b.

2.   Any effort aimed at improving the human condition, at making life more fulfilling and meaningful, may be considered part of _____ prevention of mental or emotional disturbance. (p. 596)

   a.   universal

   b.   selective

   c.   indicated

   d.   secondary

3. All of the following are sociocultural efforts toward universal intervention of mental disorders, **except** (p. 598)

    a. economic planning.

    b. penal systems.

    c. public education.

    d. social security.

4. Teenage drug and alcohol use is still viewed as one of today's (p. 598)

    a. biggest money makers for organized crime.

    b. victories over crime.

    c. most significant psychological and community problems.

    d. a and c.

5. Through their own drinking or verbalizations about alcohol, parents may (p. 600)

    a. encourage use in their children.

    b. sanction usage by their children.

    c. have little affect in their children's usage.

    d. a and b.

6. The most powerful influence on whether a teen begins to use drugs seems to be (p. 600)

    a. peers.

    b. parents.

    c. teachers and schools.

    d. Pete, the mean kid down the block.

7. Programs designed to help youngsters overcome negative pressures from peers focus on (p. 600)

    a. boxing and Kung Fu.

    b. teaching social skills and assertiveness.

    c. chess.

    d. strengthening family bonds.

8. A study in 2000 reported that _____ had had more than a few sips of alcohol. (p. 601)

    a. 80.3 percent of twelfth graders

    b. 71.4 percent of tenth graders

    c. 51.7 percent of eighth graders

    d. all of the above.

9. A persistent concern about hospitalization is that (p. 602)

    a. the mental hospital may become a permanent refuge from the world.

    b. negative feedback is used to encourage appropriate verbalizations and actions by patients.

    c. the environment, or milieu, is a crucial aspect of the therapy.

    d. b and c.

10. Milieu therapy is (p. 602)

    a. the temporary substitution of one treatment mode by another until adequate resources can be acquired to provide the treatment of choice.

    b. a general term for any form of preventive treatment.

    c. the establishment of a hospital environment itself as a therapeutic community.

    d. the integration of any two distinct forms of treatment.

PRACTICE TEST NUMBER 2

1. The rise of biological therapies has meant that (p. 602)

    a. nearly one-third of patients will be ineligible to return to the mental hospital.

    b. from 70% to 90% of patients labeled as psychotic and admitted to mental hospitals can now be discharged within a few weeks.

    c. all the activities in many mental hospitals can be brought into the total treatment program.

    d. many patients are encouraged to take responsibility for their behavior.

2. Studies have shown that in the past, up to _____% of schizophrenic patients have been readmitted within the first year after their discharge. (p. 603)

    a. 1.732

    b. 12.6

    c. 45

    d. 99.44

3. Between 1970 and 1992, the number of state mental hospitals dropped from 310 to 273, and the patient population was reduced by 73 percent due to (p. 604)

    a. the AIDS epidemic.

    b. fallout from the Vietnam war.

    c. the introduction of antipsychotic drugs.

    d. deinstitutionalization.

4. Deinstitutionalization has contributed substantially to (p. 606)

    a. mental health and general well-being in the U.S.

    b. the number of homeless people.

    c. the number of mentally ill people in prison.

    d. b and c.

5. According to recent Justice Department statistics, _____ of the people in prison in the U.S. (275,000) have a mental disorder. (p. 605)

    a.   1.732%

    b.   more than 16%

    c.   about half

    d.   almost all

6. Typically, the first step in committing an individual to a mental hospital involuntarily is (p. 606)

    a.   appointing a physician and a psychologist to examine the client.

    b.   filing a petition for a commitment hearing.

    c.   holding a commitment hearing.

    d.   notifying the police.

7. Studies have confirmed that individuals acquitted of crimes by reason of insanity typically spend _____ time in psychiatric hospitals as (than) individuals convicted of crimes spend in prison. (p. 614)

    a.   less

    b.   about the same amount of

    c.   about the same amount or more

    d.   much more

8. Violent acts are difficult to predict because these are determined as much by _____ circumstances as by the personality traits of the individual. Mental health professionals typically err on the conservative side when assessing violence proneness. (p. 609)

    a.   territorial

    b.   behavioral

    c.   situational

    d.   hostile

9. Two major source of personality information is (p. 609)

    a.   your mother and the FBI.

    b.   data from the person's previous history.

    c.   data from personality tests.

    d.   b and c.

10. Congress passed its first comprehensive mental health bill, the National Mental Health Act in (p. 615)

    a.   1789.

    b.   1865.

    c.   1946.

    d.   1993.

PRACTICE TEST NUMBER 3

1. The M'Naghten Rule of 1843 established legal defense for a person   (p. 614)

    a. if she lacked "substantial capacity" to appreciate the criminal character of her behavior.
    b. if he were "unable to appreciate" the criminality of his act and the mental disorder involved must be severe.
    c. unless it can be proven that at the time of her act, she did not know what she was doing was wrong, she is assumed to be sane.
    d. if an "irresistible impulse" caused him to commit the crime, even though he knew what he was doing was wrong.

2. The Irresistible Impulse Rule of 1887 established legal defense for a person   (p. 614)

    a. if she lacked "substantial capacity" to appreciate the criminal character of her behavior.
    b. if he were "unable to appreciate" the criminality of his act and the mental disorder involved must be severe.
    c. unless it can be proven that at the time of her act, she did not know what she was doing was wrong, she is assumed to be sane.
    d. if an "irresistible impulse" caused him to commit the crime, even though he knew what he was doing was wrong.

3. The American Law Institute (ALI) Standard of 1962 established legal defense for a person   (p. 614)

    a. if she lacked "substantial capacity" to appreciate the criminal character of her behavior.
    b. if he were "unable to appreciate" the criminality of his act and the mental disorder involved must be severe.
    c. unless it can be proven that at the time of her act, she did not know what she was doing was wrong, she is assumed to be sane.
    d. if an "irresistible impulse" caused him to commit the crime, even though he knew what he was doing was wrong.

4. The Federal Insanity Defense Reform Act (IDRA) of 1984 redefined legal defense for a person to be such that (p. 614)

    a. if she lacked "substantial capacity" to appreciate the criminal character of her behavior.
    b. if he were "unable to appreciate" the criminality of his act and the mental disorder involved must be severe.
    c. unless it can be proven that at the time of her act, she did not know what she was doing was wrong, she is assumed to be sane.
    d. if an "irresistible impulse" caused him to commit the crime, even though he knew what he was doing was wrong.

5. The National Institute of Mental Health (NIMH) was formed in Washington, D.C. in (p. 615)

    a. 1812.
    b. 1849.
    c. 1946.
    d. 1984.

6. The National Institute of Mental Health (NIMH) (p. 615)

    a. conducts and supports research.

    b. supports training in the mental health field.

    c. helps communities plan, establish, and maintain effective mental health programs.

    d. all of the above.

7. The National Mental Health Association (NMHA) (p. 616)

    a. sets and maintains the high professional and ethical standards within the psychological industry.

    b. recognizes psychological disorders as one of the 10 leading work-related health problems.

    c. works for the improvement of services in community clinics and mental hospitals.

    d. works to reduce the incidence of mental retardation and carry on a program of education.

8. The American Psychological Association (APA) (p. 616)

    a. sets and maintains the high professional and ethical standards within the psychological industry.

    b. recognizes psychological disorders as one of the 10 leading work-related health problems.

    c. works for the improvement of services in community clinics and mental hospitals.

    d. works to reduce the incidence of mental retardation and carry on a program of education.

9. The National Institute for Occupational Safety and Health (NIOSH) (p. 616)

    a. sets and maintains the high professional and ethical standards within the psychological industry.

    b. recognizes psychological disorders as one of the 10 leading work-related health problems.

    c. works for the improvement of services in community clinics and mental hospitals.

    d. works to reduce the incidence of mental retardation and carry on a program of education.

10. The National Association for Retarded Citizens (NARC) (p. 616)

    a. sets and maintains the high professional and ethical standards within the psychological industry.

    b. recognizes psychological disorders as one of the 10 leading work-related health problems.

    c. works for the improvement of services in community clinics and mental hospitals.

    d. works to reduce the incidence of mental retardation and carry on a program of education.

COMPREHENSIVE PRACTICE TEST
The following tests are designed to give you an idea of how well you understood the entire chapter. There are three different types of tests: multiple-choice, true-false, and essay.

MULTIPLE-CHOICE

1. At high risk for mental disorders are (p. 596)

    a. recently divorced people and the physically disabled.

    b. elderly people and physically abused children.

    c. persons recently uprooted from their homes and victims of severe trauma.

    d. all of the above.

2. Adequate preparation for potential problems likely to be encountered by anyone during a given life stage is a requirement for _____ health, at the _____ level of prevention (p. 597)

    a. biological, universal
    b. psychosocial, universal
    c. biological, selective
    d. psychosocial, selective

3. Grounds for commitment, in addition to mental illness, require that a person must be judged to be _____ and in need of treatment or care in a hospital. (p. 606)

    a. dangerous to themselves or to others
    b. incapable of providing for their basic physical needs
    c. unable to make responsible decisions about hospitalization
    d. any of the above

4. Which of the following patient rights was limited, according to a 1990 U.S. Supreme Court ruling? (p. 607)

    a. right to compensation for work
    b. right to refuse ECT and psychosurgery
    c. right to receive treatment
    d. right to refuse psychotropic medication

5. Violence among psychiatric patients is especially prominent for those who (p. 608)

    a. watch television.
    b. drink alcohol.
    c. do not get enough exercise.
    d. all of the above.

6. One dilemma in attempting to rehabilitate previously violent psychiatric patients is that the mental health workers must exhibit some degree of (p. 609)

    a. patience.
    b. stability.
    c. professionalism.
    d. trust.

7. A man's NGRI plea ("not guilty by reason of insanity") in a court case means (p. 611)

    a. "he couldn't have done it, because that would be an insane thing to do."
    b. "Not Getting Rightful Incarceration."
    c. "while he did do it, he lacked moral blameworthiness, because he was insane."
    d. whichever reason seems like it might work.

8. Courts have generally not considered _____ sufficient grounds for an insanity defense. (p. 612)

   a.   altered states of consciousness

   b.   being from Mississippi

   c.   having more than one personality

   d.   being married

9. An NGRI pleas was found most likely to be successful if the defendant was (p. 614)

   a.   diagnosed with a major mental disorder, or there had been prior mental hospitalizations.

   b.   a female.

   c.   accused of a violent crime other than murder.

   d.   all of the above.

10. Several states have adopted a different mentally ill plea, known as (p. 615)

   a.   Please Let Me Go (PLMG).

   b.   Guilty But Mentally Ill (GBMI).

   c.   Too Drunk to Know (TDTK).

   d.   all of the above.

11. During World War II, _____ recruits were rejected for military service for psychiatric reasons. (p. 615)

   a.   42

   b.   1.732%

   c.   two out of seven

   d.   55,734

12. Most often, in an HMO, the gatekeeper who determines which mental health treatments will be offered is a (p. 620)

   a.   psychiatric social worker.

   c.   medical generalist or business professional.

   b.   Ph.D. psychologist.

   d.   psychiatrist.

13. The World Health Organization (WHO) estimates that mental disorders affect more than _____ people worldwide. (p. 617)

   a.   42

   b.   three million

   c.   200 million

   d.   1.732 billion

14. Serious mental health risk factors, unrecognized as workplace problems, may exist in (p. 617)

    a. the work load and pace; machine-paced work in particular.

    b. the work schedule; rotating shifts and night work.

    c. role ambiguity; who has responsibility for what.

    d. all of the above.

15. It is estimated that _____ of healthcare expenditures in the United States are for managed care administration. (p. 621)

    a. 1.732%

    b. less than 10%

    c. 12%

    d. 25%

16. Other than accepting some measure of responsibility for the mental health of others through the quality of one's own interpersonal relationships, another constructive course open to each citizen is (p. 619)

    a. serving as a volunteer in a mental or other hospital.

    b. supporting realistic measures for ensuring comprehensive health services for all age groups.

    c. working toward improved public education, responsible government, the alleviation of prejudice, and the establishment of a more sane and harmonious world.

    d. All of the above, of course.

TRUE – FALSE

1. For the most part, mental health efforts have been restorative, rather than preventative. T / F (p. 596)

2. Often the most beneficial aspect of a therapeutic community is the interaction among the patients themselves.   T / F (p. 602)

3. Today, in most states, the therapist not only can violate confidentiality with impunity, but may be required by law to take action to protect persons from the threat of imminent violence against them. T / F (p. 610)

4. The new "guilty but mentally ill" (GBMI) plea requires a two-part decision. T / F (p. 615)

5. Psychological difficulties among employees may result in absenteeism, accident proneness, poor productivity, and high job turnover.   T / F (p. 616)

6. The World Federation for Mental Health was established in 1861.   T / F (p. 617)

7. The world's mental health problems are so large and so scattered that there is really nothing that an individual can do to help.   T / F (p. 619)

ESSAY QUESTIONS

1. Deinstitutionalization, the movement to close down mental hospitals and treat persons with severe mental disorder in the community, has been the source of considerable controversy. Discuss the pros and cons of deinstitutionalization. (p. 604)

2. A relatively new approach in behavioral psychology is in its prevention, as opposed to previous approaches, all aimed at treatment. Name and discuss the three subcategories of these efforts. (p. 596)

    a.

    b.

    c.

3.   The wake of the Tarasoff decision left many perplexing issues for practitioners. Discuss the decision and its aftermath. (p. 610)

WEB LINKS TO ITEMS OR CONCEPTS DISCUSSED IN THIS CHAPTER

Mental Health

        www.nimh.nih.gov/

        www.mentalhealth.org/

        www.nmha.org/

        www.mental-health-matters.com/

insanity defense

        www.psych.org/public_info/insanity.cfm

        www.forensic-psychiatrist.com/insanity.html

        www.forensic-evidence.com/site/ Behv_Evid/Finger_insanity.html

milieu therapy

        www.ohsu.edu/cliniweb/F4/F4.754.864.392.html

CRISS-CROSS

Now that you know all there is to know about this chapter, here's your opportunity to put that knowledge to work.

CRISS-CROSS CLUES
Across
5. volunteer organization for the mentally ill
6. intervention efforts aimed at a specific subgroup
7. volunteer organization working for improvement of services in community clinics
11. murder victim whose death led to "duty-to-warn" rule
12. recognizes psychological disorders as one of then leading work-related health problems
13. legal status of the mentally ill
14. total treatment program
15. NGRI

Down
1. new criminal court plea requiring two-part decision
2. professional organization for behavioral therapists
3. intervention efforts aimed at influencing the general population
4. professional organization for psychologists
7. agency serving as central research and training center
8. professional organization that sets standards for U.S. psychiatric industry
9. health services company
10. intervention efforts directed toward high-risk individuals

Puzzle created with Puzzlemaker at DiscoverySchool.com

ANSWERS TO
TEST QUESTIONS

FIND THE ANSWER HERE

CHAPTER ONE

MATCHING

Match each of the following people with her/his accomplishment or theory.

C.   Jerome Wakefield

F.   Kazdin (1998)

D.   Emil Kraeplin (1856-1926)

A.   Eugen Bleuler (1857-1939)

B.   Alois Alzheimer (1864-1945)

E.   Sigmund Freud (1856-1939)

A.   Swiss psychiatrist who worked with Kraepelin to write about schizophrenia and manic depression

B.   described disorder that was to become associated with a disorder common to elderly people

C.   proposed idea of mental disorders as being "harmful dysfunctions."

D.   German psychiatrist who worked with Bleuler to write about schizophrenia and manic depression

E.   founder of psychoanalysis

F.   "Methodology is not merely a compilation of practices and procedures. Rather it is an approach toward problem solving, thinking, and acquiring knowledge."

What's What—Match each of the following professions with its definition.

E.   Clinical Psychologist

A.   Counseling Psychologist

D.   School Psychologist

B.   Psychiatrist

C.   Psychoanalyst

F.   Psychiatric Social Worker

H.   Psychiatric Nursing

(I.) Occupational Therapist

G.   Pastoral Counselor

A.   Ph.D. in psychology and internship in mental or student counseling

B.   M.D. with residency in psychiatric hospital

C.   M.D. or Ph.D. with emphasis on psychoanalysis

D.   may or may not have Ph.D., but has extensive training regarding academic or learning problems

E.   Ph.D. in psychology with research and clinical skills

F.   M.S.W. or Ph.D. with clinical training in mental health settings

G.   ministerial background and training in psychology

H.   R.N. certification but could also have M.A. or Ph.D. specializing in care and treatment of psychiatric clients

SHORT ANSWERS *(Your answer should contain the following points.)*

1. Discuss how the Developments in Research 1.1 "Do magnets help with Repetitive-Stress Injury," demonstrate the importance of controlled research trials. (p. 4)
   a. It demonstrated that claims the magnets helped with repetitive stress injuries weren't founded, because the placebo group improved more than the group that actually had the magnets.

2. Describe the difference between inpatient and outpatient care for people with mental disorders. What are some of the changes that have occurred in treatment? (p. 13)
   a. Not all people with mental disorders receive treatment.
   b. Many people get help from general practitioners instead of seeing a specialist.
   c. Outpatients visit mental health facilities, see private therapists, or go through a hospital.
   d. The cost of hospitalization makes for shorter stays—deinstitutionalization.
   e. State hospitals are closed due to budget cuts.

3. Discuss the strengths and limitations associated with using the experimental method when conducting treatment research. (p. 20)
   a. **Strengths:** Straightforward set-up and design—proposed treatment given to one group of patients and withheld from another similar group of patients. If treated patients improve, compared to the untreated group, the treatment works. Treatment can then be given to the "waiting list" control group.
   b. **Limitations:** Withholding beneficial treatment for a period of time.

4. Explain the problem with expanding the DSM to include more kinds of behavior that are undesirable, such as "road rage." (p. 24)
   a. Economic interest of mental health professionals as related to insurance reimbursement.
   b. Mental health professionals tend to enhance the phenomenon as related to their own experiences.
   c. This could, if not checked, lead to almost any discomfort being considered a mental disorder.
   d. This inclusiveness would lose most of the scientific productive meaning.

FILL IN THE BLANKS

1. The four drawbacks to a classification system for mental disorders are: *__LOSS OF INFORMATION__*, *__STIGMATIZING__*, *__STEREOTYPING__*, and *__LABELING__*. (pp. 5-6)

2. Prevalence estimates can be determined by several different methods: *__POINT__* prevalence, estimated active cases in a given population at any instant; *__ONE-YEAR__* prevalence, number who suffered from the studied disorder at any time during a year, and *__LIFETIME__* prevalence, the number of people who suffered the studied disorder any time in their lives. (pp. 11-12)

3. Correlational research looks at variables to determine if there is a **_POSITIVE_** correlation, where things vary together in a direct, corresponding manner, a **_NEGATIVE_** correlation, where there is an inverse relationship between variables or **_UNCORRELATED_**, where the variables are independent of one another. (p. 19)

4. The authors of your textbook focus on three significant aspects of the disorders. These are the **_CLINICAL PICTURE_**, **_POSSIBLE CAUSAL FACTORS_**, and **_TREATMENTS_**. (p. 22)

5. Experimental research in values manipulating the **_INDEPENDENT_** variable and seeing what effect this has on the **_DEPENDENT_** variable. (p. 25)

6. Unfortunately, receiving a psychiatric diagnosis can lead a person to being **_STIGMATIZED_**, **_STEREOTYPED_**, and/or **_LABELED_** by others. (p. 6)

7. By referring not to the causes of mental disorders, but to their characteristics, the DSM attempts to be "**_ATHEORETICAL._**" (p. 7)

PICTURE THIS

1. Nomenclature (No "men" + Clay + TUR)
2. Comorbidity (COM + Oar + < BIB - B + D > + I + Tea)
3. Criterion Group (Cry + Tear + E + Un + Group)
4. Independent Variable (In + D + Pen + Dent)
5. Dependent Variable (Same as above, almost, of course)
6. ABAB Design (Abs to the left, Abs to the right + D + Sign)

OBSERVATIONAL AND EXPERIMENTAL RESEARCH DESIGNS

(A) In observational research, data are collected from two different samples or groups and then compared.

(B) In experimental research, participants are assessed at baseline and then randomly assigned to different groups (e.g., a treatment and a control condition). After the experiment or treatment is completed, data are then compared. (Adapted from Petrie and Sabin, 2000)

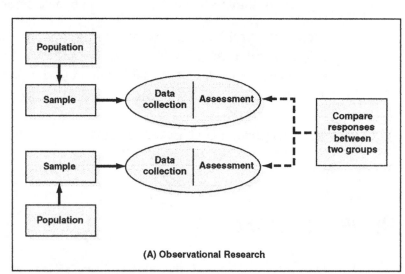

(A) Observational Research

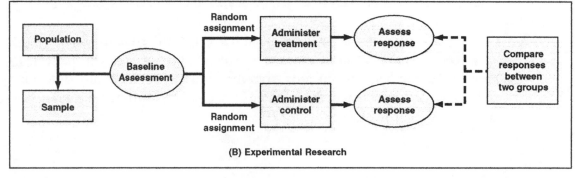

(B) Experimental Research

DOCTORAL CANDIDATE IS IN PROCESS—INTERN HELP 2.5 CENTS

You are a doctoral candidate in psychology and are starting your research. You are trying to decide what research design would be best for your work. The two you have decided to seriously consider are observational and experimental. Fill in the blanks for both methods below and write a brief description of both. (p. 20)

PRACTICE TESTS
PRACTICE TEST NUMBER 1

1. To understand mental disorders, we need to (p. 3)
    a. ask questions that will help patients and their families.

2. An example of what is abnormal or deviant changes over time is the removal of _____ as a mental disorder. (p. 5)
    c. homosexuality

3. A respectful way to classify the disorder, not the person, is by saying (p. 6)
    b. "Suzie, who has schizophrenia, in Room 627."

4. The most recent edition of the DSM is (p. 7)
    b. DSM-IV-TR

5. Mary is worrying excessively. This excessive worry is an example of a _____ which could indicate a larger problem. (p. 8)
    c. symptom

6. John has been having trouble sleeping, feeling sad, having difficulty concentrating, and is losing weight. Together, all of these behaviors are referred to as a (p. 8)
    a. syndrome.

7. Koro, an anxiety disorder, is an example of a psychopathology that is specific to which culture? (pp. 9-10)
    c. Asian

8. The World Around Us 1.3 "Personnel in Mental Health" describes professional and para-professional persons who work in the area of mental health. Two para-professionals described are (p. 11)
    c. community mental health worker and alcohol- or drug-abuse counselor.

9. The ECH and NCS epidemiology studies cited in your book found that the most prevalent kind of psychological disorder in the United States is a(n) (p. 12)

    b. anxiety disorder.

10. The NCS study found that _____ percent of people with one disorder also had one or more additional disorders. (p. 13)

    c. 56

PRACTICE TEST NUMBER 2

1. Early knowledge of psychopathological disorders come primarily from (p. 14)

    b. case studies of specific individuals.

2. Carol sits in a chair with several electrodes attached to her scalp. She is asked a series of questions. How her brain is processing this information is being recorded. The method that is being used to collect information is (p. 15)

    b. brain-imaging techniques.

3. Research in abnormal psychology is concerned with (p. 16)

    a. gaining enhanced understanding.
    b. gaining control of abnormal behavior.
    c. a and b.

4. Although single case studies can be valuable, these do have drawbacks, one of which is (p. 16)

    b. yielding enough information to make generalizations.

5. The most important thing to consider when conducting a research study is (p. 16)

    a. finding people who fit the criteria.

6. A representative sampling is (p. 17)

    a. a small group of people drawn from a larger group, which meets criteria for the research.

7. In doing research on childhood abuse experiences, David asked his subjects to recall certain incidents, but also relied on (pp. 18-19)

    b. school reports.
    c. medical records.
    d. b and c.

8. A _____ research approach collects information about a person's early life in an attempt to identify factors that lead to the development of a disorder. (p. 18)

    b. retrospective

9. The most basic experimental design in single-case research is the (p. 21)

    c. ABAB design.

10. In a single-case research design, the same _____ is studied over time. (p. 21)

    b. subject

PRACTICE TEST NUMBER 3

1. A _____ research approach focuses on individuals who have a higher-than-average likelihood of developing a psychological disorder and provide assistance before the disorder develops. (p. 18)

    a. prospective

2. Drs. Abby and Normal are conducting experimental research on the effects of sound on student concentration. They will be manipulating the sound level in their experiment. The sound is known as the (p. 19)

    b. independent variable.

3. The outcome of the above experiment is known as the (p. 20)

    a. dependent variable.

4. Pat was in a study in which she received a sugar pill instead of the experimental medication. Afterward she reported feeling better. Pat's reaction is a result of what? (p. 4)

    a. placebo treatment

5. A distinctive innovation since the DSM-III of 1980 has been the use of "operational" criteria for defining disorders. This means that the DSM now (p. 7)

    d. specifies the exact behaviors that must be observed.

6. There is strong evidence for significant overlap between anxiety and depression. Still a patient receives two diagnoses: one for anxiety and one for depression. This is an example of (p. 13)

    d. comorbidity.

7. Which of the following terms refers to a mental condition of relatively short duration? (p. 13)

    b. acute

8. In order to make sense of observed behavior, psychologists generate more or less plausible ideas called (p. 15)

    b. hypotheses.

9. The purpose of _____ is to ensure, in effect, that each member of the population has an equal chance of being included in the study's sample. (p. 17)

    d. random selection

10. A psychologist identifies 50 children who have schizophrenic mothers. At adolescence, the researcher compares those who break down with those who don't. This is an example of a _____ study. (p. 18)

    c. prospective

COMPREHENSIVE PRACTICE TEST
MULTIPLE-CHOICE

1. A classification system for mental disorders is advantageous because it gives us a way to (p. 5)
    a. structure information.
    b. advance research.
    c. create treatment plans.
    d. all of the above.

2. The DSM is published by the (p. 7)
    c. American Psychiatric Association

3. The number of active cases in a population during any given period of time is referred to as (p. 11)
    d. prevalence.

4. The number of new cases that occur over a period of time is referred to as (p. 12)
    a. incidences.

5. Research in abnormal psychology helps to (p. 13)
    a. study the nature of the disorder.
    b. understand the causes.
    c. provide the best care.
    d. all of the above.

6. Doing research on shopping behavior for her class, Sally sat on a bench in a busy mall making notes of what she saw. Sally was using what method to gather information? (p. 14)
    a. direct observation

7. Dr. Casey has what she thinks is a unique client and has done extensive data collection when working with him, including taking photographs of the behavior. she plans to present this client's behavior at a national convention. Dr. Casey is using what method to gather this information? (p. 14)

   d.   case study

8. Stan and Jim are eager to find out if college students at their school are typical with regard to the ever-increasing problem of binge drinking. To gather this information, they create a survey asking a number of questions about student's drinking habits. The method that Stan and Jim are using is (p. 15)

   c.   self-report.

9. Jennifer is doing research on the effects of violent video games on children's behavior. Her observations have lead her to believe that possibly there is a connection. She wants to test this concept. Jennifer's idea is called a(n) (p. 15)

   c.   hypothesis.

10. To test a hypothesis, researchers use _____ of people who don't exhibit the disorder being studied. (p. 17)

    b.   a control group

11. Unlike a controlled-research approach, observational or correlational research (p. 17)

    c.   does not manipulate variables.

12. The possible reason(s) two variables are highly correlated is/are (p. 18)

    a.   variable A causes B (or vice versa).
    b.   variable A and variable B are both caused by variable C.
    c.   variables A and B are both involved in a pattern of other variables that influence A and B.
    d.   all of the above.

13. Chris is studying depression in animals. He hopes that his findings may be generalized to humans. Chris's work is referred to as a(n) (p. 22)

    d.   analogue study.

14. Observational research studies things as they (p. 25)

    c.   are.

15. The New View Hospital is conducting a research study in which neither the experimenters nor the subjects know who is getting the experimental drug and who is getting the placebo. This is an example of what kind of study? (p. 4)

    d.   double-blind study

TRUE / FALSE

1. T — Two areas in which psychologists are specially trained are asking questions and doing research. (p. 3)

2. F — There is consensus regarding the definition of "abnormality." (p. 4)

3. T — Culture plays a role in how clients present mental disorders to clinicians. (p. 9)

4. T — More than 18% of the U.S. population suffers from at least one mental disorder during the course of a year. (p. 13)

5. F — People with psychological disabilities will always seek treatment from a trained psychologist. (p. 13)

6. F — Research is confined to the laboratory. (p. 14)

7. T — The greater the number of people who are sampled or studied, the better the findings will be.   (p. 14)

8. F — The less representative the sample, the more the findings can be generalized to the larger group. (p. 17)

9. F — Correlation proves causation. (p. 18)

10. T — Correlational studies can suggest causal hypotheses. (p. 18)

11. T — The experimental research methods have proven valuable in treatment research. (p. 20)

12. F — Experimental research always involves testing hypotheses by manipulating variables across groups. (p. 21)

13. T — The authors of your textbook believe it is important to be respectful of scientific principles and patients who have psychopathological conditions. (p. 23)

ESSAY QUESTIONS *(Your answer should contain the following points.)*

1. Describe the elements of abnormality. (p. 6)
    a. Suffering: psychological suffering
    b. Maladoptiveness: behavior that interferes with well-being and ability to enjoy work and relationships.
    c. Deviancy: statistically rare behavior
    d. Violation of the standards of society: failure to follow conventional social and moral rules
    e. Social discomfort: discomfort of those around a person who has violated social rules
    f. Irrationality and unpredictability: behavior is not expected, and the person is unable to control his or her behavior

2. Steve is doing research on how watching comedy will affect people who are depressed. Discuss how Steve will go about setting up his research. (pp. 15-19)
    a. Formulate a hypothesis.
    b. Find a representative sampling of depressed people.
    c. Create a control group.
    d. Show each group funny movies.
    e. Measure results-dependent variables.

CRISS-CROSS ANSWERS
Across
5. comorbidity
7. double-blind
10. epidemiology

Down
1. acute
2. sampling
3. prevalence
4. placebo
5. chronic
6. incidence
8. symptoms
9. syndrome

CHAPTER TWO

WHO'S WHO IN THE HISTORY OF ABNORMAL PSYCHOLOGY

THE ANCIENT WORLD

Plato *(429-347 B.C.)* _____ 6

Galen *(130-200 A.D.)* _____ 19

13 _____ Hippocrates *(460-377 B.C.)*

27 _____ Aristotle *(384-322 B.C.)*

Accomplishments _____

THE MIDDLE AGES

Martin Luther *(1483-1546)* _____ 1

8 _____ Avicenna *(980-1037)*

12 _____ Paracelsus *(1490-1541)*

Accomplishments _____

THE 16th THROUGH THE 18th CENTURIES

Teresa of Avila *(1515-1582)* _____ 7

Riginald Scot *(1538-1599)* _____ 2

William Tuke *(1732-1822)* _____ 11

Benjamin Rush *(1745-1813)* _____ 22

26 _____ Johann Weyer *(1515-1588)*

17 _____ Robert Burton *(1576-1640)*

15 _____ Philippe Pinel *(1745-1826)*

Accomplishments _____

THE 19th AND EARLY 20th CENTURIES

Clifford Beers *(1876-1943)* _____ 10

Emil Kraepelin *(1856-1926)* _____ 20

Wilhelm Wundt *(1832-1920)* _____ 21

Lightner Witmer *(1867-1956)* _____ 14

William Healy *(1869-1963)* _____ 9

B. F. Skinner *(1904-1990)* _____ 25

4 _____ Dorothea Dix *(1802-1887)*

5 _____ Franz Anton Mesmer *(1734-1815)*

18 _____ Sigmund Freud *(1856-1938)*

3 _____ J. McKeen Cattell *(1860-1944)*

23 _____ Ivan Pavlov *(1849-1936)*

16 _____ John B. Watson *(1878-1958)*

24 _____ E. L. Thorndike *(1874-1949)*

Accomplishments _____

SHORT ANSWERS *(Your answer should contain the following points.)*

1. Describe the contributions Hippocrates made to the understanding of mental illness. (pp. 28-29)
   a. did not believe gods and demons possessed the mentally ill
   b. mental illness had natural causes
   c. thought the brain was the central organ of intellectual activity and that brain pathology caused mental illness
   d. heredity, predisposition, and head injuries would cause sensory and motor disorders

2. The occurrence of mass madness peaked in the 14th and 15th centuries. Why, according to the text, was mass madness so common during these years? (p. 34)
   a. social oppression, famine, and epidemic diseases (Black Death)
   b. depression, fear, and wild mysticism
   c. unable to control their environment

3. Describe the atmosphere and treatment methods at the early asylums. (pp. 36-37)
   a. storage places for the insane
   b. filthy and cruel
   c. patients put on exhibition for the public
   d. forced to beg on streets
   e. shackled to walls, unable to lie down
   f. inadequate food, clothing, comforts

4. Discuss the reasons moral management of the mentally ill had been abandoned by the end of the 19th century. (p. 38)
   a. ethnic prejudice
   b. failure of the movement's leaders to train replacements
   c. overextension of hospital facilities
   d. rise of the mental hygiene movement, which focused on physical well-being
   e. advances in biomedical science

5. Explain the important events that lead to the biomedical breakthrough in discovering a cure for general paresis. (p. 44)
   a. 1825—French physician Bayle differentiated general paresis as a specific type of mental disorder.
   b. 1897—Viennese psychiatrist Richard von Krafft-Eging inoculated paretic patients with matter from syphilitic sores.
   c. 1906—von Wasserman developed a blood test for syphilis.
   d. 1917—von Wagner-Tauregg, chief of psychiatric clinic at the University of Vienna, introduced malarial fever treatment.
   e. 1978—First controlled studies of malarial treatment by Bahr and Brutsch were very successful.

FILL IN THE BLANKS

1. The four bodily fluids (humors) Hippocrates and Galen believed controlled health, and, when not in balance, caused mental illness were ***BLOOD***, ***PHLEGM***, ***BILE***, and ***BLACK BILE***. (p. 29)

2. The Middle Ages in Europe lasted from about 500-1500 A.D. The Middle Ages can be characterized as ***VOID*** with respect to scientific thinking about the causes of abnormal behavior or enlightened treatment of mentally disordered persons. (p. 32)

3. Robert Burton, who wrote ***ANATOMY OF MELANCHOLIA*** in 1621, said there were two types of demonically possessed people—those who were ***PHYSICALLY*** possessed and considered mad, and those who were ***SPIRITUALLY*** possessed and considered witches. (p. 34)

4. Henry VIII of England established a mental hospital in 1545 called St. Mary of Bethlehem, which soon became known as ***BEDLAM***, adding a new word to our language. (p. 36)

5. The first hospital in the United States devoted exclusively to the mentally ill was ***THE PUBLIC HOSPITAL*** which was constructed in Williamsburg, Virginia, in 1773. (p. 36)

6. In the early 19th century ***DRUGGING***, ***BLEEDING***, or ***PURGING*** were the acceptable medical treatment of "lunatics." These produced few objective results. (p. 39)

7. In the early 20th century, two people who were instrumental in helping Clifford Beers educate the public concerning the bad treatment still given the mentally ill were ***WILLIAM JAMES*** and ***ADOLF MEYER***. (p. 40)

8. The development in 1956 of two psychotropic medications, ***RESERPINE*** and ***CHLORPROMAZINE***, which was discussed in Developments in Research 2.3 "Historic Search for Medication to Cure Related Disorders," effected psychiatric hospitals by leveling admissions at 560,000, then dropping them to 300,000 by 1971. (p. 42)

9. In addition to an emphasis on the importance of brain pathology in mental disorders, the most important contribution of Kraepelin's 1883 textbook was his system of ***CLASSIFICATION OF MENTAL DISORDERS*** which became the forerunner of today's DSM-IV. (p. 44)

10. In disagreement with the Nancy School, Charcot insisted that ***DEGENERATIVE BRAIN DISORDERS*** led to hysteria. (p. 46)

11. The Nancy School finally triumphed in its dispute with Charcot, representing the first recognition of a ***PSYCHOLOGICALLY*** caused mental disorder. (p. 46)

12. The debate between the Nancy School and Charcot was a step in recognizing that mental disorders could have a ***PSYCHOLOGICAL*** basis or a ***BIOLOGICAL*** basis or ***BOTH***. (p. 46)

13. The behavioral perspective is organized around a central theme: the role of *LEARNING* in human behavior. (p. 48)

14. John A. Watson's (1878-1955) behavioristic approach placed emphasis on the role of the *SOCIAL* environment in *CONDITIONING* personality development and both *NORMAL* and *ABNORMAL* behavior. (p. 49)

THE DOCTOR IS IN...PSYCHIATRIC HELP—5¢

1. You are an assistant to the great Greek physician, Hippocrates. A patient comes to you and is sad, not interested in anything, sleeping badly, and unable to take part in the active Greek social life. Hippocrates asks for your opinion on what is wrong with this patient, the cause, and the treatment. What would you say? (pp. 28-29)

    a. *Diagnosis:*   the patient is melancholic

    b.. *Cause:*   the black bile is out of balance

    c. *Treatment:*   regular tranquil life
    sobriety and abstinence from excesses
    vegetable diet
    celibacy
    exercise short of fatigue
    possible bleeding

2. You and Philippe Pinel have just taken charge of the asylum of La Bicétre in Paris. What experiment do you and Pinol conduct there? (p. 37)
    a. remove chains from patients
    b. treat people with kindness, permit exercise
    c. provide sunny rooms, rather than dungeons

3. As a psychiatrist in the early 19th century, you have just become affiliated with the local asylum. A young woman comes to the asylum and tells you she is feeling low, lacks energy, and has several physical symptoms: crying and pain in several areas of her body. How would you diagnose her and what would you consider the cause of her affliction. (p. 39)
    a. *Diagnosis*: shattered senses of neurasthenics
    b. *Causes*: using up of precious nerve force
    excesses in living
    lifestyle problems

4. It's 1912 and you have just been referred to Dr. Sigmund Freud. You have had symptoms of hysteria and he is the leading expert in the field. What would you expect Dr. Freud to tell you about the cause of your disorder and what treatments would he use? (p. 45)
    a. *Cause*: thoughts/experiences in the unconscious
    b. *Treatment:* hypnosis, emotional release through catharsis, free association, and dream analysis

PRACTICE TESTS
PRACTICE TEST NUMBER 1

1. Stone-age cave dwellers treated mental illness by performing a crude operation known as (p. 28)

    b. trephining.

2. Abnormal behavior was attributed to what by the ancient Chinese, Egyptians, Hebrews, and Greeks? (p. 28)

    c. demon or god possessions

3. A person who "spoke with a god" in ancient China would have been considered to be (p. 28)

    d. possessed by good spirits.

4. If a person were considered possessed by a demon, treatment usually was (p. 28)

    c. exorcism.

5. Hippocrates and, later Galen, supported an early paradigm that stated _____ bodily humors were responsible for human behavior. (p. 29)

    d. four

6. The first person to consider dreams an important tool in understanding a patient's problem was (p. 29)

    c. Hippocrates.

7. The first person to propose that people with mental disorders weren't responsible for their criminal behavior was (p. 29)

    d. Plato.

8. The first to provide descriptions of consciousness and to write extensively on mental disorders was (pp. 29-30)

    a. Aristotle.

9. The ancient Roman physician, Galen, maintained a very scientific approach to psychological disorders by dividing their causes into _____ categories.   (p. 31)

    d. physical and mental

10. _____, known as the "prince of physicians," wrote *The Canon of Medicine* during the Middle Ages. (p. 31)

    b. Avicenna

PRACTICE TEST NUMBER 2

1. During the Middle Ages in Europe, people with mental disorders were (p. 32)

   d. void of humane treatment.

2. Johann Weyer, one of the first physicians to specialize in mental disorders, is also know as the founder of (p. 35)

   a. modern psycholopathology.

3. Who is considered the first person to begin humane treatment of the mentally ill in French asylums? (p. 37)

   b. Philippe Pinel

4. This man established the York Retreat, a country house where the mentally ill could live, work, and rest in a religious atmosphere. (p. 37)

   b. William Tuke

5. He is the founder of American psychiatry. (p. 38)

   c. Benjamin Rush

6. *The Snake Pit* was written in 1946 by _____. It called attention to the need for more humane mental health care in the _____, not overcrowded mental hospitals. (p. 40)

   a. Mary Jane Ward; community

7. The National Institutes of Mental Health was organized in (p. 40)

   b. 1946

8. Beginning in the last part of the 19th century, technological discoveries helped start what is known today as the _____ view of abnormal behavior. (p. 43)

   a. scientific
   b. experimentally oriented
   d. a or b

9. Emil Kraepelin, in his work to classify mental disorders, distinguished between mental disorders and thought the course of each was (p. 45)

   b. predictable and predetermined.

10. Freud's method of treatment, psychoanalysis, has its roots in the study of (p. 45)

    a. hypnosis.

PRACTICE TEST NUMBER 3

1. Franz Anton Mesmer (1734-1815), in his belief that people possessed magnetic fields that could be used to cure mental disorders, demonstrated most of the phenomena later associated with (pp. 45-46)

    c.   hypnosis.

2. Who was the first person to attempt to systematically answer the question as to how psychologically based mental disorders develop? (p. 46)

    d.   Freud

3. Toward the end of the 19th century, another school of thought, called _____ about abnormal behavior began to emerge that challenged the dominant theory. (p. 48)

    d.   behaviorism

4. Ivan Pavlov (1849-1936) is noted for his work with dogs in which he demonstrated what was to become known as (pp. 48-49)

    a.   operant conditioning.

    c.   classical conditioning.

    d.   a and c.

5. Operant conditioning theory, developed by E. L. Thorndike (1874-1949) and B. F. Skinner (1904-1990), explores how behaviors are influenced by (p. 49)

    d.   consequences.

6. All of the following are reasons that have been offered as explanations for the abandonment of moral treatment in the latter part of the 19th century, **except** (p. 38)

    c.   general loss of faith among the general population.

7. Classical and operant conditioning differ primarily with respect to (p. 49)

    a.   the types of reinforcers involved.

8. To understand current events in psychology, or any area, for that matter, it is important to have an understanding of the _____ developments. (p. 52)

    a.   historical

9. It is often difficult to study historical information and form accurate pictures. Why is this the case? (p. 53)

    a.   events are open to reinterpretation

    b.   bias on part of researchers

    c.   cannot rely on direct observation

    d.   all of the above

10. In 1917, Wagner-Jauregg introduced a treatment for general paresis involving (p. 44)

  d.   infecting the sufferer with malaria.

COMPREHENSIVE PRACTICE TEST
MULTIPLE-CHOICE

1.   Information dating back to the 16th century B.C. on the treatment of disease and mental disorders appear on the (p. 28)
  a.   Edwin Smith and Ebers papyri.

2.   Early Chinese, Egyptians, Hebrews, and Greeks believed person who became excited or overactive and perhaps exhibited strange behavior to be (p. 28)
  a.   possessed by evil spirits or demons.

3.   Hippocrates said that mental illness could be classified into three general categories: (p. 29)
  d.   mania, melancholic, and phrenitis.

4.   According to ancient Greek and Egyptian medicine, hysteria was a result of a(n) (p. 30)
  b.   wandering womb.

5.   _____ has been called the "Hippocates of China." (p. 33)
  c.   Chung Ching

6.   Who is considered a pioneer in the humane treatment of the mentally ill in England? (p. 37)
  d.   William Tuke

7.   Dorothea Dix is noted for her highly successful campaign to do something about the (p. 39)
  a.   inhuman treatment accorded the mentally ill.

8.   In the early part of the 19th century, psychiatrists were known as (p. 39)
  c.   alienists.

9.   The last half of the 20th century saw a change in the mental hospital environment because of what scientific development? (p. 41)
  c.   effective medication

10. Believing that mentally disturbed people were better off in the community, which could provide integrated and humane treatment, the latter decades of the 20th century began a movement of (p. 41)
  b.   deinstitutionalization.

11. Advancing knowledge of anatomy, physiology, neurology, chemistry, and general medicine lead to the identification of _____ pathology underlying many physical ailments, as well as mental illnesses. (p. 44)

    c.   biological

12. He is acknowledged as the most frequently cited psychological theorist of the 20th century. (p. 45)

    c.   Freud

13. Who is considered the founder of clinical psychology? (p. 48)

    c.   Lightner Witmer

14. Who was the first person to expand the causes of abnormal behavior beyond inner psychological problems to include environmental or sociocultural factors? (p. 48)

    b.   William Healy

15. Behaviorism emerged out of (p. 48)

    a.   experimental psychology.

TRUE – FALSE

1. T — What was known as hysteria, is referred to today as conversion disorder. (p. 30)

2. T — Contrariis contrarius was a treatment plan used by ancient Roman doctors to treat patients. (p. 31)

3. F — During the Middle Ages, Europe was more enlightened in its treatment of the mentally ill than the Middle East. (p. 31)

4. F — Scientific questioning didn't emerge again until the first part of the 19th century. (p. 35)

5. T — Johann Weyer (1515 - 1588) was a German physician and writer who used the pseudonym, Joannus Wierner, when he wrote *The Deception of Demons*. (p. 35)

6. T — Asylums are often referred to as sane houses. (p. 36)

7. F — Moral management was a success because antipsychotic drugs were used to help patients. (p. 38)

8. T — The early period of the Middle Ages in Europe saw the mentally ill treated with kindness by the clergy. This later gave way to much more inhumane treatment. (p. 34)

9. T — Early 19th century psychiatrists/alienists became the purveyors of morality by saying that Victorian morality was good for mental health. (p. 39)

10. F — By the end of the 19th century, mental hospitals were accepted by society as well-run facilities. (p. 40)

11. F — Wilhelm Wundt and Carl Jung are two names associated with the early rigorous efforts to objectively study psychological processes. (p. 47)

ESSAY QUESTIONS *(Your answer should contain the following points.)*

1. Discuss the motives behind and problems with deinstitutionalization. (pp. 41-42)

   a. **Motives**: –more humane treatment

   –more cost effective

   –eliminate the possibility of people becoming "chronically sick" in institutions

   –new medication would allow people to lead productive lives outside the hospital

   b. **Problems** –"abandonment" of chronic patients to harsh existence of living on the streets

   –no planned community efforts to fill the gaps in community services

2. Explain the disagreement between the Charcot and the Nancy School. (p. 46)

   a. **Nancy School**—Bernheim and Liebeault hypothesis that hypnotism and hysteria were related and due to suggestion.

   Basis for hypothesis—symptoms of hysteria could be produced by hypnosis and eliminated by hypnosis

   b. Charcot believed hysteria caused by degenerative brain changes

   c. Debate between physiological cause and psychological cause

   d. **Nancy School triumphed**—first recognition of a psychologically caused mental disorder

CRISS-CROSS ANSWERS

Across

10. deinstitutionalization

Down

1. classical conditioning
2. operant conditioning
3. free association
4. unconscious
5. tarantism
6. mesmerism
7. psychoanalysis
8. lycanthropy
9. behaviorism
11. asylums

CHAPTER THREE

Who's Who—Match each of the following people with her/his accomplishment or theory.

C. Karen Horney

E. Harry Stack Sullivan

D. Erik Erikson

B. Erich Fromm

A. Alfred Adler

A. believed that people are inherently social beings motivated primarily by the desire to belong to and participate in a group.

B. focused on dispositions that people adopt in their interactions.

C. vigorously rejected Freud's demeaning female psychology.

D. broadened Freud's psychosexual stages into more socially-oriented concepts.

E. maintained that the term, "personality" was best defined in terms of an individual's characteristic way of relating to others.

What's What—Match each of the following people with her/his accomplishment or theory.

E. Discrimination

C. Generalization

B. Intermittent

D. Reinforcement

A. Avoidance conditioning

A. A person, previously bitten, avoids dogs.

B. An occasional win at gambling keeps the behavior going.

C. A person, beaten as a child by an authority figure, has an involuntary fear of anyone in authority.

D. A child performs a response that produced candy in the past.

E. A child learns that although red and green strawberries look somewhat similar, only the red ones taste good.

What's What—Match each of the following people with her/his accomplishment or theory.

C. Authoritative

D. Authoritarian

A. Permissive-indulgent

B. Neglecting-uninvolved

A. impulsive and aggressive; spoiled, selfish, inconsiderate, and demanding; exploit people for their own purposes.

B. disruptions in attachment in childhood; moodiness, low self-esteem, and conduct problems later in childhood; problems with peer relations and academic performance.

C. energetic and friendly, competent in dealing with others and the environment.

D. conflicted, irritable, moody; poor social and cognitive skills.

SHORT ANSWERS *(Your answer should contain the following points.)*

1. List the five methods used in behavior genetics to study the heritability of mental disorders and give description of each. (pp. 65-68)

   a. **pedigree or family-history method**—observation of samples of relatives of each proband case to see whether the incidence increases in proportion to the degree of hereditary relationship.

   b. **twin method**—the study of monozygotic and dizygotic twins to look at concordance rates for mental disorders.

   c. **adoption method**—the study of adopted offspring of parents with a mental disorder and those who parents did not have a disorder to see if a disorder develops.

   d. **linkage analysis**—studies that capitalize on currently known locations of chromosomes of genes for physical characteristics or biological processes to see if the same could apply for mental disorders.

   e. **association studies**—studies of large groups of people with and without a disorder, followed by a comparision of the frequencies of certain genetic markers that are known to be located on particular chromosomes in the people with and without the disorder.

2. Briefly explain the cultural differences between Western and Japanese perspectives on attachment relationships. (pp. 98-99)

   a. **Western**—attachment occurs when mother's respond in a sensitive fashion to children's signals. Children are to show exploration and autonomy, discuss strong feelings and disagree, have positive self-views.

   b. **Japanese**—parents anticipate children's needs, thus avoid children being exposed to stress. Children are dependent on their mothers, emotionally restrained, express feelings indirectly, are self-critical and self-effacing.

3. Define and give an example of each of the following defense mechanisms (see chart on page 75)

   a. acting out

   b. denial of reality

   c. displacement

   d. fixation

   e. projection

   f. rationalization

FILL IN THE BLANKS

1. A *NECESSARY* cause is one that must exist for a disorder to occur, but it is not always a sufficient cause. (p. 56)

2. A *SUFFICIENT* cause guarantees the occurrence of a disorder, but it may not be necessary for the disorder to occur. (p. 56)

3. A *CONTRIBUTORY* cause increases the probability of a disorder but is neither necessary nor sufficient. (p. 57)

4. Causal factors occurring relatively early in life that do not show their effects for many years are considered *DISTAL* causal factors that may contribute to a *PROXIMAL* to develop a disorder. (p. 57)

5. Causal factors that operate shortly before the occurrence of symptom onset would be considered *PROXIMAL* causal factors that, in some cases, may be no more than the "straw that breaks the camel's back." (p. 57)

6. A condition that tends to maintain maladaptive behavior that is already present is a *REINFORCING* cause (e.g., the extra attention, sympathy, and removal from unwanted responsibility that may be secondary to becoming ill). (p. 57)

7. Being raised by a parent who is warm and supportive is an example of a *PROTECTIVE* factor. (p. 58)

8. Thomas Kuhn noted that theoretical orientations in science typically remain strong even in the face of evidence or alternate explanations. A theory typically lasts until a fundamental insight is achieved that appears to resolve problems left unsolved by existing theories. The new insights, also called *PARADIGM* shifts, are complete reorganizations of the way people think about a particular issue or field of science. (p. 60)

9. The electrical nerve impulse travels from the cell body of a neuron to the terminal buttons via the *AXON* (p. 62)

10. The *AXON ENDINGS* or *TERMINAL BUTTONS* are the sites where neurotransmitter substances are stored until needed. When the nerve impulse reaches the axon endings, the transmitter is released into the *SYNAPSE* a tiny fluid-filled gap between the axon endings of the *PRESYNAPTIC NEURON* neuron and the *DENDRITES OR ALL BODY* of the postsynaptic neuron. (p. 62)

11. The neurotransmitter substances act on the dendrite of the postsynaptic neuron at specialized places called *RECEPTOR* sites. (p. 62)

12. The effect of the neurotransmitter on the postsynaptic neuron can be either _**EXCITATORY**,_ which means it increases the probability that the neuron will fire, or _**INHIBITORY**,_ which means that it decreases the probability that the neuron will fire. (p. 62)

13. The action of the neurotransmitter substance is time-limited either by deactivation by an _**ENZYME**,_ such as monoamine oxidase, in the synaptic cleft or by a process called _**RE-UPTAKE**,_ which takes it back into the presynaptic neuron and stores it in the synaptic storage vesicles. (p. 61)

14. Highly intelligent parents provide an intellectually stimulating environment. This is an example of what has been termed a(n) _**PASSIVE**_ effect of the child's genotype on the environment, resulting from the genetic similarity of parents and children. (p. 65)

15. Happy babies evoke more positive responses from others than do passive, unresponsive infants. This is an example of a(n) _**EVOCATIVE**_ effect of the child's genotype from the social and physical environment. (p. 65)

16. Extroverted children may seek the company of others, thereby enhancing their own tendencies to be sociable. This is an example in which the child's genotype plays a more _**ACTIVE ROLE**_ in shaping the environment. (p. 65)

17. If a given disorder were completely heritable, the _**CONCORDANCE RATE**_ for identical twins with the disorder would be 100%. (pp. 65-66)

18. Those factors that would affect all children in a family similarly are known as _**SHARED ENVIRONMENTAL INFLUENCES.**_ (p. 67)

19. The id operates according to the _**PLEASURE**_ principle. (p. 72)

20. The id generates mental images and fantasies referred to as _**PRIMARY PROCESS**_ thinking. (p. 72)

21. The ego operates according to the _**REALITY**_ principle. (p. 74)

22. The ego uses reason and intellectual resources to deal with the external world, which is referred to as _**SECONDARY PROCESS**_ thinking. (p. 74)

23. The superego is the outgrowth of internalizing the _**TABOOS**_ and _**MORAL VALUE**_ of society. (p. 74)

24. Freud's views replaced brain pathology with intrapsychic conflict and exaggerated ego defenses against anxiety as the cause of at least some mental disorders. One of his most noteworthy contributions was to emphasize the extent to which ***UNCONSCIOUS*** motives and ***DEFENSE*** mechanisms affect behavior, the importance of ***EARLY CHILDHOOD*** experiences in later personality adjustment and maladjustment, and the importance of ***SEXUAL*** factors in human behavior and mental disorders. The second particularly noteworthy contribution was the realization that the same psychological principles apply to both ***NORMAL*** and ***LEARNED*** behavior. (pp. 78-79)

25. Two important criticisms of psychoanalytic theory have been offered. First, it fails to recognize the scientific limits of ***PERSONAL REPORTS OF EXPERIENCE*** as the primary mode of obtaining information. Second, there is a lack of ***EVIDENCE*** to support many of its explanatory assumptions or the effectiveness of its therapy. (p. 79)

26. The roots of the behavioristic approach can be traced to the study of ***CLASSICAL CONDITIONING*** by a Russian physiologist named Ivan Pavlov and to the study of ***INSTRUMENTAL CONDITIONING*** by Edward Thorndike. Promotion of the behavioral approach is credited to a young American psychologist named ***WATSON***. (p. 78-80)

27. Identify the following statements as referring to classical conditioning (C) or instrumental (I) conditioning (i.e., place a "C" or "I" after each) as appropriate. (pp. 80-81)

    a. As we mature, this type of learning becomes more important. ***I***

    b. Many responses, particularly those related to fear or anxiety, are learned through this type of learning. ***C***

    c. As we grow up, this type of learning becomes an important mechanism for discriminating the desirable from the undesirable. ***I***

    d. Consists of simple strengthening of a stimulus-response connection. ***I***

    e. The person learns a response-outcome expectancy. ***I***

28. In operant or instrumental conditioning, initially a high rate of reinforcement may be necessary, but thereafter, it is especially persistent when reinforcement is ***INTERMITTENT*** (p. 81)

29. Behaviorism has been praised for its precision and objectivity, its wealth of research, and its demonstrated effectiveness in ***CHANGING SPECIFIC BEHAVIOR.*** (p. 82)

30. According to Beck, different forms of psychopathology are characterized by different ***MALADAPTIVE SCHEMAS*** that have developed as a function of adverse early ***LEARNING EXPERIENCE*** and that lead to the ***DISTORTION IN THINKING***, characteristic of certain disorders, such as anxiety, depression, and personality disorders. (pp. 83-84)

31. Cognitive-behavioral clinicians have shifted their focus from overt behavior to the *UNDERLYING COGNITIONS* assumed to be producing that behavior. Then the clinician's goal becomes one of altering maladaptive *COGNITIVE.* (p. 84)

32. Each psychosocial viewpoint of abnormal behavior depends on *GENERALIZATIONS* from limited observations and research. (p. 84)

33. Bowlby found that, when children age 2 to 5 years are separated from their parents during prolonged periods of hospitalization, the acute effects include significant *DESPAIR* during the separation and *DETACHMENT* upon reunion. (p. 90)

34. *DIATHESIS-STRESS* models of abnormal behavior state that many mental disorders or believed to develop as the result of some kind of stressor operating on a person who has a predisposition for that disorder. (p. 58)

35. The *BIOPSYCHOSOCIAL* viewpoint acknowledges the idea that biological, psychosocial, and sociocultural factors all interact and play a role in psychopathology and treatment. (p. 60)

36. The four neurotransmitters that have been studied most extensively in relationship to psychopathology are: *NOREPINEPHRINE, DOPAMINE, SEROTONIN,* and *GAMMA AMINOBUTRYIC ACID (GABA).* (p. 61)

37. When looking at shared and nonshared environmental influences, it was found that for many important psychological characteristics and forms of psychopathology, *NONSHARED* environmental influences appear to be more important. (p. 67)

38. The effects of deprivation and rejection on a child was delineated by Bullard and his colleagues, as a "*FAILURE TO THRIVE*" syndrome in which normal growth and development are seriously impaired and frequently required admission to a hospital. (p. 88)

39. Although some universal symptoms and patterns of symptoms appear for mental disorders, *SOCIOCULTURAL FACTORS,* often influence which disorders *DEVELOP,* the *FORMS* they take and their *COURSES.* (p. 96)

THE DOCTOR IS IN...PSYCHIATRIC HELP—5¢

1. Roger comes to your office because he has recently been laid off from his job as a store manager. He is concerned because he has started to drink heavily as a result of this and finds himself feeling incredibly sad and depressed. His wife is supportive but he is afraid she will get tired of dealing with his moods and leave. Although she says she won't, he is becoming preoccupied with the idea of her leaving him. He tells you that his father abused alcohol and that his mother ended up leaving when she couldn't take it any more.

His father always drank, according to Roger, would get really down, and, on at least one occasion, talked about suicide. Roger doesn't want to become like his father but finds himself acting in similar ways. He is thinking that maybe he should just tell his wife to leave him, then move to another state, and start all over

a. Look at Roger's situation from a psychodynamic, behavioral, and cognitive-behavioral perspective. What in Roger's story would you emphasize from each of these perspectives and how would you treat him?

b. **Psychodynamic:** (p. 72)

Emphasize the unconscious motives for Roger's behaviors—hurtful memories from his childhood about his mother and father. You might also say that his drinking is a result of the breakdown of his ego—an ego-defense mechanism

Treatment:

Use free association and dream analysis to become acquainted with the conscious and the unconscious, also might want to include interpersonal therapy.

c. **Behavioral:** (p. 79)

Look at Roger's behavior and the stimuli, and reinforcing conditions that control it. For instance, his drinking is getting him attention from his wife and because he is drinking so much it reinforces that he can't get a job. His drinking also reinforces his sadness and depression (alcohol is a depressant).

Treatment: Create a situation where alcohol is not a reinforcement but is substituted for something else that is positive, e.g. Roger and his wife walking together or looking through employment opportunities together. Attendance of AA meetings to continue to strengthen the behavior of not drinking.

d. **Cognitive-Behavioral:** (p. 83)

Look at Roger's basic information-processing mechanisms, his internal reinforcements, and how these are distorted. Explore his attributional style and the meaning he gives to his wife's behavior about leaving him and his thoughts of leaving her.

Treatment: Change thought patterns through logical reanalysis and by having Roger experiment with different behaviors/actions that would then be looked at in therapy.

PRACTICE TESTS

PRACTICE TEST NUMBER 1

1. Disorders could be classified and diagnosed better if their causes could be better understood instead of relying on (p. 56)

   a. clusters of symptoms.

2. The etiology of abnormal behavior means the (p. 56)

   c. causal pattern.

3. The response of an individual to demands that he or she perceives as taxing or exceeding his or her personal resources is referred to as (p. 58)

    a.   stress.

4. The diathesis is a relatively _____ necessary or contributory cause. (p. 58)

    b.   distal

5. Jimmy's parents use drugs and his father is often abusive toward his mother. In spite of this, Jimmy is doing well in school and has made the football team. Jimmy's success is a form of (p. 58)

    c.   resilience.

6. Jimmy had an uncle who took him under his wing and helped him get through some rough times. This uncle provided the warmth and support that Jimmy lacked at home. Jimmy's uncle provided a (p. 58)

    a.   protective factor.

7. When Sharon went to school, she was taught the theory and practice of the psychoanalytical viewpoint. The methods she used in her practice reflected this viewpoint and she believed totally in this perspective. At a conference, she was introduced to the cognitive-behavioral viewpoint and became intrigued by it. She went on to study this perspective and incorporate it into her practice. Sharon's new insights constituted a (p. 60)

    b.   paradigm shift.

8. Malfunction of the negative feedback system in the hypothalamic-pituitary-adrenal-cortical axis, has been implicated in such psychopathologies as (p. 63)

    a.   post-traumatic stress disorder.
    b.   depression.
    d.   a and b.

9. The fact that a number of disorders, such as depression, schizophrenia, and alcoholism, show a heredity as an important predisposing causal factor, is consistent with which perspective? (p. 63)

    a.   Biological

10. The observed structural and functional characteristics that result from an interaction of the person's total genetic endowment and the environment are referred to as a person's (p. 63)

    a.   phenotype.

PRACTICE TEST NUMBER 2

1. An example of a constitutional liability is (pp. 68-70)

   b. physical handicaps.

   c. temperament.

   d. b and c.

2. At what age can we identify approximately five dimensions of temperament development that may affect personality? (p. 69)

   b. two to three months

3. The _____ acknowledges that genetic activity influences neural activity, which, in turn, influences behavior, which in turn influences the environment, and that these influences are bidirectional. (p. 70)

   c. developmental systems approach

4. Because biological treatments seem to have more immediate results than other available therapies, these have been seen as a possible (p. 71)

   a. cure-all.

5. When we adopt a perspective, it will influence (p. 85)

   a. our perceptions of maladaptive behavior.

   b. the types of evidence we look for.

   c. the way in which we interpret data.

   d. all of the above.

6. The process of working new experiences into existing cognitive frameworks, even if the new information has to be reinterpreted or distorted to make it fit, is known as (p. 86)

   c. assimilation.

7. The process of changing existing frameworks to make it possible to incorporate discrepant information is known as (pp. 86-87)

   b. accommodation.

8. Amato and Keith (1991a, 1991b) found that the negative effects of divorce seemed to be decreasing, particularly since 1970, because divorce was decreasing in (p. 93)

   a. stigmatization.

9. Jill, who is 20 years old, is popular with many people and is comfortable in all settings. Jill has a good deal of (p. 94)

   c. social competence.

10. Jennifer, who is five years old and in kindergarten, is clueless when it comes to reading her peer's emotions, especially fear and sadness. This behavior can predict aggressive behavior toward peers in the (p. 95)

    a.   third grade.

PRACTICE TEST NUMBER 3

1. Studies done by sociocultural researchers made it clear that there is a relationship between mental disorders and (p. 96)

    c.   sociocultural conditions.

2. In our society, the lower the SES, the higher the incidence of (p. 99)

    c.   mental disorder.

3. Many more women than men suffer from various emotional disorders. This may be in part due to sexual discrimination. The primary types of discrimination are (pp. 100-01)

    b.   access and treatment.

4. Estimates are that approximately _____ of the homeless are affected by mental illness. (p. 101)

    d.   one-third

5. Since Kleinman and Good consider cultural factors so important to understanding depressive disorders, they have urged the psychiatric community to do what? (p. 101)

    c.   incorporate another axis in the DSM

6. Dr. Smith combines many different approaches/techniques when assessing and working with clients. What is Dr. Smith's approach? (p. 102)

    b.   eclectic

7. A factor that increases the probability of developing a disorder without being either necessary or sufficient is a _____ cause. (p. 57)

    d.   contributory

8. Which type of anxiety is a signal to the ego that the id's unacceptable impulse is threatening to break out? (p. 74)

    b. neurotic anxiety

9. The ability to discriminate may be brought about by (p. 81)

    c.   responding differently to similar stimuli, based on which ones are reinforced.

10. Which of the following was not proposed as a strong factor in popularity among juveniles? (pp. 94-95)

    a.   parents' income

COMPREHENSIVE PRACTICE TEST
MULTIPLE-CHOICE

1. A predisposition toward developing a disorder is termed (p. 58)

    d. diathesis.

2. The stressor is a more _____ cause. (p. 58)

    a. proximal

3. A rapidly growing field of psychology that focuses on determining what is abnormal at any point in development by comparing and contrasting it with normal and expected changes that occur in the course of development is called (p. 59)

    c. developmental psychopathology.

4. The belief that ——————— in the brain can result in abnormal behavior is one of the basic tenets of the biological perspective today. (p. 61)

    c. neurotransmitter imbalances

5. This is referred to as the master gland of the body. (p. 63)

    d. pituitary gland

6. A person's total genetic endowment is referred to as her or his (p. 65)

    b. genotype.

7. This perspective views human nature as basically "good." (p. 73)

    d. humanistic

8. This perspective places more emphasis on the irrational tendencies and the difficulties inherent in self-fulfillment—particularly in a modern, bureaucratic and dehumanizing mass society. (p. 73)

    a. existential

9. Evidence suggests that disordered _____ make a significant contribution to child and adolescent psychopathology, especially to problems such as depression, conduct disorder, delinquency, and attention deficit disorder. (p. 91)

    d. fathers

10. Your book mentions that, at present, the only unified perspective is called the (p. 103)

    d. biopsychosocial viewpoint.

11. The specialized structure on the postsynaptic neuron at which the neurotransmitter exerts its effect is the _____. (p. 62)

   c. receptor site

12. After being released into the synaptic cleft, the neurotransmitter substance may be reabsorbed into the presynaptic axon button, a process called _____. (p. 62)

   a. re-uptake

13. In genetic studies the subject, or carrier, of the trait or disorder in question who serves as the starting point is known as the (p. 65)

   a. proband.

14. According to Freud's psychoanalytic perspective, the source of all instinctual drives is the (p. 72)

   b. id.

15. Margaret Mahler focused on the process by which children come to understand that they are different from other objects. This process involves a developmental phase called (p. 76)

   d. separation-individuation.

16. Instead of Freud's concept of fixation, Erikson proposed that parental deprivation might interfere with the development of _____. (p. 78)

   d. basic trust

17. The form of learning in which an individual learns to achieve a desired goal is (p. 80)

   b. operant conditioning.

18. The behavioristic tradition has been criticized for (p. 82)

   d. its over concern with symptoms.

19. The tendency to explain one's success as due to luck—as compared to hard work—is best categorized as an example of a specific (p. 83)

   a. attributional style.

20. A basic goal of psychosocial therapies is (p. 87)

   a. accommodation.

21. Bowlby found that when young children were separated from their parents during prolonged periods of hospitalization, their reaction upon reunion was (p. 90)

   b. detachment.

22. A _____ parental style is likely to produce a child who is impulsive and aggressive, spoiled, selfish, inconsiderate, and demanding, and who will exploit people for his/her own purposes. (p. 92)

    c. permissive-indulgent

23. Epidemiological studies that have linked psychopathology with social class are

    b. correlational in nature. (p. 99)

24. According to the authors, the problematic proliferation of diverse viewpoints about psychopathology can best be solved by (pp. 84-85)

    c. developing a unified point of view.

True – False

1. F — The behavioral sciences have no difficulty distinguishing between what is cause and effect. (p. 57)

2. T — Protective factors are not necessarily positive experiences. (p. 58)

3. T — Some forms of psychopathology have been linked to hormonal imbalances. (p. 63)

4. F — Genes affect behavior directly. (p. 63)

5. T — The most common birth difficulty associated with later mental disorders is low birth weight. (p. 68)

6. F — Assimilation is the basic goal of psychosocial therapies. (p. 86)

7. T — Children deprived of needed resources normally supplied by parents or parental surrogates may be left with irreversible psychological scars. (p. 87)

8. F — Candy is a loner and Brian is a bully. Each of them will probably have healthy mental health outcomes. (p. 94)

9. T — When social roles are conflicting, unclear, or difficult to achieve, unhealthy personality development may occur. (p. 99)

10. T — Prejudice against minority groups may play a role in explaining why these groups sometimes show increased prevalence of certain mental disorders. (p. 100)

11. T — The sociocultural viewpoint has been readily embraced by the therapeutic community and incorporated into treatment. (p. 101)

ESSAY QUESTIONS *(Your answer should contain the following points.)*

1. List the misconceptions and stereotypes that exist about studies of genetic influences on behavior, traits and psychopathology, and give examples of each. (p. 67)

   a. **Myth:** Strong genetic effects mean that environmental influences must be unimportant

   Example: Height—genetically determined but nutrition can play a role.

   b. **Myth:** Genes provide a limit to potential.

   Example: Children born to socially disadvantaged parent and adopted by and reared by socially advantaged parents.

   c. **Myth:** Genetic strategies are of no value for studying environmental influences.

   Example: Monozygotic twins with less than 100% concordance rates for mental illness and personality.

   d. **Myth:** Nature and nurture are separate.

   Example: Babies born with PKU only develop the disease if exposed to diets with phenylalanine.

   e. **Myth:** Genetic effects diminish with age.

   Example: Dizygotic twins show greater differences over time than monozygotic twins.

   f. **Myth:** Disorders that run in families must be genetic and those that do not run in families must not be genetic.

   Example: Autism doesn't run in families but shows a very powerful genetic effect.

CRISS-CROSS ANSWERS

Across

3. ego
4. discrimination
5. introjection
6. libido
10. extinction
13. superego
14. assimilation
15. etiology
16. attributions

Down

1. reinforcement
2. accommodation
7. temperament
8. schema
9. generalization
11. id
12. resilience

CHAPTER FOUR

Who's Who and What's What—strengths and weaknesses of projective and objective tests

Test	Strengths	Weaknesses
Projective	• *unstructured* • *focus on unique aspects of personality (p. 118)*	Interpretations are subjective, unreliable, and difficult to validate; require trained staff to administer and score.
Objective	Cost effective, reliable, objective, administered and scored by computer	• *too mechanistic* • *people unable to read can't take test* • *individual cooperation needed* • *distorted answers to create impression* • *computers print blindly (p. 120)*

Psychological tests and appropriate description of each test's purpose

Psychological Test	Purpose
D. Rorschach Test	A. Rating scale based on standardized interview
E. Thematic Apperception Test	B. Intelligence scale for children
F. Minnesota Multiphasic Personality Inventory (MMPI)	C. Intelligence scale for adults
B. WAIS-III	D. Projective test using inkblots
C. WISC-III	E. Projective test using pictures
A. Brief Psychiatric Rating Scale (BPRS)	F. Structured personality test
G. Sentence Completion Test	G. Test that pinpoints topics that should be explored

SHORT ANSWERS   *(Your answer should contain the following points.)*

1. Discuss the benefits of using computers in psychological testing and why some clinicians are reluctant to use these. (p. 115)

   a. **Benefits:**
      - effective assessment function by getting together and evaluating all the information gathered
      - can perform with a wide range of assessment tasks by comparing information in the memory banks

- can supply probable diagnosis
- indicate likely behavior
- suggest appropriate treatment
- predict outcome
- print summary reports
- low cost

b. **Reluctance:**
   - some clinicians are uncomfortable with computers
   - some practitioners do not do extensive pretreatment assessments
   - the computers are impersonal and mechanical
   - computer-bases assessment a threat to clinicians and will replace human functionality

2. Compare the functions, advantages, and disadvantages of the CAT, MRI, fMRI, and the PET scans. (pp. 108-10)

   a. **CAT—Computerized Axial Tomography**
      Function: • uses X-rays across patients brain to produce images and locate abnormalities
      Advantage: • don't need surgery to look at brain abnormalities
      Disadvantage: • exposes patients to prolonged radiation
                     • images not as clear

   b. **MRI—Magnetic Resonance Imaging**
      Function: • measurement of variations in magnetic fields caused by varying amounts of water in various organs
                     • to look at the anatomical structure of any cross-section of an organ
      Advantage: • less complicated than a CAT scan
                     • very clear and able to give a look at all but the smallest brain abnormalities
                     • noninvasive
      Disadvantage: • some patients claustrophobic in narrow cylinder

   c. **fMRI—function Magnetic Resonance Imaging**
      Functions: • used to measure brain activity
                     • measures oxygenation (blood flow) of specific areas of brain tissue
      Advantages: • less expensive than PET scans
                     • can map on-going psychological activity, e.g., sensations, images, and thoughts
      Disadvantage: • some minor problems with distraught psychiatric patients

   d. **PET—Postiron Emission Tomography**
      Function: • shows how an organ is functioning by measuring metabolic processes
      Advantages: • images of metabolic activity allow for better diagnosis
                     • can see problems that aren't just anatomical
      Disadvantages: • low fidelity pictures
                     • better as a research technique than the clinical diagnostic procedure

3. Explain the purpose of classifying abnormal behavior. (p. 127)

    a. provides clear communication

    b. attempts to delineate meaningful side variations of maladaptic behavior

    c. introduces order into discussion of the nature, causes, and treatment of abnormal behavior

    d. allows communication about particular clusters of abnormal behavior

    e. gathers statistics on how common are various disorders

    f. meets needs of medical insurance companies

4. Discuss the problem of labeling. (pp. 133-34)

    a. psychiatric diagnosis, as a label, applies to a category of socially disapproved, problematic behavior

    b. label is too easily accepted as description of an individual, rather than a person's behavior

    c. individuals may accept the label and redefine themselves to play out that role

    d. labeling can effect a person's morale, self-esteem, and relationships with others

FILL IN THE BLANKS

1. Data from clinical assessment is used for two purposes. First, it serves as a basis for treatment decisions. A less obvious, but equally important, function is that of establishing a *BASELINE* against which to evaluate progress made during and following treatment.   (p. 106)

2. For clinical purposes, knowledge about an individual's *HISTORY*, *INTELLECTUAL FUNCTIONING*, personality characteristics, and environmental pressures and resources is more important than a formal diagnosis. (p. 106)

3. Medical examinations are necessary in some situations to rule out physical abnormalities or to determine the extent to which physical problems are involved. The two types of medical examinations that may be performed include the general *PHYSICAL* examination and the *NEUROLOGICAL* examination, aimed at assessing the *STRUCTURAL (ANATOMICAL)* and *FUNCTIONAL (PHYSIOLOGICAL)* integrity of the brain as a behaviorally significant physical system. (p. 108)

4. An EEG is a graphic record of the *BRAIN'S ELECTRICAL ACTIVITY*. Significant divergences from the normal pattern of brain impulses can reflect abnormalities of brain function, such as might be caused by a brain tumor or other lesion. (p. 109)

5. Neurological tests identify abnormalities in the brain's physical properties. In contrast, neuropsychological assessment identifies gross impairments in *BEHAVIOR* and varied psychological *DEFICIT*. (p. 110)

6. The Halstead-Reitan battery consists of a standard set of tests that have been preselected so as to sample in a systematic and comprehensive manner a ***BROAD RANGE*** known to be adversely affected by various types of brain injury. (p. 111)

7. Psychosocial assessment attempts to provide a realistic picture of the individual in interaction with the ***SOCIAL ENVIRONMENT***. (p. 112)

8. The main purpose of direct observation is to learn more about the person's psychological functioning through the objective description of behavior in various contexts. Ideally, such observations would occur in the individual's ***NATURAL ENVIRONMENT***, but are typically confined to ***CLINIC*** or ***HOSPITAL*** settings. In addition, many clinicians ask their patients to report their own behavior, thoughts, and feelings as these occur in various natural settings—a procedure called ***SELF-MONITORING***. (p. 112-13)

9. Psychological tests are standardized sets of procedures to obtain samples of a subject's behavior that can be compared to the behavior of other individuals, usually through the use of established test ***NORMS*** or test score ***DISTRIBUTION***. (p. 114)

10. Among the characteristics about which the clinician can draw inferences from psychological tests are coping patterns, motive patterns, personality characteristics, role behaviors, values, levels of depression or anxiety, and ***INTELLECTUAL FUNCTIONING***. (p. 114)

11. 27. Projective tests are aimed at discovering the ways in which an individual's ***PAST LEARNING*** and ***PERSONALITY STRUCTURE*** may lead him or her to organize and perceive ***AMBIGUOUS*** information from the environment. (p. 115)

THE DOCTOR IS IN...PSYCHIATRIC HELP—5¢

1. You are a famous neuropsychologist, and a new patient has been referred to you. This patient's history leads you to believe that some sort of brain injury has occurred. You believe that preselected battery of standard tests is the most beneficial. What test battery would you sue? What are its component parts, and what are its limitations? (pp. 110-11)
    a. **Use:**   *Holstead-Reitan battery*
    b. **Components:**   *Factual Performance Test*—measures motor speed
                          Rhythm Test—measures attention and sustained concentration
                          Speech Sound Perception Test—identification of spoken words, measurers concentration, attention, and comprehension
                          Finger Oscillation Test—speed of which person can depress a lever
                          Holstead Category Test—measures person's ability to learn and remember material
    c. **Limitations:** Takes about six hours to administer; cost of time, examination fatigue

2. Tim, a 21-year-old man, has just been admitted to the hospital. He had been found wandering the streets, talking to himself. It looks as if he has been homeless for some time. You are called in to do a clinical observation. What would you include in your observation of Tim? (p. 112)

   a. objective description of Tim's appearance and behavior

   b. personal hygiene, emotional responses, depression, anxiety, aggression, hallucination, or delusions

   c. could also include staged role playing, event re-enactment, family interaction assignments—analogue situations

3. You are seeing a new patient who has been referred to you by his primary-care doctor. Ben, a 29-year-old truck driver, went to his doctor thinking he was having a heart attack. When he drove across bridges, his heart would pound, his hands got sweaty, he would feel short of breath, and begin to hyperventilate. Several months ago, Ben was involved in an accident that left three people dead and several injured. Though it wasn't his fault (there had been heavy fog), he felt that as an experienced truck driver, he should have been able to prevent the accident. The symptoms began shortly after the accident and have lasted for six months. His primary doctor reports that Ben is not having any heart problems and is generally in good health.

   As Ben's psychologist, what type of interview would you conduct? What diagnosis would you give him on Axis I, II, and III? Why? (p. 130)

   either structured interview (SCAN) or unstructured interview

   - Axis I: a. Post Traumatic Stress Disorder. Symptoms occurred after an accident and have lasted more than a month.

              b. Panic or disorder (could also be phobia). Rapid heart beat, sweaty hands, shortness of breath in a specific situation.

   - Axis II: None
   - Axis III: None

PICTURE THIS

   1. Computerized Axial Tomography (CAT Scan) — Cat + Scanner - R
   2. Personality Test—Purse + Sun + ALI + [Golf] Tee
   3. Rorschach Test—Roar + Shock + Test
   4. Thematic Appreception Test (TAT)—Tea + A + Tee
   5. Validity—Veil + Lid + i + Tee {Please forgive us}
   6. MMPI—MM + Pea [in a pod] + Eye
   7. Rating Scales—Rake - K + T + ing + Scales
   8. Reliability—RE + Lie [down] + A + Bill + i +Tee

PRACTICE TESTS
PRACTICE TEST NUMBER 1

1. Formal diagnosis is necessary after assessment for (p. 106)

    a.   insurance claims.

    b.   planning treatment.

    c.   deciding on which treatment facilities would be best for the client.

    d.   all of the above.

2. When taking a social history, the clinician notes key dimensions that help her/him to understand the individual's problem. The key dimensions are (p. 107)

    a.   excesses, deficits, and approp.rietness.

3. After the assessment data is integrated into a consistent, meaningful picture, a _____ is developed about the client's behavior? (p. 107)

    d.   hypothesis

4. A significant divergence of normal brain patterns recorded on an EEG, that may be a result of some abnormality is referred to as (p. 109)

    b.   dysrhythmia.

5. Mrs. Smith, 73, is experiencing some significant difficulty with cognitive activities and has lost some coordination. She is referred to a specialist who will test her cognitive, perceptual, and motor performance. This specialist is a (p. 110)

    a.   neuropsychologist.

6. Mrs. Smith is administered a battery of tests, consisting of a standard set of tests designed to systematically and comprehensively sample psychological competencies known to be affected by types of brain injuries. The test she probably was given was a (pp. 110-11)

    d.   Halstead-Reitan.

7. You have scheduled an assessment interview for a new client. You have chosen a standardized interview format that you hope will yield a clear picture of your client's situation. This will be a(n) _____ interview. (p. 112)

    a.   structured

8. You have scheduled an assessment interview for another new client. You have scheduled an assessment interview. There are several questions you want the client to answer, but you want to be free to explore responses in more depth. This format is considered a(n) _____ interview. (p. 112)

    b.   unstructured

9. Tim has been admitted to the hospital, and you, a renowned doctor, are about to administer several clinical observations using a rating scale. It is called the (p. 113)

    c. BPRS.

10. You are going to conduct research on depression. You use what instrument to select your research subjects? (p. 113)

    b. HRSD

PRACTICE TEST NUMBER 2

1. Which of the following is an example of an intelligence test? (p. 114)

    a. WISC-III
    b. WAIS-III
    c. Standard-Binel Intelligence Scale
    d. All of the above.

2. Holding an inkblot picture in front of her client, Dr. Taylor asked the client to respond to what she saw in the picture. Dr. Taylor was administering the _____ test. (p. 115)

    b. Rorschach

3. Holding a series of pictures in front of his client, Dr. Zimmer asked the client to make up a story based on the picture. Dr. Zimmer was administering the _____ test. (p. 117)

    a. Thematic Apperception

4. Dr. Jones gives her client the beginning of sentences and asks that she complete each one. This is known as the _____ test. (p. 118)

    c. Sentence completion

5. Unlike projective testing devices, these tests are non-controlled and objective. This type of test is a(n) _____ personality test. (p. 119)

    c. objective

6. The MMPI consists of _____ clinical scales, each designed to measure terolemies to respond in psychologically client ways. (p. 119)

    a. 10

7. As a psychiatrist in a large mental hospital, you and several of your colleagues often work together to evaluate assessment data. You are part of a (p. 126)

    d. interdisciplinary team.

8. The degree to which a measuring device produces the same results each time it is used to measure the same thing is referred to as (p. 128)

    a. reliability.

9. The extent to which a measuring instrument actually measurers what it is supposed to measure is referred to as (p. 128)

    b. validity.

10. Good reliability in diagnostic classification does not in itself guarantee (p. 128)

    b. validity.

PRACTICE TEST NUMBER 3

1. The psychiatric classification system widely used in Europe is the (p. 129)

    a. ICD-10.

2. The psychiatric classification system used in the United States is the   (p. 129)

    b. DSM.

3. Although purporting to be a categorical model of classification, the authors of the book say the DSM is, in fact, a   (p. 129)

    a. prototypal.

4. A diagnostic interview that follows no preexisting plan is called a(n) (p. 134)

    b. unstructured interview.

5. A diagnostic interview that follows a sort of master plan is called a(n)   (p. 134)

    a. structured interview.

6. A neurological diagnostic aid that reveals how an organ is functioning by measuring metabolic processes is the (p. 109)

    a. PET scan.

7. Which of the following is the most highly regarded six-hour neuropsychological test? (p. 110)

    a. Halstead-Reitan

8. According to the text, the rating scale specifically targeted for depression that has almost become the standard for selecting clinically depressed research subjects is the (p. 113)

    d. Hamilton Rating Scale for Depression.

9. Which of the following is a structured personality test? (p. 119)

    a. MMPI

10. Which of the following personality tests would most likely be used for personnel screening for a dangerous job? (p. 119)

    b. MMPI

COMPREHENSIVE PRACTICE TEST
MULTIPLE-CHOICE

1. The initial clinical assessment is used to (p. 106)

    a. identify the main dimensions of the problem.
    b. predict the likely course of events.
    c. establish a baseline.
    d. all of the above.

2. When assessing an individual, the clinician integrates information concerning the person's personality traits, behavior patterns, environmental demands, etc. into a consistent, meaningful picture often called a(n) (p. 107)

    c. dynamic formulation.

3. _____ testing provides a clinician with behavioral information on how organic brain damage affects a person's functions. (p. 110)

    d. Neuropsychological

4. A classification system's usefulness depends upon its (p. 128)

    a. reliability.
    b. validity.
    c. a and b.

5. A _____ approach for classifying abnormal behavior assumes that human behavior can be divided into either healthy or disordered, and that within the disordered category there are non-overlapping types with a high degree of homogeneity in both symptoms displayed and underlying organization of the disorder. (p. 128)

    d. categorical

6. A _____ approach for classifying abnormal behavior assumes that a person's typical behavior is the product of different strengths of behaviors along several definable dimensions. (p. 128)

    a. dimensional

7. A _____ approach to classifying abnormal behavior is a conceptual entity depicting an idealized combination of characteristics that access together in a standard way at the level of actual observation. (p. 128)

    b. prototypal

8. A limitation of the DSM classification system is that (p. 130)

    c. real patients often don't fit into the precise lists of signs and symptoms.

9. Individuals are evaluated according to five axes. The first three deal with (p. 130)

    c.   assessing an individual's present clinical status.

10. The fourth and fifth axes of the DSM-IV TR deal with (pp. 130-31)

    b.   global assessment of functioning.

    c.   assessing an individual's present clinical status.

    d.   b and c.

11. Clinical interviews have been criticized as unreliable and evidence of this unreliability includes the finding that different clinicians often arrive at different formal diagnoses. For this reason, recent versions of the DSM have emphasized an approach that   (p. 112)

    d.   employs "operational" assessment.

12. Two general categories of psychological tests used in clinical practice are (p. 114)

    a.   intelligence and personality.

13. Personality tests are often grouped into two categories (p. 114)

    c.   projective and objective.

14. The aim of a projective test is to (p. 114)

    c.   assess the way a patient perceives ambiguous stimuli.

15. Behaviorists have criticized the MMPI for being too (p. 120)

    b.   "mentalistic."

TRUE – FALSE

1. T — In cases of severe disorders, decisions regarding treatment may be made about a client with his or her consent or consultation with family members. (p. 107)

2. T — Assessment of an individual may involve coordinated use of physical, psychological, and environmental assessment procedures. (p. 107)

3. F — Confidentiality is not an important issue for clients, because they want as many people as possible to know about their problems. (p. 108)

4. T — Rating scales, when used in clinical observation and self-reports, encourages reliability, objectivity, and allows the rater to indicate the presence, absence, or prominence of a behavior.   (p. 113)

5. F —Two general categories of psychological tests used for clinical practice are general medical exams and intelligence tests. (p. 114)

6. T — An agreed-upon classification system allows clinicians to be confident of communicating clearly. (p. 127)

7. F — The classification of mental disorders is intended to give direct insight into their problems.   (p. 127)

8. F —A classification system, once completed, is not changed.   (p. 127)

9. T — Validity presupposes reliability.   (p. 128)

10. F —The number of recognized mental disorders has remained constant from the first DSM-I to the DSM-IV.   (pp. 129-30)

11. T — Acute mental disorders are relatively short in duration. (p. 133)

12. F —Chronic mental disorders are relatively short in duration. (p. 133)

ESSAY QUESTIONS   *(Your answer should contain the following points.)*

1. What assessment techniques would be favored by the following? (p. 107)
    a. Biologically oriented clinician
        - biological assessment focusing on underlying organic malfunctioning
    b. Psychoanalytically oriented clinician
        - use of TAT or Rorschach Test
        - focuses on intrapsychic conflicts
    c. Behaviorally oriented clinician
        - looks at functional relationships between environmental events or reinforcements and abnormal behavior
        - uses behavioral absencations and self-monitoring techniques to identify maladaptive learned patterns
    d. Cognitively oriented behaviorist
        - would shift to dysfunctional thoughts rethinking maladaptive learned patterns
    e. Humanistically oriented clinician
        - interview techniques to uncover blocked or distorted personal growth
    f. Interpersonally oriented clinician
        - use of personal confrontations and behavioral observations to pinpoint difficulties in interpersonal relationships

2.   What are the elements of psychological assessment? (p. 112)

   a.   identify presenting problem
   - situational
   - more persuasive and long-term
   - combination of the above

   b.   recent deterioration in cognitive faculties

   c.   how long the person has been dealing with the problem

   d.   whether prior help has been sought

   e.   self-defeating behavior and personality deterioration

   f.   whether the problem is affecting the person's performance in social roles

   g.   whether the symptoms fit DSM-IV-TR diagnostic patterns

CRISS-CROSS ANSWERS

Across
   6.   analogue situations
   7.   validity
   11.   episodic
   12.   clinical assessment
   13.   acute

Down
   1.   recurrent
   2.   symptoms
   3.   objective tests
   4.   reliability
   5.   factor analysis
   6.   actuarial procedures
   8.   chronic
   9.   comorbidity
   10.   signs

CHAPTER FIVE

MATCHING

Match the following terms with their definitions.

Term	Definition
D. Post-Traumatic Stress Disorder	A. a maladoptive response within three months of a stressor
G. psychoneuroimmunology	B. one's ability to withstand stress
A. adjustment disorder	C. an adjustment demand
H. crisis	D. severe psychological and physical symptoms as a reaction to unexpected environmental crises
F. stress	E. preventative strategy, prepares people to meet stressful situations
C. stressor	F. a by-product of poor or inadequate coping
I. eustress	G. new field of study which focuses on the effects of stress on the immune system
B. stress tolerance	H. when a stressful situation excedes one's adoptive capacities
E. stress-inoculation training	I. postitive stress

SHORT ANSWERS *(Your answer should contain the following points.)*

1. Explain the Social Readjustment Rating Scale and what it predicts. (p. 143)
   a. The Social Readjustment Rating Scale is an objective method for measuring the cumulative stress to which a person has been exposed over a period of time in terms of "life-change units (LCU)."
   b. More stressful events had more LCUs assigned.
   c. Death of a spouse rates 100 LCUs; minor violation of the law is 11.
   d. An experiment found that persons with 300 or more in recent months were at significant risk for getting a major illness.

2. Name the three interactional levels in coping with stress and give examples of each. (p. 145)
   a. Biological. There are immunological defenses and damage-repair mechanisms.
   b. Psychological and interpersonal. There are learned coping patterns, self-defenses, and support from family and friends.
   c. Sociocultural. Group resources, such as labor unions, religious organizations, and law-enforcement agencies.

3. Selye (1956, 1976b) found that the body's reaction to sustained and excessive stress typically occurs in three major phases. Name and briefly explain each. (p. 147)

   a. Alarm reaction, in which the body's defensive forces are activated.

   b. Stage of resistance, in which biological adaptation is at the maximum level.

   c. Exhaustion, in which bodily resources are depleted and the organism loses its ability to resist.

4. Explain how the sympathetic nervous system (SNS) reacts when an organism is faced with danger—the fight-or-flight response. Also, explain why there may be a danger connected to this. (p. 147)

   a. The heart rate and blood flow are increased to large muscles.

   b. Pupils are dilated so that more light enters the yet.

   c. The skin constricts to limit blood loss in the event of injury.

   d. Blood sugar is increased to provide more energy.

   e. Possible problem: If the threat vanishes (usually the case), the body remains activated for physical combat, and, although it seeks to return to the previous restful state, there is a degree of wear and tear on the system, and "…each exposure leaves an indelible scar…"

5. Following a disaster, a victim's initial responses typically follow three stages. Name and briefly explain these. (p. 153)

   a. Shock—stunned, dazed, and apathetic.

   b. Suggestible stage—tends to be passive, suggestible, and willing to take directions.

   c. Recovery stage—may be tense and apprehensive, general anxiety. PTSD may develop at this point.

6. Name and explain five areas of life functioning that may be affected by a rape. (p. 156)

   a. Physical disturbances, including hyperaroulas or anxiousness.

   b. Emotional problems, such as anxiety, depression, low self-esteem.

   c. Cognitive dysfunction, including disturbed concentration and intrusive thoughts.

   d. Atypical behavioral acts, such as aggression, antisocial actions, and substance abuse.

   e. Interference in social relationships, including sexual problems, intimacy problems, and further victimization in a sexual relationship.

7. The trauma of military combat was called "shell shock" in World War II, "operational fatigue," or "combat exhaustion" in the Korean and Vietnam wars, and, currently, "acute stress disorder." Discuss its causes and effects. (pp. 157-59)

   a. Ever-present threat of death or mutilation. Experiencing or participating in horrific events during combat.

   b. The first symptoms are increasing irritability and sensitivity, sleep disturbances, and often-recurrent nightmares.

   c. The feeling of overwhelming anxiety.

ANSWERS TO FILL IN THE BLANKS

1. Three Axis 1 categories are ***ADJUSTMENT DISORDER***, ***ACUTE STRESS DISORDER***, and ***POST-TRAUMATIC STRESS DISORDER (ACUTE, CHRONIC, OR DELAYED).*** (p. 140)

2. Although a particular ***STRESSOR*** may predominate in a situation, we usually confront a continuously changing pattern of interrelated and sometimes contradictory demands. (p. 142)

3. ***SEVERE STRESS*** can exact a high cost in terms of lowered efficiency, depletion of adaptive resources, wear and tear on the biological system, and, in extreme cases, severe personality and physical deterioration—even death. (p. 146)

4. When trauma victims were exposed to trauma-related cues (an audio recording of an event similar to the one they experienced), they showed ***INCREASED DISTRESS*** and a ***HEIGHTENED RESPONSIVITY*** even years after the event. (p. 148)

THE DOCTOR IS IN...PSYCHIATRIC HELP—5¢

1. Becky came to your office because she had been sexually assaulted six months ago and is having difficulty. She tells you that she feels anxious and depressed. The rapist was an acquaintance of her's and she has been questioning her ability to judge people and trust is very difficult to develop. Her self-esteem is really low and she is having a problem concentrating at school because she keeps having thoughts about the rape. Becky has been having nightmares and feeling has started to drink a lot to help her sleep. Her friends have been supported but they seem to be getting tired of her mood swings and angry outbursts. Becky feels like she is going crazy.

   How would you diagnose Becky and why? What treatment would you recommend for her? (pp. 156-57, 166)

   Post-traumatic stress disorder: Symptoms have lasted longer than one month. She feels anxious and depressed, is having difficulty concentrating and intrusive thoughts regarding the rape. She is having mood swings and is starting to drink to keep the nightmares away.

   Treatment: Seek specialized rape crisis counseling services for short-term counseling. Services might include advocacy for Becky if she goes to court, possibly direct-exposure therapy if symptoms persist. Give her number to the telephone hotline and possibly use psychotropic medications.

PICTURE THIS

1. Stress Tolerance (No "men" + Clay + TUR)
2. Crisis (Cry + Sis)
3. Eustress (Ewe + St + <Dress-D>)
4. PTSD (Pea + Tea + Ess + D)

MULTIPLE-CHOICE PRACTICE TESTS
PRACTICE TEST NUMBER 1

1. A wide range of obstacles, such as prejudice and discrimination, loneliness, inadequate self-control, the death of a loved one, fall into the category of (p. 140)

   c. frustrations.

2. The simultaneous occurrence of two or more incompatible needs or motives, such as career versus family needs, is described as (p. 140)

   b. conflict.

3. Feeling the need to achieve goals or behave in particular ways—internal or external—is known as (p. 141)

   a. pressure.

4. The term, "_____," is used to refer to times when a stressful situation approaches or exceeds the adaptive capacities of a person or group. (p. 142)

   a. crisis

5. A crisis or trauma may occur as a result of (p. 142)

   a. a disaster, such as a flood.
   b. a nasty divorce.
   c. an injury or disease.
   d. All of the above.

6. The faster the changes, the greater the (p. 143)

   b. stress.

7. A person's _____ of the stressor has an impact—one person's stressor is another person's thrill. (p. 144)

   a. perception

8. The term, "_____," refers to a person's ability to withstand stress without becoming seriously impaired. (p. 144)

   c. stress tolerance

9. _____ can moderate the effects of stress on a person and can even reduce illness and early death (p. 144)

   b. positive social and family relationships

10. _____ can make a stressor more potent and weaken a person's capacity to cope with it. (p. 144)

   a. Lack of support

PRACTICE TEST NUMBER 2

1. When confronting stress, a challenge is (p. 145)

   a. to meet the requirements of the stressor.

   b. to protect oneself from psychological damage and disorganization.

   d. a and b.

2. Severe stress may result in alterations that can impair the body's ability to fight off (p. 146)

   b. invading bacteria and viruses.

3. In using its resources to meet one severe stressor, an organism may _____ tolerance for other stressors. (p. 146)

   a. suffer a lowering of

4. Five years after the nuclear accident at Three Mile Island, people exposed to the incident showed (p. 148)

   c. symptoms of high stress.

5. One extremely stressful situation is loss of (p. 150)

   b. gainful employment.

6. The sudden unexpected death of a loved one accounts for about _____ of all PTSD cases seen in a community. (p. 150)

   a. one-third

7. A normal grieving process typically lasts up to _____ and may involve negative health effects, such as high blood pressure, changes in eating habits, and even thoughts of suicide. (p. 151)

   c. about a year

8. In the U.S., Post-Traumatic Stress Disorder (PTSD) appears to occur in about _____ adults at some time in their lives, but the reported rates are lower in national populations with fewer natural disasters and lower crime. (p. 152)

   a. 1 in 12

9. There is a _____ ratio of female to male prevalence of PTSD, due largely to the occurrence of assaultive violence against women. (p. 152)

   b. 2:1

10.   The symptoms of PTSD may vary greatly, depending on the (p. 152)

    a.   nature and severity of the terrifying experience.

    b.   degree of surprise.

    c.   personality make-up of the person.

    d.   all of the above.

PRACTICE TEST NUMBER 3

1.   Regarding PTSD causal factors, (p. 155)

    a.   personality seems to play a role.

    b.   the nature of the event itself appears to account for most of the stress-response variance.

    c.   appears to be a greater likelihood of post-traumatic disorder among women than men.

    d.   all of the above.

2.   An extensive survey of college health behavior reported that _____ percent of female students acknowledged having been forced to have sexual intercourse. (p. 156)

    d.   20

3.   _____ is the most frequent cause of PTSD in women. (p. 156)

    b.   Rape

4.   In stranger rape, initially the victim is likely to have a strong fear of (p. 156)

    b.   physical harm or death.

5.   In acquaintance rape, the reaction may be (p. 156)

    b.   betrayal.

    c.   guilt.

    d.   b and c.

6.   Survivors of POW camps commonly showed (pp. 159-60)

    a.   impaired resistance to physical illness.

    b.   low frustration tolerance.

    c.   frequent dependence on alcohol and drugs.

    d.   all of the above.

7.   Many adults who emigrate—especially those forced to leave their homes—experience a high degree of stress and psychological adjustment problems. However, even greater degrees of stress can occur with (p. 162)

    b.   their children.

8. Torture induces psychological effects independent of other stressors, but the impact of torture could be lessened if victims were able to (p. 164)

    b. predict and ready themselves for the pain they were about to experience.

9. A process of stress-inoculation training prepares people to tolerate an anticipated threat by (p. 166)

    a. providing information about the situation and ways people can deal with such dangers.
    b. providing self-statements that promote effective adaptation are rehearsed.
    c. having the person practice making such self-statements while being exposed to stressors.
    d. All of the above.

10. A study found that brief therapy treatment _____ the traumatic event significantly reduced PTSD symptoms. (p. 169)

    b. immediately following

COMPREHENSIVE PRACTICE TEST
MULTIPLE-CHOICE

1. The term, "stress," has typically been used to refer to the _____ placed on an organism, and the organism's internal biological and psychological responses to such demands. (p. 140)

    b. adjustive demands

2. The symptoms of stress _____ when a person is more closely involved in an immediately traumatic situation. (p. 142)

    b. intensify

3. The longer a stressor operates, the _____ its effects. (p. 142)

    c. more severe

4. Encountering a number of stressors at the same time will make these _____ than when occurring separately. (p. 142)

    c. more severe

5. Stress operating through the hypothalamic-pituitary-adrenal system can result in a _____, making persons vulnerable to diseases to which they would normally be immune. (p. 149)

    d. suppression of the immune system

6. What seems to push a normal reaction into the category of post-traumatic stress disorder is (p. 150)

    c.   the inability to function as usual.

7. Acute Stress Disorder occurs (p. 153)

    b.   within four weeks and last from two days to four weeks.

8. Post-Traumatic Stress Disorder differs from Acute Stress Disorder in that it (p. 153)

    a.   lasts longer than four weeks.
    c.   may be long-lasting or late-arising.
    d.   a and c.

9. _____ following a traumatic experience is considered important is preventing conditioned fear from establishing itself and becoming resistant to change. (p. 156)

    c.   Prompt psychotherapy

10. After suffering a rape (female or male), a victim is very likely to (p. 156)

    a.   suffer anxiousness.
    b.   experience disturbed concentration and intrusive thoughts.
    c.   behave atypically, such as aggressively, or substance abuse.
    d.   all of the above.

11. Most physically wounded soldiers have shown _____ symptoms than non-physically wounded soldiers (except in cases of permanent mutilation). (p. 159)

    b.   less anxiety or less combat exhaustion

12. A study of a large sample of former POWs found that half reported symptoms of PTSD in the year following their releases, and _____ met PTSD criteria 40 to 50 years after their wartime experiences. (p. 160)

    c.   nearly a third

13. Among returning WW II POWs, within the first six years, (p. 160)

    a.   nine times as many died from tuberculosis as would have been expected in civilian life.
    b.   four times as many died from gastrointestinal disorders, over twice as many from cancer, heart disease, and suicide as the norm.
    c.   three times as many from accidents.
    d.   all of the above.

14. A causal factor in combat stress problems is (pp. 160-61)

    a.   temperament—a soldier's emotional and physical stamina.
    b.   psychosocial—personal freedom frustrations, stresses from combat, personality.
    c.   sociocultural—esprit de corps, acceptability of war goals, quality of leadership.
    d.   all of the above.

15. Psychological symptoms experienced after having been tortured include (p. 163)

    a.   pain, nervousness, insomnia, tremors, weakness, fainting, sweating, and diarrhea.

    b.   night terrors and nightmares, depression, suspiciousness, social withdrawal and alienation, irritability, and aggressiveness.

    c.   concentration problems, disorientation, confusion, memory deficits, aggressiveness, impulsivity, and suicide attempts.

    d.   all of the above.

TRUE – FALSE

1.   T — All situations, positive and negative, that require adjustment can be stressful. (p. 140)

2.   T — Stresses can be damaging if these are too severe for our coping resources—or if we believe as if they are. (p. 146)

3.   F — Severe and sustained stress on any level has very little effect on an organism's overall adaptive capacity.   (p. 146)

4.   T — People who are recently divorced or separated are markedly overrepresented among people with psychological problems.   (p. 151)

5.   F — Even though PTSD can have a large impact on a person, young persons in particular don't feel the need to avoid social situations or excitable stimuli.   (p. 152)

6.   F — Training and preparation can insulate persons from PTSD. This is why police officers never suffer from it.   (p. 152)

7.   T — PTSD can result in the traumatic event being persistently re-experienced by the person, or, conversely, deliberate avoidance of any stimuli associated with the trauma, such as cars, if the event were a car crash. (p. 153)

8.   T — Everyone has a breaking point, and at sufficiently high levels of stress, the average person can be expected to develop some psychological difficulties following a traumatic event. (p. 155)

9.   T — Being held hostage can produce disabling psychological symptoms in victims for months following the incident. (p. 162)

ESSAY

1.   Explain the three responses of personality decompensation. (p. 149)

    a.   **Alarm and mobilization**

       •   Emotional arousal, increased tension, vigilance, heightened sensitivity; first signs of maladjustment may appear.

    b.   **Resistance**

       •   Utilizing task-oriented coping measures, ego-defense mechanisms. Indications of strain may exist. May revert to previously developed defenses.

c. **Exhaustion**
- Adaptive resources are depleted; coping patterns begin to fail. May employ exaggerated and inappropriate defensive measures. Delusions and hallucinations may occur. Severe exhaustion may lead to uncontrolled violence, apathy, stupor, and perhaps even death.

2. Coping with rape: Describe the feelings and problems women experience at different points during their traumas. (pp. 156-57)

a. **Anticipatory phase:**
- Before the rape, defense mechanisms, such as denial: "This can't be happening."

b. **Impact phase:**
- Recognition that she is actually going to be raped
- Fear for her life, may lead to inability to act
- Continues until rape is over

c. **Post-traumatic recoil phase:**
- Begins immediately after rape
- May include crying and sobbing, or control masked by a calm subdued facade
- Guilt, self-blame

d. **Reconstitution phase:**
- Victim starts to make plans for the future
- Self-protective activities, changing phone number, moving
- Frightening nightmares about the rape
- Phobias develop, including fear of being alone, fear of crowds

3. Identify and briefly explain the approaches to treating the symptoms of PTSD. (pp. 166-69)

a. **Short-term therapy**—brief, focuses on the immediate problem

b. **Post-disaster debriefing sessions**—"unwind" in a safe environment following a traumatic situation

c. **Direct exposure to therapy** for those whose PTSD symptoms persist—victim is reintroduced to stimuli that have come to be feared or associated with the traumatic event

d. **Telephone hotlines**—available in most major cities and many smaller ones to help people undergoing periods of severe stress

e. **Psychotropic medications**—antidepressants and other medication focused on specific symptoms

CRISS-CROSS ANSWERS

Across
5. eustress
9. frustrations
11. stress tolerance

Down
1. acute distress disorder
2. ptsd
3. stressor
4. decompensation
6. conflicts
7. distress
8. crisis
10. stress

CHAPTER SIX

MATCHING

Psychological Test	Definition
D. Phobia	A. the transmission of a phobia from one person or animal, to another by observing a person or animal behaving fearfully
G. Neuroticism	B. credited with devising a two-process theory of avoidance learning in OCD
F. Neurotic behavior	C. panic attack that occurs during sleep
I. Inflation effect	D. persistent and disproportionate fear of some specific object or situation that Presents little or no actual danger
A. Vicarious conditioning	E. avoidance of activities that create arousal sensations
C. Nocturnal panic	F. exaggerated use of avoidance behaviors or defense mechanisms
E. Introceptive avoidance	G. basic personality trait which refers to aproneness to experience negative mood states
J. Anxious apprehension	H. cognitive psychologist who coined phrase "automatic thoughts" that are associated with panic triggers
M. CRH	I. when a person is exposed to a more intense traumatic experience (not paired with the conditioned stimulus) after a first traumatic experience thus becoming more fearful of the conditioned stimulus
L. Bed nucleus of the stria terminali	J. future-oriented mood state in which a person attempts to be constantly ready to deal with negative upcoming events
K. TKS	K. anxiety disorder found in Japan related to Western social phobia but people are concerned with doing something to embarrass or offend others
H. Aaron Beck	L. extension of the amygdala believed to be important brain area mediating generalized anxiety
B. O. H. Mowrer	M. anxiety producing hormone recently implicated as playing a role in GAD

SHORT ANSWERS *(Your answer should contain the following points.)*

1. List the five subtypes of specific phobia and give examples of each. (p. 176)
   a. Animal—snakes, spiders
   b. Natural environment—heights or water
   c. Blood-injection-injury—sight of blood or injury
   d. Situational—airplanes or elevators
   e. Atypical—choking or vomiting

2. Discuss methods used to treat social phobias. (p. 182)

    a. Behavior therapy—prolonged exposure to social situations in graduated manner

    b. Cognitive behavior therapy—identify underlying negative automatic thoughts; help change negative automatic thoughts through logical reanalysis—the challenging of the automatic thought

    c. Medication—can also be treated with beta-blockers, antidepressants, and antianxiety drugs.

3. You are a psychoanalysis and a client comes to see you with GAD. How would explain the causal factors for this disorder? (pp. 202-03)

    a. unconscious conflict between the ego and id impulses that are not being dealt with because the person's defense mechanisms have broken down or become overwhelmed

    • perhaps defense mechanisms never developed

    • inoperative defense mechanisms leave the person anxious nearly all of the time

4. Describe the different types of obsessive thoughts and compulsions. (p. 212)

    a. Obsessive thoughts: contamination fears, fears of harming self or others, lack of symmetry, pathological doubt, need for symmetry, sexual obsessions and religious or aggressive obsessions

    b. Compulsions: five primary types – cleaning, checking, repeating, ordering/arranging, counting and primary obsessional slowness

FILL IN THE BLANKS

1. The DSM-IV-TR recognizes _**SEVEN**_ primary types of anxiety disorders. (p. 176)

2. The National Cormorbidity Survey found that anxiety disorders affect approximately _**30**_ percent of the female population and _**19**_ percent of men at some point in their lives. (p. 176)

3. The three main categories of phobia are _**SPECIFIC**_ phobia, _**SOCIAL**_ phobia, and _**AGORAPHOBIA.**_ (p. 176)

4. _**ANIMAL, BLOOD-INJURY, DENTAL,**_ and _**NATURAL ENVIRONMENT**_ phobias begin in childhood, but _**CLAUSTROPHOBIA**_ and _**AGORAPHOBIA**_ tend to begin in adolescence and early adulthood. (p. 177)

5. The experiments by Mineka and Cook showed that laboratory-reared monkeys could learn to be afraid of snakes by observing a _**WILD-REARED**_ monkey behaving fearfully with snakes. It was also found that the monkeys could learn fear by watching a _**VIDEOTAPE**_ of wild monkeys responding fearfully to snakes. This suggests that _**MASS MEDIA**_ may play a role in _**VICARIOUS**_ conditioning of fears and phobias in people. (p. 181)

6. The ***PREPAREDNESS*** theory says that humans and animals are more likely to have phobias for snakes, water, heights and enclosed places because of our evolutionary history of these things being associated with trauma. (p. 181)

7. An uncued panic attack that occurs during sleep is known as ***NOCTURNAL PANIC.*** (p. 187)

8. Current estimates are that 30 to 50 percent of persons with panic disorder will experience a serious ***DEPRESSION*** at some point in their life and meet the criteria for ***DEPENDENT*** or ***AVOIDANT*** personality disorder. (p. 190)

9. Currently, two neurotransmitters systems are most implicated in panic attacks. These are the ***NORADRENERGIC*** and ***SEROTONERGIC*** systems. (p. 191)

10. The ***COMPREHENSIVE LEARNING*** theory of panic proposes that initial panic attacks become associated with initially neutral interoceptive and exteroceptive cues through a conditioning process. (p. 192)

11. Experience with controlling aspects of one's life may ***IMMUNIZE*** us from developing generalized anxiety disorder. (p. 199)

12. Fear and panic involve the activation of the ***FIGHT-OR-FLIGHT*** response while generalized anxiety is a more ***DIFFUSE*** emotional state involving ***AROUSAL*** and a ***PREPARATION*** for possible impending threat. (p. 202)

13. The behavioral model has been useful in helping to understand what ***FACTORS*** may help to ***MAINTAIN*** obsessive-compulsive behavior and in generating an effective form of ***TREATMENT***. However, it has not been as helpful in explaining why people with OCD develop ***OBSESSIONS*** in the first place. (p. 206)

14. People with OCD seem to have an overactivation of the ***ORBITAL FRONTAL CORTEX***, which delivers the "stuff of obsession," and a dysfunction of the ***CORTICO-BASAL GANGLIONIC-THALAMIC CIRCUIT*** circuit, which leads to inappropriate behavioral responses. (p. 210)

THE DOCTOR IS IN...PSYCHIATRIC HELP—5¢

1.   Teresa comes to your office. She has been referred to you by her primary care doctor who, after doing a complete work-up, could find nothing wrong with her. She tells you she feels as if she is losing control and going crazy. You ask her to explain. She says that for the last two months, she has been unexpectedly having shortness of breath, heart palpitations, dizziness, and sweating. These experiences seem to come out of the blue and make her so afraid of having other feelings like these, that she is afraid to leave her house. (pp. 186-89, 195-96)

How would you diagnose Teresa and why? Also create a treatment plan for her.
a.   **Diagnosis:** Panic disorder with agoraphobia
b.   **Treatment:** A variety of treatment methods could be used.
- Medication: not as good but could prescribe benzodiazepines or antidepressants
- Cognitive-Behavior Therapy (see Developments in Practice)

c.   **You would:**
- teach Teresa about nature of anxiety and panic, and how to self-monitor her experiences
- teach her how to control her breathing
- help her identify her automatic thoughts during panic attacks
- teach her how to decatastrophize e.g., expose her to feared situations and feared bodily sensations (interceptive fears)

2.   Ned visits your office. He is has made an appointment because his family says he needs to see you. His constant worrying is concerning them and becoming difficult to deal with. Ned tells you he has been feeling anxious about the future and says that he needs to be ready to deal with any negative thing that might come up—like his car breaking down or getting lost when trying to get to a new area. Both of these would affect his work, thus, his financial well-being, and, ultimately, his family. He tells you he can't seem to control the constant state of apprehension and always feels tense and over aroused. He hasn't been sleeping well and has had difficulty concentrating at work (which is also worrying him, as he thinks is may affect his employment). His family says he is constantly irritable and he has felt a lot of muscle tension, especially in his neck and shoulders. (pp. 197-98, 202)

How would you diagnose Ned and what would be the most effective treatment for him?
a.   **Diagnosis:** Generalized Anxiety Disorder
b.   **Treatment:**
- Medications—possibly busipirone or some antidepressants
- Cognitive-behavior therapy—training in applied muscle relaxation techniques and cognitive restructuring techniques aimed at reducing distorted cognitions, information processing biases and catastrophizing about minor events. GAD is still one of the most difficult anxiety disorders to treat.

c. One of Ned's most persistent problems is ongoing worry. You have read the study by Borkovec and colleagues (1994). What would you tell Ned about the findings regarding the benefits people with GAD derive from worrying?

Benefits are:
- superstitious avoidance of catastrophe
- actual avoidance of catastrophe
- avoidance of deeper emotional topics
- coping and preparation
- motivating device

3. Jean has over the last few months, been washing her hands 50 to 75 times a day. Her hands are now cracked and bleeding and she is unable to work. In addition to hand washing she has to constantly check her stove and door locks and she must do this in a particular way or she has to start all over again. She has come to see you because she is about to lose her marriage as a result of her behavior. Jean knows her behaviors are senseless and excessive but she can't control them. How would you diagnosis Jean and what treatment plan would you create? (pp. 202-04, 210-12)

a. **Diagnosis:** Obsessive-compulsive disorder

b. **Treatment:** Behavioral treatment involving a combination of exposure and compulsive response prevention is perhaps the most effective. SSRIs are a possibility, but there is a high relapse rate when the drugs are stopped. In severe intractable OCD, which has not responded to therapy or drugs, neurosurgical techniques may be considered.

PICTURE THIS

1. neurosis
2. phobia
3. panic
4. anxiety
5. agoraphobiqa
6. general anxiety disorder
7. compulsions

MULTIPLE-CHOICE PRACTICE TESTS

PRACTICE TEST NUMBER 1

1. Who believed that neuroses were psychological disorders that resulted when there was significant anxiety that was a result of intrapsychic conflict? (p. 174)

c. Freud

2. The components of fear and panic are (p. 174)

    a. cognitive/subjective.

    b. physiological.

    c. behavioral.

    d. all of the above.

3. Anxiety, unlike fear, is a complex blend of emotions and cognitions that is oriented to the (p. 175)

    c. future.

4. Many human and animal experiments have established that the basic fear and anxiety response patterns are highly (p. 175)

    b. conditionable.

5. Phobic behavior tends to be reinforced by the reduction in anxiety that occurs when a feared situation is (p. 177)

    c. avoided.

6. _____ percent of people with blood-injury phobia have a history of fainting when confronted with the sight of blood or injury. (p. 178)

    a. seventy-five

7. Which viewpoint believes that phobias represent a defense against anxiety? (p. 178)

    c. psychodynamic

8. By watching her older sister react in a fearful way to spiders, Keri learned to also be afraid of spiders. This is called (p. 179)

    c. vicarious conditioning.

9. John had dogs all of his life and was quite comfortable being around dogs. When John was bitten by a dog, he did not develop a phobia. Why? (p. 180)

    d. His experiences had immunized him.

10. Steve watches as his therapist goes up and down an elevator in a calm and nonchalant way. Later, he is walking into the elevator with his therapist and going up one floor. This is an example of (p. 182)

    a. participant modeling.

PRACTICE TEST NUMBER 2

1. Social phobias usually begin in (p. 183)

    c. adolescence or early adulthood.

2. Which famous performers below suffer from social phobia? (p. 183)

    a. Barbara Streisand

    b. Carly Simon

    d. a and b

3. Like other phobias, social phobias are often (p. 184)

    b. learned.

4. Unlike specific phobias, social phobia can sometimes be treated with (p. 186)

    c. medication.

5. What distinguishes panic attacks from other types of anxiety? (p. 187)

    a. brevity

    b. intensity

    d. a. and b.

6. Panic attacks are about twice as prevalent in women as in men. This is thought to be a result of _____ factors. (p. 189)

    c. sociocultural

7. In family and twin studies, panic disorders have a _____ heritable component. (p. 190)

    c. moderate

8. The _____ is the central area involved in what has been called a "fear network" with connections to lower (locus coeruleus) and higher (prefrontal cortex) areas of the brain. (p. 191)

    b. amygdala

9. Beck and Emery (1985) and Clark (1986, 1988, 1997) proposed a model of panic that says clients are hypersensitive to their bodily sensations and prone to giving them the direst possible interpretations. What is this theory called? (p. 192)

    c. cognitive theory

10. Ken often has an upset stomach. He is very anxious about this condition. Although Ken does not have any panic attacks, yet his preexisting high level of _____ makes him more prone to developing a panic disorder. (p. 194)

    d. anxiety sensitivity

PRACTICE TEST NUMBER 3

1. It is estimated that GAD is experienced by approximately _____ percent of the population in any one-year period and _____ percent at some point in their lives. (p. 198)

    d. 3 and 5

2. The role of worry for people with GAD (p. 200)

    a. has positive and negative consequences

3. A(n) _____ is a overt repetitive behavior or more covert mental act. (p. 203)

    a. compulsion

4. Cognitive factors that contribute to OCD behavior are (p. 209)

    a. attention drawn to disturbing material relevant to obsession.
    b. difficulty blocking out negative irrelevant input.
    c. low confidence in memory skills.
    d. All of the above.

5. Biological causal factors are _____ implicated in the causes of OCD. (p. 209)

    a. strongly

6. According to biological psychiatrists, panic disorder is qualitatively different from generalized anxiety because of an apparent finding that a _____ drug appeared to block panic attacks in agoraphobics without affecting their anticipatory anxiety. (p. 195)

    b. tricyclic antidepressant

7. Which of the following is not typically a part of cognitive-behavior therapy for panic disorder? (p. 195)

    d. carbon dioxide inhalation and/or lactate infusion

8. The benzodiazepines, minor tranquilizers that reduce generalized anxiety, probably exert their effects through stimulating the action of (p. 201)

    b. GABA.

9. An impulse the person cannot seem to control is called a(n) (p. 203)

    a. compulsion.

10. The personality disorders with which OCD most often occurs are (p. 205)

    d. avoidant and dependent.

COMPREHENSIVE PRACTICE TEST
MULTIPLE-CHOICE

1. The term, "neurosis," was dropped in the DSM–III in the year (p. 174)

    b.   1980.

2. The most common way of distinguishing between fear and anxiety is that fear involves a(n) (p. 174)

    d.   obvious source of danger.

3. Paula has extreme irrational fear. She feels anxious and has physical responses such as a racing heart and dizziness. Paula will probably first be seen by her (p. 176)

    a.   primary care doctor.

4. Specific phobias were formerly known as _____ phobias. (p. 176)

    d.   simple

5. At the age of 21 months, Karen, was a very timid and shy child. She hid behind her mother and rarely ventured over to play with other children in her play group. Based on the study done by Kagan and his colleagues, what can you predict about the risk of Karen developing multiple specific phobias by the age of seven or eight? It is (p. 181)

    c.   higher because of temperamental factors.

6. The most common specific social phobia is fear of (p. 183)

    a.   public speaking.

7. From an evolutionary perspective, social phobia are a by-product of (p. 184)

    a.   dominance hierarchies.

8. Billy, who is 25 months old, is behaviorally inhibited. What can you predict, based on the Hayward et. al. and Kagan research, will be the likelihood of Billy developing a social phobia by the age of 13? He (p. 184)

    a.   has increased risk.

9. An early hypothesis about the origins of agoraphobia was that it was a (p. 192)

    a.   fear of fear.

10. Unlike other anxiety disorders that usually have an acute onset, people with GAD report (p. 198)

    b.   a slow and insidious onset.

    c.   sudden onset.

    d.   a and b.

11. Something that may account for why people with GAD feel constantly tense and vigilant for possible threats is their relative lack of (p. 199)

    c.   safety signals.

12. GAD seems to share a common genetic diathesis with (p. 201)

    c.   major depressive disorder.

13. A(n) _____ is a persistent and recurrent intrusive thought, image or impulse that is experienced as disturbing and inappropriate. (p. 203)

    b.   obsession

14. With OCD, what factors seem consistent in almost all the different clinical presentations? (p. 205)

    a.   Anxiety is the affective symptom.
    b.   Compulsions usually reduce the anxiety.
    c.   Nearly all people afflicted with OCD fear they will be responsible for something terrible happening to themselves or others.
    d.   All of the above.

15. OCD may be characterized by excessively high levels of (p. 210)

    c.   Serotonin.

TRUE – FALSE

1. T — Fear or panic is a basic emotion that involves activation of the "flight or fight" response. (p. 174)

2. F — Anxiety involves a positive mood, worry about the future and the ability to predict the future threat. (p. 175)

3. F — It has been proven that classical conditioning does not produce fears and phobias. (p. 178)

4. T — Life experiences influence a person's likelihood of developing a phobia. (p. 180)

5. F — The best treatment for specific phobia is cognitive therapy. (p. 182)

6. T — The treatment of choice for specific phobias is exposure therapy. (p. 182)

7. T — The term, "social anxiety disorder," is increasingly preferred by researchers and clinicians, instead of social phobias. (p. 183)

8. F — Social phobics have a deep sense of control over events in their lives. (p. 185)

9. T — Agoraphobia can occur in the absence of full-blown panic attacks. (p. 189)

10. F — Seven to 30 percent of adults who have experienced panic attacks will go on to develop panic disorder. (p. 190)

11. T — The learning theory model is better able to explain why panic attacks often occur without any preceding negative automatic thoughts or during sleep at night than the cognitive model. (p. 194)

12. F — People with panic disorder have their attention automatically drawn to pleasant information in their environment. (p. 194)

13. T — Most people with GAD manage to function in spite of their high levels of worry and anxiety. (p. 198)

14. F — People with GAD have a history of experiencing many important events in their lives in which they feel are predictable and controllable. (p. 199)

15. T — GABA, a neurotransmitter, is now strongly implicated in generalized anxiety. (p. 201)

16. F — OCD is different from other anxiety disorders in that there is a large gender difference in adults. (p. 204)

17. T — When OCD clients were asked to suppress intrusive thoughts, they reported twice as many intrusive thoughts on those days as opposed to the days they were given no instructions. (p. 209)

ESSAY QUESTIONS *(Your answer should contain the following points.)*

1. Discuss the criteria for diagnosing generalized anxiety disorder (GAD). (pp. 198-99)
    a. chronic excessive worry about a number of events or activities—formerly used to be called free-floating anxiety
    b. worry must occur more days than not for at least six months and be difficult to control
        • cannot be associated with another concurrent Axis I disorder
        • subjective experience of worry must be accompanied by at least three of the following symptoms
            • restlessness, being keyed up
            • sense of being easily fatigued
            • difficulty concentrating or mind going blank
            • irritability
            • muscle tension
            • sleep disturbance

2. Give examples of cultural differences in sources of worry. (p. 212)

    a. Yoruba culture of Nigeria—three primary clusters of symptoms associated with generalized anxiety:

- worry focusing on creating and maintaining a large family and fertility
- dreams may indicate the person is bewitched
- bodily complaints—water in my brain, "ants creeping in my brain," etc.

    b. China—Koro, fear of penis shrinking or nipples retracting

    c. Japan—Taijin Kyofusho—concern of doing something that will embarrass or offend others

CRISS-CROSS ANSWERS

Across

1. fear
3. compulsions
5. neurosis
7. social phobia
8. panic
9. amygdala

Down

2. anxiety
4. specific phobia
6. obsessions

CHAPTER SEVEN

MATCHING

Match each of the following people with her/his accomplishment or theory.

C. Martin Seligman

F. Emile Durkheim

A. Aaron Beck

B. Sigmund Freud

E. Emil Kraepelin

D. Abramson et al., 1989

A. depressogenic schemas/negative automatic thoughts

B. "Mourning and Melancholia"

C. learned helplessness theory

D. hopelessness theory

E. introduced term, " manic-depressive insanity"

F. French sociologist who studied the sociocultural factors in suicide

SHORT ANSWERS *(Your answer should contain the following points.)*

1. A friend of yours recently lost a grandparent. You have just finished studying mood disorders in your Abnormal Psychology class. What could you tell him about the normal response phases to the loss? (p. 218)

    Four phases—

    a. Numbing and disbelief; a few hours to a week

    b. Yearning and searching; weeks or months

    c. Disorganization and despair

    d. Some level of reorganization

2. In the Brown and Harris 1978 study, what factors were associated with the women who experienced stressful life events but did not become depressed? (p. 230)

    Four factors—

    a. Having an intimate relationship with spouse or lover

    b. Having no more than three children

    c. Having a part-time or full-time job

    d. Having a serious religious commitment

3. Discuss the ways interpersonal problems can play a causal role in depression and how depression affects others. (pp. 236-37)

    a. Lack of social support: more vulnerable to depression

    b. Lack of social skills: Speak more slowly or monotonously, maintain less eye contact, difficulty solving interpersonal problems

    c. Behavior elicits negative feelings in others

d.   Negative feelings make people less willing to interact with depressed person

e.   Depression can lead to marital discord and marital discord, can lead to depression

f.   Depression in one family member extends to infants, children, and adolescents

4.   Explain the emphasis suicide prevention centers have when working with someone who is contemplating suicide. (p. 260)

a.   Maintain supportive and directive contact with person for short period of time

b.   Help the person realize acute distress is impairing his or her ability to access the situation accurately

c.   Help the person see that present distress and emotional turmoil will not be endless

FILL IN THE BLANKS

1.   The life-time prevalence for dysthymia is nearly **_5_** percent for men and **_8_** percent for women. (p. 220)

2.   Three specifiers connected with major depression are major depressive episode with **_MELANCHOLIC_** features, severe major depressive episode with **_PSYCHOTIC_** features, and major depressive episode with **_TYPICAL_** features. (p. 222)

3.   When delusions or hallucinations with psychotic features are present during a major depressive episode, these must be **_MOOD-CONGRUENT,_** with content portraying a negative tone. (p. 222)

4.   Depression may **_RECUR_** at sometime following a period of remission, or it may **_RELAPSE,_** which refers to the return of symptoms within a short period of time. (p. 223)

5.   Whybrow et. al. suggested that psychosocial stressors may play a role in the development of mood disorders by causing long-term changes in **_BRAIN_** functioning. (p. 246)

6.   The reformulated helplessness theory proposes three critical dimensions on which attributions are made: **_INTERNAL/EXTERNAL_**, **_GLOBAL/SPECIFIC_**, and **_STABLE/UNSTABLE_**. (pp. 234-35)

7.   **_BIPOLAR_** disorders are distinguished from **_UNIPOLAR_** disorders by the presence of manic or hypomanic symptoms. (p. 216)

8.   Although the symptoms listed are the same for manic and **_HYPOMANIA_** episodes, there is much less impairment in social and occupational functioning in **_HYPOMANIA_**, and, to qualify, hospitalization must not be required. (p. 241)

9. ***ADJUSTMENT DISORDER WITH DEPRESSED MOOD*** and ***DYSTHYMIA*** are considered the mild-to-moderately-severe main categories of depressive disorders. (p. 220)

10. ***CYCLOTHYMIA*** is considered the mild-to-moderately-severe category of bipolar disorders. (p. 241)

11. A person who experiences a ***MANIC EPISODE*** has markedly elevated euphoric and expansive moods, often interrupted by occasional outbursts of intense irritability, or even violence. (p. 241)

12. Someone who meets the criteria for a major mood disorder and at least two major symptoms of schizophrenia is diagnosed with ***SCHIZOAFFECTIVE DISORDER***. (p. 244)

13. ***"MOOD STABILIZER"*** is used to describe lithium and related drugs, because these have anti-manic and anti-depressant effects. (p. 251)

14. Electroconvulsive therapy is often used with severely depressed, suicidal patients because antidepressants often take ***THREE*** to ***FOUR*** weeks to produce significant improvement. ECT is also used with patients who have not responded to other forms of ***PHARMACOLOGICAL*** treatment. When selection criteria are carefully observed, a complete remission of symptoms occurs after about six to 12 treatments. (p. 244)

15. Fill in the missing information in the following questions about the risk of suicide. (p. 254)
    a. The vast majority of those who commit suicide do so during the ***RECOVERY*** phase of depression.
    b. The risk of suicide is just ***ONE*** percent during the year a depressive episode occurs but rises to ***FIFTEEN*** percent over the entire lifetime of an individual who experiences recurrent episodes.
    c. Experts agree that the actual number of suicides is probably ***TWO TO FOUR*** times as high as the official number.

THE DOCTOR IS IN...PSYCHIATRIC HELP—5¢

1. **Helen**

    Diagnosis: Dysthymia—persistent depressed mood for at least two years with symptoms of poor appetite, sleep disturbances, low energy, low self-esteem and fleeting periods of feeling normal.

    Additional information: Family history of mood disorders, relationship with husband, last time she had a physical check-up, outside interests and how often the periods of feeling normal appear and how long do these last. (p. 220-21)

2. **Expert you**
    a. Conduct disorders and substance abuse common among completers

b.   Mood disorders common among non-fatal attempts

c.   Those with two or more disorders are at higher risk for completion

d.   Availability of fire arms in the home more common for completers

e.   Adolescents more sensitive to lack of control and may have maladaptive family settings

f.   Limited problem-solving abilities

g.   Exposure to suicide in media (pp. 254-60)

3.   **Miles**

Diagnosis: Seasonal affective disorder—depressed for two winters in a row with symptoms disappearing in the spring.

Additional information: Did Miles have any depressive episodes at other times of the year? Did he experience anything similar where he use to live? (p. 223)

4.   **Ed**

Diagnosis: Bipolar. Manic behavior—excessive ideas, violent when wife wouldn't give him a credit card. Mania lasted a week. Depression had preceded the manic episode. (p. 241)

PICTURE THIS

1.   Mania (Mane + IA)

2.   Hypomania (Hypo + Mane + IA)

3.   Hemlock Society (Hem + Lock + Sews + Eye + A + Tea)

4.   *Listening to Prozac* (Listening + 2 + PRO + Sack)

5.   Bi Polar (Two Poles)

6.   Dysthmia (Disk + Thigh + MIA)

7.   Rapid Cycling (Need we explain?)

PRACTICE TESTS

PRACTICE TEST NUMBER 1

1.   In 1990, out of the 150 health conditions that were considered to be a "disease-burden" to society, depression ranked (p. 216)

b.   fourth.

2.   Mania is characterized by (p. 216)

c.   excitement and euphoria.

3.   Depression is characterized by (p. 216)

a.   sadness and dejection.

4.   Mood disorders are differentiated by (p. 216)

a.   severity.

c.   duration.

d.   a and c.

5. A person who has been diagnosed with dysthymia may experience normal mood periods that may last (p. 220)

    a. a few days or weeks up to a maximum of two months.

6. Sue meets the criteria for being diagnosed with major depressive disorder. However, her therapist also notes some patterns of symptoms that she feels are important for understanding the disorder and treating Sue effectively. These additional patterns are called (p. 222)

    d. specifiers.

7. Mood disorders were previously called (p. 216)

    c. affective disorders.

8. Twin studies have provided evidence that there may be a _____ genetic component to unipolar depression. (p. 224)

    c. moderate.

9. In the 1960s and 70s, research was focused on the following neurotransmitters and their effect on depression: (p. 225)

    a. norepinephrine, dopamine and serotonin.

10. Originally, diathesis-stress models assumed that diatheses were biological. Recently, depression researchers have begun to propose diatheses that are (p. 230)

    a. cognitive.
    b. social.
    d. a and b.

PRACTICE TEST NUMBER 2

1. Two personality variables that may contribute to a diathesis for depression are (p. 230)

    b. neuroticism and low positive affectively.

2. The cognitive diatheses that have been studied for depression focus on _____ patterns of thinking. (p. 230)

    c. negative

3. Research has found that a person may have a vulnerability to depression if he/she experiences an early childhood loss of a parent and (p. 230)

    a. poor parental care.

4. One of the most important contributions of the psychodynamic approach to depression has been to point out the (p. 231)

    c. importance of early loss (real or imagined).

5. According to the behavioral theories of depression, people become depressed when their responses no longer produce positive reinforcement or when (p. 232)

    b.   their rate of negative reinforcement increases.

6. A psychological theory on reasons why these are sex differences in unipolar depression proposes that women are more prone to experience (p. 236)

    a.   a lack of control over negative life events.
    b.   discrimination in the workplace.
    c.   poverty.
    d.   all of the above.

7. The mild-to-moderate range of bipolar disorder is known as (p. 241)

    b.   cyclothymia.

8. Who introduced the term, "manic-depressive insanity," to describe a series of attacks of elation and depression? (p. 242)

    c.   Kraepelin

9. Even without formal therapy, the great majority of manic and depressed patients recover from a given episode within less than (p. 250)

    b.   one month.

10. In suicides associated with depression, most often suicide is committed during the _____ phase of a depressive episode. (p. 254)

    d.   recovery

PRACTICE TEST NUMBER 3

1. A disorder that involves mood swings between subclinical levels of depression and mania is (p. 241)

    d.   cyclothymic disorder.

2. Bipolar mood disorder is distinguished from major depression by (p. 243)

    a.   at least one episode of mania.

3. The original learned helplessness theory refers to the depressed patient's perception that (p. 234)

    b.   there is no control over aversive events.

4. Since about 1990, the type of antidepressants increasingly prescribed because of fewer side effects are (p. 251)

    b.   selective serotonim re-uptake inhibitors (SSRIs).

5. _____ is a brief form of treatment for unipolar depression that is highly structured and attempts to each people to evaluate their beliefs and negative automatic thoughts. (p. 252)

    a. CBT

6. This treatment for unipolar depression focuses on current relationships issues, trying to help the person understand and change maladaptive interaction patterns. (p. 253)

    c. IPT

7. Two main thrusts of suicide prevention efforts are the treatment of the person's mental disorder(s) and (p. 260)

    c. crisis intervention.

8. A disorder that involves mood swings between subclinical levels of depression and mania is (p. 220)

    c. dysthymic disorder.

9. Bipolar mood disorder is distinguished from major depression by (p. 243)

    a. at least one episode of mania.

10. All of the following are symptoms of the manic phase of bipolar mood disorder **except** (p. 241)

    d. deflated self-esteem.

COMPREHENSIVE PRACTICE TEST
MULTIPLE-CHOICE

1. Simultaneous symptoms of both mania and depression is referred to as (p. 216)

    c. mixed episode.

2. Unipolar and bipolar mood disorders, while not completely separate, are different in (p. 216)

    a. symptoms.
    b. causal factors.
    c. treatment.
    d. all of the above.

3. Which of the following mood disorders is more common and has actually increased in recent years? (p. 218)

    b. major depression

4. Mild depression may be seen as "normal and adaptive" if (p. 218)

    a. it is brief and mild.
    b. involves looking at issues that would normally be avoided.
    c. keeps us from using energy to obtain futile goals.
    d. all of the above.

5. A diagnosis of major depressive disorder *cannot* be made if the person has experienced (p. 220)

    c. hypomania.

6. Depression occurs during which of the following life cycle stages? (pp. 221-22)

    a. infancy.
    b. adolescence.
    c. middle adulthood.
    d. all of the above.

7. Depression in infants is known as (p. 221)

    b. anaclitic depression.

8. When major depression and dysthymia coexist in an individual, it is referred to as (p. 222)

    b. double depression.

9. Because depressive episodes are time-limited, they are usually specified as (p. 223)

    c. single and recurrent.

10. A neurophysiological finding that damage to the _____ but not the _____ anterior cortex, often results in depression. (p. 225)

    b. left; right

11. Circadian rhythms, which may play a causal role in depression, are controlled by strong and weak (p. 227)

    c. oscillators

12. John is not looking forward to the fall. This is the time when his appetite increases and he experiences hypersomnia. He also starts to feel pretty low. John suffers from seasonal affective disorder. Treatment for John will include (p. 227)

    d. light therapy.

13. Gary has fallen further and further behind in his rent. His roommates are threatening to kick him out. This stressful life event is known as a(n) (p. 229)

    b. dependent life event.

14. Women who are at a genetic risk for depression will experience more (p. 229)

    c.   stressful life events.

15. In the brains of depressed patients, abnormalities have been detected in the (p. 227)

    a.   anterior cingulate cortex.

    b.   hippocampus.

    c.   amygdala.

    d.   all of the above.

TRUE – FALSE

1. F — Major depression is more common in men (21% lifetime prevalence rate) than women (13% lifetime prevalence rate). (p. 218)

2. T — It is normal to feel depressed as a result of a recent loss or stress. (p. 218)

3. F — Postpartum blues and postpartum depression are the same thing and very common in women who have recently given birth. (p. 219)

4. F — Dysthymia and major depression sufferers have periods of normal moods. (p. 220)

5. F — When a person suffers from double depression, recovery is very likely to occur and not reoccur, once a person has been treated. (p. 222)

6. T — Seasonal affective disorders are an example of recurrent depressive episodes. (p. 223)

7. T — Findings for genetic contribution to mild forms of unipolar depressions are not as consistent as for major depression. (p. 224)

8. F — Hormones play a significant role in causing depression in women. (p. 236)

9. T — Bipolar is distinguished from major depression by at least one episode of mania or a mixed episode. (p. 242)

10. T — A recent survey documented that more than 75% of people with depression don't receive treatment or receive inappropriate care. (p. 250)

11. F — Tricyclies have been the antidepressants most commonly prescribed since about 1990. (p. 250)

12. T — Discontinuing antidepressants when symptoms have remitted may cause relapse. (p. 251)

13. T — Women are about three times as likely to attempt suicide as are men, but three times more men than women die by suicide each year. (p. 254)

14. F — Marital therapy has not been shown to be as effective as cognitive therapy for people who have unipolar depression and marital discord. (p. 253)

15. T — Children are at increased risk for suicide if they have lost a parent or have been abused. (p. 255)

16. T — Genetic factors, as well as alterations in serotonia functioning, can contribute to causal factors for suicide. (p. 255)

17. F — Suicidal ambivalence means the person wants to die. (p. 259)

18. F — Those who threaten suicide seldom do. (p. 259)

ESSAY QUESTIONS *(Your answer should contain the following points.)*

1. Describe Aaron Beck's cognitive theory of depression. (pp. 232-34)
   a. Depressogenic schemas or dysfunctional beliefs—rigid, extreme and counterproductive thoughts
   b. Negative automatic thoughts—thoughts just below the surface and are unpleasant pessimistic predictions
   c. Negative cognitive triad—what negative automatic thought focus on. These are negative thoughts about self, negative thoughts about one's experience and surrounding world, and negative thoughts about one's future
   d. The above is maintained by negative cognitive biases, which are dichotomus reasoning, selective abstraction, and arbitrary inference

2. Discuss the issues associated with the controversy regarding a person's right to die. (p. 261)
   a. Has always been an issue with some cultures/societies supporting a person's right to commit suicide, e.g. classical Greece, the Netherlands, Hemlock Society, and the Oregon Death with Dignity Act
   b. A terminally ill person has a right to die with dignity—legislative pressure to pass laws to allow physician assisted suicide, e.g. Dr. Kervorkian
   c. Some people fear that people who are terminally ill will be pressured into taking their own lives
   d. Another issue is someone who isn't terminally ill who wants to take his/her own life and the use of prevention tactics, such as involuntary hospitalization
   e. Civil right suits, if a person is restrained against his/her will, thus raising legal issues

3. Discuss the causal factors in bipolar disorder.   (pp. 245-47)

    Biological

    - Genetic component—80% of the variance in the tendency to develop bipolar depression
    - Abnormalities in the hypothelamic, pituitary, thyroid axis
    - Disturbance in biological rhythms
    - Shifting patterns of brain activity

    Biochemical

    - Perhaps excesses of neurotransmitters norepinephrine, serotonin, and dopamine

    Psychosocial

    - Stressful life events
    - Personality and cognitive variables interacting with stressful life events associated with relapse
    - Extreme defense against or reaction to depression

4. Explain the sociocultural factors affecting unipolar and bipolar disorders. (pp. 247-49)

    a. Depression occurs in all cultures, but form and prevalence vary.

    b. China and Japan: some time and vegetative manifestations. No Western concept of guilt, self-recrimination.

    c. Australian aborigines: no guilt or self-recrimination and no suicide. Vent hostility on to others.

    d. Kaluli of New Guinea: relieve losses prevents hopelessness.

    e. U.S.: unipolar depression higher in lower socioeconomic groups; bipolar more common in higher socioeconomic classes.

CRISS-CROSS ANSWERS

Across
6. mood disorders
11. reoccurence
13. hypomania

Down
1. dysthymic
2. suicide
3. cyclothymic
4. bipolar
5. positive affect
7. relapse
8. specifiers
9. manic
10. schizoaffective disorder
12. unipolar
14. attributions

CHAPTER EIGHT

MATCHING

Match the following psychological disorders with their descriptions.

Disorder	Description
D. somatoform disorder	A. severe pain but no medical pathology to explain it
B. hypochoncriasis disorder	B. anxious preoccupation with having a disease based on a misinterpretation of bodily signs or symptoms
E. somatization disorder	C. patterns of symptoms affecting sensory or voluntary motor functions, even though medical examination reveals no physical basis for these
A. pain disorder	D. psychological problems are manifested in physical disorders that often mimic medical conditions, for which no medical evidence can be found
C. conversion disorder	E many different complaints of physical ailments in four symptom categories spreading over several years
J. body dysmorphic disorder	F. inability to recall previously sorted information that cannot be accounted for by ordinary forgetting; common initial reaction to severe stress
H. dissociative disorders	G. person manifests two or more distinct identities or personality states that alternate in some way in taking control of behavior
K. depersonalization disorder	H. normal processes regulating awareness and multichannel capacities of the mind apparently become disorganized, leading to various anomalies
I. dissociative fugue	I. a person not only goes into an amnesic state, but also leaves home surroundings and becomes confused about his or her identity
G. dissociative identity disorder	J. an obsessive preoccupation with some perceived flaw in one's appearance
F. dissociative amnesia	

SHORT ANSWERS (*Your answer should contain the following points.*)

1. Four criteria must be met for somatization disorder to be present: (p. 269)
   a. Four pain symptoms. The patient must report a history of pain experienced in at least four different sites or functions.
   b. Two gastrointestinal symptoms. The patient must report a history of at least two symptoms, other than pain, pertaining to the gastrointestinal system.
   c. One sexual symptom. The patient must report at least one reproductive system symptom other than pain.
   d. One pseudoneudrological symptom. The patient must report a history of at least one symptom, not limited to pain, suggestive of a neurological condition.

2. Conversion disorder's four categories of symptoms: (pp. 273-74)

   a. Sensory—most often visual, auditory, or sensitivity to feeling

   b. Motor—paralysis of an arm or leg

   c. Seizures—resemble epileptic seizures

   d. Mixed presentation from 1-3

3. One way of telling the difference between people with malingering/factitious disorders and other somatoform disorders is by the response given when asked to describe the symptoms. Fakers are inclined to be defensive, evasive, and suspicious, but individuals with conversion disorders are very willing to discuss them, often in excruciating detail. (p. 274)

4. Four types of psychologenic amnesia are recognized: (p. 280)

   a. localized—a person remembers nothing that happened during a specific period

   b. selective—a person forgets some, but not all, of what happened during a given period

   c. generalized—a person forgets his or her entire life history

   d. continuous—a person remembers nothing from a certain point in the past until the present

5. In very rare cases, called dissociative fugue, a person is not only amnesic for some or all aspects of his or her past, but also departs from home surroundings. During the fugue these persons are unaware of memory loss for prior stages in their life, but their memory for what happens during the fugue state itself is intact, during which they may live a quite normal life. Days, weeks, or ever years later, such persons may suddenly come out of the fugue state and find themselves in strange places working in a new occupation and not knowing how they got there. (p. 280)

FILL IN THE BLANKS

1. People with hypochondriasis are most often anxious and preoccupied with ***BODILY FUNCTIONS,*** other minor physical abnormalities or with ***VAGUE AND AMBIGUOUS*** physical sensations. (p. 266)

2. There seems to be a familial linkage between ***ANTISOCIAL PERSONALITY DISORDER*** in men and ***SOMATIZATION DISORDER*** in women. (p. 269).

3. To persons suffering pain disorder, the pain experienced is ***VERY REAL*** and it can hurt as much as pain with ***PURELY MEDICAL CAUSES***. (p. 270)

4. A symptom, such as partial paralysis or a pseudoseizure, which may appear to have a medical or neurological basis until medical examination reveals these cannot be fully explained by any known medical condition, is known as ***CONVERSION DISORDER***. (p. 271)

5. People with body dysmorphic disorder frequently will engage in excessive grooming behavior, often trying to _**CAMOUFLAGE THEIR PERCEIVED DEFECT**_ through their hair style, clothing, or makeup. (p. 275)

6. Often persons suffering from depersonalization disorder report feeling like they are living in _**A DREAM OR A MOVIE**_—quite unpleasant and aversive—and the person may feel as if he or she is _**GOING CRAZY**_, even though insight into what is happening is retained. (p. 278)

7. Dissociative identity disorder (DID) is a dramatic dissociative disorder in which a patient manifests at least _**TWO OR MORE DISTINCT IDENTITIES**_ or personality states that alternate in some way _**IN TAKING CONTROL OF BEHAVIOR**_. (p. 281)

8. In DID, _**TWO OR THREE**_ identities is usually the case, but a large series of cases showed an average of _**15**_ with some claiming as many as _**100**_. (p. 282)

THE DOCTOR IS IN...PSYCHIATRIC HELP—5¢

1. As the psychiatrist in a large hospital, you have been called in to evaluate a patient who had been admitted two days before. The patient, Cathy, had awakened in the morning and had been unable to see. She was blind. After being admitted to the hospital and the doctors determining there had been no accident, a complete medical and neurological exam was done. The results turned up nothing that would cause the blindness. You were called in to see if there could be a psychological cause. After talking to her for a while, you find out that husband had died unexpectedly about three months ago, leaving her with financial problems. She was going to have to get a job and she was worried about her employability. You ask if she has a picture of her husband. She says, "Yes," and walks to the shelf skirting a chair that is in her way.

    How would you diagnose Cathy and why. How would you treat her? (pp. 271-75)

    Diagnosis: Conversion disorder, blind with no medical or neurological cause, recent large stressors in life, doesn't seem to be faking it, walks around a chair but is blind

    Treatment: behavioral approaches, possibly hypnosis combined with other problem-solving therapies

2. Frank comes to see you because he has been urged him to talk to somebody. He is wearing sunglasses, even though he is in your office and it is dark outside. When you ask him about the glasses, he tells you that his eyelids are horrible and ugly. He doesn't want anyone to see them—ever. Frank tells you that he spends much of the day checking his eyelids and trying to make them look better. He is saving for another surgery, his third, because he just can't stand the way his eyes look. You ask if he dates, has friends or a job. Frank says that he doesn't date (Who would want to be with someone as ugly as he is?), so he has started to withdraw even from his few friends. He recently lost his job because he was unable to meet clients, looking the way he does.

How would you diagnose Frank and why? How would you treat him? (pp. 275-78)

Diagnosis: Body dysmorphic disorder, preoccupation with eyelids to the point of interfering with his life; two surgeries and saving for a third

Treatment: antidepressants and cognitive-behavioral therapy that focuses on having Frank identify and change distorted perceptions about his body.

3. Jackie comes to see you because she has been feeling rather odd lately. She tells you that she is feeling "unreal"—like she is not a part of her body. Jackie says that she is beginning to see her life as a movie because she feels so isolated from her self. She explains that when this experience occurs, it is like looking at the world through someone else's eyes. Her friends and even herself are viewed through these eyes as "automatons." These experiences are now happening two or three times per week and lasts for several hours.

What would be your diagnosis for Jackie and why? How would you treat her and what would you expect treatment outcomes to be? (pp. 278-79)

Diagnosis: Depersonalization disorder—Jackie feels separate from her body and like she is in a movie. She feels unreal and sees herself and her friends as automatons.

Treatment: no real controlled research has been done on treatment for depersonalization disorder. This disorder is thought to be resistant to treatment making outcome difficult to predict. Treatment has focused on other psycopathology that may be associated with the disorder. Hypnosis and teaching self-hypnosis techniques may be useful but again no controlled research has been done.

PICTURE THIS

1. Somatoform (Sew + Mat + O + Form)
2. Dissociative Disorders (Disk + Sew + C + A + TIV   Disc + Oar + 2 DERs)
3. Hypochondriasis (Hypo + Con + DRE + A + Sis)
4. Dissocioative Amnesia (Disk + Sew + SEE + AT + IF AM + Knee + Z + A)

MULTIPLE-CHOICE PRACTICE TESTS

PRACTICE TEST NUMBER 1

1. Dissociative disorders are some of the more dramatic phenomena to be observed in the entire domain of psychopathology, for example, (p. 266)

   a. people who cannot recall who they are or where they may have come from.

   b. people who have two or more distinct identities or personality states that alternatively take control of the individual's behavior.

   d. a and b.

2. People with _____ are preoccupied with fears of having a serious disease, based on misinterpretation of one or more bodily signs or symptoms, and is not reassured when medical examination can find no physical problem. (p. 266)

   c. hypochondriasis

3. Somatization disorder very commonly occurs with (p. 266)

   a. major depression.
   b. panic disorder and phobic disorders..
   c. generalized anxiety disorder.
   d. all of the above.

4. Evidence exists that somatization disorder (p. 270)

   a. runs in families.

5. Patients with somatization disorder tend to think of themselves as (p. 270)

   a. physically weak.
   b. unable to tolerate stress.
   c. unable to tolerate physical activity.
   d. all of the above.

6. All of the following are part of a chain of events in the development of a conversion disorder, **except** (p. 271)

   a. a conscious plan to use illness as an escape.

7. A typical example of symptoms of conversion disorder would be (p. 271)

   a. partial paralysis.
   b. blindness or deafness.
   c. pseudoseizures.
   d. all of the above.

8. Freud used the term "conversion hysteria" because he believed the symptoms were an expression of (p. 272)

   c. repressed sexual energy.

9. Conversion disorder occurs _____ often in women than in men. (p. 272)

   b. two-10 times more

10. Although it can develop at any age, conversion disorder most commonly occurs (pp. 272-73)

    a. between early adolescence and early adulthood.

PRACTICE TEST NUMBER 2

1. Early studies showed that perhaps _____ of patients diagnosed with conversion disorders were later diagnosed with an organic illness. (p. 274)

   c. 25-50%

2. People with _____ disorders are intentionally producing or grossly exaggerating psychological or physical symptoms for external reasons, such as avoiding work or military service. (p. 274)

   a. malingering and formfactitious

3. A person with _____ disorder is obsessed with a perceived or imagined flaw or flaws in his or her appearance. It is so intense that it causes clinically significant distress and/or impairment in social or occupational functioning. (p. 275)

   d. body dysmorphic

4. People with body dysmorphic disorder (BDD) may think (p. 276)

   a. their skin has ugly blemishes.
   b. their breasts are too small.
   c. their face is too thin.
   d. all of the above.

5. Dissociative disorders are methods in which individuals avoid stress by (p. 278)

   a. escaping from their personal identities.

6. It is likely that some people may have certain _____ that make them more susceptible to developing dissociative symptoms than others. (p. 278)

   d. personality traits.

7. In _____, one's sense of one's own self and one's own reality is temporarily lost, usually occurring during or after periods of severe stress. (p. 278)

   c. depersonalization

8. When episodes of depersonalization become persistent and recurrent and interfere with normal functioning, _____ may be diagnosed. (p. 278)

   b. depersonalization disorder

9. If _____ is caused by brain pathology, it most often involves failure to retain new information and experiences, that is, the information contained in experience is not registered and does not enter memory storage. (p. 279)

   c. retrograde amnesia

10. _____ is a fairly common initial reaction to intolerably stressful circumstances. (pp. 279-80)

  a. Dissociative amnesia

PRACTICE TEST NUMBER 3

1. In very rare cases, called _____, a person is not only amnesic for some or all aspects of his or her past, but also departs from home surroundings. (p. 280)

  b. dissociative fugue

2. Dissociative identity disorder (DID) was formerly known as (p. 281)

  c. multiple personality disorder.

3. The identity switches in DID typically occur (p. 282)

  a. very quickly (in a matter of seconds).

4. DID's alter identities may differ in (p. 282)

  a. gender, age,and sexual orientation,
  b. handedness, handwriting, and prescription for eyeglasses.
  c. foreign languages spoken and general knowledge
  d. all of the above.

5. _____ may or may not be aware of each other, or may attempt to take over control from the host identity. (p. 282)

  c. Alter identities

6. DID was rare until around _____, but now thousands of cases have been reported. (p. 283)

  c. 1979

7. DID has now been identified throughout the world. It has been found (p. 283)

  a. in all racial groups.
  b. in all cultures.
  c. in countries ranging from Nigeria and Ethiopia, to Turkey, Australia, and the Carribean.
  d. all of the above.

8. A major cause of DID appears to be (p. 283)

  b. childhood sexual abuse.

9. For _____ patients, most therapists set integration of the previously separate alters, together with their collective merging into the host personality, as the ultimate goal of treatment.

    c.   DID (p. 289)

10. A controversy exists concerning DID, including (p. 290)

    a.   how it develops.

    b.   whether it is real or faked.

    c.   whether memories of childhood abuse are real, and if the memories are real whether the abuse played a causal role.

    d.   all of the above.

COMPREHENSIVE PRACTICE TEST
MULTIPLE CHOICE

1. Body dysmorphic disorder (BDD) age of onset is usually in adolescence when many people start to become preoccupied with their appearance and appears to be (p. 277)

    b.   approximately equal in men and women.

2. Treatment approaches for BDD focus on

    a.   getting patients to identify and change distorted perceptions of their body.

    b.   exposure to anxiety-provoking situations (e.g., wearing something that highlights, rather than disguises, their defect).

    c.   prevention of checking responses (e.g., mirror checking, reassurance seeking, and repeatedly examining their imaginary defect). (p. 277)

    d.   all of the above.

3. Only in the past _____ has the concept of dissociation become a major research area in the field of cognitive psychology. (p. 278)

    c.   quarter-century

4. Like somatoform disorders, _____ disorders appear mainly to be ways of avoiding anxiety and stress and of managing life problems that threaten to overwhelm the person's usual coping resources. (p. 278)

    a.   dissociative

5. In _____ people may feel they are floating above their physical bodies, which may suddenly feel very different—as if drastically changed or unreal. (p. 278)

    a.   depersonalization disorder

6. Circumstances, for example those occurring during wartime combat conditions or immediately after a catastrophic event, such as a serious car wreck, may cause failure to recall previously stored personal information that cannot be accounted for by ordinary forgetting. This is called (pp. 279-80)

    b.   dissociative amnesia.

7. In DID, the primary or host identity is most frequently encountered, but alter identities may (p. 282)

   b.   take control at different points in time.

8. People with DID often show (p. 282)

   a.   moodiness and erratic behavior.

   b.   headaches, hallucination, and substance abuse.

   c.   post-traumatic symptoms and other amnesic and fugue symptoms.

   d.   all of the above.

9. In _____ amnesia, the individual forgets his/her entire life history. (p. 280)

   c.   generalized

10. Approximately _____ more females than males are diagnosed as having the DID, believed by some to be due to the greater proportion of abuse among females than males. (p. 283)

    c.   3-9 times

11. One of the primary techniques used in most treatments of DID is (p. 289)

    b.   hypnosis.

12. DID patients who recover memories of abuse (often in therapy) have sued _____ for inflicting abuse. (p. 290)

    b.   their parents

13. DID patients have also sued _____ for implanting memories or abuse they later came to believe had actually not occurred. (p. 290)

    c.   therapists and institutions

14. Some parents, asserting they had been falsely accused, formed an international support organization called _____ and have sometimes sued therapists for damages, alleging the therapists induced false memories of parental abuse in their child. (p. 290)

    a.   The False Memory Syndrome Foundation

15. Alter personalities would be expected in cases of (p. 282)

    d.   dissociative identity disorder.

TRUE – FALSE

1. T — Somatoform disorders share one key feature: all are expressions of psychological difficulties in the "body language" of medical problems that, on careful examination, cannot be documented to exist. (p. 266)

2. F — Somatization disorder is not extremely difficult to treat because much systematic research has been conducted. (p. 270)

3. T — Indications exist that people with hypochondriasis often had an excessive amount of illness in their families while growing up. (p. 268)

4. T — Contemporary views of conversion disorder see it as serving the function of providing a plausible excuse, enabling the individual to escape or avoid an intolerably stressful situation without having to take responsibility for doing so. (p. 272)

5. F — Conversion disorder was not very common in the past and and hardly ever occurred prior to World War II. (p. 272)

6. F — Normally, conversion disorder involved men who would ordinarily be considered unstable. (p. 272)

7. T — Most of us have concerns about our appearance; but people with body dysmorphic disorder are far more extreme, leading, in many cases, to complete preoccupation and significant emotional pain. (p. 276)

8. T — We all dissociate to a degree, occasionally. (p. 278)

9. T — Like somatoform disorders, dissociative disorders appear mainly to be ways of avoiding anxiety and stress and of managing life problems that threaten to overwhelm the person's usual coping resources. (p. 278)

10. T — Some have proposed that both eating disorders and BDD are variants of a "body image disorder" (not an official category). People with both BDD and eating disorders are preoccupied with their appearance and overemphasize their importance for relationships. (p. 277)

ESSAY QUESTIONS *(Your answer should contain the following points.)*

1. Pain disorder essay: (pp. 270-71)
    a. Two types:
        - pain disorder associated with psychological factors. Psychological factors are judged to play a major role in the onset or maintenance of the pain.
        - pain disorder associated with psychological factors and a general medical condition. The pain experienced is considered to result from psychological factors and some medical condition that could cause pain.
    b. Pain may be acute (duration of less than six months) or chronic (duration of more than six months).
    c. Unknown in the general population; fairly common among patients at pain clinics.
    d. More frequently diagnosed in women.
    e. Frequently comorbid with anxiety and/or mood disorders.
    f. Can lead to a vicious cycle of patient not being able to work or exercise and resulting inactivity may lead to depression and loss of physical strength and endurance. The loss of strength and fatigue can, in turn, exacerbate the pain.

g. Cognitive-behavior treatment techniques have been widely used. They generally include relaxation training, support and validation that the pain is real, scheduling of daily activities, cognitive restructuring, and reinforcement of "no-pain" behaviors.

2. Criteria commonly used for distinguishing between conversion disorders and true organic disturbances: (pp. 273-74)

a. Patient must receive a thorough medical and neurological examination.

b. The frequent failure of dysfunction to conform clearly to the symptoms of the particular disease or disorder simulated—no wasting away or atrophy of a "paralyzed" limb.

c. The selective nature of the dysfunction—"paralyzed" muscles can be used for some activities but not others.

d. Under hypnosis or narcosis, the symptoms can be removed, shifted, or reinduced at the suggestion of the therapist.

3. At least four serious controversies concerning DID: (pp. 285-87, 290-91)

1. Concern whether DID is a real disorder or whether it is faked, and even if it is real, can it be faked?

2. How does DID develop? a) DID is caused by early childhood trauma and b) the development of DID involves some kind of social enactment of multiple different roles that have been inadvertently encouraged by careless clinicians.

3. Those who maintain DID is caused by childhood trauma cite mounting evidence that the vast majority of individuals diagnosed with DID report memories of an early history of abuse. But are these memories of early abuse real or false?

4. If abuse has occurred in most individuals with DID, did the abuse play a causal role, or was something else correlated with abuse actually the cause?

5. Controversy rages.

a. Believers usually take DID and the idea of abuse as its cause to be established beyond doubt.

b. Disbelievers are sympathetic to people suffering from DID symptoms, but have tended to doubt that it is usually caused by childhood abuse, and have challenged the validity or accuracy of recovered memories of abuse.

CRISS-CROSS ANSWERS
Across
7. dissociative identity disorder
Down
1. somatoform disorders
2. dissociative fugue
3. dissociation
4. pain disorder
5. conversion disorder
6. malingering
7. Derealization
8. dissociative amnesia

CHAPTER NINE

WHO'S WHO AND WHAT'S WHAT—MATCHING

Name/Term	Definition
C. Princess Diana	A. published the first medical account of anorexia nervosa in 1689
E. Karen Carpenter	B. comes from the Greek words meaning "ox" and "hunger"
A. Richard Morton	C. suffered from bulima nervosa
D. Charles Lasegue and Sir William Gull	D. instrumental in naming the eating disorder, anorexia nervosa, in 1873.
F. Anorexia nervosa—restricting type	E. suffered from anorexia nervosa which ultimately lead to her death
H. Anorexia nervosa—binge-eating purging type	F. low weight is maintained by tightly controlling how much food is eaten
B. Bulima nervosa	G. proposed the term, " bulima nervosa," in 1979
G. Russell, a British psychiatrist	H. breakdown of eating restraint, resulting in periods of binge-eating and efforts to purge

SHORT ANSWERS *(Your answer should contain the following points.)*

1. Describe risk factors for eating disorders in males. (p. 295)
    a. homosexuality
    b. pre-morbid obesity
    c. being teased as a child
    d. subgroups who need to "make weight" in order to work

2. What are the DSM-IV-TR criteria for bulimia nervosa? (p. 298)
    a. frequent occurrence of episodes of binge-eating
    b. lack of control over eating
    c. recurrent inappropriate behavior that is intended to prevent weight gain
    d. person's self-evaluation has to be excessively influenced by weight and body shape

3. Mary was diagnosed with an eating disorder, anorexia nervosa. She sought treatment for the disorder. Based on the research done by Lowe in 2001, what can you say about her recovery possibilities? (p. 303)

    Very difficult to treat—Lowe's study looked at outcomes 21 years after patients sought treatment. He found that 16% of women with anorexia nervosa had died from starvation or suicide, 10% were still suffering from anorexia 21% partially recovered, and 51% were fully recovered. Mary has a little better than 50% chance of recovery.

4. Explain how the study done by Anne Becker of the women in Fiji illustrates the impact the media has on thinness. (pp. 305-06)

> In early 1990s when Becker was first conducting her research, fat was associated with being strong, capable of work, and being kind and generous. Being thin was considered negative, thought to be sickly, incompetent, or having received poor treatment. There was no such thing as an eating disorder. In 1998, when Becker returned to Fiji, television has been introduced to Fiji, and the people were able to see such shows as *Beverly Hills 90210* and *Melrose Place*. The young women were expressing concerns about their weight and dislike of their bodies and dieting in earnest. This research provides anecdotal information about how the introduction of Western values about thinness might insinuate themselves into different cultures.

FILL IN THE BLANKS

1. At the heart of anorexia nervosa is an intense fear of *GAINING WEIGHT*, a refusal to maintain a body weight that is *NORMAL*, a distorted perception of body *SHAPE* and *SIZE*, and an absence of at least three consecutive *MENSTRUAL PERIODS*. (p. 296)

2. Unlike patients with anorexia nervosa, bulimic patients are typically of *NORMAL* weight and may even be slightly *OVERWEIGHT*. (p. 298)

3. A 21-year follow-up of patients with anorexia nervosa suggests that patients tend not to maintain a *RESTRICTING* form of the disorder but tend to make a progression to *BINGING* and *PURGING* over time. (p. 301)

4. Research suggests that some personality traits in eating disordered patients might both *PREDATE* the onset of the disorder and *REMAIN* when the eating disorder remits and the patient has recovered. (p. 302)

5. Research is now suggesting that even *ANTICIPATING* going on a diet can itself be a *TRIGGER* for overeating. (p. 309)

6. When treatment for anorexia nervosa does not address the *PSYCHOLOGICAL* issues that fuel the behavior, any weight gain will be *TEMPORARY*. (p. 310)

7. Unlike patients with anorexia or bulimia, most binge-eating disorder patients do not overvalue *THINNESS*, although they do *DISPARAGE* their own bodies. (p. 312)

THE DOCTOR IS IN...PSYCHIATRIC HELP—5¢

1. Mary is 5'6" tall and weighs 96 pounds. She tells you that whenever she looks in the mirror, all she sees is a fat person. Mary has restricted her eating to just a few pieces of celery and carrots each day. There is a ritual to her eating pattern. Mary's hair is thin and her nails are brittle. She is still having regular menstrual periods.

   How would you diagnose Mary and why? (p. 301)

   a. **Eating Disorder Not Otherwise Specified**: because she meets the criteria for anorexia except that she is still having menstrual periods.

2. Glenn, a 45-year-old male, comes to your office. His wife insisted that he come in to see you. Glenn is 5'8" tall and weight 350 pounds. Even though his health is in jeopardy, he finds himself binging on all kinds of food from cakes and cookies to pizzas, fried chicken and hamburgers. He feels disgusted with his behavior. You ask if he purges and he tells you that he does not. He says that sometimes he will exercise excessively after binging but not every time.

   How would you diagnose Glenn and why? (p. 301)

   a. **Binge-Eating Disorder.** Glenn binges at a level comparable to someone with bulimia but does not regularly engage in any form of behavior to limit weight gain.

3. Diane, a 14-year-old girl, is referred to you because she has anorexia nervosa. Her parents are very concerned but a bit shocked when you suggest that you would like to see the whole family in therapy, not just Diane. What would you expect to see as family characteristics when you talk to Diane's family? How would you proceed with treatment? (pp. 309-11)

Diagnosis:

   a. Limited tolerance of disharmonious affect or psychological tension
   b. An emphasis on propriety and rule-mindedness
   c. Parental overdirection of the child or subtle discouragement
   d. Subtle discouragement of autonomous strivings
   e. Poor skills in conflict resolutions
   f. Long standing preoccupations regarding desirability
   g. Thinness, dieting and good physical appearance
   h. Perfectionist tendencies

Treatment:

   a. Work with parents to get child to eat
   b. Help parents to function as a team
   c. Address other family issues and problems after child has started to gain weight
   d. Work with child and parents to develop more independent and healthy family relationships
   e. Provide family therapy for one year

MULTIPLE-CHOICE PRACTICE TESTS
PRACTICE TEST NUMBER 1

1. One eating disorder that is found almost exclusively in men is (p. 295)

   d. reverse anorexia

2. In this type of anorexia nervosa, every effort is made to limit how much food is eaten and caloric intake is tightly controlled. (p. 296)

   c. restricting type

3. This type of anorexia nervosa involves a breakdown of restraint that results in periods of binge eating. (p. 296)

   a. binge-eating purging type

4. Karen has the eating disorder, bulimia nervosa. During her average binge, she could consume as much as _____ calories. (p. 298)

   c. 4,800

5. The DSM-IV distinguishes between two types of bulimia nervosa. They are (p. 298)

   a. purging and nonpurging

6. The difference between a person with bulimia nervosa and a person with the binge-eating/purging type of anorexia nervosa is (p. 298)

   c. weight

7. A newer eating disorder diagnosis that is currently not found in the DSM but is listed in the Appendix and warrants further study is (p. 301)

   a. BED

8. Sally has an eating disorder. She also engages in self-harming behavior. Sally's behavior is similar to how many other people with eating disorders. (p. 302)

   c. more than one-third

9. A common disorder found in relatives of patients with eating disorders is (p. 304)

   b. mood disorders

10. This neurotransmitter, in addition to being linked with mood disorders and impulsivity, also modulates appetite and feeding behavior. (p. 304)

    a. Serotonin

PRACTICE TEST NUMBER 2

1. The majority of girls and women who have anorexia seem to come from a (p. 305)

    c.   higher social class background

2. The first model to exemplify the current sociocultural ideal of extreme thinness was (p. 305)

    d.   Twiggy

3. Internalizing the _____ is associated with a range of problems that are thought to be risk factors for eating disorders. (p. 306)

    d.   Thin-ideal

4. There seems to be a perceptual discrepancy between how young girls and women regard their own bodies and the media representation of the (p. 306)

    a.   "ideal" female form

5. The average age that young women start to diet is now between (p. 308)

    c.   12-13

6. This is a causal risk factor for body dissatisfaction. (p. 308)

    a.   negative affect

7. Until her death in 1984, who was considered the the world's leading authority on the pychotherapy of anorexic disorders? (p. 310)

    b.   Hilde Bruch

8. The phenomenon of eating disorder patients learning from other patients about how to deceive hospital staff into thinking they are complying with treatment is known as (p. 310)

    c.   contagion

9. With many young women seeing anorexia as a life style choice and not recognizing the danger involved, they are turning to _____ web sites for validation. (p. 311)

    a.   pro-ana

10. This type of treatment has proven to be effective in treating anorexia and bulimia by helping to modify distorted beliefs about weight, food and self. (p. 310)

    d.   CBT

PRACTICE TEST NUMBER 3

1. The _____ component of CBT for bulimia is focused on normalizing eating patterns. (p. 312)

    a.   behavioral

2. The _____ component of CBT for bulimia challenges the dysfunctional thought patterns that perpetuate a binge cycle. (p. 312)

   b. cognitive

3. When patients with bulimia stop trying so hard to restrain their eating, they seem to (p. 312)

   c. improve

4. Significant depression is a comorbid condition for binge-eaters, affecting around _____during their lifetime. (p. 312)

   d. 60%

5. Obesity is defined based on a statistic called the (p. 313)

   b. BMI

6. From a diagnostic perspective, obesity is not a(n) (p. 314)

   c. eating disorder

7. Adult obesity is related to the number and size of the _____ in the body. (p. 314)

   c. adipose cells

8. A key influence on excessive eating and obesity is (p. 314)

   b. family behavior patterns.

9. If you were a psychoanalyst and were treating a patient who was obsessed, you would view him or her as fixated in what stage of psychosexual development? (p. 314)

   a. oral

10. This type of obesity was defined by Bruch as obesity that occurs in adults as a response to trauma or stress. (p. 315)

   d. reactive

COMPREHENSIVE PRACTICE TEST
MULTIPLE-CHOICE

1. At the heart of anorexia nervosa and bulimia nervosa is an intense and pathological fear of becoming (p. 294)

   b. overweight and fat

2. Another component of anorexia and bulimia is a pursuit of _____ that is relentless and sometimes deadly. (p. 294)

   c. thinness

3. Although people of all different ages have been known to develop eating disorders, the period of greatest risk is in the (p. 294)

    a. teenage years.
    b. early adulthood.
    d. a and b.

4. The clinical picture of the binge-eating/purging type of anorexia give it much in common with (p. 297)

    c. Bulimia nervosa

5. If a person meets the criteria for anorexia nervosa they can't be diagnosed with bulimia nervosa because (p. 298)

    b. there is a greater mortality associated with anorexia than with bulimia.

6. Eating disorders are no longer confined to industrialized Western countries but can be found in (p. 302)

    a. India
    b. Africa
    c. Asia
    d. all of the above.

7. The-long term mortality rate for bulimia nervosa is around (p. 303)

    c. 0.5%

8. People with anorexia and bulimia often show a long-standing pattern of excessive (p. 308)

    d. perfectionism

9. Although implicated in the development of eating disorders, currently there is not enough empirical evidence that _____ is a risk factor for eating disorders. (p. 309)

    c. childhood sexual abuse

10. Family therapy has been found to be most effective when it is used to treat this group whose eating disorder has a fairly recent onset. (p. 311)

    a. adolescents

11. Because many patients with bulimia also suffer from mood disorders, they are often treated with (p. 312)

    c. antidepressants

12. On average, how many patients with bulimia, who were treated with cognitive behavioral therapy, stopped binging and purging after treatment? (p. 312)

    c. 50%

13. Obesity can result in (p. 314)

     a. diabetes.

     b. high blood pressure.

     c. musculoskeletal problems.

     d. all of the above.

14. The rates of obesity are rising too quickly to be only a result of genetics. This rise implies what has become a significant influence. (p. 314)

     c. unhealthy lifestyles

15. Being obese is defined as having a body mass index of _____ or above. (p. 313)

     a. 30

16. An extreme method for treating obesity involves (p. 316)

     d. gastric bypass surgery.

TRUE – FALSE

1. F — Eating disorders in the elderly are easily diagnosed because doctors are aware of the problem. (p. 294)

2. T — Patients with anorexia nervosa, even if they are painfully thin or emaciated, often deny having any problems. (p. 296)

3. T — Thirty to fifty percent of patients transition from the restricting type to the binge-eating purging type of anorexia nervosa during the course of their disorder. (p. 296)

4. F — Death is often a direct outcome of the eating disorder bulimia nervosa. (p. 298)

5. T — There is a great deal of comorbidity associated with eating disorders and other diagnosable psychiatric conditions. (p. 301)

6. F — Recent work has proven, and it has been widely accepted, that the restrictive type of anorexia has a genetic base. (p. 304)

7. T — Body dissatisfaction is an important risk factor for pathological eating. (p. 307)

8. F — Dieting is not regarded as a risk factor for the development of eating disorders in young women. (p. 307)

9. T — About 17% of patients with severe eating disorders have to be committed to a hospital for treatment against their will. (p. 310)

10. F — The most immediate concern with patients with anorexia is to restore their weight to a level that is not life-threatening. (p. 310)

11. T — Obesity tends to persist over time. (p. 314)

ESSAY QUESTIONS   *(Your answer should contain the following points.)*

1. Discuss the medical complications of anorexia nervosa and bulimia nervosa. (p. 300)

    Anorexia

    a. hair thins; nails and hair become brittle

    b. skin becomes dry and downy hair grows on face neck, arms, back and legs (langugo)

    c. skin develops a yellowish tinge

    d. hands and feet feel cold

    d. low blood pressure

    e. Vitamin B1 deficiency, which could lead to depression and cognitive changes

    f. sudden death from heart arrhythmias

    g. low levels of potassium can result in kidney damage and renal failure

    Bulimia

    a. purging can cause electrolyte imbalances and hypokalemia

    b. risk for heart abnormalities

    c. damage to heart muscle caused by ipecac used to induce vomiting

    d. callouses on their hands from sticking their fingers down their throat

    e. damage to teeth from acid in stomach when throwing up

    f. mouth ulcers and dental cavities

    g. small red dots around eyes, caused by the pressure of throwing up

    h. swollen parotid glands, caused by repeatedly vomiting

2. Describe Garner's set-point theory and its relation to eating disorders. (p. 304)

    Weight is physiologically regulated around a weight that the body tries to defend, a set-point. If a person tries to radically deviate from this weight, there are "physiological compensations" that take place in order to restore the weight. Hunger drive is an example of a compensation. The more weight a person loses, the greater the hunger levels. This is an attempt to encourage eating, gain weight and return to a state of equilibrium. People with anorexia think about food all the time and try very hard to suppress their hunger. Chronic dieting increases likelihood of person having periods of binging impulses—eating very high-caloric foods.

CRISS-CROSS ANSWERS

Across

5. obesity
7. serotonin
8. perfectionism
9. meta-analysis

Down

1. bulima nervosa
2. negative affect
3. set-point theory
4. anorexia nervosa
6. Body Mass Index

CHAPTER TEN

MATCHING

Terms

E. psychoneuroimmunology

G. health psychology

B. behavioral medicine

A. positive psychology

C. biofeedback

F. Type A behavior pattern

I. Type B behavior pattern

Definition

A. a focus on human traits and resources that might have direct implications for our physical and mental well-being

B broad interdisciplinary approach involving many disciplines

C. focus on altering physiological states

D. pattern relaxed, more laid-back, and less time pressured people

E. the study of the interactions between behavior, the nervous system, and the immune system

F. excessive competitive drive, extreme commitment to work, impatience or time urgency, and hostility

G. subspecialty deals with psychology's contributions to diagnosis, treatment, and prevention of psychological components of physical problems

SHORT ANSWERS *(Your answer should contain the following points.)*

1. Cortisol is a good hormone to have around in an emergency. But there is also a down side to cortisol. Explain. (pp. 325-26)
    a. It prepares the body for the fight or flight response, inhibits the innate immune system…
    b. If the cortisol response is not shut off, it can damage brain cells.

2. Optimism and its opposite, hopelessness, can have a significant impact on one's health. Explain. (pp. 330-33)
    a. Hopelessness can accelerate the progression of atherosclerosis, the underlying process leading to heart attacks and strokes.
    b. Optimism seems to serve as a buffer against disease.
    c. People with too little optimism experience a psychological sense of helplessness.

3. Explain the prevalence of hypertension in the African-American community in the United States. (p. 334)
    a. Probably stresses of inner-city life, poverty, and explicit racial prejudice.
    b. Diet. African-American women are more likely to be overweight
    c. High salt use in the diet, and blacks, as a group, excessively retain ingested sodium.
    d. Less likely to exercise as a group.

4. What is the importance of asking yourself, "In the past month, have I felt so sad, discouraged, hopeless or had so many problems that I wondered if anything was worthwhile?" (p. 337)

    Not to make you feel bad, but in a study, those who said, "Yes," had twice the risk of CHD than did those who said, "No."

5. Why should depression and CHD be linked? (p. 337)

    a. Depressed people may engage in more behaviors known to put people at risk—not eating well, exercising, or smoking, etc.

    b. Depression may be linked to CHD through biochemical mechanisms, such as elevated levels of cortisol and norepinephrine.

FILL IN THE BLANKS

1. Organic malfunctions causing hypertension account for only a small percentage; the large majority of hypertension cases is called *ESSENTIAL HYPERTENSION*. (p. 334)

2. Key factors in work-related stress seem to be *BEING IN A HIGHLY DEMANDING JOB* and *HAVING LITTLE CONTROL OVER DECISION-MAKING*. (p. 338)

3. It appears that any sociocultural conditions that markedly increase life stress tend to play havoc with the biological human organism and lead to *AN INCREASE IN DISEASE*, as well as *OTHER PHYSICAL AND MENTAL PROBLEMS*. (p. 342)

4. It may turn out that the greatest contribution of *BEHAVIORAL APPROACHES* will be in the area of altering self-injurious habits, such as smoking and excessive alcohol use. (p. 344)

MULTIPLE-CHOICE PRACTICE TESTS
PRACTICE TEST NUMBER 1

1. The emphasis of _____ is on the role that psychological factors play in the occurrence, maintenance and prevention of physical illness. (p. 322)

    b. behavioral medicine

2. Antigens in the blood stream are searched out and destroyed by (p. 327)

    a. B-cells.

    b. T-cells.

    c. macrophages.

    d. all of the above.

3. Gastric ulcers (p. 324)

    c. may have psychological or physical, as well as common lifestyle factors.

4. A person who is depressed due to having an underactive thyroid would be a victim of (p. 324)

    a. Mental Disorder Due to a General Medical Condition.

5. Cortisol (p. 325)

    a. is necessary in an emergency, as it prepares the body for a fight or flight response.

    b. can damage brain cells, especially in the hippocampus if not shut off.

    d. a and b.

6. Long-term stress (p. 326)

    a. might compromise the body's ability to heal and fight infections.

    b. is being linked to diminished immune reactivity.

    d. a and b.

7. The immune system has been likened to a police force, in that (pp. 326-27)

    a. if it is too weak, it cannot function effectively, and the body succumbs to damage from invading viruses and bacteria.

    b. if it is too strong and unselective, it can turn on its own normal cells.

    d. a and b.

8. In an experiment where self-evaluations of the subjects were manipulated negatively, the power of the killer cell cytotoxicity to eradicate an antigen was (p. 328)

    c. significantly diminished.

9. Unexpectedly, it was found that, just as Pavlov's dogs learned to salivate to a tone, immunosuppression can be (p. 328)

    b. classically conditioned.

10. Conditions demonstrated to be associated with diminished immune function include (p. 330)

    a. sleep deprivation.

    b. space flight.

    c. death of a spouse.

    d. all of the above.

PRACTICE TEST NUMBER 2

1. Lifestyle factors—habits or behavior patterns presumable under our own control—play _____ role in three of the leading causes of death in this country: coronary heart disease, automobile accidents, and alcohol-related deaths. (p. 330)

    b. a major

2.   It is widely known that use of the latex condom is an effective measure for preventing transmission of the HIV-1 retrovirus, (p. 330)

   a.   yet very large numbers of sexually active persons do not use them.

3.   Considering optimism as it affects health, (pp. 330-31)

   a.   many surgeons will delay a major operation until they are convinced that a patient is reasonably optimistic about the outcome.

   b.   in an everyday sense, it seems to serve as a buffer against disease.

   c.   people with too little optimism experience a psychological sense of helplessness.

   d.   all of the above.

4.   Chronic anger and hostility in a person (p. 331)

   a.   can be risk factors for coronary heart disease and death.

5.   Neuroticism, anxiety, and depression are known as _____ emotions. (p. 331)

   b.   negative

6.   Positive psychology has shown the health benefits of (p. 331)

   a.   humor and laughter.

   b.   positive affectivity.

   c.   forgiving people as opposed to harboring a grudge.

   d.   all of the above.

7.   With stress, the normal heartbeat, regular pulse, and relatively low blood pressure (pp. 333-34)

   b.   become part of the "flight-or-fight" pattern and must work harder.

   c.   increase and usually return to normal when the crisis passes, although under continuing emotional strain, high blood pressure may become chronic.

   d.   b and c.

8.   High blood pressure is insidious and dangerous, due to the fact (p. 334)

   a.   its regulation is so complex that when it goes awry, identifying the causal factors can be extremely difficult.

9.   Studying the relationship between anger and blood pressure showed that participants who _____ had the lowest blood pressure. (p. 335)

   c.   used constructive anger

10. Investigating patients who had had heart attacks, researchers found that clinically depressed patients were _____ more likely to die in the next six months than were their nondepressed counterparts. (p. 337)

   c.   five times

PRACTICE TEST NUMBER 3

1. Another study that followed 1,500 men and women with no prior history of heart disease for 14 years found that persons who had suffered major depression were _____ more likely to have had a heart attack. (p. 337)

    c. four times

2. People with low levels of emotional support (unmarried, small social network, lack of friends) are _____ likely to develop CHD, and _____ likely to have another cardiac event, and _____ likely to die over the next five years. (p. 337)

    a. more, three times more, three times more

3. Mental stress is known to (p. 338)

    a. raise systolic blood pressure.
    b. cause an elevation in epinephrine.
    c. reduce the oxygen supply to the heart muscle.
    d. all of the above.

4. In a study of twins where only one had CHD, it was found that the twin suffering from heart disease was _____ work-oriented, took _____ leisure time, had _____ home problems and, in general, experienced greater _____ in his lives than his healthier twin brother. (p. 339)

    b.   more, less, more, dissatisfactions

5. Death rates from varied causes, including physical disease, are _____ in people who have recently undergone marital problems or divorce than in the general population. (p. 340)

    b. markedly higher

6. People who have a good social support system (p. 340)

    a. have lower blood pressure.
    b. have higher natural killer cell activity in the blood.
    d. a and b.

7. For patients with CHD, appropriate treatment might include (p. 342)

    a. lipid lowering medications.
    b. anxiolytic (anxiety reducing) medications.
    c. anticoagulants.
    d. all of the above.

8. In the first study of emotional disclosure in people with rheumatoid arthritis, it was found that those who had engaged in emotional disclosure had _____ physical dysfunction than people in the control condition. (p. 343)

    c. significantly less

9. Why emotional disclosure provides clinical benefits is not clear. However, possibly it is because (p. 343)

    a.   patients are given an opportunity for emotional catharsis or "blowing off steam."

    b.   writing provides an opportunity for people to re-think and re-appraise their problems.

    d.   a and b.

10. Biofeedback (pp. 343-44)

    b.   generally has failed to live up to the enthusiasm it originally generated.

    c.   may prove to be effective in the control of musculoskeletal pain.

    d.   b and c.

MULTIPLE-CHOICE COMPREHENSIVE

1. It is becoming more apparent that a disorder (p. 322)

    a.   may be entirely physical in origin.

    b.   may be entirely psychological in origin.

    d.   a. and b.

2. Studies examining the association between stress and immune functioning established an association between the occurrence of stressful circumstances and (p. 326)

    b.   diminished immune reactivity.

3. A man hearing voices telling him to refuse dialysis for his kidney disease is an example of (p. 324)

    d.   what DSM-IV references as Psychological Factor Affecting a General Medical Condition.

4. A stress response involves biological responses, including (pp. 325-26)

    a.   the hypothalamus, which stimulates the sympathetic nervous system which stimulates the adrenal glands to secrete adrenaline and noradrenaline.

    b.   an increase in heart rate and a preparation to metabolize glucose more rapidly.

    c.   the pituitary gland secretes adrenocorticotropic hormone which activates the adrenal cortex into producing the stress hormone called cortisol.

    d.   all of the above.

5. While stress has not been found to cause specific physical diseases, it (p. 326)

    a.   is becoming a key underlying theme in our understanding of the development and course of virtually all organic illness.

    b.   may serve as a predisposing, precipitating, or reinforcing factor in the causal pattern.

    c.   may interfere with the body's normal defensive forces or immunological system.

    d.   all of the above.

6. In studies of groups of uninfected high-risk and early stage HIV-infected gay men, it was found that (p. 328)

    a.   behavioral interventions, such as aerobic exercise, had positive psychological and immunocompetence effects.

    b.   depressed mood was associated with enhanced HIV-1 activity.

    c.   psychological depression compromised immune function.

    d.   all of the above.

7. Psychoneuroimmunology, the study of the interactions between behavior, the nervous system, and the immune system (pp. 328-29)

   a.   has shown that, unlike previously thought, the immune system is not "closed" and responsive only to external challenges.

   b.   the nervous system and the immune system communicate.

   c.   the brain influences the immune system and the immune system influences the brain.

   d.   all of the above.

8. Research has shown that depression (or negative affect) shows (p. 330)

   a.   a strong association between dysphoric mood and compromised immune function.

   b.   the state of being depressed in itself adds something beyond any negative effects of the stressors precipitating this mood.

   c.   that depressive affect reliably associated with lowered numbers of white cells following foreign protein challenge lowered natural killer cell activity, and lowered quantities of several varieties of circulating white cells.

   d.   All of the above.

9. Concerning negative emotions—the negative affect—it has been shown that (p. 331)

   a.   negative emotions can be damaging to our health.

   b.   depression is associated with measurable and undesirable changes in immune functioning and even seems to increase mortality from all causes in medical inpatients.

   c.   anxiety seems to be associated with the development of coronary heart disease, both in men and women and to delay recovery from surgery.

   d.   all of the above.

10. In 1996, the number of sudden cardiac deaths in the United States in people ages 15 to 34 was (p. 332)

   d.   3,000.

11. A group of men identified as either Type A or Type B was followed for eight and a half years. Compared to Type B personality, Type A personality was associated with _____ coronary artery disease and risk of recurrent myocardial infarction. (p. 335)

   c.   much more

12. In a two-year study of 34,000 male professionals with panic disorder, agoraphobia, and generalized anxiety, men with the highest levels of phobic anxiety were _____ likely to have a fatal heart attack and _____ likely to suffer sudden cardiac death than were men with the lowest levels. (p. 337)

   b.   three times more, six times more

13. Genetic contributions to disease may involve (p. 338)

   a.   an underlying physical vulnerability for acquiring a disease.

   b.   the psychological make-up of the individual and his/her stress tolerance.

   c.   an interaction between a and b.

   d.   all of the above.

14. If a particular environmental stressor may have been a key causal factor in the development of a physical illness, removal of this stressor (p. 342)

    c.   may not be enough to bring about recovery if organic changes have already taken place.

15. _____ is based on the assumption that because autonomic responses can be learned, they can be unlearned. (p. 344)

    c.   Behavior therapy

TRUE – FALSE

1. T — The ailments to which people are most vulnerable—whether physical, psychological, or both—are determined in no small part by who we are, where we live, and how we live. (p. 322)

2. T — The "fight-or-flight response" involves primarily the sympathetic division of the autonomic nervous system. (p. 325)

3. T — Stress appears to speed up the onset or increase the severity of a disorder, and to interfere with the body's immunological defenses and other homeostatic repair functions. (p. 326)

4. F — The immune system and the nervous system are separate, closed systems which operate independently of each other. (pp. 328-29)

5. F — Depression has little or no effect on the immune system. (p. 330)

6. T — Stress has been shown to slow down the healing of wounds by as much as 24-40%. (p. 330)

7. F — Usually, if shown a clear relationship between lifestyle and health risk, people can make lasting lifestyle changes. (p. 330)

8. T — Had it not been for the placebo effect, the medical profession, as we know it, might not have survived to the twentieth century, because until the early 1900s, medical practitioners had little else to offer disease sufferers. (p. 332)

9. T — Heart attack patients who are depressed at the time of their heart attacks or shortly afterward show a greatly increased risk for future coronary events and cardiac death. (p. 336)

10. T — Stress does not have to be extreme or severe in order to have potentially lethal consequences down the road. (p. 338)

11. T — Some physical disorders may be acquired, maintained, or both in much the same way as other behavior patterns. (p. 342)

ESSAY QUESTIONS *(Your answer should contain the following points.)*

1. In "Developments in Research 10.1 Cytokines: The Link Between the Brain and the Immune System," these newly discovered small protein molecules allow the immune system to communicate with itself and with the brain. Discuss Cytokines, what these are, what these do, and what the promise is. (p. 329)

  a.   Like hormones of the immune system

  b.   Mediating the inflammatory and immune response

  c.   Two main categories—pro-inflammatory and anti-inflammatory

  d.   Through the cytokines, the brain and immune system can communicate

  e.   Means that the brain is capable of influencing immune processes. This could be huge.

2. Chronic fatigue syndrome can leave a person physically exhausted for months or even years. Discuss this disorder. (p. 345)

  a.   Often begins with sudden flu-like illness or similar

  b.   Debilitating fatigue that cannot be explained medically

  c.   Fluctuating disability, may be bedridden for months

  d.   Unremitting fever, chills, soaking sweats, acute light sensitivity, balance and cognitive problems.

3. Discuss the behavioral medicine approach to physical illness. (p. 322)

  a.   The psychological factors that may predispose an individual to physical illness

  b.   The ways in which the negative effects of stress can be reduced or buffered by personal resources

  c.   The biological mechanisms by which human physiology is altered by stressors

  d.   The psychological processes involved in health choices individuals make

  e.   The factors that determine compliance with sound medical advice

  f.   The effectiveness of psychological measures in altering unhealthy lifestyles

CRISS-CROSS ANSWERS
Across
9. essential hypertension
Down
1. psychoneuroimmunology
2. immunosuppression
3. health psychology
4. placebo effect
5. antigen
6. biofeedback
7. behavioral medicine
8. cytokines
10. T cells

CHAPTER ELEVEN

MATCHING

Match the following personality disorders with the appropriate description.

Personality Disorder	Description
D. Paranoid	A hypersensitivity to rejection, shyness, insecurity
F. Schizoid	B. overconcern with attractiveness; self-dramatization
J. Schizotypal	C. impulsive, drastic mood shifts, self-mutilation
B. Histrionic	D. suspicious and mistrustful; blames others
H. Narcissistic	E. persistent unhappiness or dejection; feelings of inadequacy, guilt, and self-criticism
K. Antisocial	F. lacks desire to form attachments; poor relationships
C. Borderline	G. negative attitudes, passive resistance; complaining, sullen, and argumentative
A. Avoidant	H. grand preoccupation with self, lack of empathy
L. Dependent	I. excessive concern with order, rules; perfectionistic
I. Obsessive-Compulsive	J. peculiar thought patterns; odd perception & speech
G. Passive Aggressive	K. lacking morals or ethics, deceitful, manipulative
E. Depressive	L. discomfort being alone, indecisive, difficulty ending relationships

SHORT ANSWERS

Provide brief answers to the following questions.

1. Give the five criteria in the DSM-IV-TR definition of personality disorder. (p. 351)
    A. The pattern must be manifested in at least two areas.
    B. The pattern must be inflexible and pervasive.
    C. Leads to clinically significant distress or impairment in functioning.
    D. Pattern is stable and of long duration.
    E. Pattern is not better accounted for as another mental disorder.

2. Discuss the possible biological and psychological casual factors for personality disorders. (pp. 352-53)
    a. **Biological factors**
        • Infants' temperament may predispose them to develop certain disorders
        • Increasing evidence for genetic contributions to certain disorders

b. **Psychological factors**
- Learning-based habit patterns and maladaptive cognitive styles
- May originate in disturbed parent-child attachment relationships
- Role of parental psychopathology and ineffective parenting practices
- Early emotional, physical, and sexual abuse

3. Many studies have found that people with borderline personality disorder report a large number of negative, even traumatic, events in childhood, including abuse and neglect, separation and loss, and parental psychopathology. However, it is difficult to say childhood trauma plays a causal role. Why? (p. 361)

    a. most children who experienced early abuse and neglect do not end up with any serious personality disorders

    b. the studies that suggested this has serious shortcomings

    c. childhood abuse is not a specific risk factor, because it also is reported at relatively high rates with other personality disorders

    d. childhood abuse nearly always occurs in families with other pathological dynamics that actually may be more important than the abuse per se

4. Discuss the difference between a loner with schizoid personality disorder and the loner who is avoidant. (p. 362-63)

    a **Schizoid**

    primary focus is on avoiding humiliation and rejection

    b. **Dependent**

    primary focus is on being taken care of

FILL IN THE BLANKS
Read the following and fill in the blanks. These questions are designed to help you focus on specific details.

1. Two of the general features characterizing most personality disorders are ***CHRONIC INTERPERSONAL DIFFICULTIES,*** and ***PROBLEMS WITH ONE'S IDENTITY OR SENSE OF SELF***. (p. 350)

2. People who tend to see themselves as blameless, finding fault for their own mistakes and failures in others, even to the point of ascribing evil motives to others, suffer from ***PARANOID PERSONALITY DISORDER***. (p. 353)

3. Teenagers who have a ***SCHIZOTYPAL*** personality disorder have been shown to be at increased risk for developing schizophrenia and schizophrenia-spectrum disorders in adulthood. (p. 356)

4. Those with ***NARCISSISTIC*** personality disorder tend to overestimate their abilities and accomplishments and behave in stereotypical ways to gain acclaim and recognition and feed their fantasies of unlimited success, power, beauty, or brilliance. (p. 358)

5. Those with **_ANTISOCIAL_** personality disorder tend to be impulsive, irritable, and aggressive, and sow a pattern of generally irresponsible behavior. (p. 359)

6. There is substantial co-occurrence of borderline personality disorder with other personality disorders— especially **_HISTRIONIC_**, **_DEPENDENT_**, **_ANTISOCIAL_**, and **_SCHIZOTYPAL_**. (p. 361)

7. Histrionic and dependent personalities have strong needs for reassurance and approval, but the **_HISTRIONIC_** personality is gregarious, flamboyant, and actively demanding of attention, whereas the **_DEPENDENT_** personality is more docile and self-effacing. (p. 364)

8. Borderline and dependent personalities fear abandonment, but the **_BORDERLINE_** personality, who usually has intense and stormy relationships, reacts with feelings of emptiness or rage if abandonment occurs, where the **_DEPENDENT_** personality reacts initially with submissiveness and appeasement, but finally with an urgent seeking of a new relationship. (p. 364)

9. Persons with **_OBSESSIVE-COMPULSIVE PERSONALITY DISORDER_** personality disorder have difficulty in interpersonal relationships because of excessive devotion to work and because of difficulty expressing emotions. (p. 364)

10. The person who is pessimistic, prone to worry, with an emphasis on distorted cognitions and interpersonal traits, may be a **_DEPRESSIVE_** personality. (p. 365)

11. The primary goal of treatment for **_BORDERLINE_** personalities is seen as strengthening the weak egos of these individuals, with a particular focus on their primary primitive defense mechanism of splitting, which leads them to see other people as "all good" or "all bad." (p. 367)

12. People with **_ANTISOCIAL_** personality disorder have a lifelong pattern of unsocialized and irresponsible behavior, with little regard for safety—either their own or that of others. (p. 368)

13. Psychopathic personalities exhibit the antisocial and aggressive behaviors of antisocial personalities, and, in addition, are selfish, callous, exploitative, and lacking in **_EMPATHY_** or **_REMORSE_**. (p. 369)

THE DOCTOR IS IN...PSYCHIATRIC HELP—5¢

1. Helen, a 31-year-old waitress, comes to the office of a male therapist, seeking help trying to understand why she doesn't have a relationship. She tells him about her life in a very dramatic and lively manner and makes flirteous comments like, "I can't understand why no one likes me—what I wouldn't do to have some cute guy like you just sweep me off my feet." She then looks at the therapist and smiles seductively. Helen told the therapist

that she feels so comfortable with him after just five minutes, that she is sure they will become friends. Although Helen presents her life in a very dramatic way, she does not tell the therapist many details.

How would Helen be diagnosed and why? (p. 357)

> **Histrionic personality disorder**—very dramatic, is flirtatious, wants approval, moves to be closer to therapist than would be considered healthy

2. Jack, a computer software engineer, comes to your office because he is having problems at work and possibly is going to lose his job if things don't change. You ask him what has happened. He looks at you suspiciously, and asks you who else you have been talking to. You assure him you haven't talked to anyone. He tells you that others at work are talking about him behind his back, and he knows they are responsible for his having to see a therapist. Jack tells you he has no friends at work or any place else. He had two friends once, but he stopped seeing them when they couldn't go out to dinner with him once, because of "other commitments." Jack believed that the two of them plotted together against him. Jack was coherent and seemed in contact with reality—as he saw it.

How would you diagnose Jack and why? (p. 353)

> **Paranoid personality disorder**—pervasive suspiciousness and distrust, interpersonal difficulties, others are to blame for his problems, is not psychotic

3. Pam sits in your office not saying much and having a difficulty talking about herself. She manages to tell you that she is alone much of the time—something she doesn't like—and would like to feel comfortable meeting people. Pam tells you that she is so afraid of people not liking her or criticizing her, that she hardly ever goes out. She is extremely self–conscious and avoids situations in which she might be criticized or rejected.

How would you diagnose Pam and why? (p. 362)

> **Avoidant personality disorder**—extreme social inhibition and introversion. Hypersenstivity to criticism. She is aware of a problem but is afraid of rejection if she were to get involved socially, and is self-conscious.

4. As a therapist, what issues will you face in treating the three patients above? (pp. 366-68)

  a. Personality disorders difficult to treat because these are enduring, pervasive, and inflexible patterns of behavior.

  b. There are many different goals of treatment, such as reducing subjective distress and enhancing well-being, changing specific dysfunctional behaviors, changing whole patterns of behavior, and changing the entire structure of the personality.

  • Therapeutic techniques must be modified

  • Possible hospitalization or partial hospitalization

  • Use of new cognitive approach, which assumes that the dysfunctional feelings and behavior associated with the personality disorder are the result of schema that produce biased judgments and the tendency to make cognitive errors in many situations

MULTIPLE-CHOICE PRACTICE TESTS
PRACTICE TEST NUMBER 1

1. Personality disorders were formerly known as (p. 350)

   b. character disorders.

2. Studies estimate that _____ persons meet criteria for at least one personality disorder at some point in their lifetime. (p. 350)

   c. about 13% of

3. Most personality traits have been found to be (p. 353)

   b. moderately heritable.

4. Many studies have suggested that _____ may be an important factor in a subset of causes for several different personality disorders. (p. 353)

   c. early emotional, physical, and sexual abuse

5. Persons with _____ personality disorder commonly bear grudges, are unwilling to forgive perceived insults and slightest, and are quick to react with anger (p. 353).

   b. paranoid

6. Persons with _____ personality disorder rarely experience strong positive or negative emotions, are unable to express their feelings, appear as cold and distant, and can be classified as loners or introverts. (p. 355)

   a. schizoid

7. Persons with _____ personality disorder are excessively introverted with pervasive social and interpersonal deficits, as in question 6, but, in addition, they have cognitive and perceptual distortions and eccentricities in their communication and behavior. (p. 356)

   b. schizotypal

8. Persons with _____ personality disorder exhibit excessive attention-seeking behavior, using their lively, dramatic, and often excessively extroverted styles, and tend to feel unappreciated if not the center of attention. (p. 357)

   a. histrionic

9. Persons with _____ personality disorder show an exaggerated sense of self-importance, a preoccupation with being admired, and a lack of empathy for the feelings of others. (p. 358)

   b. narcissistic

10. Narcissistic personality disorder may be more frequently observed in (p. 358)

    b. men than in women.

PRACTICE TEST NUMBER 2

1. Persons with _____ personality disorder continually violate and show disregard for the rights of others through deceitful, aggressive, or antisocial behavior, typically without remorse or loyalty to anyone. (p. 359)

    d.   antisocial

2. Persons with _____ personality disorder show a pattern of behavior characterized by impulsivity and instability in interpersonal relationships, self-image, and moods. (p. 360)

    c.   borderline

3. Persons with _____ personality disorder display extreme affective instability, which often leads to erratic self-destructive behaviors, such as binges of gambling, sexual promiscuity, and suicide attempts. (p. 360)

    c.   borderline

4. Overall, about _____ of patients with borderline personality disorder reported some type of childhood abuse or neglect (p. 361).

    d.   90%

5. A study (Paris, 1999) suggests that borderline personality disorder may be more prevalent in our society today than in the past and in many other cultures, because of (p. 362)

    b.   the weakening of the family structure in our society.

6. Persons with _____ personality disorder have a pattern of extreme social inhibition and introversion leading to lifelong patterns of limited social relationships. (p. 362)

    a.   avoidant

7. Persons with _____ personality disorder show an extreme need to be taken care of, which leads to clinging and submissive behavior (p. 363).

    b.   dependent

8. Dependent personality disorder occurs in about 2-4% of the population and is (p. 364)

    c.   more common in women than men.

9. Persons with _____ personality disorder are characterized by the need for perfectionism and an excessive concern with maintaining order and control. (p. 364)

    c.   obsessive-compulsive

10. The obsessive-compulsive personality (p. 364)

    b.   is quite rigid and stubborn.

    c.   has difficulty delegating tasks to others.

    d.   b and c.

PRACTICE TEST NUMBER 3

1. Persons diagnosed with _____ personality disorder show a pervasive pattern of passive resistance to demands in social or work situations, sometimes being highly critical or scornful of authority. (p. 365)

   b. passive-aggressive

2. Persons diagnosed with _____ personality disorder show a usual mood state of unhappiness, gloominess, or dejection. (p. 365)

   b. depressive

3. Treatment of borderline personality disorder using drugs is controversial because (p. 367)

   b. it is so frequently associated with suicidal behavior.

4. Persons diagnosed with _____ personality disorder persistently disregard and violate the rights of others through a combination of deceitful, aggressive, or antisocial behavior. (p. 368)

   b. antisocial

5. The prevalence of antisocial personality disorder in the general population is estimated to be about _____% for males and _____% for females. (p. 368)

   a. 3, 1

6. Persons diagnosed with _____ are characterized by callousness, selfishness, and an exploitative use of others, as well as being antisocial, impulsive, and socially deviant lifestyle. (p. 369)

   a. psychopathy

7. Released prison inmates who were diagnosed as psychopaths were estimated to be _____ than those without a psychopathy diagnosis. (p. 369)

   a. three times more likely to reoffend
   b. four times to reoffend violently
   d. a and b.

8. An important factor in the probability that a child with a genetic or constitutional liability will develop conduct disorder, and later adult psychopathy or ASPD is (p. 375)

   a. poor and ineffective parenting skills, especially ineffective discipline, monitoring, and supervision.
   b. parents' own antisocial behavior.
   c. divorce and other parental transitions.
   d. all of the above.

9.   A "burned-out psychopath" is one who (p. 377)

   c.   is an older, wiser person whose criminal activities have lessened after age 40.

10.   The best multifaceted cognitive-behaviorally oriented treatment programs (p. 377)

   b.   generally produce changes of only modest magnitude.

COMPREHENSIVE PRACTICE TEST
MULTIPLE-CHOICE

1.   In their study, Widiger and colleagues found that _____ patients who qualified for one or more personality disorder diagnosis also qualified for at least one more. (p. 352)

   c.   85% of

2.   The ultimate goal would be to achieve a biopsychosocial perspective on the origins of each personality disorder, (p. 352)

   b.   but we are far from that goal today.

3.   Cluster A personality disorders are described as (p. 366)

   a.   odd/eccentric.

4.   People with narcissistic personality disorder do not, as a rule, seek psychological treatment because (p. 358)

   b.   they view themselves as nearly perfect and in no need of change.

5.   To be considered an antisocial personality disorder, the pattern of behavior must have been occurring since the age of 15, and before age 15, the person must have shown (p. 359)

   a.   destruction of property, deceitfulness or theft.
   b.   persistent patterns of aggression toward people or animals.
   c.   serious violation of rules at home or in school.
   d.   all of the above.

6.   Approximately 20-40% of borderline personalities have cognitive symptoms that include (p. 360)

   a.   relatively short or transient episodes in which they appear to out of contact with reality.
   b.   experiencing delusions or other psychotic-like symptoms, such as hallucinations, paranoid ideas, body image distortions, or dissociative symptoms.
   d.   a and b.

7.   People with avoidant personality disorder (p. 362)

   a.   do not seek out other people but do not enjoy their aloneness.

   b.   have great anxiety due to their inability to relate comfortable to other people.

   c.   tend to be hypersensitive and may see ridicule or disparagement where none was intended.

   d.   all of the above.

8.   A person with dependent personality disorder (p. 363)

   a.   may remain in an abusive relationship due to a fear that defending herself might cause her to lose her partner.

   b.   may not function well on his own.

   c.   has great difficulty making even simple everyday decisions due to a lack of self-confidence.

   d.   all of the above.

9.   A person with passive-aggressive personality disorder (p. 365)

   b.   commonly complains about personal misfortunes or of being misunderstood or unappreciated.

10.   Personality disorders are generally very difficult to treat, in part because (p. 366)

   b.   these are, by definition, enduring, pervasive, and inflexible patterns of behavior.

11.   People who suffer from _____ personality disorder may experience transient psychotic symptoms, believe that they have magical powers, and may engage in magical rituals. (p. 356)

   c.   schizotypal

12.   Psychopaths are (p. 370)

   a.   often charming, spontaneous, and likeable on first acquaintance.

   b.   deceitful and manipulative, callously using others to achieve their own ends.

   c.   prone to acting out impulses in remorseless and often senseless violence.

   d.   all of the above.

13.   Psychopaths (p. 370)

   a.   seem to have good insight into other people's needs and weaknesses and are adept at exploiting them.

   b.   are irresponsible and unfaithful mates, being manipulative and exploitative in sexual relationships.

   c.   have learned to take, rather than earn, what they want and seldom forgo immediate pleasure for future gains and long-range goals.

   d.   all of the above.

14.   _____ in childhood is the single best predictor of who develops and adult diagnosis of psychopathy or antisocial personality. (p. 374)

   c.   The number of antisocial behaviors exhibited

15. The criminal activities of many psychopathic and antisocial personalities declines after the age of _____, but the egocentric, callous, and exploitative dimension does not. (p. 377)

     b.   40

TRUE – FALSE

1.   T — Rather than stemming from debilitating reactions to stress, personality disorders seem largely to come from gradual development of inflexible and distorted personality and behavioral patterns. (p. 350)

2.   T — In milder cases of these disorders, we find people who generally function adequately, but who would be described by their relatives, friends, or associates as troublesome, eccentric, or difficult to get to know. (p. 350)

3.   T — People with personality disorders do not usually learn from previous mistakes and troubles. (p. 351)

4.   F — Although many patients have a mix of personality disorders, it is not uncommon to find individuals to fit the "ideal" descriptions in the textbook. (p. 353)

5.   F — The prevalence in the general population of histrionic personality disorder is estimated at 20-30% and never occurs in women. (p. 357)

6.   T — In a sense, all children begin life as narcissists and only gradually acquire a perspective-taking ability. (p. 358)

7.   T — Self-mutilation is one of the most characteristic features of borderline personality. (p. 360)

8.   T — Approximately 75% of individuals diagnosed as borderline personalities are women. (p. 361)

9.   T — There are cases of generalized social phobia without avoidant personality disorder, but very few cases of avoidant personality disorder without generalized social phobia. (p. 363)

10. T — A person with dependent personality disorder may fail to get appropriately angry with others because of a fear of losing their support. (p. 363)

11. T — People with obsessive-compulsive personality disorder have lifestyles characterized by overconscientiousness, inflexibility, and perfectionism. (p. 364)

12. T — No systematic studies of treating people yet exist for paranoid, schizoid, narcissistic, or histrionic disorders. (p. 368)

13. T — The psychopath's conscience seems to be severely retarded or nonexistent. (p. 370)

ESSAY QUESTION   *(Your answer should contain the following points.)*

1. Perhaps more misdiagnoses occur in diagnosing personality disorders than any other category. Why is this? Explain. (pp. 351-52)

    a. Criteria not as sharply defined

    b. Categories are not mutually exclusive

    c. Personality characteristics are dimensional in nature—that is, these can range from normal to severe, which can lead to unreliable diagnoses

2. Antisocial personality disorder can be an extremely serious affliction, and persons suffering from it can be a danger to society. Name and explain the criteria that need to be met before a diagnosis can be made. (p. 368)

    a. At least three behavioral problems occurring after age 15

    b. At least three instances of deviant behavior before age 15

    c. The antisocial behavior is not a symptom of another mental disorder

3. People with psychopathic and antisocial personalities are extremely difficult to treat. Why is this so? (pp. 376-77)

    a. biological treatments (drugs) do not seem to have any substantial impact on the disorder as a whole

    b. individuals have little motivation to take their medications

    c. inherent factors in the psychopath's personality—the inability to trust, to learn from experience, to accept responsibility for one's actions

    d. information given by psychopaths is not reliable

CRISS-CROSS ANSWERS
Across
2. borderline
6. paranoid
8. histrionic
9. antisocial
10. pschopathy
11. obsessive-compulsive

Down
1. schizotypal
3. avoidant
4. narcissistic
5. schizoid
7. dependent

CHAPTER TWELVE

WHO'S WHO AND WHAT'S WHAT — MATCHING

Match the following drugs with their effects.

Drug		Effects
G.	Alcohol	A. intoxicant found in coffee and chocolate
A.	Caffeine	B. mild hallucinogen from a plant; can produce mild euphoria or unpleasant experiences depending upon the mood of the user
E.	Nicotine	C. synthesized drug first used in inhalant for stuffy noses; recalled when discovered that customers were chewing the wicks for "kicks;" newer, more powerful preparation is methedrine, also known as speed
D.	Ecstasy	D. a hallucinogen and a stimulant; popular among young adults
I.	Opium	E. poisonous alkaloid associated with 14% of all deaths in the U.S.
K.	Morphine	F. hallucinogen distorts sensory images, causing users to see or hear things differently and unusually
L.	Heroin	G. the major problem drug in the U.S.; associated with over half of highway deaths, 50% of all rapes, 40-50% of murders, 40% of all assaults
M.	Methadone	H. drug from a plant, costly, a "high" for the affluent
H.	Cocaine	I. a mixture of about 18 alkaloids; morphine and heroin made from this
C.	Amphetamine	J. derived from peyote cactus; hallucinogen used for centuries
N.	Barbiturates	K. derived from opium; was used during Civil War as pain killer; legal as prescription only
F.	LSD	L. derived from opium; first used in cough syrup around 1900; highly addictive; illegal in U.S.
J.	Mescaline	M. addictive drug used as substitute for heroin during treatment
B.	Marijuana	N. sedatives, depressants that slow down the nervous system; large doses produce immediate sleep or death

SHORT ANSWERS *(Your answer should contain the following points.)*

1. Discuss the relationship between being pregnant and drinking alcohol. (p. 388)
   a. even moderate amounts of alcohol believed dangerous
   b. fetal alcohol syndrome (FAS)
   c. birth defects, such as mental retardation

2. Discuss the two factors apparently involved in the overpowering hold that occurs in some people after only a few uses of a drug, such as opium, cocaine, or alcohol. (pp. 390-91)
   a. some drugs activate areas of the brain that produce pleasure
   b. person's genetic and biological make-up

3. Discuss the neurochemical process underlying addiction is the role the drug plays in activating the "pleasure pathway."   (p. 391)
    a. the mesocorticolumbic dopamine pathway (MCLP)
    b. alcohol and other drugs produces euphoria by stimulating this area in the brain

4. The development of alcohol-related problems includes living in an environment that promotes use of the substance. Explain. (p. 393)
    a. lack of stability in family relationships and parental guidance
    b. children witness parents using alcohol or drugs
    c. negative parental models have long-range negative consequences
    d. role models and media promote alcohol as stress reducer
    e. alcohol promoted to increase popularity and acceptance in younger persons

5. Is there an "alcoholic personality"—a type of character organization that predisposes a person to use alcohol, rather than some other defensive pattern of coping with stress? Explain. (p. 394)
    a. self-medicate with alcohol or reduce discomfort
    b. emotionally immature, expect a great deal of the world, require praise, feel inferior, low frustration tolerance, unsure of abilities to fulfill expected male or female roles.
    c. tends to be impulsive and aggressive

6. Discuss the immediate effects of mainlined or snorted heroin. (p. 407)
    a. euphoric spasm (60 seconds or so)
    b. followed by a high; lethargic, withdrawn (typically four to six hours)
    c. negative phase that produces a desire for more

7. The view that cocaine users did not develop physiological dependence has changed over the past 20 years. Explore this change of view. (p. 409)
    a. acute tolerance has now been demonstrated
    b. a significant increase in knowledge of cocaine's addictive properties
    c. a new disorder is described—cocaine withdrawal
    d. the psychological and life problems experienced by cocaine users are often great—often related to the considerable amount of money required to support their habits

FILL IN THE BLANKS

1. **_DEPENDENCE_** occurs when an individual develops a tolerance for a substance or exhibits **_WITHDRAWAL SYMPTOMS_** when it is not available. (p. 384)

2   Two major diagnostic classifications of addictive or substance-related disorders are those that involve **_ORGANIC IMPAIRMENT_** from prolonged and excessive ingestion of psychoactive substances and **_SUBSTANCE-INDUCED ORGANIC MENTAL DISORDERS AND SYNDROMES_**. (p. 384)

3. Two major categories of substance abuse disorders are substance ***DEPENDENCE*** disorders and substance ***ABUSE*** disorders. (p. 384)

4. Alcohol abuse is associated with more than ***50***% the deaths and major injuries suffered in automobile accidents each year, with about ***40 TO 50***% of all murders, ***40***% of all assaults, and more than ***50***% of all rapes. (p. 385)

5. People who abuse alcohol following periods of sobriety are known as ***BINGE DRINKERS***. (p. 384)

6. Organic impairment, including brain shrinkage, occurs in a high proportion of people with alcohol dependency, especially among ***BINGE DRINKERS***. (p. 385)

7. Associated with a lower incidence of alcoholism are ***MARRIAGE***, ***HAVING HIGHER LEVELS OF EDUCATION***, and ***BEING OLDER***. (p. 387)

8. Not only do alcoholics become physiologically dependent on alcohol, they develop a powerful ***PSYCHOLOGICAL DEPENDENCE*** as well. (p. 393)

9. In acute intoxication, the initial focus is on ***DETOXIFICATION***, ***THE TREATMENT OF WITHDRAWAL SYMPTOMS***, and ***A MEDICAL REGIMEN FOR PHYSICAL REHABILITATION***. (p. 398)

10. After a physiological craving for opium or one of its derivatives has been established, users find that they have become physiologically dependent on the drug in the sense that they ***PHYSICALLY ILL*** when they don't take it. (p. 407)

11. In our society, a narcotics subculture exists in which addicts can obtain drugs and protect themselves against society's sanctions. Once young addicts join, they become ***INCREASINGLY WITHDRAWN***, indifferent to their friends, and become ***PROGRESSIVE ISOLATED***, seeing drugs as a means of ***REVOLT AGAINST AUTHORITY*** and conventional values. (p. 408)

12. A person going through barbiturate withdrawal becomes ***ANXIOUS AND APPREHENSIVE*** and manifests coarse tremors of the hands and face. Also ***INSOMNIA***, weakness, ***NAUSEA***, vomiting, ***ABDOMINAL CRAMPS***, rapid heart rate, ***ELEVATED BLOOD PRESSURE***, and loss of weight may occur. An acute ***DELIRIOUS PSYCHOSIS*** may develop. (p. 413)

13. Ecstasy (MDMA) is both a ***HALLUCINOGEN*** and a ***STIMULANT*** and is considered to be a "***DANGEROUS***" drug. (p. 414)

THE DOCTOR IS IN...PSYCHIATRIC HELP—5¢

1. You have been working with Tony, who is dependent on alcohol. He has had several problems with the law and has lost his job as a result of his drinking. His wife has told him that if he doesn't get help, she is going to leave. As Tony's therapist, how would you treat him? (pp. 398-403)

    a. Possible use of medications to reduce cravings and ease detoxification process

    b. Group therapy—peers who will provide a confrontational give-and-take atmosphere; possibly have Tony's wife take part in a group for spouses of alcohol abusers

    c. Family therapy/treatment—to work out the family dynamics

    d. Behavioral therapy—aversive conditioning, behavioral couples therapy

    e. Cognitive-behavioral approach recommended by Marlatt—combines cognitive-behavioral strategies of intervention with social-learning and modeling of behavior

    f. Possibly look at controlled drinking or AA meetings

    g. Be sure to look at relapse prevention

2. Lupe brings her father, Martin, into to see you. She had gone to his house and found him asleep on the kitchen table, a bottle of pills and an alcoholic drink sitting near by. He is an older gentleman who about a year ago lost his wife to cancer. As you are talking, he tells you that he had been having difficulty sleeping until his doctor had given him something. These helped, but he found that having a drink made these work faster, and, since he was on a fixed income, the pills lasted longer even though the label said not to drink. Lupe tells you that her father has become very sluggish and is having sudden mood shifts. Lately, it seems that she is finding him this state more often.

    What do you think Martin is taking and why? What are the potential dangers involved if something isn't done to help Martin? (p. 411-413)

    Martin is taking barbiturates. His behavior, not sleeping, then being able to do so with the pill, sluggishness; impaired cognition and mood swings, all indicate the use of sedatives.

    Potential danger is death, since he is taking the barbiturates and drinking.

PICTURE THIS

1. Barbiturates (Bar <chart> + Bit + UR + 3 Eights)
2. Substance Abuse (Sub + ST + Ants + ABU + SSS)
3. Caffeine (Calf + EEN)
4. Heroin (Hair + O + In <door>)
5. Cocaine (KO + Cane)
6. Ecstasy (XTC)
7. Hallucinogens (HAL + <Noose -N+L> +In door again + O + Gin)

MULTIPLE-CHOICE PRACTICE TESTS

PRACTICE TEST NUMBER 1

1. As a problem facing our society today, addictive behavior is (p. 384)

    b. one of the most pervasive and intransigent mental health problems.

2. Substance abuse generally involves (p. 384)

    a. use of a substance, resulting in potentially hazardous behavior.

    b. a continued use despite persistent social, psychological, occupational, or health problems.

    d. a and b.

3. Substance dependence involves (p. 384)

    b. a continued use, despite persistent social, psychological, occupational, or health problems.

    c. a marked psychological need for increasing amounts of a substance to achieve the desired effects.

    d. b and c.

4. The need for increased amounts of a substance to achieve the desired effects, resulting from biological changes in the body, is (p. 384)

    c. tolerance.

5. Depression ranks high among the mental disorders often comorbid with alcoholism, not surprisingly, since alcohol (p. 385)

    c. is a depressant.

6. When the blood-alcohol level reaches approximately 0.5 percent, the individual passes out, which is a good thing, because (p. 387)

    c. concentrations above 0.55 percent are usually lethal.

7. The effects of alcohol vary for different drinkers, depending on (p. 387)

    a. their physical condition.

    b. the amount of food in their stomach.

    c. the duration of their drinking.

    d. all of the above.

8. A physiological effect of alcohol is (p. 387)

    a. a tendency toward decreased sexual inhibition, but lowered sexual performance.

    b. a lapse of memory—a blackout.

    c. headache, nausea, and fatigue of a hangover.

    d. all of the above.

9. Researchers believe that genetics may have a role in one's susceptibility to alcoholism because (p. 391)

    a. almost one-third of alcoholics in a study had at least one parent with an alcohol problem.

    b. females in a study were five times more likely to be alcoholic if both of their parents were alcoholic.

    c. children of alcoholic parents who had been adopted by nonalcoholic foster parents had nearly twice the number of alcohol problems by their late 20s as did a control group.

    d. all of the above.

10. Certain ethnic groups, particularly Asians and Native Americans, have abnormal physiological reactions to alcohol, known as "_____," including flushing of the skin, a drop in blood pressure, heart palpitations, and nausea. (p. 392)

    b. alcohol flush reaction

PRACTICE TEST NUMBER 2

1. Stable family relationships and parental guidance are extremely important molding influences for children, and this stability is often _____ in families of substance abusers (p. 393).

    a. lacking

2. About _____% of persons with schizophrenia have either alcohol or drug abuse dependency as well. (p. 394)

    c. 50

3. About _____ people die each year in the United States of alcohol poisoning. (p. 396)

    c. 4,000

4. In cultures whose religious values restrict or prohibit the use of alcohol, the incidence of alcoholism is (p. 396)

    b. minimal.

5. In the Alcoholics Anonymous (AA) view (p. 401)

    b. one is never cured but an alcoholic for life, whether or not one is drinking.

6. Drug abuse and dependence are most common during (p. 403)

    a. adolescence and young adulthood.

7. A study of job satisfaction found that multiple drug use (polydrug), predicted impaired work functioning and job dissatisfaction (p. 404)

    d. four years later.

8. Because morphine is so addictive, a chemical, called acetic anhydride, was added to it around the turn of the 20th century in hopes of converting it into a more controllable substance. This new mix was called (p. 406)

   b.   heroin.

9. Opium and its derivatives, morphine, codeine, and heroin were outlawed in 1914 by (p. 406)

   c.   The Harrison Act.

10. In a recent survey about _____ Americans acknowledged having tried heroin and almost _____ people admitted using it withing the past 12 months. (p. 407)

   d.   2.4 million, 250,000

PRACTICE TEST NUMBER 3

1. Typically the life of a narcotic addict becomes increasingly centered on obtaining and using the drugs, so the addiction usually (p. 408)

   a.   leads to socially maladaptive behavior.
   b.   forces the addict to lie, steal, and associate with undesirable contacts.
   c.   causes females to turn to prostitution as a means to finance their addiction.
   d.   all of the above.

2. The most frequently cited reason for beginning to use heroin was (p. 408)

   a.   pleasure.
   b.   curiosity.
   c.   peer pressure.
   d.   all of the above.

3. Cocaine, in contrast to opiate derivatives, which depress the action of the central nervous system, (p. 409)

   a.   speeds it up.

4. In 2000 about _____% of emergency room visits were cocaine related. (p. 409)

   d.   29

5. Many life problems experienced by cocaine abusers result in part from _____. (p. 410)

   b.   the considerable amounts of money required to support their habits.

6. The earliest amphetamine—Benzedrine—was first synthesized in 1927 and soon available in drugstores as an inhalant to relieve stuffy noses. However, it was soon withdrawn because (p. 410)

   b.   some customers were chewing the wicks in the inhalers for "kicks."

7. Curiously, amphetamines have _____ effect on many youngsters. (p. 411)

   b. a calming

8. Methedrine, used in large amounts, can raise blood pressure (p. 411)

   a. enough to cause immediate death.

9. A common effect of barbiturates is (p. 411)

   a. slow speech.
   b. impaired decision making and problem solving.
   c. sudden mood shifts.
   d. all of the above.

10. Psychedelic drugs do not, in fact, "create" sensory images, but (p. 413)

    b. distort these, so that a person sees or hears things in different and unusual ways.

COMPREHENSIVE PRACTICE TEST
MULTIPLE-CHOICE

1. Alcohol abuse and dependency are _____ in the United States. (p. 385)

   b. one of the most destructive and psychiatric disorders

2. The life expectancy with alcohol dependency is about _____ than that of the average citizen. (p. 385)

   a. 12 years shorter

3. In addition to various physical problems, an excessive drinker usually suffers from (p. 388)

   a. chronic fatigue, oversensivitity and depression.
   b. lowered feelings of adequacy and worth, impaired reasoning and judgement, and gradual personality deterioration.
   c. coarse and inappropriate behavior, lowered pride and personal appearance, becoming generally touchy, and irritable.
   d. all of the above.

4. A number of investigators have pointed out that the typical alcohol abuser is (p. 394)

   a. unable or unwilling to tolerate tension and stress.
   b. discontented with his or her life.
   d. a and b.

5. Many young people begin to use alcohol, because they expect that it will (p. 395)

    a.   lower tension and anxiety.

    b.   increase their popularity.

    c.   increase sexual desire and pleasure in life.

    d.   all of the above.

6. Alcohol abuse and dependence are difficult to treat because (p. 398)

    a.   many alcoholics refuse to admit they have a problem.

    b.   they refuse to seek assistance before they "hit bottom."

    c.   many leave treatment before therapy is completed.

    d.   all of the above.

7. A multidisciplinary approach to the treatment of drinking problems appears to be most effective because (p. 398)

    a.   the problems are often complex.

    b.   researchers really aren't sure what works yet.

    d.   a and b.

8. Caffeine and nicotine are (p. 403)

    a.   drugs of dependence.

9. In 2000, heroin overdose accounted for _____% of all drug episodes of emergency room admissions. (p. 407)

    d.   16

10. The use of opium derivatives over a period of time usually results in a physiological craving for the drug. The time required varies, but it has been estimated that continual use over a period of _____ is sufficient. (p. 407)

    c.   30 days

11. Strong doses of barbiturates cause sleep almost immediately. Excessive doses (p. 411)

    a.   are lethal.

12. A person undergoing a "bad trip" on LSD may (p. 414)

    b.   set himself afire.

    c.   jump off a building.

    d.   b and c.

13.   Ecstasy users have been found to be more likely to (p, 414)

    a.   use marijuana.

    b.   engage in binge drinking.

    c.   have multiple sexual partners.

    d.   all of the above.

14.   Until the late 1960s, marijuana use in the United States was confined largely to (p. 415)

    a.   members of lower socioeconomic minority groups.

    b.   people in the entertainment and related fields.

    d.   a and b.

15.   Continued use of high dosages of marijuana over time tends to produce (p. 416)

    c.   lethargy and passivity.

TRUE – FALSE

1.   F — Tolerance for a substance is the need for less and less to achieve the desired effect. (p. 384)

2.   T — Substance dependence means that an individual will show tolerance for a drug and/or withdrawal symptoms when the drug is unavailable. (p. 385)

3.   T — One in seven people meet the criteria for alcohol abuse. (p. 385)

4.   T — Men are about five times more likely to have an alcohol problem then women. (p. 386)

5.   T — In a study, college freshmen from families with alcohol abusing parents viewed their families as less healthy and had more problematic family relationships than those with nonalcohol abusing parents. (p. 393)

6.   T — There is a strong association between antisocial personality disorder and alcohol, aggression, and high rates of substance abuse. (p. 394)

7.   T — Excessive use of alcohol is one of the most frequent causes of divorce in the United States.   (p. 395)

8.   T — Users of opium derivatives gradually build up a tolerance to the drug, so that increasingly larger amounts are needed to achieve the desired effects. (p. 407)

9.   T — The ill health and general personality deterioration often found in opium addiction do not result directly from the pharmacological effects of the drug, but are usually products of the sacrifice of money, proper diet, social position, and self-respect as an addict becomes more desperate to procure the required daily dosage. (p. 408)

10. T — Opiate addicts were found to be highly impulsive and showed an inability to delay gratification. (p. 408)

11. T — Addicts often dread the discomfort of withdrawal, but in a hospital setting it is less abrupt and usually involves the administration of a medication that eases the distress. (p. 408)

12. T — Amphetamines were initially considered to be "wonder pills" that helped people stay alert, and were used by both the Allied and German soldiers to ward off fatigue during World War II. (p. 410)

ESSAYS QUESTIONS *(Your answer should contain the following points.)*

1. Alcohol has complex and seemingly contradictory effects on the brain from the activation of the brain's "pleasure areas" to the health risks and degradation that can result from heavy and long-term usage. Discuss this, particularly in relation to the items below. (pp. 387-91)

   a. physiological effects—depresses brain functioning, inhibiting glutamate, affects higher brain center, impairing judgement and other rational processes and lowering self control.

   b. mood and realities—decreased sexual performance, blackouts (lapses of memory), hangover

   c. pregnancy—possible fetal alcohol syndrom, producing birth defects, such as mental retardation

   d. chronic use—suffers chronic fatigue, oversensitivity, and depression

   e. dependence—can produce lowered feelings of adequacy and worth

   f. organic damage—alcohol must be assimilated by the liver, which may suffer irreversible damage; 26,000 annual cirrhosis deaths from alcohol

   g. physical and mental decline—impaired reasoning and judgment, and gradual personality deterioration

2. A controversy exists between whether alcoholics need to give up drinking altogether or whether they can learn to drink moderately, with some new research on one side and groups like AA on the other. Discuss this. (pp. 400-01)

   a. controlled drinking, the ability to start drinking after drying out, is possible, it seems, in some cases of less severe situations

   b. AA view is that once a person is an alcoholic, that person is always at risk and always in recovery, one day at a time.

3. Withdrawal from heroin can range from agonizing to not being even very painful. At the very least, it does appear to be an interesting experience. Explore heroin withdrawal. (pp. 407-08)

   a. addicted users find they feel physically ill when they do not take it

   b. after approximately eight hours withdrawal symptoms begin

      • severity depends on many factors: amount used, duration of addiction, addict's health and personality

    c.   can be agonizing with symptoms, including runny nose, tearing eyes, perspiration, restlessness
- symptoms get worse as time rolls on: chilliness alternates with flushing and excessive sweating, vomiting, diarrhea, abdominal cramps, pains, dehydration
- occasionally, symptoms include delirium, hallucinations, manic activity
- cardiovascular collapse and death is a possibility

    d.   symptoms are usually on the decline by the third or fourth day, gone by seventh or eighth

CRISS-CROSS ANSWERS

Across
3. dependence
5. heroin
7. tolerance
9. nicotine
10. methadone
11. toxicity
12. opium

Down
1. substance abuse
2. addictive behavior
4. caffeine
6. Ecstasy
8. alcoholic

CHAPTER THIRTEEN

MATCHING Match the following person or term with the appropriate answer.

Person / Term

G. Simon Tissot

D. Reverend Sylvester Graham

H. Dr. John Harvey Kellogg

C. Onania, or the Heinous Sin
    of Self Pollution

E. Havelock Ellis and Magnus
    Hirschfeld

I. Evelyn Hooker

B. autoerotic asphyxia

A. statutory rape

F. priapism

Answer

A. sexual activity with a person who is legally defined to be
    under the age of consent

B. dangerous form of masochism that involves self-strangulation
    to the point of oxygen deprivation

C. anonymously published book in London that started the
    hypothesis that masturbation caused insanity

D. advocated the abstinence theory during the 1830s

E. said, during the late nineteenth and early twentieth centuries,
    that homosexuality was natural and nonpathological

F. erectile problem in young men where erection will not
    diminish, even after a couple of hours

G. Swiss physician who developed the "degeneracy theory"

H. wrote about the 39 signs of the "secret vice" (masturbation)
    and made a fortune publishing books discouraging
    masturbation; also urged people to eat more cereal

I. demonstrated that psychologists could not tell the difference
    between psychological test results of homosexuals and
    heterosexuals

Match the dysfunction with its characteristic.

Dysfunction

of Sexual Desire

D. Hypoactive sexual desire disorder

H. Sexual aversion disorder

of Sexual Arousal

A. Male erectile disorder

E. Female sexual arousal disorder

of Orgasm

I. Premature ejaculation

F. Male orgasmic disorder

B. Female orgasmic disorder

Sexual Pain Disorders

G. Vaginismus

C. Dyspareunia

Characteristics

A. inability to achieve or maintain an erection

B. difficulty in achieving orgasm, either manually or
    during sexual intercourse

C. painful coitus; may have either organic or psychological
    basis

D. little or no sexual drive or interest

E. nonresponsiveness to erotic stimulation, physically and
    emotionally

F. inability to ejaculate during intercourse

G. involuntary muscle spasm at the entrance to the vagina
    preventing penetration

H. total lack of interest in sex and avoidance of sexual
    contact

I. unsatisfactorally brief period between the beginning of
    sexual stimulation and ejaculation

SHORT ANSWERS *(Your answer should contain the following points.)*

1. Why has research about childhood sexual abuse increased in the past decade? (p. 436)
   a. much more common than once was assumed
   b. possible links between childhood sexual abuse and some mental disorders
   c. some dramatic and well-publicized cases involving allegations of childhood sexual abuse have raised issues concerning validity of children's testimony and accuracy of recovered memories

2. What are the differences between intrafamilial and extrafamilial child molesters? (p. 441)
   Intrafamilial: tend to have some pedophiliac arousal patterns suggesting they are partly motivated by sexual arousal to children and adult women; majority of offenses are against girls; will offend with one or a few children in the family
   Extrafamilial: victims are more equally distributed between boys and girls (more likely to be victims)

FILL IN THE BLANKS

1. Despite the substantial *VARIABILITY* in sexual *ATTITUDES* and *BEHAVIOR* in different times and places, people typically behave as though the sexual *STANDARDS* of their time and place were the only correct approach, and they tend to be *INTOLERANT* of sexual *NONCONFORMITY*. (p. 423)

2. Many people probably have some *VOYEURISTIC* inclinations, which are checked by practical considerations, such as the possibility of being *CAUGHT*, and by the *ETHICAL* attitudes concerning the right to *PRIVACY*. (p. 430)

3. Paraphilic *SADISM* and *MASOCHISM,* including activities, such as pinching, biting, whipping, sticking with a needle, or slashing with a razor, are the *PREFERRED* or *EXCLUSIVE* means to *SEXUAL* gratification seem to be rare. (p. 431)

4. Two etiological facts, which are important concerning paraphilia, are that nearly all persons with paraphilias are *MALE,* and that people with paraphilias often have *MORE THAN ONE*. (pp. 432-33)

5. Many researchers believe that male vulnerability to forming *SEXUAL* associations with *NONSEXUAL* stimuli is a result of *CLASSICAL* and *INSTRUMENTAL* conditioning and/or social learning through *OBSERVATION* and *MODELING*. (p. 433)

6. The research by Ceci and colleagues on what influences children's testimony concluded: "*REPEATEDLY* thinking about a *FICTITIOUS* event can lead some preschool children to produce *VIVID, DETAILED* reports that *PROFESSIONALS* are unable to discern from their reports of actual events." (p. 438)

7. Perhaps the most common type of pedophile is someone who is _**SHY**_, _**UNASSERTIVE**_, and _**PASSIVE**_ and may be drawn to children because he feels in _**CONTROL**_ only relative to them. (p. 440)

8. Incest is more common than is generally believed, in part, because many _**VICTIMS**_ are reluctant to report it or do not consider themselves _**VICTIMIZED**_. (p. 441)

9. Feminist scholars have challenged the view that the rapist is motivated by _**LUST**_ and believe that rape is motivated by the need to _**DOMINATE**_, assert _**POWER**_, and to _**HUMILIATE**_ the victim. (p. 442)

10. What characterizes both date rapists and incarcerated rapist is _**PROMISCUITY, HOSTILE MASCULINITY**_ and an _**EMOTIONAL DETACHED, PREDATORY PERSONALITY**_. (p. 443)

11. Barlow and colleagues believe that sexually dysfunctional men and women get distracted by _**NEGATIVE THOUGHTS**_ about their _**SEXUAL**_ performance, not _**ANXIETY**_ per se. (p. 449)

THE DOCTOR IS IN...PSYCHIATRIC HELP—5¢

1. Jim was referred to you by the courts. He was caught after breaking into a woman's house to steal her underwear. Jim says that he is almost relieved at being caught as his problem was getting worse. He used the underwear to fantasize while he masturbated. You ask him how long this behavior has been going on and he tells you that he has had these feelings since as an adolescent, he found one of his sister's girlfriend's underwear in the bathroom (he had a crush on her).

   How would you diagnosis Jim and why? (p. 428)

   > **Jim has a fetish.** He uses an inanimate (women's underwear) to obtain sexual gratification and has had the problem for over six months. Also, it is causing him distress, and he seems to be concerned that it is getting worse.

2. Darla comes to your office. She is an attractive female in her late 40s. She begins by telling you that she was born a boy but always felt like a girl. She never wanted to play boy games, preferred to be with girls, and often wished she would wake up in the morning and find that she had become a girl. She began cross-dressing almost 20 years ago and has lived full-time as a female for the last 10 years. Darla has been on hormones for several years and is looking to have surgery. She is employed as a secretary and has passed as a woman for many years.

   How would you diagnose Darla? Why and what would you recommend as treatment? (pp. 433-436)

   a. **Gender identity disorder/Transsexualism:** Darla meets the criteria for gender identity disorder. She has had a strong cross-gender identification (desire and insistence on being the opposite sex) and gender dysphoria (discomfort about her biological sex). She is now an adult and considered a transsexual.

b. **Treatment:** Psychotherapy is not effective in resolving gender dysphoria, so the best treatment would be to help Darla obtain sexual reassignment surgery.

3. Susan and Ben come to your office seeking couple's counseling. They are both frustrated with their sexual relations. Susan experiences involuntary spasms around her vagina when they attempt to have intercourse. It is very painful and she can't go on. This has begun to affect Ben and he has started to have erectile dysfunctions. They love each other very much and want to work this out.

How would diagnose the problem, and what else would you want to know about the couple? (p. 452)

a. **Diagnosis:** Vaginismus for Susan and situational erectile dysfunction for Ben

b. **What else to know:** Any past traumatic sexual experience for Susan, when did the problem start and how have they handled the problem so far

PICTURE THIS

1. Gender Dysphoria (<Fender F=G> + Disk + 4 + IA)
2. Orgasm (Oar + Gas + M)
3. Sadism (Sad + ISM)
4. Premature Ejaculation (PRE + Mat + UR E + Jack + YOU + Lay + SHUN)

PRACTICE TESTS

PRACTICE TEST NUMBER 1

1. This society in the South Pacific holds two beliefs that are reflected in their sexual practices: semen conservation and female pollution. (p. 424)

    c. Sambia

2. Homosexuality was removed as a sexual deviation from the DSM in (p. 424)

    b. 1973.

3. Glenn is a 35-year-old married man who cross-dresses. He becomes sexually aroused while looking at himself dressed as a woman. His wife is aware of his cross-dressing and doesn't have a problem with it. Glenn is considered to have a (pp. 428-29)

    a. transvestic fetish.

4. A Peeping Tom is another name for someone who is a(n) (p. 430)

    d. voyeur.

5. The legal term for _____ is "indecent exposure." (p. 430)

    a. exhibitionism

6. Steve finds great sexual pleasure in being bound by his lover and humiliated—and sometimes whipped. He has participated in this behavior for over two years now. Steve would be considered a(n) (pp. 431-32)

    d.   masochist.

7. The most common outcome of boys with gender identity disorder appears to be (p. 433)

    d.   homosexuality.

8. _____ appears in genetic males and is a paraphilia characterized by sexual arousal at the thought or fantasy of being a woman. (p. 435)

    b.   Autogynephilic

9. The accuracy of children's testimony is an issue, because children (p. 437)

    a.   are susceptible to the influence of others.
    b.   can't always distinguish fact from fantasy.
    d.   a and b.

10. _____ is one of the most important and interesting contemporary controversies in the domain of psychopathology and mental health. (p. 440)

    a.   Recovered memory

PRACTICE TEST NUMBER 2

1. _____ is diagnosed when an adult has recurrent, intense sexual urges or fantasies about sexual activity with a prepubertal child. (p. 440)

    b.   Pedophilia

2. The typical victim of a pedophile is a girl between the ages of (p. 440)

    d.   8 and 11.

3. _____ is sexual activity that occurs under actual or threatened forcible coercion of one person by another. (p. 441)

    b.   Rape

4. According to your textbook, who of the following was most likely to force a woman to perform a sexual act? (p. 441)

    d.   someone she was in love with

5. What percentage of rapes are committed in the rapist's neighborhood? (p. 442)

    b.   80

6. About how many rapes are single-offender rapes in which the victim may know the offender? (p. 442)

    c.   two-thirds

7. The psychological impact of rape was first called (p. 442)

    d.   rape trauma syndrome.

8. The psychological impact of rape is now called (p. 442)

    a.   post-traumatic stress disorder.

9. _____ rape is a favorite tactic of defense attorneys, which some police and court jurisdictions still believe, even though it is a myth. (p. 442)

    c.   Victim-precipitated

10. Rapists show some deficits in their cognitive appraisals of women's (p. 444)

    a.   feelings.
    b.   intentions.
    d.   a and b.

PRACTICE TEST NUMBER 3

1. Recently, both explanations and treatments of sexual dysfunction have become increasingly (p. 447)

    c.   physiological.

2. The DSM-IV-TR says that sexual dysfunction can occur in which phase? (p. 447)

    a.   desire
    b.   excitement
    c.   orgasm
    d.   all of the above

3. Hypoactive sexual desire disorder seems to have a very strong _____ component, especially for women. (p. 448)

    a.   psychological

4. In this type of sexual desire dysfunction, the person shows extreme avoidance of all genital sexual contact with a partner. (p. 448)

    b.   sexual aversion disorder

5. Sexual interest in men and women depends on (p. 448)

    d.   testosterone.

6. The general neglect of research and treatment of female sexual dysfunction is an implicit attitude that women don't care about (p. 448)

    c.   sex.

7. _____ was formerly called impotence. (p. 448)

    b.   Male erectile disorder

8. Masters, Johnson and Kaplan, believed that erectile dysfunction was primarily a function of _____ about sexual performance. (p. 449)

    c.   anxiety

9. Viagra will promote an erection only if _____ is present. (p. 450)

    b.   sexual desire

10. Female sexual arousal depends more on the neurotransmitter known as (pp. 450-51)

    c.   VIP.

COMPREHENSIVE PRACTICE TEST
MULTIPLE-CHOICE

1. The major reason there are fewer sex researchers than other researchers is (p. 422)

    a.   sexual taboos.
    b.   sexual issues are controversial.
    d.   a and b.

2. The _____ theory, developed in the 1750s, had the central belief that semen was necessary for masculine characteristics and physical and sexual vigor in men, thus masturbation and patronizing prostitutes were considered harmful. (p. 423)

    a.   degeneracy

3. During what decade did the American Medical Association declare that masturbation was a normal part of adolescent behavior, and the Boy Scouts do away with their antimasturbation warnings? (p. 424)

    d.   1970s

4. The DSM-IV-TR criteria for this group of disorders is a persistent pattern, lasting at least six months, that causes significant distress or impairment, in which unusual objects, rituals, or situations are required for full sexual satisfaction. (p. 428)

    b.   paraphilias

5. Ted Bundy and Jeffrey Dahmer were sighted in your book as extreme examples of this paraphilia. (p. 431)

   b. sadism

6. Sexual abuse includes (p. 436)

   a. pedophilia.
   b. rape.
   c. incest.
   d. all of the above.

7. Although short-term consequences of childhood sexual abuse include fears, PTSD, sexual inappropriateness, and poor self-esteem, approximately _____ of sexually abused children show no symptoms. (p. 436)

   d. one-third

8. Long-term consequences of childhood sexual abuse may include (p. 436)

   a. dissociative symptoms.
   b. somatization disorder.
   c. borderline personality disorder.
   d. all of the above.

9. Culturally prohibited relations between family members, such as brother and sister or a parent and child, are known as (p. 441)

   c. incest.

10. This is the most common form of incest but it is rarely reported. (p. 441)

    d. brother-sister

11. According to the FBI Uniform Crime Reports, the greatest concentration of rapist arrested are between _____ years old. (p. 443)

    a. 18 and 24

12. It is difficult to establish the prevalence rates for rape because studies may (p. 442)

    a. vary in the definitions used.
    b. vary in the way information is gathered.
    d. a and b.

13. Studies done by Raymond Knight and Robert Prentky have shown that all rapists actually have _____ motives. (p. 442)

    b. aggressive
    c. sexual
    d. b and c.

14. _____ is most likely to occur after a lengthy abstinence and is the most common male sexual dysfunction. (p. 451)

    d.   Premature ejaculation

15. When treating female orgasmic disorder, it is important to distinguish between a _____ and a _____ dysfunction. (p. 452)

    c.   lifelong, situational

16. _____ in women is more likely to have an obvious organic basis. (p. 452)

    d.   Dyspareunia

TRUE – FALSE

1. T — Special caution must be taken when classifying sexual practices as "abnormal" or "deviant." (p. 422)

2. T — The belief that homosexuality is a mental illness has been associated with people's discomfort concerning the sexual behaviors of homosexual people. (p. 427)

3. F — Nearly all of the people with paraphilias are female. (p. 428)

4. T — Fetishes only cause overt harm to others when accompanied by illegal acts like theft or destruction of property. (p. 430)

5. F — Voyeurism is the most common sexual offense reported to the police in the United States, Canada, and Europe.   (p. 430)

6. F — The vast majority of the studies concerning paraphilias have been with men who have not committed any offense, but have come into clinics to participate in research.   (p. 433)

7. T — Sexual abuse is sexual contact that involves physical or psychological coercion or at least one individual who cannot reasonably consent to the contact. (p. 436)

8. F — Research has shown that the use of anatomically correct dolls greatly increases the accuracy of three- and four-year olds' reports of what happened to them. (p. 439)

9. T — The incest taboo is virtually universal among human societies. (p. 441)

10. F — If the partner is under 18, but consents, it can't be considered statutory rape. (p. 442)

11. T — Women who are repeat victims of rape, tend to be victims in situations other than rape. (p. 443)

12. T — Conviction rates for rape are low. (p. 444)

13. T — Megan's Law, intended to protect potential victims, has also encouraged harassment of sex offenders. (p. 445)

14. F — A high percentage of people never experience a sexual dysfunction in their life time. (p. 448)

ESSAY QUESTIONS   *(Your answer should contain the following points.)*

1. Discuss the types of treatment that are used with sex offenders (psychological, biological, surgical), the goals and effectiveness,. (pp. 444-46)
   Goals:
   - modify patterns of sexual arousal
   - modify cognitions and social skills
   - change habits or behaviors that increase the chance of reoffending
   - reduce sexual drive

   Therapies:
   - Aversion therapy—growing skepticism about its efficacy as sole form of treatment
        aversion therapy can involve these methods
        covert sensitization
        assisted covert sensitization
        satiation
   - Cognitive restructuring—attempts to eliminate cognitive distortions
        often involves
        social-skills training—learning to process information from women more effectively
        relapse prevention—helps offender to understand the antecedents of his decision to offend

   Cognitive behavioral techniques appear more effective than aversion therapy
   - Surgical and chemical castration—lower the testosterone level, which lowers the sex drive, allowing the offender to resist any inappropriate impulses
        relapse rates when the drugs/chemicals are discontinued are very high
        recidivism rates of castrated offenders are typically less than three percent

2. What were some of the conclusions of Bruce Rind's research on the association between early sexual experiences and mental health in young adulthood? (p. 453)

   a. correlations between childhood sexual abuse and later problems were of surprisingly small magnitude, suggesting that such experiences are not typically very harmful

   b. after statistically controlling for general family problems, the small association between CSA and adult problems were reduced to essentially zero—suggesting family problems might play a greater problem

   c. incest and forced sex both associated with more problems than sex between nominally consenting nonrelated individuals

   d. age at which CSA was experienced was unrelated to adult outcome

CRISS-CROSS ANSWERS

Across
3. incest
4. orgasm
6. fetishism
7. sadism
9. pedophilia
10. transsexualism
11. autogynephilia
12. exhibitionism

Down
1. vaginismus
2. voyeurism
5. masochism
8. sexual abuse

CHAPTER FOURTEEN

MATCHING Match the following names and terms with their correct definitions or descriptions.

Name/Term	Description/Definition
D. Genain quadruplets	A. imitation of the act of others
F. John Haslam	B. Swiss psychiatrist who in 1911 used the term, "schizophrenia," to characterize a split within the intellect and between the intellect and emotion and external reality
K. John Tilly Matthews	C. completely new made-up words by a patient with schizophrenia
L. Benedict Morel	D. Studied by David Rosenthal at NIMH in the mid-1950s, because all developed schizophrenia but were discordant with severity
J. Emil Kraepelin	E. theory that schizophrenic individuals find themselves unable to maintain a job or maintaining relationships; thus, they are likely to to end up at the lower end of the socioeconomic ladder
B. Eugen Bleuler	F. An apothecary in London who in 1810 gave the first detailed clinical description of schizophrenia
C. Neologisms	G. theory that the lower the SES, the higher the prevalence of schizophrenia, because the conditions of lower-class existence are stressful, increasing the risk for schizophrenia
A. echopraxia	H. The first person described in detail in 1810 with schizophrenia
K. echolalia	I. measure of how understandable and "easy to follow" the speech of a family member is
I. communication deviance	J. German psychiatrist who used the term, "dementia praecox," to refer to a group of conditions that feature mental deterioration beginning early in life
G. sociogenic hypothesis	K. mimicking of another's phases
E. social drift hypothesis	L. Used the term, "demence precoce," to describe the symptoms of a 13-year-old boy in 1860

Match the following types of schizophrenia with their definitions.

Schizophrenia	Definition
E. Undifferentiated	A. Those persons who are in remission following a schizophrenic episode and show only mild signs of schizophrenia.
D. Paranoid type	B. A form of schizophrenia that occurs at an early age and includes blunting, inappropriate mannerisms, and bizarre behavior.
G. Catatonic type	C. A person in whom symptoms of schizophrenia have existed for six months or less.
B. Disorganized type	D. A person who shows absurd, illogical, changeable delusions and frequent hallucinations.
A. Residual type	E. A form of schizophrenia in which all the primary indications of schizophrenia are seen in a rapidly changing pattern.
F. Schizoaffective disorder	F. A person who shows some schizophrenic signs, as well as obvious depression or elation.
C. Schizophreniform disorder	G. A type of schizophrenia characterized by alternating periods of extreme excitement and extreme withdrawal.

SHORT ANSWERS *(Your answer should contain the following points.)*

1. Describe the types of delusions common in schizophrenia. (p. 461)
   a. **made feelings or impulses:** thoughts, feelings, or actions are being controlled by external agents
   b. **thought insertion** thoughts are being inserted into one's brain by some external agency
   c. **thought withdrawal:** some external agency has robbed one of one's thoughts
   d. **delusions of reference:** neutral environmental event (television program or song) is believed to have special and personal meaning intended only for the patient
   e. **delusions of bodily changes:** (e.g., bowels don't work) or removal of organs

2. Give examples of the prenatal factors that could trigger or cause schizophrenia. (pp. 473-74)
   a. **Prenatal viral infection:** More people with schizophrenia are born between January and March, in a study done in Finland after a flu epidemic. It was found that there was a higher rate of schizophrenia in children born to mothers who had the flu in the second trimester of pregnancy.
   b. **Rhesus incompatibility:** A study done by Hollister, Laing and Mednick showed that the rate of schizophrenia is about 2.1 percent in males who are Rh-incompatible with their mothers, as opposed to 0.8 percent of males who were compatible.
   c. **Birth complications:** Research has shown that mothers of patients with schizophrenia were more likely to have had some sort of problems with pregnancy or delivery. One possibility is the problem might have caused oxygen deprivation.

    d. **Nutritional deficiency:** The results of Dutch Hunger Winter's study, in which people suffered severe famine as a result of a Nazi blockade, found that children who were conceived at the height of the famine had a two-fold increase in their risk of later developing schizophrenia.

3. List examples of the positive and negative symptoms of schizophrenia. (p. 461)

Positive:
    a. delusions
    b. hallucinations
    c. disorganized speech
    d. grossly disorganized behavior
    e. sudden onset
    f. derailment of associations

Negative:
    a. flat or blunted emotional expressiveness
    b. alogia
    c. avolition
    d. asociality
    e. significant cognitive impairment

4. Discuss the three types of prevention programs with relation to schizophrenia. (pp. 490-91)

    a. **primary prevention:** to prevent new cases; improve obstetric care for women with schizophrenia and first-degree relatives of schizophrenic patients

    b. **secondary prevention:** early intervention with people at risk; possible screening of at-risk people; problem with how to identify people and how harmful to tell someone they might develop schizophrenia

    c. **tertiary prevention:** early treatment for those who already have the illness; vocational rehabilitation, family support and cognitive therapy

FILL IN THE BLANKS

1. The vast majority of schizophrenia cases begin in late ***ADOLESCENCE*** or early ***ADULTHOOD***. (p. 459)

2. A delusion involves a disturbance in the ***CONTENT*** of thought. (p. 460)

3. Patients with auditory hallucinations show an increase of activity in the ***BROCA'S*** area of the brain involved with speech ***PRODUCTION***, not the ***WERNICKE'S*** area of the brain involved with speech ***COMPREHENSION***. (p. 462)

4. ***BRIEF PSYCHOTIC DISORDER*** involves the sudden onset of ***PSYCHOTIC*** symptoms or of grossly ***DISORGANIZED*** or ***CATATONIC*** behavior that cause great turmoil, but the episodes are usually quite brief. This disorder is often triggered by ***STRESS***. (p. 467)

5. According to Torrey et al. (1994), the overall pairwise concordance rates for schizophrenia are ***28***% in MZ twins and ***6***% in DZ twins. Thus, a reduction in shared genes from 100% to 50%, reduces the risk of schizophrenia nearly ***80***%. Also, ***50***% gene-sharing with a schizophrenic proband is associated with a lifetime risk of ***6***%. In absolute terms, though this is low, it is still markedly higher than that of the general population. (p. 468)

6. The Danish adoption study found a preponderance of schizophrenia in ***BIOLOGICAL*** relatives—as compared to ***ADOPTIVE*** relatives—of schizophrenic adoptees. (p. 471)

7. The Danish adoption study, however, did not include independent assessments of the ***CHILD-REARING ADEQUACY*** of the ***ADOPTIVE FAMILIES*** into which index (those who became schizophrenic) and control (those who did not) youngsters had been placed. (p. 471)

8. The Wahlberg and colleagues study raises the possibility that certain kinds of ***ENVIRONMENTS*** may protect people with ***GENETIC RISK***. (p. 472)

9. Schizophrenia is a genetically ***INFLUENCED***, not a genetically ***DETERMINED*** disorder. (p. 474)

10. Recent research efforts have moved toward exploring the idea that the problem of schizophrenia lies not in overall dopamine levels but in ***RECEPTOR SENSITIVITY***. (p. 479)

11. When the diagnostic criteria for schizophrenia changed in 1980 and became more ***STRINGENT***, some of the ***POSITIVE*** trends in recovery were ***DIMINISHED***. (p. 479)

12. The best predictor of long-term outcome for patients with schizophrenia is the percentage of time they spend experiencing ***PSYCHOTIC*** symptoms in the ***EARLY*** years of their illness. (p. 485)

13. ***COGNITIVE REMEDIATION*** training is an emphasis on helping patients deal with their neurocognitive deficits. (p. 488)

THE DOCTOR IS IN...PSYCHIATRIC HELP—5¢

1. Sharon comes to visit you. She has been referred by her sister. Sharon had been picked up by the police outside of Tom Hanks' house. She told the police that she and Tom were getting married and that she was the love of his life. Sharon said that his latest movie was dedicated to her, and that he conveyed it through a secret message on the screen that only she could pick up. With Sharon's permission, you talk to her sister and discover that other than this behavior, Sharon seems normal. How would you diagnosis Sharon and why? (pp. 466-67)

   Delusional disorder with erotomania subtype. Sharon's actions and beliefs are completely false and absurd. She seems normal outside of the belief that she and Tom Hanks are getting married. Sharon also seems to be stalking him.

2. You are a family therapist. A family comes to see you, bringing their 23-year-old son who suffers from schizophrenia. How would you treat this family, and, based on studies, what would you expect the son's outcome to be? (p. 487)

    Treatment:

    a. work to change the patient-relative relationship

    b. educate the patient and family about schizophrenia

    c. help to improve coping and problem-solving skills

    d. enhance communication skills especially the clarity of family communications

    Outcome:

    would expect the patient to do better clinically and have a low relapse rate

PICTURE THIS

1. Antipsychotics (Ant + Eye + S + Eye + Cot + ICS)
2. Catatonic Schizophrenia (Cat + Ton + IC)
3. Dementia Praecox (De + Men + Tea + A)
4. Disorganized Schizophrenia (Disc + Oar + GAN + Eyes + D)
5. Psychosis (S + Eye + KO + Sis)
6. Paranoid Schizophrenia (Pear + A + No + OID   Skis + O + Free + Knee + A)

PRACTICE TESTS

PRACTICE TEST NUMBER 1

1. The hallmark of schizophrenia is a significant loss of contact with reality, referred to as (p. 458)

    b. psychosis.

2. Symptoms of schizophrenia include oddities in (p. 458)

    a. perception.

    b. thinking.

    c. sense of self.

    d. all of the above.

3. Schizophrenia is about as prevalent as (p. 458)

    a. epilepsy.

4. Schizophrenia tends to develop earlier in _____ than in _____. (p. 459)

    b. men, women

5. Schizophrenia is becoming more common and severe in males than females. This could be a result of female hormones playing a (p. 459)

    d. protective role.

6. Late-onset schizophrenia is much more likely to strike women than men around (p. 459)

    b.   menopause.

7. _____ is an erroneous belief that is fixed and firmly held despite clear and contradictory evidence. (p. 460)

    b.   Delusion

8. _____ is a sensory experience that occurs in the absence of any external perceptual stimulus. (p. 461)

    a.   Hallucination

9. Disorganized speech is the external manifestation of a disorder in thought (p. 462)

    a.   form

10. _____ symptoms reflect behavioral excesses or distortions in schizophrenic patients. (p. 463)

    c.   Positive

PRACTICE TEST NUMBER 2

1. _____ symptoms reflect behavioral deficits in schizophrenic patients. (p. 463)

    b.   Negative

2. Delusions of grandeur are common in _____ schizophrenia. (p. 464)

    d.   paranoid

3. In the past, _____ schizophrenia was called hebephrenic. One of its characteristics is flat or inappropriate affect. (p. 464)

    a.   disorganized

4. _____ schizophrenia was once common in Europe and North America but has become less prevalent in recent years. It is still found in less industrialized regions of the world. (p. 465)

    b.   Catatonic

5. _____ schizophrenia is considered by the authors as something of a wastebasket category, because a patient may meet the the criteria for schizophrenia but not fit into one of the other types. (p. 466)

    a.   Undifferentiated

6. The _____ category is used for people who have suffered from at least one episode of schizophrenia but now don't have positive symptoms but clinically show negative symptoms. (p. 466)

    b.   residual

7. Most instances of acute, reactive schizophrenic breakdown occurring for the first time appear to be (p. 466)

    a.   undifferentiated.

8. The central feature of _____ schizophrenia is pronounced motor symptoms. (p. 465)

    b.   catatonic

9. In the attempt to overcome the difficulty of separating hereditary from environmental influences, researchers have used the (p. 469)

    a.   adoption strategy.

10. Something that was not included in the Danish adoption studies, which proved to be significant in future studies done by Tienari and colleagues and Wahlberg, was an independent assessment of (p. 471)

    d.   child-rearing adequacy of the adoptive families.

PRACTICE TEST NUMBER 3

1. As a genetic researcher, you have decided to move away from the family, twin,, and adoption schizophrenia studies you had been focusing on and become involved in a new paradigm. This paradigm shift would probably be a study of (p. 472)

    d.   molecular genetics.

2. In addition to prenatal viral infections, researchers are looking at _____ as a factor that could cause or trigger schizophrenia. (p. 473)

    a.   rhesus incompatibility
    b.   early nutritional deficiency
    c.   perinatal birth complications
    d.   all of the above.

3. Researchers now accept that schizophrenia is a _____ disorder, wherein vulnerability to schizophrenia stems from a brain lesion that lies dormant until normal maturation of the brain occurs. (p. 475)

    d.   neurodevelopmental

4. Studies by Elaine Walker and her colleagues, found what differences between preschizophrenic children and their healthy siblings? (p. 475)

    a. motor abnormalities

    b. less positive facial emotions

    c. more negative facial emotions

    d. all of the above

5. Because the brain normally occupies the skull fully, the enlarged ventricles of some schizophrenics imply a(n) (p. 476)

    b. loss of brain tissue mass.

6. Postmortem studies show that there are more _____ receptors in the brains of patients with schizophrenia than in controls (p. 479)

    d. D2

7. This is an excitatory neurotransmitter that researchers suspect might be involved in schizophrenia. (p. 480)

    c. Glutamate

8. A significant percentage of patients with schizophrenia are deficient in their ability to track a moving target. The skill required to do this task is called (p. 481)

    b. smooth-pursuit eye movement.

9. Theories on the causes of schizophrenia that no longer are applicable, because of the lack of empirical support, are (p. 481)

    a. double-bind hypothesis.

    b. schizophrenogenic mother.

    c. gross parental ineptitude.

    d. All of the above.

10. These people help patients find the services they need in order to function in the community. (p. 487)

    b. case managers

COMPREHENSIVE PRACTICE TEST
MULTIPLE-CHOICE

1. The most common form of hallucination is (p. 461)

    c. auditory.

2. Modern research has found support for the idea that auditory hallucinations are really misperceived (p. 462)

    d. self-talk.

3. Type I schizophrenia is associated with this subsyndrome. (p. 463)

    c. positive.

4. Type II schizophrenia is associated with this subsyndrome. (p. 463)

    d. negative

5. Carlos is referred to you with psychotic symptoms that meet the criteria for schizophrenia. However, he also exhibits clear mood changes. What would your diagnosis of Carlos be? (p. 466)

    d. schizoaffective

6. Jennifer comes into your office for an appointment. For the past two months she has been experiencing schizophrenia-like psychoses but really not severe enough yet for her to be diagnosed with schizophrenia. How would you diagnose Jennifer? (p. 466)

    a. Schizophreniform

7. A person in whom symptoms of schizophrenia have existed for six months or less would be diagnosed as the (p. 466)

    a. undifferentiated type.

8. Shared psychotic disorder, in which one person passes on or shares a delusion with someone he or she is close to, is also known as (p. 467)

    d. folie á deus.

9. An assumption that can create some problems when interpreting the findings of twin studies is (p. 469)

    c. MZ and DZ twins have equally similar environments.

10. If schizophrenia were exclusively genetic, the concordance rate for identical twins would be _____ percent. (p. 469)

    d. 100

11. The prevalence of schizophrenia in the first-degree relatives of a proband with schizophrenia is about what percent? (p. 468)

    b. 10

12. Wahlberg and colleagues found that children who were at genetic risk and lived with families that had high _____ showed high levels of thought disorder (p. 472).

    b.   communication deviance

13. The Finnish Adoption Study has provided strong confirmation of what model for the origins of schizophrenia. (p. 472)

    c.   diathesis-stress

14. Focusing on MZ concordance rates has perhaps caused an overestimation of the heritability of schizophrenia, because MZ and DZ twins do not have equally similar _____ environments. (p. 474)

    a.   prenatal

15. In 1995 Davis, Phelps and Bracha, found that MZ twins who were monochorionic, as opposed the MZ twins who were dichorionic, had about what percent concordance rate with schizophrenia? (p. 474)

    c.   60

16. Negative symptoms of schizophrenia seem to be linked to which part of the brain? (p. 478)

    a.   frontal lobe

17. Positive symptoms of schizophrenia seem to be linked to which part of the brain, especially on the left side? (p. 478)

    a.   temporal lobe
    b.   hippocampus
    c.   amygdala
    d.   all of the above

18. The overall organization of the cells in the brain is called the brain's (p. 478)

    c.   cytoarchitecture.

19. Some evidence points to patients with schizophrenia as missing particular types of neurons known as (p. 478)

    a.   inhibitory interneurons.

20. The first antipsychotics, developed over 50 years ago to treat schizophrenia, are called (p. 486)

    a.   conventional antipsychotics.
    b.   typical antipsychotics.
    d.   a and b.

21. The newer class of antipsychotics are referred to as (p. 486)

    b.   novel antipsychotics.
    c.   atypical antipsychotics.
    d.   b and c.

22. Betty, who is schizophrenic, goes to a group everyday where she learns employment skills, relationship skills, and skills in managing medication. This type of training is referred to as (p. 487)

    c.   social-skills.

23. The goal of cognitive-behavioral therapy when treating schizophrenia is (p. 488)

    a.   decrease intensity of positive symptoms.
    b.   reduce relapse.
    c.   decrease social disability.
    d.   all of the above.

24. This type of therapy is staged, which means that it comprises different components that are administered at different points in the patient's recovery. (p. 490)

    a.   personal therapy

TRUE – FALSE

1. T — Schizophrenia is a single, discrete illness. (p. 458)

2. T — People who have a parent with schizophrenia have a statistically higher risk of developing the disorder than those who do not. (p. 458)

3. T — Delusions reflect a disorder of thought content. (p. 462)

4. F — A preponderance of negative symptoms in the clinical picture is considered a good sign for the patient's future outcome. (p. 463)

5. T — The prognosis for someone diagnosed with schizophreniform disorder is better than for established forms of schizophrenia. (p. 466)

6. F — The terms, "familial" and "genetic," are synonymous. (p. 468)

7. T — Schizophrenia probably involves several, or perhaps many, genes working together to make a person susceptible. (p. 472)

8. T — The first signs of schizophrenia may be found in the way that children move. (p. 476)

9. F — Schizophrenics are very sensitive to pain. (p. 477)

10. T — Schizophrenia manifests itself more in defective cognition that in defective biology. (p. 480)

11. F — Patients living in more industrialized countries do better than patients living in less industrialized countries. (p. 485)

12. T — Patients who were treated with a "befriending" intervention in the Sensky and colleagues study did unexpectedly well. (p. 489)

ESSAY QUESTIONS *(Your answer should contain the following points.)*

1. Discuss how dopamine became implicated in schizophrenia. (p. 479)
   a. mental changes associated with LSD had scientists interested in schizophrenia consider a possible biochemical basis for the disorder
   b. the observation that chlorpromazine's therapeutic benefits were linked to its ability to block dopamine receptors
   c. the abuse of amphetamines in the 50s and 60s lead to the discovery that, if too much dopamine is produced, a form of psychosis that includes paranoia and auditory hallucinations occurs that looks a lot like schizophrenia
   d. actual clinical studies that treated patients by giving them drugs, which increased the availability of dopamine

2. Define and explain expressed emotion (EE) and its connection to patient relapse. (p. 483)
   a. EE is a measure of the family environment which is based on how the family member speaks about the patient during a private interview with a researcher. There are three main elements: criticism, hostility, and emotional over involvement (EOI).
   b. Criticism, the most important, reflects dislike or disapproval; hostility, dislike, or rejection of patient as a person; EOI dramatic or overconcerned attitude with illness.
   c. It predicts relapse in patients.
   d. When EE levels in families are lowered, rates of patient relapse rates decrease.
   e. High EE behaviors exhibited by family members are perceived as stressful by patients and possibly triggering the release of cortisol, which triggers dopamine activity.
   f. Studies show that an increase in patients' unusual thinking occurred immediately after the patient was criticized by a family member.

3. Compare the conventional antipsychotics with the newer novel ones in terms of effectiveness and side effects. (p. 486)

    Conventional: Haldol and Thorazine

    a. work because these are dopamine antagonists

    b. benefits appear within 1-3 weeks, with maximum results in 6-8 weeks

    c. work best for positive symptoms

    d. side effects: drowsiness, dry mouth, weight gain, extra-pyramidal side effects, tardive dyskinesia, and neuroleptic malignant syndrome

    Novel: Clozal, Risperday, Zyprexa, Seroquel, Geodon

    a. cause fewer extrapyramidal symptoms

    b. don't block D2 receptors well but block a much broader range of receptors, including D4 dopamine receptor

    c. relieve positive and negative symptoms

    d. patients less likely to be rehospitalized

    e. side effects: drowsiness and weight gain, diabetes, and, rarely, agranulocytosis

CRISS-CROSS ANSWERS

Across

1. glutamate
3. schizophrenia
4. dopamine
8. catatonic
9. delusion
10. antipsychotics

Down

2. expressed emotion
5. psychosis
6. hallucination
7. negative symptoms

CHAPTER FIFTEEN

WHO'S WHO AND WHAT'S WHAT—MATCHING

Label the brain structures using the correct terms from the list below.

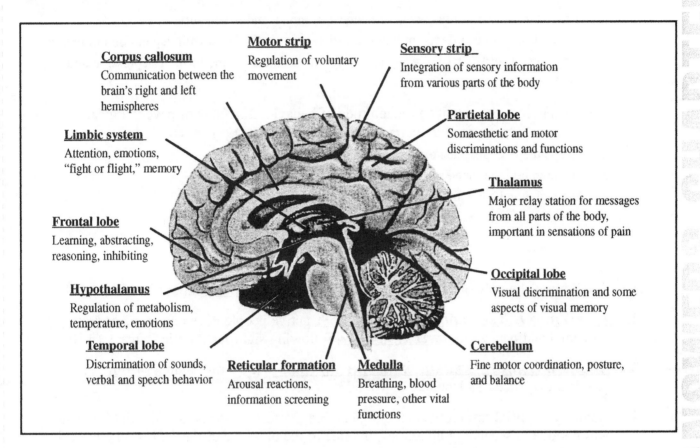

Corpus callosum
Communication between the brain's right and left hemispheres

Motor strip
Regulation of voluntary movement

Sensory strip
Integration of sensory information from various parts of the body

Partietal lobe
Somaesthetic and motor discriminations and functions

Limbic system
Attention, emotions, "fight or flight," memory

Thalamus
Major relay station for messages from all parts of the body, important in sensations of pain

Frontal lobe
Learning, abstracting, reasoning, inhibiting

Hypothalamus
Regulation of metabolism, temperature, emotions

Occipital lobe
Visual discrimination and some aspects of visual memory

Temporal lobe
Discrimination of sounds, verbal and speech behavior

Reticular formation
Arousal reactions, information screening

Medulla
Breathing, blood pressure, other vital functions

Cerebellum
Fine motor coordination, posture, and balance

Match the term or name with the correct answer.

Term/Name	Answer
D. Anosognosia	A. genes on chromosome 14 and 1 that are associated with very early onset Alzheimer's disease
C. Alois Alzheimer	B. famous historical victim of a traumatic brain injury
A. Presenilin 1 and presenilin 2	C. German neuropathologist who first described AD
E. Apolipoprotein (APOE)	D. inability for realistic self-appraisal
B. Phineas Gage	E. gene on chromosome 19 that plays a great role in late onset Alzheimer's

SHORT ANSWERS   *(Your answer should contain the following points.)*

1. Why are cognitive disorders discussed in the textbook? (p. 494)

    a. These disorders are regarded as psychopathological conditions.

    b. Some brain disorders cause symptoms that look remarkably like other abnormal psychology disorders.

    c. Brain damage can cause changes in behavior, mood, and personality.

    d. Many people who suffer from brain disorders react to the news with depression or anxiety.

    e. Cognitive disorders take a heavy toll on family members in the form of depression and anxiety.

2. What determines the extent and magnitude of behavioral deficits or psychological impairments in persons with damage to brain tissue? (p. 495)

    a. the nature, location, and extent of neural damage

    b. the premorbid competence and personality of the individual

    c. the individual's life situation

    d. the amount of time since the first appearance of the condition

FILL IN THE BLANKS

1. The brain is the only organ capable of ***STUDYING*** and ***READING*** about itself. (p. 494)

2. ***INTELLIGENT***, ***WELL-EDUCATED***, ***MENTALLY*** active people have enhanced ***RESISTANCE*** to mental and behavioral ***DETERIORATION*** following significant brain injury.   (p. 499)

3. ***AMYLIOD PLAQUES***, ***NEUROFIBRILLARY TANGLES*** and overall brain ***ATROPHY*** are physical evidence of Alzheimer's. (p. 503)

4. Contrary to initial assumptions, the organic brain effects associated with AIDS patients was not due to secondary infections, but due to the presence of the ***HIV-1 VIRUS*** itself. (p. 507)

5. AIDS-related dementia damage appears to be concentrated in ***SUBCORTICAL*** regions, notably the ***CENTRAL WHITE MATTER***, the tissue surrounding the ***VENTRICLES***, and deeper gray matter structures, such as the ***BASED GANGLIA*** and ***THALAMUS***. (p. 508)

6. The later phases of AIDS dementia include ***BEHAVIORAL*** regression, ***CONFUSION***, ***PSYCHOTIC*** thinking, ***APATHY***, and marked ***WITHDRAWAL***. (p. 508)

7. A sudden interruption of the blood supply to parts of the brain is a ***CEREBRAL INFARCT***. (p. 508)

8. The characteristics between VAD and AD are similar, but the decline in VAD is not as smooth because a) the discrete character of an ***INFARCT EVENT*** , b) variations over time in the volume of blood delivered by a ***SEVERELY CLOGGED ARTERY***, and c) a tendency for VAD to be associated with more severe ***BEHAVIOR COMPLICATIONS***. (p. 508)

9. Disorders that result from traumatic injuries to the brain are more common than any other forms of ***NEUROLOGICAL*** disease, except ***HEADACHE***. (p. 509)

THE DOCTOR IS IN...PSYCHIATRIC HELP—5¢

1. Glen is an 82-year-old man who suddenly became very confused, not able to remember things and very agitated—pacing his room endlessly at night. In addition, he was unable to stay on tasks long enough to even complete dressing himself. The morning would find him cooperative, but that could change quickly to anger. Glen had been taking several medications and was recently given another.

    How would you diagnose Glen and why? Also, what treatment would you use? (pp. 499-500)

    a. **Glen suffers from delirium.** The sudden onset, age considerations, and behaviors point to this diagnosis. He has also been given another medication, so the delirium may be brought on by the interactions of the medicines. For treatment: neuroleptics, environmental manipulations, family support, and orienting techniques.

2. Terry is a 44-year-old man who has a long history of alcohol abuse. He has come to see you at the insistence of his sister with whom he is staying. In your interview with Terry, he is very capable of telling you about his life and past experiences while working on oil rigs around the world. You had asked him to look a picture in a magazine and tell you what he saw. He was able to do this as he looked at the picture. However, when you asked him to recall what the picture was about a few minutes later, he had no idea what you were talking about and made up a story—that seemed to him a reasonable explanation as to why he didn't recall the picture.

    How would you diagnose Terry and why? (p. 509)

    a. **Amnestic syndrome.** Terry had a long history of alcohol abuse and his memory for remote events is intact as is immediate recall. However, his short-term memory is impaired as he can't remember events that took place a few minutes before.

3. What six factors in the case below suggest that your patient has an unfavorable prognosis? (p. 513)

    > *"An 18-year-old male who had several run-ins with the law during high school, received a serious head injury in a motorcycle accident. He was in a coma for almost a month. He is currently suffering some paralysis, and is very angry and depressed. He refuses to cooperate with is physical therapist. His parents, who live in a remote rural area where no rehabilitation facilities are available, will take him back home, but are rather unenthusiastic about the prospect."*

    a. in a coma for a month

    b. cognition impairment

    c. only graduated from high school (he is young)

    d. didn't have well-functioning, promising personality

    e. refuses to cooperate with physical therapist

    f. not returning to favorable situation

PICTURE THIS

1. Delirium (D + L + Ear + E + UM))
2. Dementia (D + Men + Tea + A)
3. Anterograde Amnesia (Ant + Ear + O + Grade <a pretty good one>   Am + Knee + C + A)

MULTIPLE-CHOICE PRACTICE TESTS

PRACTICE TEST NUMBER 1

1. Before the DSM-IV was published, delirium, dementia, and other amnestic and cognitive disorders, were considered (p. 495)

    c. organic mental disorders.

2. When structural defects in the brain occur before birth or at a very early age, the typical result is (p. 494)

    a. mental retardation.

3. To distinguish the possibility of a brain disorder from mood disorder, the clinician will look to see if the client has (p. 494)

    a. headaches.
    b. a major change in behavior.
    c. a prior history of psychopathology.
    d. all of the above.

4. The diagnostic coding of various neuropsychological disorders is done by what is causing the _____ problem. (p. 495)

    c. cognitive

5. The screening test that clinicians often use to determine the possibility of cognitive impairment is the (p. 496)

    c. MMSE.

6. The _____ hemisphere of the brain is mostly responsible for language and solving mathematical equations. (p. 497)

    b. left

7. The study by LoSasso et. al. (2001) found that nail salon technicians had significantly more cognitive and neurological impairments, probably due to an exposure to (p. 497)

    c. neurotoxic substances.

8.   After a traumatic brain injury caused by an accident or a fall, for example, around _____ percent of patients make a suicide attempt. (p. 499)

     b.   18

9.   Most people who have neuropsychological disorders do not develop _____ symptoms. (p. 499)

     d.   psychopathological

10.   A rapid and widespread disorganization of complex mental processes caused by a generalized disturbance in brain metabolism is called (p. 499)

     d.   delirium.

PRACTICE TEST NUMBER 2

1.   Delirium is treated with (p. 500)

     a.   neuroleptic medications.

     b.   benzodiazines.

     d.   a and b.

2.   What is the correct order for the continuum of level of consciousness? (p. 500)

     c.   alert awake, delirium, stupor, coma

3.   Children are at high risk of delirium, because their brains are not yet fully (p. 500)

     b.   developed.

4.   At least _____ different disorders are known to cause dementia. (p. 501)

     c.   50

5.   Alzheimer's cannot be absolutely confirmed until the patient's (p. 502)

     d.   death.

6.   Which of the following is the most common behavioral manifestation of Alzheimer's disease? (p. 503)

     a.   slow mental deterioration

7.   Since there is no cure for Alzheimer's, _____ care seems to help with diminishing the patient's and caregiver's distress and some of the complications that come with the disorder. (p. 506)

     b.   palliative

8.   These drugs have been shown to slow the rate at which patients with Alzheimer's deteriorate. (p. 506)

     b.   tacrine

     c.   donepezil

     d.   b and c

9. Environmental factors that could contribute to Alzheimer's include (p. 505)

   a. diet.
   b. aluminum.
   c. head trauma.
   d. all of the above.

10. Most people with Alzheimer's live (p. 507)

   a. with family members in the community.

PRACTICE TEST NUMBER 3

1. Vascular dementia involves a(n) (p. 508)

   b. continuing recurrence of small strokes.

2. Laura has been diagnosed with VAD and AD. As a clinician you would refer to this condition as (p. 508)

   b. mixed dementia.

3. Patients with VAD are more likely to suffer from _____ disorders than patients with Alzheimer's. (p. 508)

   d. mood

4. A person with VAD is vulnerable to sudden death from a (p. 508)

   a. stroke.
   b. cardiovascular disease.
   d. a and b.

5. Traumatic brain injury affects more than _____ people each year in the United States. (p. 509)

   b. 2 million

6. The general types of TBI recognized by clinicians are (p. 510)

   a. closed-head injuries.
   b. penetrating head injuries.
   c. skull fractures.
   d. all of the above.

7. If a head injury is sufficiently severe to result in unconsciousness, the person may experience retrograde amnesia or an inability to recall (p. 511)

   c. events immediately preceding the injury.

8. In a study of TBI in boxers, it was found that the presence of the _____ genetic-risk factor was associated with more chronic neurological deficits. (p. 511)

   b. APOE-4

9. A recent study has shown that older individuals and individuals who have TBI share several changes in (p. 511)

    c. information-processing speed.

10. Common after effects of moderate brain injury are (p. 513)

    a. chronic headaches.
    b. anxiety.
    c. impaired memory.
    d. all of the above.

COMPREHENSIVE PRACTICE TEST
MULTIPLE-CHOICE

1. The thick outer membrane that protects the brain and literally means "hard mother" is called the (p. 494)

    d. dura mater.

2. When the brain is damaged or brain functioning is in some way compromised, _____ changes result and are the most obvious signs of a damaged brain. (p. 494)

    a. cognitive

3. The _____ hemisphere of the brain is mostly responsible for grasping overall meanings in novel situations, reasoning on a nonverbal, intuitive level, and appreciation of spatial relations. (p. 497)

    a. right

4. In contrast to diffuse damage that results in dementia, focal lesions are _____ areas of abnormal change in brain structure. (p. 496)

    b. circumscribed

5. The most common cause of delirium is (p. 500)

    c. drug intoxication.

6. _____ has a gradual onset, but even in the early stages, memory for recent events is affected. (p. 501)

    a. Dementia

7. Data from a large Canadian study suggest that, after the first contact with a doctor for memory problems, a person with AD may live as little as (p. 504)

    c. 3.3 years.

8. Cases of early on-set AD appear to be caused by rare (p. 504)

    c. genetic mutations.

9. The widespread use of antiviral therapy has reduced the prevalence of dementia due to HIV to around _____ percent. (p. 508)

    c. 20

10. Cerebral arteriosclerosis can be medically managed by decreasing the likelihood of further (p. 508)

    c. strokes.

11. Amnestic syndrome is most commonly caused by chronic (p. 509)

    d. alcohol use.

12. Post-trauma epilepsy is common in (p. 510)

    b. penetrating head injuries.
    c. skull fractures.
    d. b and c.

13. The TBI that could result from a roller coaster ride is (p. 510)

    a. closed-head injury.
    b. penetrating head injury.
    c. skull fracture.
    d. none of the above.

14. The _____ a child, who has a significant traumatic brain injury, the more likely to be adversely affected they are. (p. 513)

    b. younger

15. Oken and colleagues concluded in 1998 that patients with Alzheimer's who took _____ performed better cognitively. (p. 514)

    a. ginkgo

TRUE – FALSE

1. T — Alzheimer's disease is the most common cause of dementia. (p. 502)

2. F — Alzheimer's disease usually begins after about age 65. (p. 503)

3. T — AD is not an inevitable consequence of aging. (p. 504)

4. T — People who are the caregivers for Alzheimer's patients are at high risk for depression. (p. 507)

5. T — Brain damage is the root cause of amnestic disorders. (p. 509)

6. F — Sports injuries are the most common cause of TBI. (p. 509)

7. F — In a majority of brain injury cases, notable personality changes occur. (p. 513)

ESSAY QUESTIONS   *(Your answer should contain the following points.)*

1. Discuss the progressively diffuse damage that may occur when a brain disorder has a mainly focal origin but gradually spreads over a greater area to become diffuse. (p. 499)

    a. Impairment of memory: notable trouble remembering recent events but not necessarily remote past events

    b. Impairment of orientation: unable to locate him or herself accurately

    c. Impairment of learning, comprehension and judgement: thinking becomes clouded, sluggish, and/or inaccurate

    d. Impairment of emotional control or modulation: emotional overreactivity

    e. Apathy or emotional blunting: emotional underrractivity

    f. Impairment in the initiation of behavior: lack of self-starting capability and may have to reminded about what to do next

    g. Impairment of controls over matters of propriety and ethical conduct: marked lowering of personal standards in appearance, personal hygiene, etc.

    h. Impairment of receptive and expressive communication: inability to comprehend written or spoken language or to express his or her own thoughts

    i. Impaired visuospatial ability: difficulty coordinating motor activity with the characteristics of the visual environment

2. List and describe the brain abnormalities that are characteristic of Alzheimer's disease. (p. 505)

    a. **Senile plaques:** made of deformed nerve cell terminals that, at their core, contain beta amyloid, which has been shown to be neurotoxic, causing cell death

    b. **Neurofibrillary tangles:** webs of abnormal filaments within a nerve cell that contain protein called tau, thought to be caused by increasing burden of amyloid, thus the presence of tau indicates the disease is progressing

    c. **Abnormal appearance of small holes in the neuronal tissue:** called granulovacuoles and caused from cell degeneration—the earliest and most severely affected structures are a cluster of cell bodies located in the basal forebrain and involved in reducing the release of ACh, a neurotransmitter involved in mediation of memory

CRISS-CROSS ANSWERS

Across
5. anterograde (amnesia)
7. delirium
8. amnestic (syndrome)

Down
1. vascular (dementia)
2. dementia
3. retrograde (amnesia)
4. plaques
5. Alzheimer
6. AIDS-related (dementia)

CHAPTER SIXTEEN

MATCHING
Match the following with the appropriate description.

G. Imipramine

H. intranasal hormone replacement used to treat enuresis

F. somnambulism

I. NREM

L. Asberger's disorder

D. Tourette's syndrome

A. Kanner

K. autistic-savant

B. Siegel

C. "Eden Model"

J. Integrative Strategy Instruction

M. hypoxia

N. Langdon Down

E. Children's Defense Fund

A. the first to describe autism in infancy and childhood

B. author of the book, *The World of the Autistic Child*

C. an approach to assisting people with autism over the course of their lifespan

D. an extreme tic disorder invloving multiple motor and vocal patterns

E. a public-interest group based in Washington D.C. that advocates for children

F. sleepwalking

G. medication used to treat enuresis

H. DDAVP

I. a period during sleep when sleepwalking takes place

J. a comprehensive intervention model to facilitate learning in LD children offered by Ellis

K. autistic children who show markedly discrepant and relatively isolated abilities

L. pervasive developmental disorder that appears later than autism

M. lack of sufficient oxygen to the brain

N. the first person to describe the best known clinical conditions associated with moderate and severe mental retardation

SHORT ANSWERS   *(Your answer should contain the following points.)*

1. What are the three subtypes of ADHD now recognized in the DSM-IV-TR? (p. 521)
   a. **Attention:** Deficit/Hyperactivity Disorder, Combined Type
   b. **Attention:** Deficit/Hyperactivity Disorder, Predominantly Inattentive Type
   c. **Attention:** Deficit/Hyperactivity Disorder, Hyperactive/Impulsive Type

2. What are the clinical signs of separation anxiety? (p. 525)
   a. excessive anxiety about separation from major attachment figure
   b. lack of self-confidence
   c. unrealistic fears
   d. oversensitive

   e.   self-conscious

   f.   nightmares

   g.   chronic anxiety

3. Describe the clinical picture of a child with autism. (pp. 534-536)

   a.   difficulties in relating to others

   b.   problems with perceptual-cognitive functioning

   c.   absence of speech

   d.   lack of development of sense of identity

   e.   engage in bizzare and repetitive activities

   f.   fascinations with unusual objects

   g.   obsession with maintaining environmental sameness

4. What two groups do children who are institutionalized fall into? (p. 546)

   a.   those who in infancy and childhood, manifest severe mental retardation and associated physical impairment and are institutionalized at an early age

   b.   those who have no physical impairments but show relatively mild mental retardation and a failure to adjust socially in adolescence and are institutionalized because of behavior problems

FILL IN THE BLANKS

1. Zill and Schoenborn in 1990, reported that boys have a higher rate of _EMOTIONAL_ problems over the _CHILDHOOD_ and _ADOLESCENT_ years but _EATING DISORDERS_ rates are higher for girls. (p. 518)

2. Hyperactive children are highly _DISTRACTIBLE_ and often _FAIL_ to _FOLLOW_ instructions or _RESPOND_ to demands placed on them. (p. 520)

3. Pelham and colleagues (1993) found that _BEHAVIOR MODIFICATION_ and _MEDICATION THERAPY_ significantly reduced ADHD. (p. 522)

4. The essential feature of oppositional defiance disorder is a recurrent pattern of _NEGATIVISTIC_, _DEFIANT_, _DISOBEDIENT_, and _HOSTILE_ behavior toward _AUTHORITY_ figures that persist for at least _SIX_ months. (p. 522)

5. Children who develop a conduct disorder at an _EARLIER_ age are much _MORE_ likely to develop _ANTISOCIAL_ personality disorder as adults than are _ADOLESCENTS_ who develop coduct disorders suddenly in _ADOLESCENCE_. (p. 523)

6. _PSYCHOPHARMACOLOGICAL_ treatment of anxiety disorders in children and adolescents is becoming more _COMMON_ today, although the _EFFECTIVENESS_ of drugs in treating these disorders is _QUESTIONABLE_. (p. 527)

7. Before ***ADOLESCENCE*** rates of depression are somewhat ***HIGHER*** in boys, but depression occurs at about ***TWICE*** the rate for ***ADOLESCENTS*** girls as boys. (p. 528)

8. Children who have ***PRIMARY FUNCTIONAL*** enuresis have never been ***CONTINENT***; children who have ***SECONDARY ENURESIS*** enuresis have been ***CONTINENT*** for at least a year but have regressed. (p. 531)

9. The term, "functional enuresis," refers to the habitual involuntary discharge of urine after the age of expected continence, which is age **5**, that is not ***ORGANICALLY*** caused. What is the difference between primary and secondary functional enuresis? (p. 531)

10. In a review of the treatment of bedwetting, Houts, Berman, and Abramson (1994) concluded that treated children were ***MORE IMPROVED*** at follow-up than nontreated children and that learning-based procedures were ***MORE*** effective than were medications. (p. 531)

11. Sleepwalking involves repeated episodes in which a person leaves his or her bed and walks around without ***BEING CONSIOUS OF THE EXPERIENCE*** or ***REMEMBERING IT LATER***. (p. 532)

12. The diagnosis of learning disorder is restricted to those cases in which there is a clear ***IMPAIRMENT*** in ***SCHOOL*** performance, or if the person is not a student, in ***DAILY LIVING*** activities, and impairment is not due to ***MENTAL RETARDATION*** or to a pervasive ***DEVELOPMENTAL DISORDER***. (p. 538)

13. Mild mental retardation, where IQ range is ***50/55*** to ***70*** is considered ***EDUCABLE***. Moderate mental retardation, where IQ range is ***35/40*** to ***50/55***, is considered ***TRAINABLE***. In severe mental retardation, where IQ range is ***20/25*** to ***35/40***, is considered ***DEPENDENT RETARDED*** and profound mental retardation where IQ range is ***BELOW 20/25***, is considered ***LIFE-SUPPORT RETARDED***. (pp. 540-41)

THE DOCTOR IS IN...PSYCHIATRIC HELP—5¢

1. Mark, who is seven years old, is referred to your office by his school. He comes to the session with his mother. The school report says that Mark is defiant, disobedient, and has tried to punch his teacher and the principal on more than one occasion. This behavior has been getting worse for the last year. In fact, Mark was suspended last year for spitting at his teacher. You note that the mother is also hostile and believes that coming to see you is a waste of time. You find out that the household is in turmoil, as the parents are always fighting, and get the feeling that the children are often the reason for the fighting.

   How would you diagnose Mark and what treatment would you recommend? (pp. 522-25)
   Diagnosis: Oppositional defiant disorder

Treatment: Work on getting the family in for therapy; use the cohesive family model as a treatment strategy, along with behavioral therapy techniques, and possibly remove Mark from his home as a last resort

2. Gary is a four-year-old boy who has started wetting the bed. Up until his new sister arrived, this hadn't been a problem. However, for the last two months since the new baby came home from the hospital, he has been wetting the bed and occasionally his pants. His parents are troubled and don't know what to do. (p. 531)

How would you diagnose Gary and what would you do to treat him?

Diagnosis: secondary functional enuresis

Treatment: use medication, such as imipramine; also conditioning procedures, but the incidence of enuresis tends to decrease significantly with age and as he comes to accept his baby sister

PRACTICE TESTS
PRACTICE TEST NUMBER 1

1. Until the twentieth century, children were seen as being (p. 518)
   b. miniature adults.

2. Clinicians now realize that to understand childhood disorders, they must take into account (p. 518)
   a. developmental processes.

3. Cindy is two years old, has temper tantrums, and puts everything she finds into her mouth. This behavior, for her age, is (p. 518)
   a. appropriate.

4. The DSM-I, which provided the first limited classification system to include childhood disorders, was published in (p. 519)
   c. 1952.

5. A problem with the early classification system for childhood disorders is that it was (p. 519)
   b. the same one used for adults.

6. Attention-deficit/hyperactivity disorder, conduct disorder, anxiety disorders of childhood, depressive disorders, symptom disorders, and autism are coded on which Axis? (p. 520)
   a. Axis I

7. Learning disabilities and mental retardation are coded on which Axis? (p. 520)
   b. Axis II

8. Perhaps because of their behavioral problems, children with ADHD are often lower in intelligence by about _____IQ points. (p. 520)

   c. 7 to 15

9. ADHD is thought to occur in about _____ percent of the school-aged children. (p. 520)

   a. 3 to 5

10. ADHD is more frequently found in boys before the age of (p. 520)

    d. 8.

PRACTICE TEST NUMBER 2

1. ADHD first appeared in the DSM-II in (p. 521)

   c. 1968.

2. Oppositional defiant disorder is apparent by about the age of (p. 522)

   a. 8.

3. Conduct disorder is apparent by about the age of (p. 522)

   b. 9.

4. Risk factors that oppositional defiant and conduct disorders have in common include (p. 523)

   a. family discord.
   b. socioeconomic disadvantage.
   c. antisocial behavior in parents.
   d. all of the above.

5. Conduct disordered children and adolescents are frequently comorbid for (p. 523)

   a. depressive symptoms.
   b. substance abuse disorder.
   d. a and b.

6. An effective treatment strategy for conduct disorder is the (p. 524)

   b. cohesive family model.

7. The goal of teaching behavior therapy techniques to the parent or parents of children with conduct disorder is so they can (p. 525)

   a. function as therapists in reinforcing desirable behavior.

8. _____ is the most common childhood anxiety disorder. (p. 525)

    c.   Separation anxiety

9. Selective mutism is rare in clinical populations and is seen most typically at what age? (p. 526)

    d.   preschool

10. Although childhood and adult depression essentially use the same DSM diagnostic criteria, a recent modification to the childhood diagnosis is (p. 528)

    c.   irritability.

PRACTICE TEST NUMBER 3

1. Depression in children has been related to depression in (p. 530)

    b.   their mothers.

    c.   their fathers.

    d.   b and c.

2. Andrea is five years old has been diagnosed with childhood depression. She could benefit from what type of therapy? (p. 530)

    b.   play therapy

3. A tic is a persistent, intermittent muscle twitch or spasm, usually limited to a (p. 532)

    d.   localized muscle group.

4. Tommy has been diagnosed with Tourette's syndrome. He is typical of other children with Tourette's. Tommy is probably how old? (p. 533)

    d.   7

5. _____ was a pioneer in the development of behavioral treatment for autistic children. (p. 537)

    b.   Ivar Lovaas

6. Many famous and successful people have overcome their learning disabilities. Which of the following people had a learning disability? (p. 539)

    a.   Sir Winston Churchill

    b.   Woodrow Wilson

    c.   Nelson Rockerfeller

    d.   all of the above

7. Ionizing radiation may harm a child by acting directly on the _____ or may damage the sex chromosomes of either parent. (p. 542)

    a.   fertilized egg

8.   Research has shown that a person with Down syndrome have the greatest deficits in (p. 544)

  c.   verbal and language-related skills.

9.   Treatment without parental consent is permitted in all of the following cases, **except** (p. 548)

  a.   immature minors.

10.   Haney and Gold found that most delinquent acts were committed (p. 553)

  b.   in association with one or two other persons.

COMPREHENSIVE PRACTICE TEST
MULTIPLE-CHOICE

1.   Children are vulnerable to psychological problems because they (p. 519)

  a.   have less self-understanding.
  b.   haven't developed a stable sense of identity.
  c.   haven't a clear understanding of what is expected of them.
  d.   All of the above.

2.   _____ is devoted to studying the origins and course of individual maladaptation in the context of normal growth processes. (p. 518)

  d.   Developmental psychopathology

3.   Recent research, although inconclusive, has pointed to ADHD being a result of (p. 521)

  a.   biological factors.
  b.   social environmental factors.
  d.   a. and b.

4.   The medication Ritalin is often used to decrease overactivity and distractibility in children with ADHD. Side effects of this medication include (p. 521)

  a.   decreased blood flow to brain.
  b.   disruption of growth hormone.
  c.   psychotic symptoms.
  d.   All of the above.

5.   Which of the following is the most common developmental sequence for conduct disorder (CD), antisocial personality (ASP), delinquency, and/or oppositional defiant disorder (ODD)? (p. 522)

  a.   CD, ODD, ASP

6.   Anxiety disorders are more common in which group? (p. 525)

  b.   girls

7. Causal factors for childhood depression are also implicated in (p 529)

    a.   childhood anxiety disorders.

8. Children's exposure to early _____ events can increase their risk for developing depression. (p. 529)

    b.   traumatic

9. Enuresis and encopresis are known as (p. 530)

    a.   elimination disorders.

10. The onset of sleepwalking disorder is usually between the ages of six and 12. It is classified under _____ in the DSM-IV-TR, rather than disorders of infancy, childhood, and adolescence. (p. 532)

    c.   sleep disorders

11. Causal factors in autism include (p. 536)

    a.   genetic factors.
    b.   disturbance in the central nervous system.
    c.   chromosome abnormalities.
    d.   all of the above.

12. All of the following are true of infantile autism, **except** (p. 534)

    d.   most cases are found in the upper classes.

13. The drug(s) used most often in autism is/are _____; however, the effects have not been very impressive. (p. 536)

    a.   haloperidol

14. Dana has trouble in school. He has difficulty spelling and in word recognition. Often Dana will omit, add, or distort words. Dana probably has (p. 538)

    b.   dyslexia.

15. Mental retardation is coded on (p. 540)

    b.   Axis II.

16. Which of the following degrees of retardation is, by far, the most common? (p. 540)

    d.   mild

17. One of the major factors that needs to be taken into account when studying or treating children is (p. 548)

    b.   children are dependent on those around them.

18. The goal of early intervention programs for children is to (p. 551)

  a.   reduce the stressors in the child's life.

  b.   strengthen the child's coping mechanisms.

  d.   a and b.

19. Many habitual delinquents share the traits typical of the _____ personality. (p. 553)

  a.   antisocial

20. Alienation from family and the broader society cause juveniles to become more vulnerable to (p. 553)

  c.   the psychological support afforded by membership in a delinquent gang.

TRUE – FALSE

1.   F — Progress in child psychopathology has caught up with that in adult psychopathology.   (p. 518)

2.   T — Young children, if they attempt suicide or act violently toward another person, probably do so without any understanding of the finality of death.   (p. 519)

3.   T — Hyperactive children are not anxious.   (p. 520)

4.   F — Pemoline, when used to treat children with ADHD, has as many side effects as Ritalin. (p. 521)

5.   T — Not all children with conduct disorder will go on to become antisocial personalities. (p. 522)

6.   F — Kazdin (1995) said that family and social context factors are not as important causal factors in conduct disorders as genetics.   (p. 524)

7.   T — Selective mutism should be diagnosed only if the child actually has the ability to speak and knows the language.   (p. 526)

8.   F — Typically, children with anxiety disorders grow up to be adults who don't fit in. (p. 527)

9.   T — Depression in children and adolescents occurs with high frequency.   (p. 528)

10.   T — Children can learn to be depressed. (p. 529)

11.   F — The average age of children with encopresis is three years. (p. 532)

12.   T — If a baby is to inherit PKU, both parents must carry the recessive gene. (p. 545)

13. T — The treatment of children has come to mean family therapy for all members, including both parents, the child, and his or her siblings. (p. 549)

14. T — Play therapy, when used with children, is an effective tool that can be used to reduce problems and promote adjustment. (p. 549)

ESSAY QUESTIONS   *(Your answer should contain the following points.)*

1. Explain the causal factors in childhood anxiety disorders. (p. 526)

   Unusual constitutional sensitivity that makes them easily conditionable by aversive stimuli
   - early illnesses, accidents, or losses that involved pain and discomfort
   - modeling effect of an overanxious and protective parent who sensitizes a child to the dangers and threats of the outside world
   - indifferent, detached, or rejecting parents
   - possibly cultures that favor inhibition, compliance, and obedience
   - exposure to violence leading to a reduced sense of security and psychological well-being

2. Discuss the causal effects of mental retardation. (pp. 542-43)

   a. Genetic—chromosomal factors; mental retardation tends to run in families and is in the moderate to severe categories

   b. Infections and toxic agents

   c. Trauma (physical injury)—physical injuries at birth

   d. Ionizing radiation—radiation acting on fertilized egg or parents' eggs and sperm

   e. Malnutrition and other biological factors—may affect child more indirectly by altering child's responsiveness, curiosity and motivation

CRISS-CROSS ANSWERS
Across
2. encopresis
3. autism
5. ritalin
8. microcephaly
9. tic
10. echolalia
11. Pemoline
12. enuresis
13. phenylketonuria

Down
1. down syndrome
4. hydrocephaly
6. dyslexia
7. selective mutism

CHAPTER SEVENTEEN

MATCHING

Psychological Test	Purpose
H. John Cade	A. involves coordinated efforts of medical, psychological, social work, and other mental health personnel working together as each case warrants.
I. Albert Ellie	
E. psychoactive	B. a relationship between client and therapist that is essential to psychotherapuetic gain
N. Carl Rogers	
J. Ugo Cerletti and Lucio Bini	C. what Binder and Strupp refer to as a rupture in the therapeutic alliance
A. team approach	D. efficacy trials
C. negative process	E. mind-altering
B. working alliance	F. antipsychotic medications administered in a long-acting injectable form
M. Aaron Beck	G. author of *Listening to Prozac*
G. Peter Kramer	H. discovered that lithium salts were effective in treating manic disorders
O. Virginia Satir	I. regarded as the modern originator of inducing convulsions to treat mental disorders
K. Antonio Moniz	
I. Ladislas von Meduna	J. Italian physicians who after visiting a slaughter house and seeing electric shock used on animals, passed electric current through a patient's head, a method which became known as ECT
D. randomized clinical trials	
F. depot neuroleptics	K. introduced the frontal lobotomy in 1935
	L. founder of REBT
	M. his cognitive therapy assumes that client's problems stem from illogical thinking
	N. founder of client-centered therapy
	O. founder of conjoint family therapy

SHORT ANSWERS *(Your answer should contain the following points.)*

1. What are the elements of a therapeutic alliance? (p. 560)

    a. agreement between patient and therapist about goals and tasks of therapy

    b. an affective bond between patient and therapist

    c. sense of working collaboration on the problem

    d. clear communication

2. When evaluating treatment success, what sources of information are important? (p. 561)

    a. therapist's impression of changes that have occurred

    b. client's report of change

    c. reports from client's family and friends

    d. comparisons of pre- and post-treatment scores on tests or other relevant measures

    e. measure of change in selective overt behaviors

3. Discuss the advantages and disadvantages of Buspirone in treating anxiety. (p. 572)

    a. acts on serotonergic functioning

    b. as effective as the benzodiazepines in treating GAD

    c. low potential for abuse

    d. no withdrawal effects

    e. not as effective for those who had previously taken benzodiazepines

    f. takes two to four weeks to take effect; therefore, not effective in acute situations

4. Compared with some other forms of therapy, behavior therapy has some distinct advantages. Briefly explain. (p. 580)

    a. treatment approach is precise

    b. explicit learning principles is a sound basis

    c. economy of time and costs is quite good

5. According to cognitive therapies, clients' errors in the logic behind their thinking leads them to problems like depression. Briefly explore this. (p. 582)

    a. they selectively perceive the work as harmful while ignoring evidence to the contrary

    b. overgeneralize on the basis of limited examples

    c. magnify the significance of undesirable events

    d. engage in absolutistic thinking

6. Briefly explain why the humanistic-experiential therapies have been criticized. (pp. 585-86)

    a. lack of highly systematized models of human behavior

    b. lack of agreed-upon therapeutic procedures

    c. vagueness about what is supposed to happen between client and therapist

FILL IN THE BLANKS

1. The belief that people with **_PSYCHOLOGICAL_** problems can learn more **_ADAPTIVE_** ways of **_PERCEIVING_**, **_EVALUATING_** and **_BEHAVING_** is the conviction underlying all **_PSYCHOTHERAPY_**. (p. 558)

2. The half-life is the time it takes for the **_LEVEL_** of **_ACTIVE_** drug in the body to be **_REDUCED_** by **_50_** percent. (p. 565)

3. Patients taking SSRIs tend to improve after about **_3_** to **_5_** weeks of treatment and are considered to have had a **_POSITIVE_** response to treatment if they show at least a **_50_** percent improvement in their symptoms. (p. 568)

4. If a patient remains symptom free for **_6_** to **_12_** months or more, they are considered to have **_RECOVERED_**. (p. 570)

5. In spite of their side effects, MAO inhibitors are still used in certain cases of ***ATYPICAL DEPRESSION*** that are characterized by ***HYPERSOMNIA***, and ***OVEREATING***, and do not respond well to other classes of antidepressants. (p. 570)

6. Side effects of lithium include increased ***THIRST***, ***GASTROINTESTINAL DIFFICULTIES***, ***WEIGHT GAIN***, ***TREMOR***, and ***FATIGUE***. It can also be ***TOXIC*** if the recommended dose is exceeded. (p. 573)

7. Instead of exploring past traumatic events or inner conflicts, the ***BEHAVIOR THERAPIST*** focuses on the problem or symptom that is causing the distress. (p. 577)

8. The suppression of problematic behavior may be as simple as ***REINFORCEMENTS THAT SUPPORT IT***, provided, of course, ***THAT THEY CAN BE IDENTIFIED***. (p. 579)

9. One basic assumption underlying Beck's cognitive therapy approach is that problems like ***DEPRESSION*** result from clients' ***ILLOGICAL THINKING*** about ***THEMSELVES***, the ***WORLD***, and ***FUTURE***. (p. 581)

10. Many of us have learned ***UNREALISTIC*** beliefs and ***PERFECTIONISTIC*** values that cause us to expect too much of ourselves, leading us to ***BEHAVE IRRATIONALLY*** and then to feel that we are ***WORTHLESS FAILURES***. (p. 581)

11. Existential therapists do not follow any rigidly prescribed procedures but, rather, emphasize the ***UNIQUENESS OF EACH INDIVIDUAL*** and his or her "***WAY OF BEING IN THE WORLD***." (p. 585)

12. Although gestalt therapy is commonly used in a ***GROUP SETTING***, the emphasis is on ***ONE PERSON AT A TIME***. (p. 585)

13. Analytic interpretation involves a therapist's tying together a client's often ***DISCONNECTED IDEAS BELIEFS, AND ACTIONS*** into a ***MEANINGFUL EXPLANATION*** to help the client ***GAIN INSIGHT*** into the relationship between his or her ***MALADAPTIVE BEHAVIOR*** and the ***REPRESSED EVENTS AND FANTASIES*** that drive it. (p. 587)

THE DOCTOR IS IN...PSYCHIATRIC HELP—5¢

1. Bernice is a 47-year-old woman who recently lost her job in an auto factory. She is depressed and very concerned about how she is going to make ends meet when her unemployment insurance runs out. All she has ever done was to work factory jobs. She married right out of high school and supported her husband through school, as did her parents. Her husband was killed in an auto accident seven years ago. She has two children, 22 and 15 years old. Bernice tells you that she is concerned about her drinking.

Her father was an alcoholic and her mother was always sad and withdrawn. She believed this was the reason her father drank, but wasn't certain, since he drank for as long as she could remember. Right now she finds herself wanting to drink, but trying not to give in to it, because she feels it might be bad for her. Her self-esteem is very low as she feels that she is not smart enough—since she only has a high school diploma—to do anything but work in a factory. Her kids are supportive and doing well, but she still feels like a bad mother, because she can't give them all the things she sees other kids have. She feels this way in spite of her children telling her they don't need or want those things.

After reading the above scenario, pretend that you are a therapist and decide what aspects of the scenario would be emphasized/important for each of the following approaches. Also, discuss one aspect of treatment from each approach you would use with Bernice.

Pharmacological (pp. 563, 567)

Treatment:

focus on possible genetic connection with depression and prescribe antidepressants

Behavior (p. 579)

Treatment:

Bernice learned her behavior from her family and is modeling the behavior she learned. Treatment focus on modeling the behavior of someone she admires and feels is successful and reinforcing behavior that might be beneficial, e.g., taking a few college classes, looking for a job, etc.

Cognitive and Cognitive-Behavioral (pp. 581-83)

Treatment:

Bernice's difficulties are a result of dysfunctional beliefs about herself and her situation.

Use Ellis' REBT to restructure her belief system and self-evaluation, e.g., feeling like a bad mother in spite of her children saying otherwise.

Use Beck's cognitive therapy to challenge her illogical thinking about the present and the future, e.g., all she can ever do is factory work or stress-inoculation therapy, changing the way Bernice talks to herself about her current situation and how she is dealing with it.

Humanisitic—Experiential (p. 584)

Treatment:

Bernice's difficulties stem from problems with alienation, depersonalization, loneliness and failure to find meaning and genuine fulfillment. Using Rogerian therapy you would help Bernice become able to accept and be herself by establishing a psychological climate in which she can feel comfortable and accepted

Psychodynamic (pp. 586-88)

Treatment:

Classical psychoanalysis—search for repressed memories, thoughts, fears, and conflicts stemming from Bernice's early psychosexual development that would have to do with her experiences and relationships with her father and mother

Psychoanalytical oriented psychotherapy—attempt would be to help Bernice clarify distortions and gaps in the client's construction of the origins and consequences of her problem, thus challenging her "defenses"

Methods used:

Classical psychoanalysis—free association, resistance, transference, and dream analysis

Psychoanalytically oriented psychotherapy—active conversational style in which you would attempt to clarify distortions, such as her feelings about being family and if she is like her parents, schedule fewer sessions and face Bernice as you talked to her

You could also talk about existential therapy or gestalt therapy.

PRACTICE TESTS
PRACTICE TEST NUMBER 1

1. Who are the most obvious candidates for psychological treatment? (p. 558)
    a. Susan, whose husband left her
    b. Andre, who lost his job
    c. Carlos, whose wife just died from cancer
    d. all of the above

2. A new drug developed by a pharmaceutical company must obtain approval from what agency before it can be marketed? (p. 563)
    c. FDA

3. In the case of *Osherhoff vs. Chestnut Lodge*, Osherhoff received a settlement out of court, because Chestnut Lodge (p. 564)
    b. had not administered drug therapy.

4. The unique quality of antipsychotic drugs is their ability to (p. 565)
    d. reduce the intensity of delusions and hallucinations.

5. Virtually all of the antipsychotic drugs accomplish the same biochemical effect, which is (p. 565)
    a. blocking dopamine receptors.

6. Tardive dyskinesia is a side effect of taking conventional (p. 566)
    a. antipsychotic medication.

7. In 1988, this became the first SSRI to be released in the United States. (p. 567)
    c. Prozac

8. The immediate short-term effects of the tricycic antidepressants serve to (p. 567-68)

   d. increase the availability of serotonin and norepinephrine in the synapses.

9. The first antidepressant medications to be developed in the 1950s were (p. 570)

   c. MAO inhibitors

10. Antidepressants are also being widely used to treat (p. 571)

    a. bulimia.
    b. panic disorders.
    c. GAD.
    d. all of the above.

PRACTICE TEST NUMBER 2

1. Benzidiazepines are used to treat (p. 571)

   b. anxiety.

2. Lithium compounds are used in the treatment of (p. 573)

   c. bipolar mood disorders.

3. Which of the following caused an immediate decrease in the widespread use of psychosurgical procedures in this country? (p. 576)

   c. the advent of the major antipsychotic drugs

4. Psychosurgery is sometimes used for patients with debilitating (p. 576)

   a. obsessive-compulsive disorders.
   b. severe self-mutilation.
   d. a and b.

5. In _____, positive reinforcement is often used to establish, by gradual approximation, a response that was initially resisted. (p. 580)

   a. response shaping

6. Systematic desensitization is aimed at teaching a person, in the presence of an anxiety-producing stimulus to relax, because (p. 596)

   b. it is difficult, if not impossible, to feel pleasant and anxious at the same time.

7. In systematic desensitization, a patient confronting a feared real stimulus, as opposed to an imaginal one, is called (p. 578)

   c. in vivo exposure.

8. Using a form of the old-fashioned method of punishment to modify undesirable behavior is called (p. 578)

    a. aversion therapy.

9. Aversion therapy has been used successfully in the treatment of (p. 578)

    a. bizarre psychotic behavior.
    b. sexual deviance.
    c. smoking, drinking, overeating, drug dependence, and gambling.
    d. all of the above.

10. A therapist who believes it possible to take away something without putting something in its place is likely to be (p. 579)

    b. ineffective.

PRACTICE TEST NUMBER 3

1. In 1964, Bandura found that the most effective treatment for snake phobia was (p. 579)

    b. live modeling of fearlessness, combined with instruction and guided exposure.

2. Generally, behavioral therapy has been found to be less useful for (p. 580)

    b. the more pervasive and vaguely defined the client's problem is.

3. Behavioral techniques are the backbone of modern approaches to treating (p. 580)

    a. sexual dysfunctions.

4. Albert Ellis' _____ posits that a well-functioning individual behaves rationally and in tune with empirical reality. (p. 581)

    b. rational emotive behavior therapy (REBT)

5. Stress-inoculation therapy is a type of self-instructional training focused on (p. 582)

    b. altering the self-statements an individual routinely makes in stress-producing situations.

6. During therapy, a gestalt therapist is likely to ask, (p. 585)

    a. "What are you aware of in your body now?"
    c. "What does it feel like in your gut when you think of that?"
    d. a and c.

7. Therapists must constantly beware of developing negative feelings toward the client, which is known as (p. 588)

    c. counter-transference.

8. In integrative behavioral couple therapy (IBCT), _____ are integrated with change strategies to provide a form of therapy that is more tailored to individual characteristics and the needs of the couple. (p. 590)

   a. acceptance strategies

9. Most family therapists believe that _____—not just the designated "client"—must be directly involved in the therapy if lasting improvement is to be achieved. (p. 590)

   c. the family

10. The _____ are based on the assumption that we have the freedom and the responsibility to control our own behavior. (p. 584)

   b. humanistic-experiential therapies

COMPREHENSIVE PRACTICE TEST
MULTIPLE-CHOICE

1. It is estimated that _____ percent of patients receive medications and psychotherapy (p. 564)

   a. 55.

2. Patients who received both had an overall positive response rate of _____ percent. (p. 563)

   c. 85

3. Which of the following would you see as making substantial gains in personal growth as a result of therapy? (p. 558)

   a. Louis, who feels he would like to go back to school to finish his degree.

4. Research suggests that about _____ percent of patients show clinically significant change after 21 therapy sessions. (p. 562)

   b. 50

5. A particularly harmful unethical behavior on the part of the therapist toward his or her client is (p. 562)

   c. engaging in sexual relationship.

6. A new drug that seems to bne more effective in treating major depression, is (p. 568)

   b. Effexor, a SNRI

7. Carl Rogers client-centered therapy focuses on (p. 584)

   b. natural power of the organism to heal itself.

   c. removing the constraints and restrictions that grow out of unrealistic demands that people tend to place on themselves.

   d. b and c.

8. The view of the existential therapist is that human beings, being aware of their own existence, are responsible for (p. 585)

    a. deciding what kind of person to become.

    b. establishing their own values.

    c. actualizing their own potentialities.

    d. all of the above.

9. The main two basic forms of psychodynamic therapy are (p. 586)

    d. classical psychoanalysis and psychoanalytically oriented psychotherapy.

10. According to psychoanalysis, a dream has two kinds of content: (p. 587)

    c. manifest content and latent content.

11. In _____, the therapist is careful to maintain a neutral manner, to allow the client to "work though" the conflict. (p. 587)

    c. psychoanalysis

12. The original version of Freud's psychoanalysis is practiced only rarely today, because it (p. 588)

    a. is arduous.

    b. is costly in time, money, and emotional commitment.

    c. may take several years before all major issues have been resolved.

    d. all of the above.

13. The interpersonal therapy model developed by Klerman and associates, originally targeted for the problem of depression, has since been shown to be a promising treatment for (p. 589)

    b. bulimia nervosa.

14. Structural family therapy's approach is that family members will have altered experiences in the family and behave differently if (p. 590)

    b. they change the organization of the family in such a way that members will behave more supportively and less pathogenically toward each other.

    c. the family context can be changed.

    d. b and c.

15. Today, clinical practice is characterized by a relaxation of the boundaries previously found between disciplines, and most psychotherapists (pp. 590-91)

    b. try to borrow and combine concepts and techniques from various schools.

TRUE – FALSE

1. F — Therapy can offer magical transformations. (p. 558)

2. T — A client's motivation and the seriousness of the problem are important to the outcome of therapy. (p. 559)

3. T — Effective therapy depends, to some extent, on a good match between the client and therapist. (p. 561)

4. F — Whites metabolize antidepressants and antipsychotic medications more slowly than African Americans. (p. 565)

5. T — Atypical antipsychotics may effectively treat the positive and negative symptoms of schizophrenia. (p. 567)

6. F — SSRIs are chemically related to the older tricyclic antidepressants. (p. 567)

7. T — A patient is in remission when treatment removes all symptoms. (p. 568)

8. T — Prozac, Paxil, and Zoloft are now among the drugs most often prescribed by physicians. (p. 569)

9. F — Benzodiazepines are widely prescribed, because these aren't addictive. (p. 571)

10. T — A variety of behavioral techniques have developed to help patients unlearn maladaptive behaviors. (p. 577)

11. T — In token economy programs, patients earn tokens good for privileges by demonstrating appropriate ward behavior. (p. 580)

12. T — Psychoanalysis is not easy to describe, and the problem is complicated because of inaccurate conceptions based on cartoons and other forms of caricature. (p. 586)

13. T — The greatest contribution of the interpersonal approach may be its role in the developing movement toward "integration" of the various forms of therapy. (p. 588)

14. T — Although it is quite routine at the start of couples therapy for each partner to secretly harbor the idea that only the other will have to do the changing, it is nearly always necessary for both do so. (p. 589)

15. T — Often wives can see clearly what is "wrong" with their husbands, but not what attitudes and behaviors of their own are contributing to the marital impasse. (p. 589)

16. T — Husbands tend to have remarkable "insight" into their wives' flaws, but not their own. (p. 589)

17. T — The criticism has been raised that psychotherapy can be viewed as an attempt to get people adjusted to a "sick" society rather than to encourage them to work toward its improvement. (p. 591)

18. T — Even though there is little or no solid evidence that psychotherapeutic outcomes are diminished when client and therapist differ in race or ethnicity, most members of minority groups state a strong preference for therapists who share their ethnic background. (p. 592)

ESSAY QUESTIONS   *(Your answer should contain the following points.)*

1. Explain current views of ECT from the public view and a therapeutic view. Also discuss the types and the effectiveness. (pp. 574-75)

    a. public sees ECT as horrific and primitive primarily because of lawsuits where patient consent was not obtained before treatment.

    b. may be the only way of dealing with severely depressed and suicidal patients who have not responded to other forms of treatment

    c. used as treatment for severely depressed pregnant women or the elderly who cannot take the antidepressant drugs

    d. ECT is 80 percent effective with difficult-to-treat patients

    e. Types

        • bilateral ECT—electrodes are placed on either side of patient's head and brief electrical pulses are passed from one side of head to other for 1.5 seconds; bilateral more effective than unilateral, but has more severe cognitive side effects and memory problems

        • unilateral ECT—involves limiting current flow to one side of the brain, typically nondominant side

    f. patients are given anthemia and a muscle relaxant

    g. patient has amnesia for a period preceding the therapy and is confused for the next hour or so

    h. treatment administered three times weekly with patient becoming disoriented, which will clear when treatment terminates

    i. recommended to start with unilateral and switch to bilateral if no improvement is seen

2. Evaluate cognitive-behavioral therapies. (pp. 583-84)

    a. appears inferior to exposure-based therapies in the treatment of anxiety disorders

    b. may be most useful in helping basically healthy people to cope

    c. stress-inoculation therapy successfully used with anger, pain, Type A behavior, mild forms of anxiety

    d. extremely beneficial in alleviating many types of disorders: depression, panic disorder, generalized anxiety disorder, bulimia

3. Name and discuss the four basic techniques of Freud's psychoanalysis. (pp. 586-88)
   a. Free association
      • individual says whatever comes into his mind
   b. Analysis of dreams
      • procedure for uncovering unconscious material
   c. Analysis of resistance
      • the unwillingness or inability to talk about certain painful or threatening material
   d. Analysis of transference
      • client brings and unconsciously applies to her therapist, attitudes and feelings

CRISS-CROSS ANSWERS
Across
2. neurosurgery
5. in vivo exposure
8. marital
12. electroconvulsive
14. resistance
15. placebo
16. efficacy

Down
1. double-blind
3. Sigmund Freud
4. manualized
6. psychodynamic
7. behavior
9. modeling
10. psychotherapy
11. REBT
13. transference

CHAPTER EIGHTEEN

SHORT ANSWERS *(Your answer should contain the following points.)*

1. Briefly discuss the three requirements for psychosocial "health." (p. 597)

   a. develop the skills needed for effective problem solving, expressing emotions constructively, and engaging in satisfying relationships

   b. an accurate frame of reference on which to build his or her identity

   c. be prepared for the types of problems likely to be encountered during life

2. Our government has approached the drug abuse problem with three broad strategies, all of which have proven insufficient. Name these and discuss. (p. 599)

   a. Interdicting and reducing the supply of drugs available.
   - War on drugs has had little impact on the availability of drugs.

   b. Providing treatment services for those who develop drug problems
   - Perhaps the least effective way to reduce the problem

   c. Encouraging prevention
   - Most desirable; teaching young people ways to avoid use; hasn't worked because efforts have not been powerful enough or been well implemented

3. Discuss the three general therapeutic principles that guide the "milieu therapy" approach. (p. 602)

   a. staff expectations are clearly communicated to patients

   b. patients are encouraged to become involved in all decisions

   c. patients belong to social groups on the ward

4. A large study compared the relative effectiveness of three treatment approaches. Discuss what was discovered. (pp. 602-03)

   a. Milieu therapy
   - more successful releases than traditional
   - 70% of released patients remained in the community

   b. Social-learning treatment program
   - more successful releases than traditional
   - more than 90% of released patients remain out

   c. Traditional mental hospital treatments
   - fewer than 50% released patients remained out

5. An overcontrolled hostile person can become dangerous. Explain. (p. 609)

   Often exhibits an unusually low level of manifestly aggressive behavior prior to the commission of an aggressive act—very often an extremely violent one.
   - i.e., the high school honor student who kills several of his classmates with a gun.

FILL IN THE BLANKS

1. Without a supportive community, individual development is _**STIFLED**_. (p. 598)

2. Prominent social forces promoting the early use of alcohol in young people are attractive _**TELEVISION ADVERTISING**_, the influence of _**PEER GROUPS**_, negative _**PARENTAL ROLE MODELS**_, and the ready _**AVAILABILITY OF MANY DRUGS**_. (p. 598)

3. Attempts to effect psychologically desirable social change are likely to involve ideological and political issues that may inspire _**POWERFUL OPPOSITION**_, including _**OPPOSITION FROM THE GOVERNMENT ITSELF**_. (p. 598)

4. Recent estimates suggest that there are some _**TWO TO THREE MILLION**_ chronically mentally ill individuals in America, of whom _**ABOUT HALF**_ reside in mental hospitals, with the remainder living in nursing homes. (p. 602)

5. The Tarasoff decision spelled out a therapist's _**RESPONSIBILITY**_ in situations where there has been an explicit threat on a specific person's life. (p. 610)

6. An important contribution of the World Health Organization (WHO) is its _**INTERNATIONAL CLASSIFICATION OF DISEASES**_, which enables clinicians and researchers in different countries to use a uniform set of diagnostic categories. (p. 617)

7. Job dissatisfaction and poor mental health have been associated with work assignments involving _**FRAGMENTED, NARROW, UNVARYING**_ tasks that allow for _**LITTLE CREATIVITY**_ and give the worker _**LITTLE SENSE**_ of having contributed to the ultimate product. (p. 617)

THE DOCTOR IS IN...PSYCHIATRIC HELP—5¢

1. Stuart, a 26-year-old man you had been seeing for several years, comes into your office demanding to see you immediately, even though he doesn't have an appointment. He hasn't seen you for more than a month, because he had a job and was trying to go to school. Stuart is diagnosed with schizophrenia and is fine as long as he takes his medications; his behavior indicates he is not taking his medication. You try explaining to him that you have other appointments, but he becomes more and more agitated, talking about the people at work who are out to get him—but that he is going to get them first. Stuart is dishelved and looks like he hasn't bathed in several days. He tells you that you have to help him or he will do something awful.

    As Stuart's therapist, what would you do and why? (p. 606)

    > Have Stuart committed to the hospital as an emergency. There isn't time to get a court order, and Stuart is dangerous to himself or others; incapable of providing for his basic physical needs; unable to make responsible decisions about hospitalization, and is in need of treatment.

2. Jack had been friends with Jill for two years. He was madly in love with her although, she had made it clear that she liked him only as a friend and didn't want a romantic relationship. About five months ago, Jill met Brian and they started dating. Jack felt jealous and left out. He had been through other "boyfriends" and always managed to wait them out until Jill stopped seeing them. This time is different, and Jill is talking about possibly marrying Brian. Jack is beside himself and is consumed with anger and jealousy. He is talking about killing Brian and making it look like an accident. He reasons that Jill will then have to seek him out again for comfort. When asked how he would make it look like an accident, Jack replies that he would fix the breaks on Brian's car. Jack has the knowledge to do such a thing.

As Jack's therapist, how would you respond, and what are your legal responsibilities? (p. 610)

a. First, you would discuss the consequences of such behavior and what it could mean to his life and others. If, as the therapist, you believe that Jack is capable of carrying out his threat, you have a duty-to-warn. This means that client/therapist confidentiality can be broken to inform police and to make "reasonable efforts" to inform the potential victim.

MULTIPLE-CHOICE PRACTICE TESTS
PRACTICE TEST NUMBER 1

1. Universal interventions are concerned with (p. 596)

   a. altering conditions that can cause or contribute to mental disorders.
   b. establishing conditions that foster positive mental health.
   d. a and b.

2. Any effort aimed at improving the human condition, at making life more fulfilling and meaningful, may be considered part of _____ prevention of mental or emotional disturbance. (p. 596)

   a. universal

3. All of the following are sociocultural efforts toward universal intervention of mental disorders, **except** (p. 598)

   b. penal systems.

4. Teenage drug and alcohol use is still viewed as one of today's (p. 598)

   c. most significant psychological and community problems.

5. Through their own drinking or verbalizations about alcohol, parents may (p. 600)

   a. encourage use in their children.
   b. sanction usage by their children.
   d. a and b.

6. The most powerful influence on whether a teen begins to use drugs seems to be (p. 600)

    a.   peers.

7. Programs designed to help youngsters overcome negative pressures from peers focus on (p. 600)

    b.   teaching social skills and assertiveness.

8. A study in 2000 reported that _____ had had more than a few sips of alcohol. (p. 601)

    a.   80.3 percent of twelfth graders

    b.   71.4 percent of tenth graders

    c.   51.7 percent of eighth graders

    d.   all of the above

9. A persistent concern about hospitalization is that (p. 602)

    a.   the mental hospital may become a permanent refuge from the world.

10. Milieu therapy is (p. 602)

    c.   the establishment of a hospital environment itself as a therapeutic community.

PRACTICE TEST NUMBER 2

1. The rise of biological therapies has meant that (p. 602)

    b.   from 70% to 90% of patients labeled as psychotic and admitted to mental hospitals can now be discharged within a few weeks.

2. Studies have shown that in the past, up to _____% of schizophrenic patients have been readmitted within the first year after their discharge. (p. 603)

    c.   45

3. Between 1970 and 1992, the number of state mental hospitals dropped from 310 to 273, and the patient population was reduced by 73 percent due to (p. 604)

    d.   deinstitutionalization.

4. Deinstitutionalization has contributed substantially to (p. 606)

    b.   the number of homeless people.

    c.   the number of mentally ill people in prison.

    d.   b and c.

5. According to recent Justice Department statistics, _____ of the people in prison in the U.S. (275,000) have a mental disorder. (p. 605)

    b.   more than 16%

6. Typically, the first step in committing an individual to a mental hospital involuntarily is (p. 606)

    b.   filing a petition for a commitment hearing.

7. Studies have confirmed that individuals acquitted of crimes by reason of insanity typically spend _____ time in psychiatric hospitals as (than) individuals convicted of crimes spend in prison. (p. 614)

    a.   less

8. Violent acts are difficult to predict because these are determined as much by _____ circumstances as by the personality traits of the individual. Mental health professionals typically err on the conservative side when assessing violence proneness. (p. 609)

    c.   situational

9. Two major source of personality information is (p. 609)

    b.   data from the person's previous history.
    c.   data from personality tests.
    d.   b and c.

10. Congress passed its first comprehensive mental health bill, the National Mental Health Act in (p. 615)

    c.   1946

PRACTICE TEST NUMBER 3

1. The M'Naghten Rule of 1843 established legal defense for a person (p. 614)

    c.   unless it can be proven that at the time of her act, she did not know what she was doing was wrong, she is assumed to be sane.

2. The Irresistible Impulse Rule of 1887 established legal defense for a person (p. 614)

    d.   if an "irresistible impulse" caused him to commit the crime, even though he knew what he was doing was wrong.

3. The American Law Institute (ALI) Standard of 1962 established legal defense for a person (p. 614)

    a.   if she lacked "substantial capacity" to appreciate the criminal character of her behavior.

4. The Federal Insanity Defense Reform Act (IDRA) of 1984 redefined legal defense for a person to be such that (p. 614)

    b.   if he were "unable to appreciate" the criminality of his act and that the mental disorder involved must be severe.

5. The National Institute of Mental Health (NIMH) was formed in Washington, D.C. in (p. 615)

   c. 1946.

6. The National Institute of Mental Health (NIMH) (p. 615)

   a. conducts and supports research.
   b. supports training in the mental health field.
   c. helps communities plan, establish, and maintain effective mental health programs.
   d. all of the above.

7. The National Mental Health Association (NMHA) (p. 616)

   c. works for the improvement of services in community clinics and mental hospitals.

8. The American Psychological Association (APA) (p. 616)

   a. sets and maintains the high professional and ethical standards within the psychological industry.

9. The National Institute for Occupational Safety and Health (NIOSH) (p. 616)

   b. recognizes psychological disorders as one of the 10 leading work-related health problems.

10. The National Association for Retarded Citizens (NARC) (p. 616)

   d. works to reduce the incidence of mental retardation and carry on a program of education.

COMPREHENSIVE PRACTICE TEST
MULTIPLE-CHOICE

1. At high risk for mental disorders are (p. 596)

   a. recently divorced people and the physically disabled.
   b. elderly people and physically abused children.
   c. persons recently uprooted from their homes and victims of severe trauma.
   d. all of the above.

2. Adequate preparation for potential problems likely to be encountered by anyone during a given life stage, is a requirement for _____ health, at the _____ level of prevention. (p. 597)

   b. psychosocial, universal

3. Grounds for commitment, in addition to mental illness, require that a person must be judged to be _____ and in need of treatment or care in a hospital. (p. 606)

   a. dangerous to themselves or to others
   b. incapable of providing for their basic physical needs
   c. unable to make responsible decisions about hospitalization
   d. all of the above.

4. Which of the following patient rights was limited, according to a 1990 U.S. Supreme Court ruling? (p. 607)

    d. right to refuse psychotropic medication

5. Violence among psychiatric patients is especially prominent for those who (p. 608)

    b. drink alcohol.

6. One dilemma in attempting to rehabilitate previously violent psychiatric patients is that the mental health workers must exhibit some degree of (p. 609)

    d. trust.

7. An NGRI plea ("not guilty by reason of insanity") in a court case means (p. 611)

    c. "while he did do it, he lacked moral blameworthiness because he was insane."

8. Courts have generally not considered _____ sufficient grounds for an insanity defense. (p. 612)

    a. altered states of consciousness

9. An NGRI pleas was found most likely to be successful if the defendant was (p. 614)

    a. diagnosed with a major mental disorder, or there had been prior mental hospitalizations.
    b. a female.
    c. accused of a violent crime other than murder.
    d. All of the above.

10. Several states have adopted a different mentally ill plea, known as (p. 615)

    b. Guilty But Mentally Ill (GBMI).

11. During World War II, _____ recruits were rejected for military service for psychiatric reasons. (p. 615)

    c. two out of seven

12. Most often, in an HMO, the gatekeeper who determines which mental health treatments will be offered is a (p. 620)

    c. medical generalist or business professional.

13. The World Health Organization (WHO) estimates that mental disorders affect more than _____ people worldwide. (p. 617)

    c. 200 million

14. Serious mental health risk factors, unrecognized as workplace problems, may exist in (p. 617)

    a. the work load and pace; machine-paced work in particular.

    b. the work schedule; rotating shifts and night work.

    c. role ambiguity; who has responsibility for what.

    d. all of the above.

15. It is estimated that _____ of health care expenditures in the United States for managed are care administration. (p. 621)

    d. 25%

16. Other than accepting some measure of responsibility for the mental health of others through the quality of one's own interpersonal relationships, another constructive course open to each citizen is (p. 619)

    a. serving as a volunteer in a mental or other hospital.

    b. supporting realistic measures for ensuring comprehensive health services for all age groups.

    c. working toward improved public education, responsible government, the alleviation of prejudice, and the establishment of a more sane and harmonious world.

    d. All of the above, of course.

TRUE – FALSE

1. T — For the most part, mental health efforts have been restorative, rather than preventative. (p. 596)

2. T — Often the most beneficial aspect of a therapeutic community is the interaction among the patients themselves. (p. 602)

3. T — Today, in most states, the therapist not only can violate confidentiality with impunity, but may be required by law to take action to protect persons from the threat of imminent violence against them. (p. 610)

4. T — The new "guilty but mentally ill" (GBMI) plea requires a two-part decision. (p. 615)

5. T — Psychological difficulties among employees may result in absenteeism, accident proneness, poor productivity, and high job turnover. (p. 616)

6. F — The World Federation for Mental Health was established in 1861. (p. 617)

7. F — The world's mental health problems are so large and so scattered that there is really nothing that an individual can do to help. (p. 619)

ESSAY QUESTIONS   *(Your answer should contain the following points.)*

1. A relatively new approach is in the prevention arena. Name and discuss the three subcategories of these efforts. (p. 596)

   a. **Universal Interventions:** General population
      - Biological measures

        lifestyles, diet, physical exercise, good health habits
      - Psychosocial measures

        develop physical, intellectual, emotional, and social competencies
      - Sociocultural measures

        relationship between an individual and his or her community

   b. **Selective Interventions:** Specific subgroup
      - Selective prevention strategies

        Education programs for high-risk teens

        Parent and family-based intervention

        Peer group programs

        Increase self-esteem

        Mass media

   c. **Indicated Interventions:** high-risk individuals
      - Mental hospital as therapeutic community

        Aftercare programs

2. Deinstitutionalization, the movement to close down mental hospitals and treat persons with severe mental disorder in the community, has been the source of considerable controversy. Discuss the pros and cons of deinstitutionalization. (p. 604)

   a. Significant improvement versus "abandonment"
   b. Seemed a workable plan
   c. Problems arose
      - substandard homes and services
      - many became homeless
      - lack of follow-up

3. The wake of the Tarasoff decision left many perplexing issues for practitioners. Discuss the decision and its aftermath. (p. 610)

   a. decision held therapists responsible to warn authorities if a specific threat emerges during a session with a client
   b. calls into question the patient confidentiality
   c. ethical dilemmas

CRISS-CROSS ANSWERS
Across
5.   NAMI
6.   selective (interventions)
7.   NMHA
11.   tarasoff
12.   NIOSH
13.   forensic psychology
14.   milieu therapy
15.   insanity defense
Down
1.   GBME
2.   AABT
3.   universal (interventions)
4.   APS
7.   NIMH
8.   APA
9.   HMO
10.   indicated (Interventions)

CHAPTER NOTES

Use the next few pages for any random notations....

CHAPTER NOTES

CHAPTER NOTES

CHAPTER NOTES

CHAPTER NOTES

CHAPTER NOTES